D0944594

Digital Compression for Multimedia

The Morgan Kaufmann Series in Multimedia Information and Systems
Series Editor, Edward Fox

Digital Compression for Multimedia: Principles and Standards
Jerry D. Gibson, Toby Berger, Tom Lookabaugh, Dave Lindbergh,
and Richard L. Baker

Practical Digital Libraries: Books, Bytes, and Bucks
Michael Lesk

Readings in Information Retrieval
Edited by Karen Sparck Jones and Peter Willett

Introduction to Data Compression
Khalid Sayood

Forthcoming

Multimedia Servers: Design, Environments, and Applications
Asit Dan and Dinkar Sitaram

DIGITAL COMPRESSION
for
MULTIMEDIA

Principles and Standards

Jerry D. Gibson — *Southern Methodist University*

Toby Berger — *Cornell University*

Tom Lookabaugh — *DiviCom*

Dave Lindbergh — *PictureTel Corporation*

Richard L. Baker — *PictureTel Corporation*

Morgan Kaufmann Publishers, Inc.
San Francisco, California

Senior Editor   Jennifer Mann
Production Manager   Yonie Overton
Production Editor   Elisabeth Beller
Cover Design   Martin Heirakuji
Cover Photos   image copyright © 1998 PhotoDisc, Inc.
Copyeditor   Ken DellaPenta
Illustrator   Cherie Plumlee
Proofreader   Jennifer McClain
Compositor   Windfall Software, using ZzTeX
Indexer   Steve Rath
Printer   Courier Corporation

Designations used by companies to distinguish their products are often claimed as trademarks or registered trademarks. In all instances where Morgan Kaufmann Publishers, Inc. is aware of a claim, the product names appear in initial capital or all capital letters. Readers, however, should contact the appropriate companies for more complete information regarding trademarks and registration.

Morgan Kaufmann Publishers, Inc.
Editorial and Sales Office
340 Pine Street, Sixth Floor
San Francisco, CA 94104-3205
USA
Telephone 415 / 392-2665
Facsimile 415 / 982-2665
Email mkp@mkp.com
WWW http://www.mkp.com

Order toll free 800 / 745-7323

Library of Congress Cataloging-in-Publication Data

Digital compression for multimedia : principles and standards / Jerry
    D. Gibson . . . [et al.].
        p.   cm.
    Includes bibliographical references and index.
    ISBN 1-55860-369-7
    1. Multimedia systems. 2. Video compression. 3. Image
compression.   I. Gibson, Jerry D.
    QA76.575.D535   1998
    005.74'6—dc21   97-42600
                                                           CIP

Contents

3   Universal Lossless Source Coding   63

4   Quantization   113

5 Predictive Coding 139

6 Linear Predictive Speech Coding Standards 185

11 MPEG Compression   363

Jerry D. Gibson

To Nell Alverson Gibson

Toby Berger

To my wife, Florence, for decades of love and support, and to four generations of special people: Hank and Doris Berger, Joseph and Belle Cohen; Bob and Barbara Berger, Mal and Trudy Labell; Elizabeth Berger Mandell and Jim Mandell, Larry Berger and Anouk Markovits; Joshua and Zachary Mandell

Tom Lookabaugh

To Christie, Emily, and Max for toleration and inspiration; to Mom and Dad for unending support; to friends and colleagues on the MPEG committee for a triumph of collaborative invention

Dave Lindbergh

To my parents

Preface

Overview

This book was ignited and fueled by a vital confluence of ideas, trends, and individuals. The ideas span a broad spectrum from heuristic compression methods to rigorous approaches firmly rooted in information theory. The heuristics are based on source modeling, signal processing techniques, and people's informed "intuition." The rigorous source coding techniques are motivated by entropy coding and rate-distortion theory, the branches of information theory that treat the efficient compression of data.

Huffman coding and scalar bit allocation methods for transform coding were the earliest information-theoretic techniques to be employed in practical data compression systems for computer files, speech, still images, and video. During the 1960s and 1970s extraordinary advances in scalar quantization, time domain waveform-following predictive coders, subband coders, and transform coders were achieved. In addition, enhanced understanding developed concerning perceptual effects, source modeling, channel error mechanisms, and coder performance evaluation. Since the late 1970s these and other sophisticated ideas from information theory have been increasingly incorporated into practical systems for data compression. Key developments in this regard were the introduction of techniques for universal lossless coding, especially Lempel-Ziv theory and arithmetic coding, and the use of rate-distortion theory ideas to design and evaluate quantizers and tree coders and to motivate operational designs based upon constrained optimization problems. Today heuristic ideas and information-theoretic ideas have been fully integrated, and this combination has opened up entirely new approaches to source compression.

Common to all high-performance source compression methods is the need for signal processing. Accordingly, advances in source compression have been facilitated by corresponding advances in the theory and understanding of signal processing. For example, signal processing researchers have provided multi-dimensional signal representations, adaptive algorithms, and time-frequency representations.

Many advanced signal processing techniques have burdensome computational requirements. A second enabling trend, therefore, has been the continuing extraordinary advances in microminiaturization and microelectronics that have provided performance leaps in circuit size, complexity, and power consumption. Today's application-specific integrated circuits (ASICs), digital signal processing chips (DSPs), and microprocessor CPUs offer unprecedented capabilities, and this continues unabated.

A third key trend, societally based, is the information explosion—the transformation of society from the industrial age to the information age. The mushrooming of the Internet and especially of its World Wide Web, the prevalence of corporate intranets, the advent of ISDN, the promise of ADSL and cable modems, and wireless communications and computing have radically transformed society. The international virtual community is not virtual—it's real.

A fourth trend that has significantly facilitated the incorporation of data compression technology into practical equipment is the incredible rush toward standardization of products and service offerings in telecommunications and networks. The recent, seemingly exponential, growth of standards-setting activities to ensure compatibility among various communications systems, networks, and compression methods has unleashed a cornucopia of new products and service offerings. Accordingly, standards are one of our principal concerns in this book.

The Beginning

The genesis of the book can be traced to a conversation between two of the authors, Toby Berger and Jerry Gibson, at the 1990 IEEE International Symposium on Information Theory in San Diego. They observed that, whereas the sessions on source coding in previous symposia had always been populated by a small clique of researchers, the San Diego source coding sessions overflowed their rooms to a degree that would have horrified a fire marshal. Moreover, the attendees included scores of practitioners from industry in addition to more than the usual number of theoreticians. Sensing that the previously described confluence of ideas and trends had matured to criticality, Toby and Jerry decided to propose a short course that would fuse theory, practice, and standards for engineers, technical managers, and computer scientists endeavoring to develop and build data compression systems for the burgeoning multimedia applications. They further planned that, after giving the course several times, they would convert the course notes into a book. UCLA Extension agreed to offer the proposed course, provided it was expanded to include more material on image compression and especially video compression. To achieve the desired expanded coverage, Gibson recruited two experts (and friends) from industry—Tom Lookabaugh and Rich Baker—both of whom were deeply involved in videoconferencing, high-quality video compression, and standards activities. Since 1992, the Berger-Gibson-Lookabaugh-Baker foursome has taught the short course on multimedia data compression a dozen times at UCLA, once on-site at Compaq, once on-site at NSA, and three times at Motorola University. The contract to produce this book was executed in 1995. Dave Lindbergh, an expert with encyclopedic knowledge of recent standards activities in videoconferencing, was added as a fifth author in 1996.

Intended Audience

The target audience for the book comprises several constituencies. Foremost among these are engineers and scientists engaged in the design, manufacture, and implementation of data compression systems for commercial applications. This group includes chip designers, software developers, telecommunications systems engineers, computer network designers, and signal processing engineers. We also intend the book to be helpful to engineering managers who lead groups and project teams in this area. In addition, the book can serve as a primary or secondary textbook for advanced undergraduate and graduate courses on data compression in electrical engineering and computer science.

A summary of the book's structure and content appears in Chapter 1. Depending upon the reader's background and interest, the chapters can be read in almost any order. However, we strongly suggest that everyone read Chapter 1 first for its overview of the field of data compression and the orientation it provides to the structure and spirit of the book. Some readers will be prepared to go directly to the chapters on the standards. Others desirous of more background can consult preparatory material in the earlier chapters.

Approach

We have attempted to produce a book that is comprehensive and precise yet accessible to a wide audience. Toward this end we have included mathematical foundations and algorithmic details whenever necessary but have relegated such material to appendices or special sections as much as possible. The details *are* important; our experience in the short course is that students rarely can get what they need for their particular application without some understanding of the basic principles. On the other hand, it will quickly be clear to the reader that this is not a classical academic textbook. It has what we think is the right mix of tutorial treatments and to-the-point developments for standards and their applications.

Acknowledgments

Gratitude and acknowledgments for guidance, insight, and assistance are due to many who helped us develop the material and publish this book. First we acknowledge Bill Goodin of UCLA Extension, who gave us the opportunity to teach the data compression short course through his program. As a result we came into contact with many talented engineers, scientists, and other professionals who took the class and used this material in their businesses. We also thank Elisabeth Beller and Jennifer Mann of Morgan Kaufmann Publishers. Elisabeth, our production editor, did a superb job of keeping everything and everybody on schedule while adhering to the highest professional standards. Jennifer Mann, our editor, patiently advised, coordinated, and cajoled us at length to produce this book. Not the least of her contributions was drawing upon a host of excellent reviewers who provided criticisms, comments, and direction. These reviewers were Barry Haskell (Lucent Technologies), William Pearlman (RPI), Bob Holm (Intel), Bob Safranek (AT&T), Bruce Walk (IBM), Ephraim Feig (IBM), Eve Riskin (University of Washington), John Limb (Georgia Tech), Mark Perkins (Algorithms and Applied Sciences), Michael Marcellin (University of Arizona), Ping Wah Wong (HP Labs), Richard Cox (AT&T Labs), Roger Dressler (Dolby), Roy Hoffman (IBM), and Tim Midwinter (British Telecom). Although they all provided us with valuable insights, we single out Rich Cox for diligence far above and beyond the call of duty. Rich spent dozens of hours critically reading the bulk of the manuscript in minute detail and shared generously of his experience and deep knowledge of the topics; we are especially grateful. We are also beholden to many of our students and colleagues who provided wisdom and counsel and/or detected both typographical and more egregious errors. The list of names that follows is partial; we apologize to the considerable number of individuals whom we have unintentionally omitted.

- From Toby Berger—Raymond Yeung, Ram Zamir, Victor Wei, Srikant Jayaraman, Harish Viswanathan, P. Subrahmanya, Ashok Montravadi, James Chow, Adi Wyner, Ed Mosteig, Luis Lastros, EE 562 and EE 567 at Cornell University, EE 717 at the University of Virginia.

- From Jerry Gibson—Madhukar Budagavi, Hui Dong, Mark Kokes, Justin Ridge, Roderick Maddox, Fred Ware, Wenye Yang, Mark Randolph, Sharif Sazzad, Jason Brewer, Vince Rhee, Stan McClellan, Myron Moodie, Seung Nam, Insung Lee, Yoon Chae Cheong, Hong Chae Woo, Dae Gwon Jeong, Victor Taylor, Boneung Koo, Wen Whei Chang, Steven Gray, Khalid Sayood, David Comstock, Jane Asmuth, Richard Fenwick, Charles Moore, David Purcell, John McVay, Andy Goris, Louis Sauter, Victor Berglund, and Ed Cross.
- From Tom Lookabaugh—Matt Goldman, Mike Perkins, Didier Le Gall, Bill Helms, Christie Caldwell, and Robin Wilson.
- From Dave Lindbergh—Jeff Bernstein, Suneel Bhagat, Steve Botzko, Tony Crossman, Mike Nilsson, Sakae Okubo, Mark Reid, Gary Sullivan, John Villasenor, Hong Wang, and Bob Webber.
- From all of us—students of all the incarnations of our UCLA short course.

Get Started!

The field of data compression is an exciting and vital one. Applications of data compression grow with each passing day. We hope you find reading this book enjoyable, informative, and profitable.

1 Introduction to Data Compression

CHAPTER

1.1 Why Compress?

Entertainment, telecommunications, the Internet—all are part of our daily lives. We enjoy them, use them in our businesses, surf them. We read about them in magazines and newspapers. We hear about them on television. We invest in them. But we've had radio, TV, music, and telephones for decades. What's new now? Is it all hype? Not really—at least, not all of it! The new word is "digital." Today we are talking about digital communications systems and networks and digital representations of movies, TV, music, images, and voice. Why digital? Digital signals are easy to store and easy to transmit over long distances without accumulating distortion, and stored digital representations (for example, of music) are highly resistant to minor degradations.

But there is a downside. Digital versions of important signals, like voice, music, TV, and movies, require more bits per second of signal to store or transmit, which translates into higher costs. For example, Table 1.1 presents the raw (uncompressed) data rates of several important source signals (Jayant, Johnston, and Safranek 1993). Certainly, many of the numbers seem large, but these numbers are only significant in comparison to the storage capacity available or the rate that can be sent over a chosen communications link. To get some idea of the significance of the rates in Table 1.1, note that the current common telephone modem rate is 28.8 kbps and the bit rate allocated to voice in North American digital cellular is 8 kbps, so the uncompressed 96-kbps requirement for telephone bandwidth voice is too high by about 12:1. Further, CD-ROM capacity is roughly 650 megabytes, and the capacity of one version of the evolving digital versatile (or video) disc (DVD-5) is roughly 40 gigabits.

T A B L E 1.1	Approximate Bit Rates for Uncompressed Sources
Telephony (200–3400 Hz):	8000 samples/second × 12 bits/sample = 96 kbps
Wideband speech (50–7000 Hz):	16,000 samples/second × 14 bits/sample = 224 kbps
Wideband audio (20–20,000 Hz):	44,100 samples/second × 2 channels × 16 bits/sample = 1.412 Mbps
Images:	512 × 512 pixel color image × 24 bits/pixel = 6.3 Mbits/image
Video:	640 × 480 pixel color image × 24 bits/pixel × 30 images/second = 221 Mbps
HDTV:	1280 × 720 pixel color image × 60 images/second × 24 bits/pixel = 1.3 Gbps

Thus, for uncompressed video, the CD-ROM could store 23.5 seconds, and the DVD-5 could store about 3 minutes.

If the numbers in Table 1.1 turn out to be too large, and often they do, what can we do to improve the situation and still retain the advantages of digital transmission and storage? The answer is compression. Very generally, compression is the efficient digital representation of a source signal, such as speech, still images, music, or video; that is, we use as few bits as possible to represent the source signal while still having an adequate reproduction of the original (Berger 1971). Hence, the role of compression is to minimize the number of bits needed to retain an acceptable version of the original source signal, thus reducing storage and transmission costs (Sayood 1996).

Although you may now be convinced that compression is needed, it is natural to ask, What is enabling the current proliferation of compression applications? That is, computers, digital communications systems, and telecommunications networks have all been around for decades, so why are we able to implement these compression techniques now? Five events have made this possible. First, we are picking the fruits of over a quarter of a century of extraordinary research in compression methods. Since few people anticipated the amazing array of high-technology consumer products that we have today, much of this research was conducted without these products in mind. However, without this solid foundation of basic research, the rapid progress that we have seen would have been impossible. Second, signal processing capabilities are unparalleled, from VLSI implementations through today's powerful digital signal processors (DSPs) to, more recently, high-speed microprocessors in commonly available personal computers. With such computing power, seemingly complicated equations and algorithms can be implemented without excessive expense. Third, the introduction of perceptually based distortion measures has provided the final giant step toward producing the quality needed in applications—especially important since so many of the applications involve voice, music, images, and video, where the end user is the human eye or ear. Fourth, standards-setting activities have reduced the risk of offering products and services that incorporate compression by guaranteeing product and system interoperability. Finally, evolving technological advances in networks, computers, and telecommunications all continue to open new opportunities and to increase the pace of acceptance of compression methods.

Thus, this book is about compression—the compression of all sources, including data, voice, video, still images, audio, and movies. We discuss basic principles, common algorithms, and important standards. The goal is to help you understand current compression techniques and standards and why the various design choices and trade-offs were made. We also hope to prepare you to evaluate and design new compression algorithms and standards.

In the remainder of this chapter, we pose the data compression problem more carefully and describe the main issues involved in designing, implementing, selecting, and evaluating data compression methods, algorithms, standards, and services.

1.2   The Data Compression Problem

Data compression is simply the efficient digital representation of a source. However, this definition can be embellished slightly to make it more explicit: data compression is the representation of a source in digital form with as few bits as possible while maintaining an acceptable loss in fidelity. The source can be data, still images, speech, audio, video, or whatever signal needs to be stored or transmitted. In this book we use the term "data compression" to encompass both lossless and lossy compression of sources—*lossless* means perfect reconstruction of the source and *lossy* means that the source is not perfectly preserved in the representation. Over the years, there are a host of terms that have been used as synonyms for data compression—and still are—so it is appropriate to review them briefly.

1.2.1   Synonyms for Data Compression

The two terms most often used today as synonyms for data compression are *signal compression* and *signal coding* (Jayant, Johnston, and Safranek 1993).

These terms avoid the confusion that may arise from using the word *data,* since to some people, the word *data* can be limiting and exclude the possibility that we are considering speech, audio, or video compression, for example. The adjective *signal* seems a little bit too inclusionary, perhaps, but these terms are gaining some acceptance. In the information theory literature, the terms *source coding* and *source coding with a fidelity criterion* are common, although the latter is found much less often today than 15 to 20 years ago. *Source coding* can mean both lossless and lossy compression, but it is sometimes reserved by authors to indicate lossless coding only. *Source coding with a fidelity criterion* is long and unwieldy, but absolutely explicit in specifying that the compression being considered is lossy (Shannon 1959; Berger 1971; Gray 1990).

Some researchers in speech and audio compression use the term *source coding* to mean source model based coding, which is at some variance with the original information theoretic usage (Flanagan et al. 1979). However, once aware of this ambiguity, confusion can be avoided with careful reading. Other terms used are *noiseless* and *noisy (source) coding,* which refer, respectively, to lossless and lossy coding. The "noise" referred to is reconstruction error, or reconstruction noise; the use of "noise" in this context probably evolved since channel coding for noisy channels was developed and accepted earlier than source coding. A term coined to avoid the confusion that comes with "compression" is *data compaction,* which is used to indicate lossless encoding of a source. This term is a good one but has not received widespread acceptance (Blahut 1987). More dated synonyms for data compression are *bandwidth compression* and *redundancy removal.* Bandwidth compression is interchangeable with *signal compression* and *data compression,* in general; redundancy removal refers to one step in a lossy coding process, such as prediction in speech coding.

Throughout this book, we will employ "data compression" in the most inclusive sense.

1.2.2 Components of a Data Compression Problem

The major components of a data compression problem are the source, the rate, and the fidelity criterion or distortion measure. We are interested in compressing all sources, but different approaches to compression can be taken depending on whether a good source model is available or not. For example, telephone bandwidth speech is accurately represented for many applications by what is called the *linear prediction model;* hence this structure appears explicitly in many speech coders. On the other hand, wideband audio, still images, and video lack a very structured model; hence, compression of these sources tends not to rely on a particular source model.

T A B L E   Audio Sampling Rates

1.2

Application	Bandwidth (kHz)	Sampling Rate (kHz)
Voice telephony	3.2	8
Teleconferencing (audio)	7.0	16
Compact disc (CD) audio	20.0	44.1
Digital audiotape (DAT)	20.0	48

T A B L E   Video Sampling Rates

1.3

Format	Lines/Frame × Pixels/Line × Frames/Second =	Sampling Rate (million pixels per second)
CIF (videoconferencing)	360 × 288 × 30 =	3
CCIR (TV)	720 × 576 × 30 =	12
HDTV	1280 × 720 × 60 =	60

The second component, rate (in bits/second), is important. Bit rate can be considered to be made up of sampling rate (in samples/second) times accuracy (in bits/sample). Tables 1.2 and 1.3 show sampling rates for various audio and video sources (Jayant, Johnston, and Safranek 1993). The rates in Table 1.2 roughly represent sampling at the Nyquist rate (rate equal to twice the bandwidth of the source), although various other issues cause the sampling rate to be set above the minimum possible. Table 1.3 illustrates some important differences in audio and video. For video, there is a specified number of horizontal and vertical samples per frame, and then there is a temporal sampling in terms of frames per second. In voice applications, the sampling rates specified are not varied widely. However, in video, considerable license may be taken. Specifically, common routes to lower data rates for video are to reduce the frame size and/or lower the frame rate, both with attendant loss in quality.

The third component of a data compression problem is the fidelity criterion or distortion measure. For mathematical tractability in lossy coding, a preferred choice is the squared error distortion measure, but this criterion has a well-known mismatch with both audio and video subjective performance. As noted, one of the principal areas leading to recent performance leaps in compression algorithms is the use of more perceptually based distortion measures—for voice coding, high-quality audio coding, and for quantization table design for still images and video. As it turns out, how perceptual measures are incorporated is different in each of these cases, but the overriding performance advantage that perceptually based coding provides is undebatable. Subsequent chapters will bear this out.

1.2.3   Types of Compression Problems

There are two types of compression problems of interest (Davisson and Gray 1976). One problem is specified in terms of a constraint on transmitted data rate or storage capacity, and the problem is to compress the source at or below this rate but at the highest fidelity possible. This problem is sometimes called the *distortion-rate problem*. Examples of this problem are voice mail, digital cellular mobile radio, and videoconferencing. A second type of problem consists of the requirement to achieve a certain prespecified fidelity, and to satisfy this constraint with as few bits per second as possible. This problem is called the *rate-distortion problem*. Examples of this approach are CD-quality audio and motion-picture-quality video.

1.3   Input Source Formats

We are interested in the compression of data, voice, audio, still images, and video, and the specification of the specific source format, such as sampling rate, image size, color or black-and-white, and so on, has a tremendous bearing on what rate, distortion, and complexity combination is necessary. Of course, some applications may set these specifications automatically, such as in the compression of movies and high-quality audio. However, other applications, such as forms of teleconferencing, are wide open in terms of the source formats that we desire to employ, at least until a standard is set, as in H.320 and H.324.

For facsimile, the ITU-T standard has two resolutions, as shown in Table 1.4, and expects the image to be bi-level black on white. This type of specification is clearly a tremendous aid in designing successful data compression (data compaction) systems. Tables 1.1 through 1.3 presented other typical speech, audio, still-image, and video formats; Tables 1.5 and 1.6 provide additional examples for image and video applications.

For telephony, a sampling rate of 8000 samples/second is fairly universally accepted. For wideband speech, the sampling rate is usually 16,000 samples/second. For high-quality audio, there are some differences in sampling rate, as indicated for CD audio and DAT audio in Table 1.2. For still images and video, however, there are a host of formats and applications, as is abundantly

T A B L E   ITU-T Facsimile Standards

1.4

Size	Vertical Resolution (lines/mm)	Horizontal Resolution (pixels/mm)	Lines/Frame	Pixels/Line
Normal resolution 20.7 cm (8.27 inches) by 29.2 cm (11.7 inches)	3.85	8	1188	1728
High resolution 20.7 cm (8.27 inches) by 29.2 cm (11.7 inches)	7.7	8	2376	1728

T A B L E   H.324 Video Formats

1.5

Format	Pixels	H.261	H.263
SQCIF	128 × 96	optional	required
QCIF	176 × 144	required	required
CIF	352 × 288	optional	optional
4 CIF	704 × 576	n/a	optional
16 CIF	1408 × 1152	n/a	optional

clear from Table 1.6. Not only is the image size important, but the frame rate is critical as well, and again, it can have variations. In fact, it can have a greater variation than implied by Table 1.6, since this is one of the primary parameters that is adjusted in videoconferencing applications to stay within the required bit rate.

For color images, there are also the issues of color space and subsampling ratios of the components. There are at least two very common color representation formats, one consisting of the luminance and two chrominance components, designated YCbCr, and the other consisting of the three colors red-green-blue, designated RGB. The subsampling ratios between the components also vary. For example, the CCIR-601 format has an option for NTSC that specifies a spatial resolution of 720 × 480 pixels for the luminance component and 360 × 480 pixels for each of the two chrominance components. This subsampling format is denoted as 4:2:2. Alternatively, there is the SIF (source input format) specified by MPEG-1, where the luminance spatial resolution is 360 × 240 and the two chrominance components have a resolution of 180 × 120, which is denoted as 4:2:0 subsampling.

TABLE 1.6   Image and Video Formats

Formats	Usable Horizontal Lines*	Pixels per Line	Total Pixels per Frame	Frames per Second	Required Bandwidth/ Transmission Rate
Analog video					
NTSC (Americas, Asia)	338	426	150,000	29.97	4 MHz
PAL (Europe)	411	420	172,000	25.00	5 MHz
VHS	338	280	95,000	29.97	<4 MHz
Computer image					
SVGA	1024	768	786,500	60	—
VGA	640	480	307,000	60	—
Motion picture film					
35mm	(not a raster-		500,000	24	—
16mm	scanned image)		125,000	24	—
Digital video					
QCIF (H.261)	144	176	25,000	15–30	56 kbps–2 Mbps
CIF (H.261)	288	352	100,000	15–30	56 kbps–2 Mbps
HDTV	806	1920	1,550,000	50	140 Mbps
MPEG (constrained set)	345	360	124,000	30	1.5 Mbps and higher

*Eliminates retrace lines and includes the utilization ratio.

All in all, as this short section makes clear, there is quite a variety of source formats. In later sections and chapters discussing algorithms and standards, the details of the source format being employed are clearly stated. Matching the source format to the particular application is critical to the design of an efficient data compression system and to the success of the final product for that application.

1.4   Reconstructed Source Quality

Throughout the discussion thus far, and for almost the entire range of sources, we have emphasized that quality is an important requirement. Since these are real sources and there is a vast array of standards and applications, you might certainly wonder how the quality of the reconstructed source is measured and, further, how data compression systems are designed to achieve sufficiently high quality. These are two separate, but related, issues.

1.4.1   Performance Measurement

The measurement of coder performance is a long-standing and difficult problem, since what is desired is an objective or numerical indicator of performance that translates into what the user agrees is good quality. After a great deal of research and experience, some usable indicators of performance for telephone bandwidth speech coders have been developed. These are described in additional detail in Appendix A, but we mention a few here to orient you to their importance and to the limitations inherent in such indicators. The most widely quoted measure of speech coder performance is the Mean Opinion Score (MOS). An MOS for a coder is a value from 1 to 5, indicating the listeners' assessment of the reconstructed speech quality when presented with coded speech samples and asked to rate them with respect to the following scale: excellent (5), good (4), fair (3), poor (2), bad (1). The MOS values for a coder can vary across languages and between tests, but for G.711 log-PCM, an MOS of 4.0 to 4.2 is often quoted. Thus, this value would be associated with toll quality.

Another measure used to assess the performance of speech coders is the Diagnostic Rhyme Test (DRT). This test is primarily designed to determine speech intelligibility and consists of using trained listeners to evaluate coded pairs of words that differ in beginning or ending consonant sounds. The DRT score for a "good" speech coder is usually in the 85–90 range. There is also an assessment test for quality called the Diagnostic Acceptability Measure (DAM), which is a multidimensional test intended to evaluate medium- to high-quality speech. While the DAM scores can be useful, DAM has not been as widely accepted as the MOS and DRT in speech coder evaluations. Typical values of the MOS, DRT, and DAM for common speech coders are shown in Table 1.7 (Jayant 1992). You should only regard the values in Table 1.7 as approximate, since different implementations and test conditions can cause variations.

1.4.2   Perceptual Distortion Measures

We turn now to how perceptual effects can be incorporated into the design of compression systems for speech, audio, still images, and video. The specifics of the approaches are different in each case, but some of the concepts are the same. The broad idea is that inaccuracies in the reconstructed source can be

T A B L E	DRT, DAM, and MOS Scores for Common Speech Coders			
1.7	Coder	DRT	DAM	MOS
	64-kbps PCM (Pulse Code Modulation)	95	73	4.2
	32-kbps ADPCM (Adaptive Differential PCM)	94	68	4.0
	16-kbps LD-CELP (Low-Delay Code Excited Linear Predictive Coding)	94	70	4.0
	4.8-kbps CELP (Code Excited Linear Predictive Coding)	91	65	3.2
	2.4-kbps LPC (Linear Predictive Coder—vocoder)	87	54	2.2

covered up, or *masked,* by the components in the source signal itself. The result is that by shaping the reconstruction error spectrum or spatial distribution in relation to the source, much larger errors can be absorbed without being objectionable to the user. In early telephony-based speech coding, this approach was called *noise spectral shaping,* but more recently and in high-quality audio, this approach is called *auditory masking.* The real power of the analysis-by-synthesis speech coders lies in the perceptually based distortion measure that chooses the excitation by minimizing a distortion measure that weights errors differently according to their relationship to the input spectral content.

For high-quality audio, where real-time operation may not be required and additional encoder complexity may be acceptable, even more effort is placed on exploiting the masking effects. In particular, the input audio spectrum is accurately calculated and a masking threshold is determined using known results from auditory masking experiments. The result is transparent-sounding audio at surprisingly low bit rates.

For still images and video, the incorporation of perceptual effects tends to come during the design of the encoder quantization tables. Extensive perceptual experiments are performed over a representative set of input image or video sources, and the quantizer characteristics are adjusted to minimize visual distortion. The final result can be that very simple scalar quantizers may achieve acceptable visual quality at bit rates often associated with vector quantization.

The importance of perceptually based distortion measures on data compression system performance cannot be overemphasized. Virtually all successful data compression systems today have this principle at their core.

1.5   System Issues and Performance Comparisons

In Section 1.2, we noted that the three major components of a data compression problem are the source, the rate, and the distortion measure. Further, the two types of problems of interest in compression applications, rate distortion and distortion rate, were also outlined in that section. Section 1.3 introduced several possible source formats and pointed out the importance of a clear specification of the source to the success of a compression algorithm and product. We have also mentioned in previous sections that the introduction of perceptually based distortion measures has been instrumental in the widespread utilization of compression in applications.

If the only consideration in designing and evaluating data compression systems is achieving acceptable performance at a specified rate, the problem may be very easy indeed. For example, part of the ITU-T G.726 specification is to achieve toll-quality speech coding at 32 kbps. It turns out that these two requirements alone on rate and quality are very simple to achieve. However, that is not all that is required by the specification. Other requirements include low delay, less than 5 ms (not too difficult); moderate to low complexity (still doable); tandem connections with other speech coders (probably not too hard at this rate); acceptable performance with an independent bit error rate up to 0.01 (more challenging); and pass signaling tones and some voiceband data modem signals with good performance (nontrivial). So, for most problems, if we are lucky enough only to have to address rate and distortion performance, the problem is much simplified. However, this is seldom the case, and these system and network issues, as we call them, can completely dominate the compression system approach and design. In this section, we call attention to several of the surrounding issues that become important in the subsequently considered compression standards and applications.

The voice telephony issues that have just been touched upon continue to be important today. In these telephony applications, the usual desire is toll quality, which is considered to be equivalent to 64 kbps G.711, and as low a complexity implementation as possible, although implementations on fixed or floating-point DSPs become acceptable as the rates are pushed down to 16 kbps and below. The low-delay requirement follows from the desire to eliminate or reduce the use of echo cancelers, but again, as rates are pushed below 16 kbps, the ITU-T has been more forgiving on this specification. For telephony applications, tandeming (or interoperability) is an issue that will not go away, since it will always be a requirement to operate with voice coders in other parts of the wired network and, of course, to interoperate with speech coders in various digital cellular mobile radio systems. The necessity for speech coders to perform adequately over channels that introduce bit errors is also a common requirement, whether one expects independent bit errors at rates of 10^{-9} or 10^{-2} or a fading channel that can produce burst errors.

For digital cellular mobile radio systems, the low-delay requirement is not present because burstiness of the channel requires interleaving, which already inserts substantial delay. A requirement that is implicit in telephony—and that takes on additional importance in digital cellular and, for that matter, in developing personal communications systems (PCS) applications—is the need for good speech coder performance in the presence of background noise and competing sounds such as road noise. Also, in the mobile environment, complexity is an issue in terms of battery power usage.

Not all voice coding applications have such stringent requirements. Voice messaging needs good quality, often called *communications quality,* but not toll quality; low-to-moderate complexity; and usually has no bit error rate requirements—although we might imagine the need to send digitized voice mail over a noisy channel. Additionally, low delay is not an issue, although excessive delay might be a problem because of intermediate storage needs.

One of the principal applications for wideband speech is telephony-based videoconferencing, hence many of the telephone-band voice coding requirements may carry forward. In general, however, low delay is not imposed because additional delay is often added to the coded speech to synchronize with the compressed video, which takes longer to code. Channel errors can still be a problem, but quality, rate, and complexity are dominant issues in such applications.

High-quality audio for storage applications usually involves non-real-time encoding and very low error rate channels, so the principal issues are quality, rate, and decoder complexity. Of course, the requirement might be added in some applications for remote encoding and broadcastlike transmission to users.

Still-image compression is often applied to image storage and retrieval, so the issues are quality, bit rate, and complexity, especially decoder complexity. However, as is evident from applications of the JPEG standard, compressed imagery may be transmitted over a variety of nonideal channels, and so the effects of bit errors introduced by a channel could become important.

Video compression for video telephony and videoconferencing applications needs to be the highest possible quality for the several stated bit rates, not too complex (but most coders are fairly complicated), with as low a delay as possible (but certainly not what is called "low delay" for speech coders, 5 ms or less), and able to operate with bit errors.

For MPEG-1 and MPEG-2 stored video applications, quality, rate, and decoder complexity are paramount. For most of their envisioned applications, bit errors during transmission are not a major issue, but innovative applications are already employing these standards in transmission environments. For stored video playback, issues derived from VCR-type features, such as fast forward, rewind, pause, and fast search, are critical.

This is but a brief view of systems and operational issues that may dominate a particular application of compression techniques or be part of a standards specification. The goal is not to be exhaustive, but suggestive of the types of requirements that arise in current applications and that may arise as engineers and entrepreneurs develop new products and services.

1.6   Applications and Standards

There are a host of known applications for data compression techniques and systems, and new applications are being proposed each day, creating a demand for modifications of existing compression methods or entirely new approaches. Existing applications of compression methods include facsimile, voice mail, telephony, digital cellular mobile radio, personal communications systems, CD-quality audio, still-image archival, videoconferencing, and video and movie distribution, just to name a few. These applications have led to a plethora of compression standards—agreed-upon techniques and systems-level specifications that are adopted by interested industry representatives to allow the manufacture of compatible equipment.

There are numerous active standards-setting bodies—for example, the International Telecommunication Union (ITU), the U.S. ANSI Committee T1 on Telecommunications, the Telecommunications Industry Association (TIA), the European Telecommunications Standards Institute (ETSI), the Japanese Telecommunications Technology Committee (TIC), the Institute of Electrical and Electronics Engineers (IEEE), and the International Standards Organization (ISO). Each of these has had a role in setting standards for data compression. The standards efforts have been phenomenally successful. Important standards have been produced, and in general, most of the standards development efforts have moved along at a relatively rapid pace. Additionally, the standards bodies and the particular standards committees have been responsive to perceived needs and requested modifications.

Tables 1.8 and 1.9 contain abridged lists of voice, still-image, and video coding standards. The sheer variety of standards being set and the dates of their adoption are indicative of the level of activity in source compression. Plus, most

T A B L E	Speech Coder Standards			
1.8	Description	Year of Introduction	Bit Rates (kbps)	MOS
	PCM (for PSTN)	1972	64	4.4
	LPC-10 (U.S. Fed. Std. 1015)	1976	2.4	2.7
	G.721 ADCPM (for PSTN)	1984	32	4.1
	INMARSAT (satellite)	1990	4.15	≈3.2
	GSM (European cellular)	1991	13	3.6
	CELP (U.S. Fed. Std. 1016)	1991	4.8	3.2
	G.728 (low-delay CELP)	1992	16	4.0
	VSELP (NA cellular)	1992	8	3.5
	QCELP (NA CDMA)	1993	1–8	≈3.4
	VSELP (Japanese cellular)	1993	6.8	≈3.3
	G.729 (new toll-quality)	1995	8	≈4.2
	G.723.1 (in H.323 and H.324)	1995	6.3	3.98
	Half-rate GSM	1995	5–6	≈3.4
	New low-rate U.S. Fed. Std.	1996	2.4	≈3.3

T A B L E	Image/Video Compression Standards		
1.9	Source	Standard	Rates
	Video telephone Px64	ITU-T H.261	56 kbps–2 Mbps
	Black-and-white, color, multispectral images	JPEG	0.25–2 bits/pixel
	Moving pictures and audio	MPEG-1	1.5 Mbps
	Broadcast-quality pictures and audio	MPEG-2	6–10 Mbps
	High-quality audio for MPEG	HDTV	64/128/192 kbps per channel
	Video	H.263	≤28.8 kbps

of these standards are set in response to a perceived need for a service or product. There have been some fears that setting a standard in a particular area would inhibit research and somehow stifle the field. In general, this has not been the case. The community at large is very responsive to improvements, and engineers, managers, and entrepreneurs are always finding new applications for standards that were not previously envisioned and that lead to further refinements and research. The principal challenge is the exceedingly fast pace of activity.

1.7   Outline of the Book

The major steps in data compression are summarized in Figure 1.1. The source may first go through a redundancy removal stage, which often consists of time domain prediction or frequency domain transforms or their equivalent. The parameters generated by the redundancy removal step are then passed to an entropy reduction step, which is some version of quantization. Finally, the quantizer outputs are losslessly encoded and sent to the storage device or transmitted over the channel. Reconstruction consists of decoding in the reverse direction.

The development of the basic principles in this book starts with lossless coding, then considers entropy reduction, and then finally redundancy removal. Note that if we begin with what is called a discrete memoryless source, such as independent samples from a data string, the redundancy removal and entropy reduction steps are not needed, and only lossless coding is involved. If we have discrete-time, continuous-amplitude samples of a memoryless source, then we need both the entropy reduction and lossless coding steps, but not redundancy removal. For sources like voice, video, and audio, we need all three steps, including redundancy removal, for efficient compression.

Chapter 2 covers basic details of lossless coding, along with a treatment of Huffman coding. Chapter 3 follows with a development of universal lossless coding, including Lempel-Ziv and arithmetic coding. Chapter 4 presents the essential ideas and techniques for scalar, adaptive, and vector quantization. Predictive coding, particularly as employed in the numerous telephony and digital cellular speech coding standards, is introduced in Chapter 5. Chapter 6 describes the existing and evolving speech coding standards based upon predictive coding, giving performance comparisons, system-level assumptions,

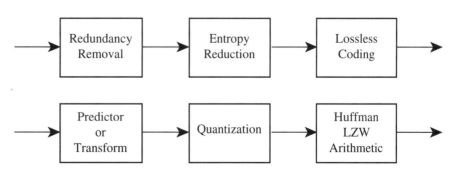

FIGURE

1.1   Major Steps in Data Compression

and their relative complexity. The fundamentals of frequency domain coding, including subband, discrete transform, wavelet, and fractal decompositions, are presented in Chapter 7. Chapter 8 then describes how these frequency domain ideas are incorporated in speech and high-quality audio compression algorithms and systems. The JPEG still-image compression standard is covered in Chapter 9 with discussions of baseline JPEG, the progressive transmission mode, and the lossless mode. The H.320, H.323, and H.324 standards for videoconferencing are presented in Chapter 10, which also contains video and audio compression capabilities as well as important system operational details. Chapter 11 discusses the MPEG-1, MPEG-2, and MPEG-4 standards, including compression details, bitstream syntax, and system-level features.

The general approach of this book is to provide the requisite background details concerning lossless coding, quantization, and redundancy removal and then go over the standards that utilize these techniques. This book is not intended to be a research monograph or an introductory textbook, so the material presented was selected based upon what is being used today, what are the fundamental underpinnings of today's methods, and what knowledge is needed to track evolving capabilities.

2 Lossless Source Coding

2.1 Introduction

Lossless coding techniques provide for exact recovery of the original data from its compressed version. A key application in which lossless coding is required is the compression of computer files to save disk space; reconstitution from the compressed representation must result in a file that is identical to the original file. At present, most hardware and software utilities that compress computer files implement variants of the Lempel-Ziv compression algorithm; examples are Unix Compress, Stacker, and gzip. Moreover, most modems operating at 14,400 baud or higher use Lempel-Ziv data compression in their default configuration. Adaptive Huffman codes are used as lossless compressors in the Unix Compact utility. Also, modified Huffman codes are used in international standards for Group 3 fax, Group 4 fax, JPEG image compression, and MPEG video compression. Another lossless coding technique, called *arithmetic coding*, has been adopted as the core compression component of the JBIG fax standard.

Lempel-Ziv algorithms, arithmetic codes, and adaptive Huffman codes all are examples of *universal* lossless compressors. A compression algorithm is considered to be universal if it can compress data efficiently despite possessing no prior statistical knowledge of the process that generated the data. We defer the treatment of universal data compression to Chapter 3. Here in Chapter 2 we limit our attention to the theory and design of lossless compression codes for sources whose statistics are known. This not only is of considerable interest in itself, but it also lays the groundwork for Chapter 3's extension to universality. From the outset, emphasis is placed on Huffman codes because of their optimality properties, their structural simplicity, and their role in fax, speech, image, and video standards.

If you are already familiar with Huffman coding, you may proceed directly to the applications in Sections 2.7 and 2.8. Group 3 and Group 4 fax standards are treated in Section 2.7, with emphasis on the modified Huffman codes that reside at their core. The design of efficient codes for effectively lossless compression of line drawings is treated in Section 2.8. This serves to exhibit the power of combining Markov modeling techniques with Huffman coding and also motivates the extension of lossless coding to sources with Markovian and other memory structures, which is the subject matter of the remaining sections of the chapter. There the entropy of a random variable and the entropy rate of a statistically stationary data source are defined precisely, culminating in Shannon's fundamental result that a source can be compressed down to, but not below, its entropy rate.

2.2   Instantaneous Variable-Length Codes

When tasked with compressing data, we often possess at least approximate knowledge of the probability distribution $p(\cdot)$ of single source letters. If no further statistical information is available, then the source should be modeled as a sequence $\{U_k, k = 1, 2, \ldots\}$ of independent, identically distributed (i.i.d.) random variables each governed by $p(\cdot)$. The fact that an i.i.d. source has no statistical dependence among its successive source symbols precludes the possibility of compressing it nearly as dramatically as can be done for sources whose memory spans many symbols; indeed, most practical situations in which data compression is used involve sources with substantial memory. However, we usually do not know the higher-order probability distributions that govern pairs, triples, and longer n-tuples of source letters. Until further notice we shall assume an i.i.d. model, not only for the above reason but also because i.i.d. models are relatively easy to understand yet general enough to illustrate most of the fundamental concepts.

Assume that the symbols of our i.i.d. source are governed by the probability distribution $\{p(u), u \in \mathcal{U}\}$. Here, the *source alphabet*, $\mathcal{U} = \{a_1, a_2, \ldots, a_M\}$, is a discrete set composed of M distinct elements called the *source letters*.

In the 1800s Samuel F. B. Morse made telegraph transmission more efficient by assigning short code strings to frequently occurring letters and longer code strings to letters that occur less often. We shall henceforth refer to this as *Morse's principle*, even though his famous Morse code does not strictly adhere to it.

T A B L E	Code A: Standard Binary Code for $M = 8$		
2.1	Source Letter	Letter Probability	Binary Codeword
	a_1	0.40	000
	a_2	0.15	001
	a_3	0.15	010
	a_4	0.10	011
	a_5	0.10	100
	a_6	0.05	101
	a_7	0.04	110
	a_8	0.01	111

Morse code maps the 26 letters of the English alphabet and a few key punctuation marks into variable-length strings from a code alphabet, $\mathcal{X}$. In Morse's case, $\mathcal{X}$ was a quaternary alphabet, $\{dot, dash, mark, space\}$. Moreover, marks and spaces can be followed directly only by dots or dashes, not by marks or spaces. Speaking strictly from the viewpoint of data compression, using marks and spaces only as separators is inefficient. However, it simplifies learning to transmit and receive and provides a measure of immunity to noise in the transmission path. Because of the unequal durations of the symbols of Morse code and the restrictions on transitions between symbols, analysis of Morse code is more difficult than analysis of the codes considered in this chapter (see Blahut 1987).

We shall index the source letters in order of decreasing probability and let p_j be shorthand for $p(a_j)$. For illustrative purposes, let's consider the example in which $p_1 = 0.4$, $p_2 = p_3 = 0.15$, $p_4 = p_5 = 0.1$, $p_6 = 0.05$, $p_7 = 0.04$, and $p_8 = 0.01$. These letter probabilities of course satisfy the requirement $p_1 + \cdots + p_8 = 1$.

Tables 2.1 through 2.4 show Code A, Code B, Code C, and Code D. Each of these codes is a prescription for assigning different binary strings, called *codewords*, to each of the eight source letters in our example. In Code A all eight codewords have the same length, namely 3. Therefore, Code A is said to be a *fixed-length code*, or *block code*. Because the codewords comprising Code B are of different lengths, it is said to be a *variable-length code* (VL code). Codes C and D also are VL codes. (Block codes are special cases of VL codes, but not vice versa.)

Representing data in binary form permits us to store it conveniently in computer memories and to send it efficiently using standard data transmission

T A B L E	**Code B: Optimum One-Shot VL Code**		
2.2	Source Letter	Letter Probability	Binary Codeword
	a_1	0.40	0
	a_2	0.15	1
	a_3	0.15	00
	a_4	0.10	01
	a_5	0.10	10
	a_6	0.05	11
	a_7	0.04	000
	a_8	0.01	001

T A B L E	**Code C: Prefix Code That Violates Morse's Principle**		
2.3	Source Letter	Letter Probability	Binary Codeword
	a_1	0.40	010
	a_2	0.15	011
	a_3	0.15	00
	a_4	0.10	100
	a_5	0.10	101
	a_6	0.05	110
	a_7	0.04	1110
	a_8	0.01	1111

T A B L E	**Code D: A Code That Is UD but Not Prefix**		
2.4	Source Letter	Letter Probability	Binary Codeword
	a_1	0.40	0
	a_2	0.15	011
	a_3	0.15	1010
	a_4	0.10	1011
	a_5	0.10	10000
	a_6	0.05	10001
	a_7	0.04	10010
	a_8	0.01	10011

equipment. Since in most modern types of computer memory, the amount of space required to store a 0 is the same as that required to store a 1, the principal aim in designing a data compression code is to reduce the average number of code symbols per source symbol, where the average is taken with respect to the statistics of the data source. Likewise, in most modern data transmission equipment, it takes the same length of time and the same amount of energy to send a 0 over the channel as it does to send a 1. Hence, for data transmission purposes, too, the driving design consideration in the selection of a data compression code is the average number of code symbols per source symbol.

If we let l_j denote the length of the binary codeword assigned to source symbol a_j, then the expected number of code symbols per source symbol is

$$\bar{l} = \sum_{j=1}^{M} p_j l_j \tag{2.1}$$

Code A uses the standard binary representations of eight distinct items—000, 001, 010, 011, 100, 101, 110, and 111. This brute-force code is referred to as the "uncompressed" binary representation. Its three binary symbols per source symbol serve as the benchmark against which the compression capability of other codes is measured. Obviously, for Code A, we have $\bar{l}_A = 3$.

Code B carries Morse's idea to its extreme. It is composed of eight short, distinct, nonempty binary strings—0, 1, 00, 01, 10, 11, 000, and 001. In keeping with Morse's principle, the string assigned to any source letter is no longer than that assigned to any less probable source letter. For Code B, we have

$$\bar{l}_B = (0.4 + 0.15) \cdot 1 + (0.15 + 0.1 + 0.1 + 0.05) \cdot 2 + (0.04 + 0.01) \cdot 3 = 1.5$$

indicating a 2:1 compression ratio relative to the brute-force approach of Code A. Similar calculations yield

$$\bar{l}_C = 0.4 \cdot 3 + 0.15 \cdot 3 + 0.15 \cdot 2 + (0.1 + 0.1 + 0.05) \cdot 3$$
$$+ (0.04 + 0.01) \cdot 4 = 2.9$$

and

$$\bar{l}_D = 0.4 \cdot 1 + 0.15 \cdot 3 + (0.15 + 0.1) \cdot 4$$
$$+ (0.1 + 0.05 + 0.04 + 0.01) \cdot 5 = 2.85$$

By construction, Code B has the minimum possible $\bar{l}$ and hence would be the code of choice if $\bar{l}$ were the only consideration. However, there are other considerations, the most important of which is unique decipherability.

2.3   Unique Decipherability

If it were the case that we knew that the source will produce one symbol at a specified instant and then never produce another symbol, then Code B would indeed be optimum for encoding the outcome of that one-shot experiment for storage or transmission. However, most data sources produce many symbols in succession, not just one. In order to encode a succession of source symbols, we must concatenate the codewords associated with these symbols. For example, suppose the source we have been considering were to produce a_3a_7 (i.e., a_3 followed by a_7). Then with code B we would concatenate the corresponding codewords, 00 and 000, thereby producing code sequence 00000. Upon receiving this code sequence, the decoder would be unable to tell whether the source had produced a_3a_7, or a_7a_3, or $a_3a_1a_3$, or any of several other possibilities. We say, therefore, that Code B is not uniquely decipherable. This problem could be circumvented by inserting "commas" between the codewords corresponding to successive source symbols. But a comma is a new code letter that is distinct from both 0 and 1, so permitting the use of commas changes the code alphabet from binary to ternary, and thereby completely changes the problem.

Instead of a comma, we could insert a special pattern of 0s and 1s, called a *flag*, between every two codewords in such a way that it could always be logically distinguished from the rest of the code string; 10 is an example of such a flag in the case of Code B. However, if a flag is employed, then the flag's length must be added to the mean codeword length calculated from the formula for $\bar{l}$ in order to obtain the actual number of code symbols per source symbol. Since the shortest viable flags for Code B have length 2, the resulting code's $\bar{l}$ balloons to 3.5.

Code A is uniquely decipherable because we know a new codeword starts every three symbols. It also has the advantage of eliminating the need for buffering in the commonly encountered situation in which the transmission channel or storage medium that is receiving the coded representation insists that binary symbols be presented to it at a fixed rate. Its disadvantages are its relatively large $\bar{l}$ and the fact that, if a code letter ever were mistakenly deleted or an extra code letter ever were mistakenly inserted, the decoder could never recover codeword synchronism.

Code C is decipherable without ambiguity because it satisfies the *prefix condition*—no short codeword may be the prefix of a longer codeword. Codes satisfying this property are called *prefix codes*. Any prefix code can be embedded in a binary tree in the manner shown in Figure 2.1 for Code C. The codewords are put in correspondence with the terminal nodes of the tree. If at each node we mark the branch exiting upward by 0 and the branch exiting downward by

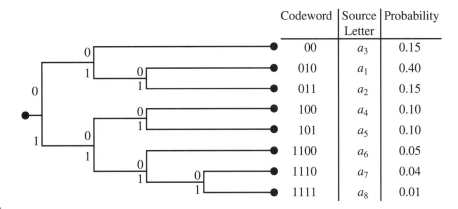

Codeword	Source Letter	Probability
00	a_3	0.15
010	a_1	0.40
011	a_2	0.15
100	a_4	0.10
101	a_5	0.10
1100	a_6	0.05
1110	a_7	0.04
1111	a_8	0.01

FIGURE

2.1   Prefix Code C Embedded in a Binary Branching Tree

1, then the codeword associated with a terminal node is the concatenation of the symbols on the branches of the path from the root to that terminal node. It is easy to recover the unique source string that gave rise to any code string obtained by concatenating words from a prefix code. For example, if you receive the string

000100110100100010101010001010100001110011011110101111

when Code C is in force, you let the received digits, starting from the left, specify a path from the root to a terminal node. When the terminal node is reached, insert an imaginary comma into the received string after the last digit used so far, return to the root, let the digits to the right of the imaginary comma specify the next path to a terminal node, and so on. For the sequence shown above, the result (with the imaginary commas displayed for clarity) is

00, 010, 011, 010, 010, 00, 101, 010, 100, 010, 101, 00, 00, 1110,

011, 011, 110, 101, 1111, . . .

which immediately translates into the source sequence

$a_3\ a_1\ a_2\ a_1\ a_1\ a_3\ a_5\ a_1\ a_4\ a_1\ a_5\ a_3\ a_3\ a_7\ a_2\ a_2\ a_6\ a_5\ a_8$ . . .

Before treating Code D, we first introduce the formal definition of *unique decipherability* (UD). Let $\underline{u} = (u_1, u_2, \ldots, u_n)$ and $\underline{\tilde{u}} = (\tilde{u}_1, \tilde{u}_2, \ldots, \tilde{u}_{\tilde{n}})$ be two sequences of source letters of possibly different lengths n and $\tilde{n}$. Let $\phi : \mathcal{U} \to \mathcal{X}^*$ be a VL code, that is, a mapping from source letters into finite-length strings from the code alphabet $\mathcal{X}$. We say ϕ is a *UD code* if the only way for the concatenation of $\phi(u_1)$, $\phi(u_2)$, . . . , and $\phi(u_n)$ to equal the concatenation of $\phi(\tilde{u}_1)$, $\phi(\tilde{u}_2)$, . . . , and $\phi(\tilde{u}_{\tilde{n}})$ is for $\underline{u}$ to equal $\underline{\tilde{u}}$.

It should be apparent that every prefix code is UD. The converse is not true. Indeed, Code D is an example of a UD code that is not a prefix code. Code D violates the prefix condition because the codeword 0, which represents a_1, is a prefix of the codeword 011, which represents a_2. To see that Code D nonetheless is UD, first observe that the other six words in Code D all start with 1, and none of them is a prefix of any other. Moreover, none of them starts with 11, so you never mistake the 11 at the end of a_2's codeword 011 for the beginning of some other codeword. The necessity to prevent codewords that start with 11 in order to preserve the crucial UD property means that certain code strings cannot possibly emerge from Code D's encoder. For example, the received code string used in the example above cannot have emanated from Code D's encoder because, after we decode the first 14 codewords, we encounter a future that begins with three successive 1s, as shown below:

0, 0, 0, 10011, 0, 10010, 0, 0, 1010, 1010, 0, 0, 1010, 10000, 11100 . . .

There is no codeword that starts this way, so there must have been a deletion, an insertion, or an error.

2.4 Huffman Codes

Code D minimizes $\bar{l}$ among the UD codes we have considered so far. However, a simple variant of Code C does even better. Note that Code C violates Morse's principle that no source letter should be assigned a codeword shorter than that assigned to a more probable source letter; a_3, which has probability 0.15, was assigned codeword 00, but a_1, which has probability 0.4, was assigned codeword 010. If we reverse these assignments, $\bar{l}_C$ drops by $0.4 - 0.15 = 0.25$, from 2.9 to 2.65, which is smaller than $\bar{l}_D = 2.85$. Since the prefix condition remains satisfied, the new code also is UD.

We can do better still. However, we don't want to be in the position of always searching for possible incremental improvements. Rather, we desire a general algorithm that, given a source letter distribution $\{p_j\}$, produces the minimum-$\bar{l}$ UD code. D. A. Huffman found such an algorithm (Huffman 1952). The optimum codes his algorithm produces are aptly called *Huffman codes*.

Huffman's algorithm iteratively generates an optimum binary-branching tree and then uses the paths to its terminal nodes as the codewords. Hence,

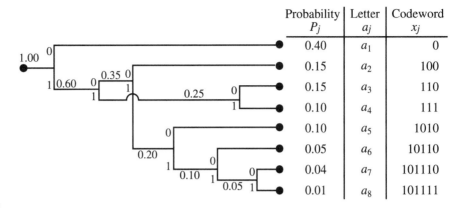

Probability P_j	Letter a_j	Codeword x_j
0.40	a_1	0
0.15	a_2	100
0.15	a_3	110
0.10	a_4	111
0.10	a_5	1010
0.05	a_6	10110
0.04	a_7	101110
0.01	a_8	101111

FIGURE

2.2   A Huffman Code for Source of the Example

Huffman codes are prefix codes. Also, Huffman's algorithm always assigns the codewords to the source letters in a manner consistent with Morse's principle.

We describe Huffman's algorithm by first applying it to our example with $p_1 = 0.40, \ldots, p_8 = 0.01$ (see Figure 2.2) and then extending to the general case. The proof that Huffman's algorithm always produces a minimum-$\bar{l}$ UD code is given in Appendix B.

The following five steps describe Huffman's algorithm in the context of our example:

1. Label each of eight nodes with one of the source letter probabilities p_j, $1 \leq j \leq 8$, as shown on the right of Figure 2.2.

2. Merge the nodes labeled by the two smallest probabilities, in this case 0.01 and 0.04, by making them the two descendants of a common ancestor node.

3. Label their ancestor with the sum of their probabilities, in this case $0.01 + 0.04 = 0.05$, as shown in Figure 2.2. For purposes of the next merge, consider that now there are only seven nodes instead of eight, namely the six original nodes not used yet and the ancestor node just created.

4. Among the seven nodes that so far have no ancestor, find two that have the smallest probability labels, in this case 0.05 and 0.05. Make them the descendants of a common ancestor, and label that ancestor with the sum of their probabilities, $0.05 + 0.05 = 0.10$.

5. Continue iteratively, at each step merging the two nodes among those that so far have no ancestor that are labeled by the smallest probabilities. Break ties any way you wish.

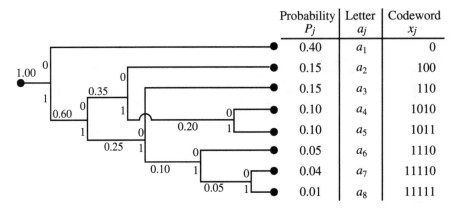

Probability P_j	Letter a_j	Codeword x_j
0.40	a_1	0
0.15	a_2	100
0.15	a_3	110
0.10	a_4	1010
0.10	a_5	1011
0.05	a_6	1110
0.04	a_7	11110
0.01	a_8	11111

FIGURE

2.3 Another Huffman Code for Source of the Example

Assigning 0 and 1 to the left and right branches, respectively, at each node yields the codeword assignments shown at the far right of Figure 2.2. There is one codeword of length 1, none of length 2, three of length 3, one of length 4, one of length 5, and two of length 6. Figure 2.3 shows an alternative Huffman tree that results from tie-breaking differently. Again there is one codeword of length 1 and none of length 2; however, this time there are two of length 3, three of length 4, two of length 5, and none of length 6. The mean codeword lengths of these two Huffman codes are

$$\bar{l}_{H_a} = 0.40 + 3(0.15 + 0.15 + 0.10) + 4 \cdot 0.10 + 5 \cdot 0.05 + 6(0.04 + 0.01)$$

$$= 0.4 + 1.2 + 0.40 + 0.25 + 0.30 = 2.55$$

and

$$\bar{l}_{H_b} = 0.40 + 3(0.15 + 0.15) + 4(0.10 + 0.10 + 0.05) + 5(0.04 + 0.01)$$

$$= 0.4 + 0.9 + 1.00 + 0.25 = 2.55$$

Although their codeword length sets are different, both Huffman codes possess the same mean codeword length; this plainly is a requirement for Huffman's algorithm to be optimum.

2.5 Nonbinary Huffman Codes

Some applications require a nonbinary code. Let us denote the cardinality $|\mathcal{X}|$ of the code alphabet $\mathcal{X}$ by D. The canonical D-ary alphabet is

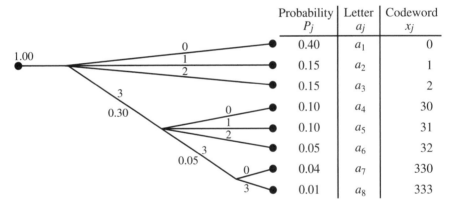

Probability P_j	Letter a_j	Codeword x_j
0.40	a_1	0
0.15	a_2	10
0.15	a_3	11
0.10	a_4	12
0.10	a_5	20
0.05	a_6	21
0.04	a_7	220
0.01	a_8	222

FIGURE 2.4   Ternary Huffman Code for Source of the Example. $J = 2 + (8 - 2) \bmod (3 - 1) = 2 + 6 \bmod 2 = 2 + 0 = 2$

Probability P_j	Letter a_j	Codeword x_j
0.40	a_1	0
0.15	a_2	1
0.15	a_3	2
0.10	a_4	30
0.10	a_5	31
0.05	a_6	32
0.04	a_7	330
0.01	a_8	333

FIGURE 2.5   Quaternary Huffman Code for Source of the Example. $J = 2 + (8 - 2) \bmod (4 - 1) = 2 + 6 \bmod 3 = 2 + 0 = 2$

$\{0, 1, \ldots, D - 1\}$. The extension from binary to general D-ary Huffman codes for a source with letter probabilities $\{p_1 \geq p_2 \geq \ldots \geq p_M\}$ is given by the following five-step algorithm. It is also illustrated in Figures 2.4 and 2.5 for $D = 3$ and $D = 4$, respectively, for the same source with $M = 8$ used in our earlier examples.

1. Label each of M nodes with one of the source letter probabilities p_j, $1 \leq j \leq M$.

2. Let $J = 2 + (M - 2)$ modulo $(D - 1)$. (For example, if $D = 3$ and $M = 8$, as in Figure 2.4, then $J = 2 + (8 - 2) \mod (3 - 1) = 2 + 6 \mod 2 = 2 + 0 = 2$; in Figure 2.5, $J = 2 + 6 \mod 3 = 2$.) Merge the nodes labeled by the J smallest probabilities $p_M, p_{M-1}, \ldots, p_{M-J+1}$ by making them the descendants of a common ancestor node. Label that ancestor node by $P_{M-J+1} + P_{M-J+2} + \cdots + P_M$.

3. Consider for the next merge only nodes that so far have no ancestor. There are $M - J + 1$ of these, namely, the $M - J$ nodes labeled by $p_1, p_2, \ldots, p_{M-J}$ and the ancestor node created and labeled in step 2.

4. Choose D nodes among those that so far have no ancestor whose labels are smallest; break ties arbitrarily. Merge the D nodes selected and assign the sum of their labels to their common ancestor.

5. Continue iteratively, at each step merging D nodes among those that so far have no ancestor whose labels are smallest.

The reason why exactly $J = 2 + (M - 2) \mod (D - 1)$ nodes are merged in the initial fan of step 2 is that this lets all the subsequent merges involve exactly D nodes and hence generate full D-ary fans. This fact, derived in Appendix B, is used there as the key step in establishing the optimality of Huffman codes for general D.

2.6   The Kraft Inequality and Optimality

There is no simple formula in terms of given source letter probabilities $\{p_j\}$ for the minimized $\bar{l}$ achieved by a Huffman code. Accordingly, there is no closed-form expression for the optimum compression ratio. However, we can develop sharp lower and upper bounds for $\bar{l}$ in terms of $\{p_j\}$. Toward this end, we first show that there exists a D-ary prefix code with word lengths $\{l_j\}$ if and only if

$$\sum_j D^{-l_j} \leq 1 \tag{2.2}$$

This condition, known as the *Kraft inequality* (Kraft 1949), is established as follows.

Given a D-ary prefix code with word lengths $\{l_j\}$, we may embed it in a D-ary tree. This embedding assigns to each codeword of length l_j a node on level l_j to serve as its terminal node. This prunes from the tree the entire structure that previously stemmed from this node; in particular, it prunes D^{L-l_j} nodes off level L. Since we cannot prune from level L more nodes than the D^L that were there in the first place, it must be that

$$\sum_j D^{L-l_j} \leq D^L \tag{2.3}$$

for every $L \geq \max_j l_j$. Dividing both sides by D^L yields the Kraft inequality.

Now suppose instead that we are given a set of integer lengths $\{l_j\}$ that satisfy the Kraft inequality. To show that there is a D-ary prefix code with these lengths, we must show that we can embed codewords of these lengths in a D-ary tree. That is, for each level l we must show that, after we have successfully embedded all words with lengths $l_j < l$, enough nodes on level l remain unpruned that we can embed a codeword there for each j such that $l_j = l$. The mathematical embodiment of this requirement is

$$D^l - \sum_{j:l_j<l} D^{l-l_j} \geq |\{j : l_j = l\}| \tag{2.4}$$

But

$$|\{j : l_j = l\}| = \sum_{j:l_j=l} 1 = \sum_{j:l_j=l} D^{l-l_j} \tag{2.5}$$

so we may recast the level-l embedding requirement in the form

$$D^l \geq \sum_{j:l_j<l} D^{l-l_j} + \sum_{j:l_j=l} D^{l-l_j} = \sum_{j:l_j\leq l} D^{l-l_j} \tag{2.6}$$

or equivalently,

$$\sum_{j:l_j\leq l} D^{-l_j} \leq 1 \tag{2.7}$$

This requirement is indeed met, since

$$\sum_{j:l_j\leq l} D^{-l_j} \leq \sum_{\text{all } j} D^{-l_j} \leq 1 \tag{2.8}$$

where in the last step we used the fact that $\{l_j\}$ satisfies the Kraft inequality.

A D-ary code for a source with letter probabilities $\{p_j, 1 \leq j \leq M\}$ is *optimum* if it is uniquely decipherable (UD) and no other UD code possesses a smaller average codeword length. Although not every UD code is a prefix code, we show in Appendix C that the codeword lengths $\{l_j\}$ of *any* UD code satisfy the Kraft inequality. It follows that, if we are given a UD code that is not a prefix code, its length set $\{l_j\}$ must satisfy the Kraft inequality, which in turn implies that there exists a prefix code that has the same $\{l_j\}$ and hence the same $\bar{l}$. This allows us to restrict our search for an optimum code to the narrower class of prefix codes. Since Huffman's algorithm generates the minimum-$\bar{l}$ prefix code (see Appendix B), it minimizes $\bar{l}$ not only over prefix codes but also over the broader class of UD codes; that is, Huffman codes are optimum.

2.7   Group 3 and Group 4 Fax Standards

The adoption of international standards for digital facsimile transmission ushered in a new era in document transmission. Now all offices and many homes are equipped with fax machines that implement these standards. It has become commonplace to transmit black-and-white documents comprised of text, line drawings, and half-toned images by fax, especially when they are needed in a hurry.

There have been three generations of digital fax standards—Group 3, Group 4, and JBIG. The Group 3 and Group 4 standards are discussed in this section. Treatment of JBIG is deferred until after the arithmetic universal coding technique has been presented in Chapter 3. Group 3 and Group 4 fax replaced Group 1 and Group 2 apparatus, which were analog in nature and did not employ any data compression. Group 1 machines required approximately 6 minutes to send a typical fax document page over a POTS line. Group 2 machines, by employing improved modulation schemes, cut this to approximately 3 minutes. Group 1 and Group 2 machines not only were temporally inefficient but also frequently produced unsatisfactory results. Today they are museum curiosities. By contrast, today's digital fax machines reliably transmit pages in a matter of seconds that are consistently accurate enough to be accepted for legal and contractual purposes.

Digital fax transmissions can be interspersed between telephone conversations on the same phone line. It is not necessary for either the transmitting or the receiving station to be attended during fax transmission.

2.7.1   Group 3 Fax

CCITT Draft Recommendation T.4 describes the standardization of Group 3 facsimile apparatus for document transmission (CCITT 1980). The standard specifies the scanning track, the dimensions of the apparatus, the transmission time, and the coding scheme. We will dispense quickly with the first three of these and then treat the coding scheme in complete detail.

G3: Scanning, Dimensions, and Transmission

Classic raster scanning is employed at both the transmitter and the receiver; that is, considering the document to be in a vertical plane facing the viewer, scanning proceeds from left to right along each line, starting at the top of the page and working to the bottom without interlacing. Each line has 1728 picture elements (pels). Each pel will be either black or white in any specific document. The standard scanning line width is 215 mm. In the vertical dimension the standard definition is 3.85 lines/mm; an optional mode with double vertical resolution (7.7 lines/mm) also is supported. Group 3 apparatus must accept documents of ISO A4 size or smaller. If one desires to send wider documents, horizontal scanning density should be reduced accordingly.

The Group 3 standard recommends a 20-ms *minimum* transmission time for the sum of the data bits, fill bits, and end-of-line (EOL) symbol that constitute the coded representation of any scan line. This requirement is imposed by mechanical limitations on the rate of advance of paper through the transmitting and receiving devices and the desire not to let the transmitter get too many lines ahead of the receiver. Because digital memory has become considerably cheaper than when the Group 3 standard originally was promulgated, today's fax machines often scan documents many times faster than the recommended 20 ms/line and store the results internally if transmission has to proceed at a lower rate. This saves the time of persons and machines at the transmitting station tasked with document handling. The Group 3 standard also provides recognized minimum transmission time options of 10 ms/line with a mandatory fallback to 20 ms if requested by the receiving machine, and of 5 ms/line with mandatory fallbacks to 10 ms and 20 ms. Finally, an option for a 40-ms/line minimum transmission time is supported, though modern equipment eschews it. Identification of the minimum transmission time of a scanning line is made during the premessage portion of the T.30 control procedure, sometimes referred to as Phase B of the call setup.

At the other extreme, no line transmission time may exceed 5 seconds. This requirement is imposed to retain synchronism and to prevent call dropping via inadvertent activation of disconnect-sensing circuitry.

G3 Coding Scheme

Group 3 fax machines use a one-dimensional runlength coding scheme. Here, "one-dimensional" refers to the fact that each successive horizontal line is coded independently of all the lines that precede and follow it, and "runlength" refers to the fact that each line is parsed into alternating runs of same-color pels— white run, black run, white run, black run, and so on.

The first run on each line is assumed to be white; if it is not white, the codeword for a white run of length 0 is sent, namely, 00110101. The sum of the lengths of all the runs on a line must be 1728. The end of each line is signaled by the EOL codeword, 000000000001. We shall see shortly that this EOL pattern (11 zeros followed by a one) can never occur anywhere else within a valid encoding other than at the end of a line. This keeps the transmitter and receiver in line synch in the absence of channel errors and allows for rapid line resynch in the event of a channel error burst that either inserts an undesired EOL or corrupts an intended one. Also, the EOL signal is sent prior to the first line of each page; that is, page breaks are signified by two successive EOLs. Accordingly, any line insertion or deletion error that might occur will not propagate beyond its page.

White runs of lengths 0 through 63 are encoded via the Terminating White Code of Table 2.5. White runs of length 64 or greater are coded by concatenating a word from the Make Up White Code of Table 2.6 with a Terminating White Code word from Table 2.5. For example, a white run of length $1362 = 64 \cdot 21 + 18 = 1344 + 18$ is encoded by concatenating the codeword 011011010 for 1344 from Table 2.6 with the codeword 0100111 for 18 from Table 2.5.

Note that both the Terminating White Code and the Make Up White Code are prefix codes—no short codeword is the prefix of a longer codeword. More importantly, note that no word in the Make Up White Code is a prefix of a word in the Terminating White Code and, conversely, no word in the Terminating White Code is a prefix of a word in the Make Up White Code. In other words, the *union* of the Terminating White Code and the Make Up White Code is a prefix code. This permits Group 3 decoders to determine unambiguously whether a terminating code (TC) or a make up code (MUC) word has been sent.

Note that greater compression could be achieved if a prefix code different from that of Table 2.5 were used to encode the residue modulo 64 of runlengths that are 64 or longer. The reasons are that, since this code would be invoked if and only if a MUC word has just been sent, its words need not be restricted not to be prefixes of any of the TC or MUC words, thereby allowing its word lengths to match better the statistics of runlengths of 64 or more calculated modulo 64. CCITT Study Group XIV chose not to do this, probably because the improvement it afforded was insufficient to justify having to store three rather than two tables for runs of a given color.

Black runs are similarly encoded by the TC and MUC words shown in Tables 2.7 and 2.8. Words from the black codes are allowed to be prefixes of words from the white codes, and vice versa. No ambiguity results because run colors always alternate and every line starts with a white run. Although there are no black runs of length 0, a black TC word for length 0 is needed because

T A B L E	Terminating White Code for Group 3 Fax				
2.5	Run	VL Word	Length	Run	VL Word	Length

Run	VL Word	Length	Run	VL Word	Length
0	00110101	8	32	00011011	8
1	000111	6	33	00010010	8
2	0111	4	34	00010011	8
3	1000	4	35	00010100	8
4	1011	4	36	00010101	8
5	1100	4	37	00010110	8
6	1110	4	38	00010111	8
7	1111	4	39	00101000	8
8	10011	5	40	00101001	8
9	10100	5	41	00101010	8
10	00111	5	42	00101011	8
11	01000	5	43	00101100	8
12	001000	6	44	00101101	8
13	000011	6	45	00000100	8
14	110100	6	46	00000101	8
15	110101	6	47	00001010	8
16	101010	6	48	00001011	8
17	101011	6	49	01010010	8
18	0100111	7	50	01010011	8
19	0001100	7	51	01010100	8
20	0001000	7	52	01010101	8
21	0010111	7	53	00100100	8
22	0000011	7	54	00100101	8
23	0000100	7	55	01011000	8
24	0101000	7	56	01011001	8
25	0101011	7	57	01011010	8
26	0010011	7	58	01011011	8
27	0100100	7	59	01001010	8
28	0011000	7	60	01001011	8
29	00000010	8	61	00110010	8
30	00000011	8	62	00110011	8
31	00011010	8	63	00110100	8

T A B L E	Make Up White Code for Group 3 Fax		
2.6	Run	VL Word	Length
	64	11011	5
	128	10010	5
	192	010111	6
	256	0110111	7
	320	00110110	8
	384	00110111	8
	448	01100100	8
	512	01100101	8
	576	01101000	8
	640	01100111	8
	704	011001100	9
	768	011001101	9
	832	011010010	9
	896	011010011	9
	960	011010100	9
	1024	011010101	9
	1088	011010110	9
	1152	011010111	9
	1216	011011000	9
	1280	011011001	9
	1344	011011010	9
	1408	011011011	9
	1472	010011000	9
	1536	010011001	9
	1600	010011010	9
	1664	011000	6
	1728	010011011	9

it must follow the MUC word whenever the length of a black run is an exact positive multiple of 64.

Note that the black TC words for lengths 1, 2, and 3 are only half as long as their white TC counterparts. This is because black runlengths have distinctly different statistics than white runlengths. In many documents, most of the black runs are only a few pels thick because they are the strokes of typed or

Terminating Black Code for Group 3 Fax

Run	VL Word	Length	Run	VL Word	Length
0	0000110111	10	32	000001101010	12
1	010	3	33	000001101011	12
2	11	2	34	000011010010	12
3	10	2	35	000011010011	12
4	011	3	36	000011010100	12
5	0011	4	37	000011010101	12
6	0010	4	38	000011010110	12
7	00011	5	39	000011010111	12
8	000101	6	40	000001101100	12
9	000100	6	41	000001101101	12
10	0000100	7	42	000011011010	12
11	0000101	7	43	000011011011	12
12	0000111	7	44	000001010100	12
13	00000100	8	45	000001010101	12
14	00000111	8	46	000001010110	12
15	000011000	9	47	000001010111	12
16	0000010111	10	48	000001100100	12
17	0000011000	10	49	000001100101	12
18	0000001000	10	50	000001010010	12
19	00001100111	11	51	000001010011	12
20	00001101000	11	52	000000100100	12
21	00001101100	11	53	000000110111	12
22	00000110111	11	54	000000111000	12
23	00000101000	11	55	000000100111	12
24	00000010111	11	56	000000101000	12
25	00000011000	11	57	000001011000	12
26	000011001010	12	58	000001011001	12
27	000011001011	12	59	000000101011	12
28	000011001100	12	60	000000101100	12
29	000011001101	12	61	000001011010	12
30	000001101000	12	62	000001100110	12
31	000001101001	12	63	000001100111	12

T A B L E	Make Up Black Code for Group 3 Fax		
2.8	Run	VL Word	Length
	64	0000001111	10
	128	000011001000	12
	192	000011001001	12
	256	000001011011	12
	320	000000110011	12
	384	000000110100	12
	448	000000110101	12
	512	0000001101100	13
	576	0000001101101	13
	640	0000001001010	13
	704	0000001001011	13
	768	0000001001100	13
	832	0000001001101	13
	896	0000001110010	13
	960	0000001110011	13
	1024	0000001110100	13
	1088	0000001110101	13
	1152	0000001110110	13
	1216	0000001110111	13
	1280	0000001010010	13
	1344	0000001010011	13
	1408	0000001010100	13
	1472	0000001010101	13
	1536	0000001011010	13
	1600	0000001011011	13
	1664	0000001100100	13
	1728	0000001100101	13

handwritten symbols or drawings. Long black runs are rare, but long white runs are commonplace. Accordingly, short black runs are assigned codewords shorter than those assigned to short white runs, and long black runs are assigned codewords longer than those assigned to long white runs.

Group 3 codeword lengths have been assigned in accord with Morse's principle that more probable events should be assigned shorter codewords. However, they have not been assigned according to Huffman's algorithm for minimizing the average codeword length. Extremely long black runs, for example, are sufficiently rare that Huffman's algorithm would assign them codewords considerably longer than those they have been assigned in Tables 2.7 and 2.8. Constraining the length of the longest word in the VL codes of Tables 2.5 through 2.8 makes them easier to store in lookup tables and faster to retrieve. The codes in these tables are often referred to as *modified Huffman codes*. (For a theory of optimum VL codes subject to a peak codeword length constraint, see Gilbert 1971.) Also, the aforementioned constraint that the EOL code must never appear anywhere within a valid code stream for any line of data would not be respected by a Huffman code. The codes of Tables 2.5 through 2.8 do respect it, though, because none of their codewords consists entirely of 0s, none has more than six consecutive 0s, and none ends with more than three consecutive 0s. It follows that valid code for a line of data never contains more than nine consecutive 0s and therefore never contains the EOL codeword, which has eleven consecutive 0s.

The minimum transmission time requirement necessitates inserting filler bits into the code for lines that would otherwise be too short (e.g., the commonly encountered all-white lines). Fill always consists of a string of 0s. Accordingly, one sends 0s until it would take only 12 more bits to reach the minimum transmission time and then sends the EOL. It is trivial for the receiver to detect and discard fill.

Finally, in the event that encoding, transmission, or decoding errors cause the lengths of the runs in a line to sum to less than 1728, the default is to fill in the rest of the line with white pels. Many encoder realizations take advantage of this default setting by intentionally not encoding the last white run on a line. Instead, they proceed directly to the EOL code, provided of course that the minimum transmission time requirement is not violated thereby. The decoder then fills white pels all the way to the right-hand margin, which indeed yields a correct representation of the document line. In the event that the sum of the runlengths in a line exceeds 1728, a fatal error usually is noted, the partial page is outputted, and the decoder proceeds to the next page.

The end of a document is signaled by sending six consecutive EOLs. This is also referred to as the return to control (RTC) signal, after which the transmitter usually sends certain postmessage commands that need not concern us here.

2.7.2   Group 4 Fax

The Group 4 fax standard was published in CCITT Recommendation T.6 (CCITT 1984). G4 is a superset of G3 in the sense that G4 receiving apparatus is required to be back-compatible with G3. G4 fax is said to be a two-dimensional coding scheme because if the document being faxed possesses spatial redundancy in the vertical direction (most documents do), Group 4 fax machines are capable of exploiting it. Whereas G3 codes each scan line independently, G4 uses the previous scan line as a reference when coding the current line. The G4 standard capitalizes on the fact that runs on the current line often begin nearly directly below the beginning of a run of the same color on the previous line. G4 apparatus codes these differences in run boundaries from line to line; of course, provision also is made for the event that the current line may be composed of either fewer or more runs than is the reference line. Most fax documents are compressed more efficiently by Group 4 than by Group 3.

Modified READ Algorithm

The first line of each page is encoded by G4 in precisely the same way as it is encoded by G3. Using this line as a reference, the G4 algorithm codes the second line by means of the relative element address designate (READ) algorithm described in the next subsection. The second line then serves as the reference for READ coding of the third line, and so on. In order to prevent errors from propagating down an entire page, some lines intentionally are coded as in Group 3; in Group 4 parlance, Group 3 is referred to as the *horizontal mode*. The encoder appends a 1 to the EOL symbol if it is going to code the next line in the horizontal mode and a 0 otherwise. Thus, the EOL symbols are 0000000000011 if the next line is to be coded as in G3 and 0000000000010 if it is to be encoded by the READ algorithm. (Note that this provides an encoding option in which both READ and G3 encodings are calculated for each line and then the shorter description is sent.) The modified READ algorithm, which we now illustrate via the example depicted in Figure 2.6, is a recursive procedure involving the updating of five parameters called a_0, a_1, a_2, b_1, and b_2. Code bits are generated in conjunction with each updating. The black-and-white pattern that appears on the bottom line of each of the two-line pairs in Figure 2.6 represents the current line (i.e., the line we are in the process of coding). The black-and-white pattern on the top line represents the reference line, which in G4 is always the scan line immediately above the current line. Let a_0 denote the pel at the beginning of the run we are about to code, a_1 denote the pel that begins the next run on the current line, and a_2 denote the pel that begins the run after that. Next, define b_1 to be the first pel on the reference line located to the right of a_0 that is the same color as a_1, and let b_2 be the pel that begins the run after that on the reference line. Hence, a_0, a_2, and b_2 are always of one color, and a_1 and b_1 are always of the opposite color (see Figure 2.6). With these conventions we see that specifying

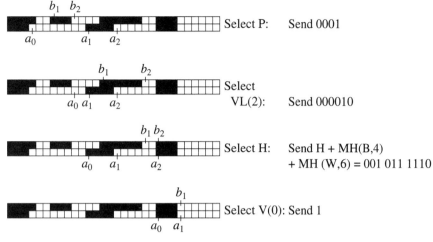

Modified READ Coding Example

Modified READ Coding Table: Modes, Codes, and Abodes

Mode	VL Codeword	Abode of New a_0
Pass: P	0001	under old b_1
Vertical:		
$\quad$ V(0)	1	
$\quad$ $V_R(1)$	011	
$\quad$ $V_R(2)$	000011	
$\quad$ $V_R(3)$	0000011	replaces old a_1
$\quad$ $V_L(1)$	010	
$\quad$ $V_L(2)$	000010	
$\quad$ $V_L(3)$	0000010	
Horizontal: H	001 + MH(a_0a_1) + MH(a_1a_2)	replaces old a_2

how a_0 gets recursively updated permits immediate updating of a_1, a_2, b_1, and b_2, too.

The modified READ procedure consists of steps 1, 2, and 3 below. The terms V(0), $V_R(k)$, and $V_L(k)$ used in step 2 are specified in Table 2.9. Figure 2.6 illustrates execution of these steps for a particular example.

1. If b_2 does not lie strictly to the left of a_1, go to step 2. When b_2 lies to the left of a_1, select the *pass mode*: send the pass mode codeword 0001, move a_0

to the column containing b_2, update the other four parameters accordingly (actually, a_1 and a_2 will remain unchanged), and repeat this step.

2. If a_1 is more than three columns away from b_1, go to step 3. Otherwise, select the *vertical mode*: send the codeword for V(0) if a_1 is in the same column as b_1. For $1 \leq k \leq 3$, if a_1 is k columns to the right of b_1, then send the codeword for $V_R(k)$, and if a_1 is k columns to the left of b_1, then send the codeword for $V_L(k)$. Move a_0 to the position that a_1 has been occupying, update the other four parameters accordingly, and return to step 1.

3. Select the *horizontal mode*: send 001, plus the Group 3 modified Huffman (MH) codeword for the length and color of the run from a_0 to a_1, plus the G3 MH codeword for the length and color of the run from a_1 to a_2. Move a_0 to the position that a_2 had been occupying and update the other four parameters accordingly. Return to step 1.

The modes, their codes, and the updated abodes for a_0 are shown in Table 2.9. In the bottom line of the table, MH($a_i a_j$) stands for the Group 3 modified Huffman codeword for the length and color of the run that starts with a_i and ends with the pixel to the immediate left of a_j.

First and Last Pel of Each Line

In order to start a line coded by the modified READ algorithm, we need to know the initial position and the initial color of a_0. The conventions are that a_0 is initialized at an imaginary location immediately preceding the first pel on the current line and is white. The length of the first run is considered to be one shorter than the run from a_0 up to but not including a_1; that is, the initial imaginary location is not included in the length of the first run. In the event that the first actual run on the line is black and the horizontal mode is invoked, then MH($a_0 a_1$) will be the code for a white run of length 0, namely 00110101, followed in turn by the MH word for the length of the black run that begins the line.

Sensing the completion of a line of modified READ coding involves the convention that a change of color takes place both on the reference line and on the current line between the final pel of the line and an imaginary pel located to its immediate right (i.e., in position 1729). a_1, a_2, b_1, and b_2 get updated to this imaginary location whenever they cannot be detected within their respective actual lines. Coding of the current line is deemed complete whenever the updating of a_0 would place it at this imaginary location. If the EOL symbol is detected by the decoder prior to the coded runs having filled the line, the remainder of the line is filled in with 0s; as in Group 3, there are situations in which compression is enhanced by intentionally sending an EOL code prematurely. Should confusion arise concerning the initialization and termination procedures described in this subsection, consult the several examples in Section 4.2.5 of CCITT (1980).

Miscellany

The Group 4 Standard, Recommendation T.6, also makes provision for entry to and exit from an uncompressed mode. In addition, a companion document, Recommendation T.10, deals with high-speed facsimile transmission over leased lines, specifying modulation, power, and phase distortion requirements and their extensions to multipoint (i.e., applications in which one transmitter sends simultaneously to several receivers). Finally, a facsimile system designer needs to appreciate that there is more to building a standards-compliant fax machine than simply implementing the recommended coding scheme(s). Issues involving terminal characteristics, character sets, control procedures, document application profiles, and call setup/teardown must be addressed. Recommendations T.503, T.521, T.563, T.73, T.62, T.62 *bis*, T.70, F.161, T.60, T.61, and T.72 treat these matters.

2.7.3   Noise and Half-Toning

If the original document being scanned is noisy, then it will tend to have many short runs, with white runs being particularly shorter than usual. This engenders a mismatch between the coding tables and the runlengths in the document. As a result, compression efficiency is reduced by even more than the increase in entropy attributable to the noise would have predicted. Sometimes it is permissible to preprocess the image with a "cleanup" routine that, for example, eliminates all runs of length 1. Such preprocessing ameliorates the detrimental effect of random noise on compression efficiency, but medical, legal, and other considerations often prevent one from "cleansing" documents in this manner before encoding them for transmission.

Compression inefficiencies also are encountered when G3 or G4 fax machines are used to transmit half-toned images. The pseudorandom dot patterns used in half-toning to represent gray levels eliminate all the long runs that are characteristic of "naturally" bi-level images (see Figure 2.7). The JBIG fax standard described in Section 3.4 is more effective at compressing half-toned images than are G3 and G4. (For information on the trade-off between quality and bit rate

FIGURE

2.7 Original (top); Half-Tone (middle); Close-up from Half-Tone (bottom)

for different methods of coding continuous-tone images using binary output devices, especially random, pseudorandom, and clumped dithering, see Bodson, Schaphorst, and Urban 1989.)

2.8   Line Drawing Compression

Let us now consider compressing a line drawing captured by a graphics tablet. Graphics tablets of modest cost can record the (x, y)-coordinates of a stylus with a spatial accuracy of 300 lines/inch and a temporal sampling rate of 300 samples/second. We shall also assume that a "lift" signal is sent each time the stylus is raised from the tablet surface. (More expensive devices also record multiple levels of pressure, as opposed to just on-off, the angle between the stylus tip and the tablet, and the movement of the stylus even when it is not in contact with the surface. We shall not assume any of those capabilities here.) Graphics tablets are particularly useful for electronically capturing a human signature during a point-of-sale or point-of-delivery transaction. Such devices commonly convey the captured data to their host (usually an electronic cash register or a personal computer) by means of a brute-force representation that consumes at least four 8-bit bytes per data point (plus one more, usually, for purposes of bookkeeping and control that we shall not count when we later compute compression ratios). In most applications we are interested only in the spatial coordinates of the points and perhaps in the *order* in which they were recorded. (In some applications, such as dynamic signature verification, it is also necessary to preserve accurately the times at which the data points were collected. PC interrupts usually are too coarse for this purpose, making it necessary to generate an enhanced clock.) We now describe a scheme that compresses the ordered data set $\{(k, x_k, y_k)\}$ effectively losslessly using far fewer bytes per data point than does the brute-force description.

Figure 2.8 depicts a nested family of squares $S_1, S_2, S_3, S_5, S_8,$ and S_{13} centered at a grid point that we shall call the origin; each side of S_j has length $4j$. We denote the origin by O_i because it is the endpoint of the ith of a sequence of straight-line segments that we have been computing as approximations to the line drawing. We now describe how to calculate the next line segment in this sequence (equivalently, the next origin O_{i+1}) in a way that ensures that there is never more than a grid point discrepancy in any direction between the line segment and the portion of the drawing that it represents. Keep in mind that, since Figure 2.8 shows approximately 24 grid lines per inch, it

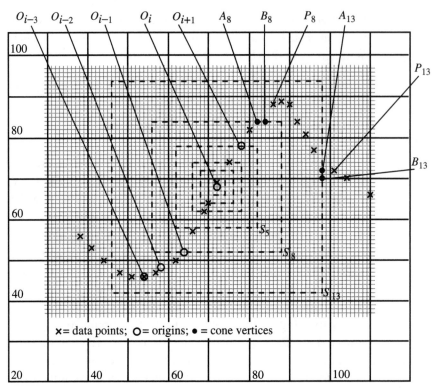

2.8   Line Drawing Compression by Fibonacci Multiring Chain Code

magnifies by 10 to 40 times what the current generation of graphics tablets actually would capture; accordingly, discrepancies smaller than one grid point are indiscernible on a computer screen nor can they be detected by the unassisted human eye.

The data points captured by the tablet are indicated in Figure 2.8 by $\times$ symbols. We shall refer to the as-yet-uncoded data points corresponding to the portion of the drawing beyond O_i but before the next lift as the "future." Assume for purposes of discussion that the data points shown in Figure 2.8 were captured in order from left to right and that there were no lifts during this portion of the line drawing; thus, the first data point in the future is $(73, 70)$ and the last one is $(110, 66)$.

Implement test T_{13}, the first step of which is to locate the first future data point, if any, that lies outside S_{13}. Denote this data point by P_{13}; for example, $P_{13} = (101, 72)$ in Figure 2.8. (If there is no P_{13}, find P_8 and implement instead test T_8, which is T_{13} as described below with all the 13 subscripts replaced by 8 subscripts; if there is no P_8, then proceed to T_5, and so forth.) Define the S-points to be those points on the nested squares that are an even number of grid points from the corner of the square on which they lie. Let A_{13} and B_{13} denote the two S-points on S_{13} nearest to the intersection I_{13} of the line segment $\overline{O_i P_{13}}$ and the square S_{13}. Consider the cone $A_{13} - O_i - B_{13}$. Test to see whether or not all the points (if any) in the portion of the future that precedes P_{13} lie within this cone.

If the data set passes T_{13}, let the next origin O_{i+1} be whichever of A_{13}, B_{13}, or the grid point midway between them is closest to I_{13}, and let the next line segment in the approximation of the drawing be $\overline{O_i O_{i+1}}$. If not, implement test T_8, T_5, and so on, until a test is passed. If all six tests are failed, locate O_{i+1} at the first data point in the future. In Figure 2.8 T_5 is passed, so O_{i+1} lies on S_5 as shown. By construction, no data point that is in the future with respect to O_i but not with respect to O_{i+1} can be more than a grid point away from the nearest point on the line segment $\overline{O_i O_{i+1}}$. (In a commercial realization [Berger and Miller 1992], determination of the next origin actually proceeds via an inside-out algorithm rather than the outside-in algorithm described here for simplicity of presentation. Also, the floating-point operations that would be needed to calculate and test the cones described here are obviated via a clever fixed-point algorithm.) The above scheme is a *modified multiring chain code* with Fibonacci spacing (Freeman 1961; Wong and Koplowitz 1992). Let's see how much compression it achieves. The total number of possibilities for the next origin is $8 \cdot (1 + 2 + 3 + 5 + 8 + 13) = 256 = 2^8$, so it takes only one 8-bit byte to describe each line segment in the approximation. Moreover, the 256 possibilities have a skewed distribution in many applications; for example, with most people's cursive handwriting, there are far fewer segments that point into quadrant 2 than into the other three quadrants. Also, almost half of the 256 possibilities lie on S_{13}, and each of these is considerably less likely to be selected as the next origin than are the points on the smaller squares. (This assumes the drawing is "sized" properly with respect to the grid spacing.) Accordingly, Huffman coding of this alphabet of cardinality 256 can appreciably reduce the number of bits needed per line segment.

Now let's see what we can do to further compress the representation. If line segment $L_i = \overline{O_i O_{i+1}}$ points in a certain direction, then most of the time L_{i+1} will point in a similar direction. That is, we may assume that (near) reversals in direction, such as those associated with cusps, occur relatively rarely. It is reasonable to expect, moreover, that the distribution for L_{i+1} given

$L_i, L_{i-1}, L_{i-2}, \ldots$ will depend little if at all on the value of $L_{i-1}, L_{i-2}, \ldots$; that is, it is reasonable to assume that the sequence $\{L_i\}$ is effectively Markovian. (See Section 2.11.2 for the definition of a Markov source.) This Markov modeling suggests that we should use a different Huffman code for each successive segment, with the words in the Huffman code for L_{i+1} being chosen according to the 256 probabilities that constitute the *conditional* probability distribution $P_{L_{i+1}|L_i}(\cdot|l_i)$ for L_{i+1} given that $L_i = l_i$. The decoder will know what Huffman code is being used for L_{i+1} by virtue of having deduced that $L_i = l_i$ by decoding the previous codeword. Therefore, we don't have to waste an 8-bit byte each time to say which code to use next; if we did have to do that, it would wholly defeat our purpose. We do, however, have to store 256 different Huffman codes at both the encoder and the decoder, so complexity has increased markedly. This complexity increase can be tempered considerably by noting that the code conditional on l_i should differ little from that associated with any rotation of l_i through a multiple of $45°$, assuming a corresponding rotation in the meaning of the codewords. Hence, we need store only $256/8 = 32$ Huffman codes; further reductions based on quasi symmetries also are possible.

Experimentation with cursive human signatures from hundreds of subjects has revealed that a multiring chain code with Fibonacci spacings followed by the above-described Markov-Huffman coding technique achieves a compression of nearly 10:1 over the representation commonly used by graphics tablets. We shall henceforth refer to this Fibonacci-Markov-Huffman scheme as FMH coding. For Kanji signatures, FMH coding achieves a compression of roughly 8:1, which can be improved upon if we take care to encode lifts more efficiently.

To ascertain what portion of the FMH compression is attributable to the Fibonacci chain code, note from Figure 2.8 that there appear to be roughly half as many origins per unit length as there are captured data points. However, this is an exaggeration because the ratio of data points to origins falls toward one as the local curvature of the drawing increases, and Figure 2.8 depicts a region of relatively low curvature. If we assume 1.5 data points per origin over the long run, then the Fibonacci scheme is responsible for a compression factor of $1.5 \times 4 = 6$, since it uses only one byte per origin as compared with four bytes per uncompressed data point. Huffman coding raises the compression ratio from 6:1 to 8:1, and Markov coding further raises it to close to 10:1.

The above description of FMH coding of line drawings not only provides a useful technique for certain practical applications but also serves to motivate the general scheme of Markov-Huffman coding for sources with stationary memory. In short, we empirically estimate the second-order joint distribution $p_{U_k,U_{k+1}}(u_k, u_{k+1})$ of the data source and then store Huffman codes for its associated conditional distributions $p_{U_{k+1}|U_k}(\cdot|u)$—one code for each possible value of $u \in \mathcal{U}$. Since in the long run the source produces each symbol $u \in \mathcal{U}$ a fraction of the time that converges to the first-order marginal distribution $p(u)$, this Markov-Huffman approach achieves compression close to $h_2 := H(U_2|U_1)$; it would actually achieve h_2 only in the unlikely event that all the probabilities in all the conditional distributions are negative powers of the size of the Huffman code alphabet. When the source itself is well approximated by a first-order Markov model, the Markov-Huffman coding scheme is quasi-optimal and effectively impossible to improve appreciably upon from the standpoint of compression performance. (See Section 2.11.2 for the mathematical justification of this claim. To enhance your understanding of Markov-Huffman compression, spend some time with Problem 5.8 in Cover and Thomas 1991.)

2.9   Entropy and a Bound on Performance

In this section we introduce the key concept of entropy and show that it serves as a lower bound on the average codeword length $\bar{l}$ of any UD code for given source letter probabilities $\{p_j\}$. In the process some inequalities are developed that not only help us establish the lower bound but also are of interest in their own right.

2.9.1 Some Inequalities

Inequalities (2.9) through (2.12) are valid, and equality prevails in them if and only if $x = 1$.

$$\ln(x) \leq x - 1 \tag{2.9}$$

$$\ln(x) \geq 1 - \frac{1}{x} \tag{2.10}$$

$$\log_D(x) \leq \log_D(e) \cdot (x - 1) \tag{2.11}$$

$$\log_D(x) \geq \log_D(e) \cdot (1 - \frac{1}{x}) \tag{2.12}$$

Figure 2.9 shows us why inequality (2.9) is true. The graph of $y = \ln(x)$, $x > 0$, passes through the point $(x = 1, y = 0)$ where its slope equals 1, so the line $y = x - 1$ is tangent to it there as shown. The second derivative of $\ln(x)$ is $-x^{-2}$, which is negative for all $x > 0$. This implies that $\ln(x)$ is strictly concave throughout this range. Therefore, it is bounded from above by each of its tangent

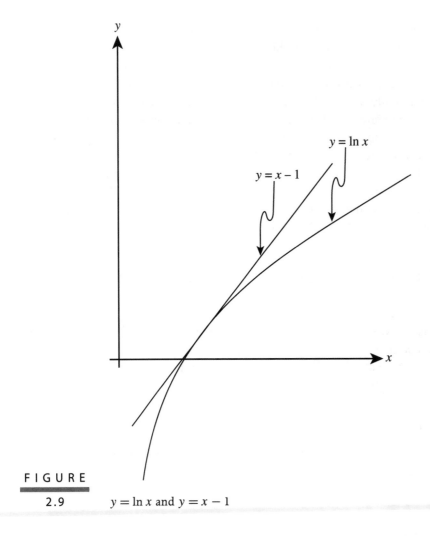

2.9 $y = \ln x$ and $y = x - 1$

lines with equality only at the point of tangency. This establishes (2.9) and the stated necessary and sufficient condition for equality. To obtain (2.10), simply replace x by $1/x$ in (2.9) and rearrange the terms. Inequalities (2.11) and (2.12) follow immediately from the identity $\log_D(x) = \log_D(e) \cdot \ln(x)$; the constant $K = \log_D(e)$ is positive for any logarithm base D because $e = 2.718\ldots > 1$.

2.9.2 Entropy

The *entropy* of the probability distribution $\{p_j\}$, denoted by $H(\{p_j\})$, or simply by H when the context permits, is defined by

$$H = -\sum_{j} p_j \log p_j \tag{2.13}$$

Zero-probability letters do not contribute to H because $p \log p \to 0$ as $p \to 0$. The base of the logarithm determines the units of H. Usually base 2 is used, in which case H is measured in *bits*. Sometimes base e is used, in which case H is measured in *nats*. We will leave the log base unspecified unless the context demands otherwise.

The entropy H of $\{p_j, 1 \le j \le M\}$ satisfies

$$0 \le H \le \log M \tag{2.14}$$

Equality holds on the left only in deterministically degenerate cases in which p_j equals 1 for some value of j and hence equals 0 for all the other values of j. There is equality on the right if and only if $p_j = M^{-1}$ for all M values of j.

To obtain the inequality on the left, note that $-p \log p \ge 0$ for $0 < p \le 1$, with equality if and only if $p = 1$. Hence, $H \ge 0$ with equality only in the degenerate cases cited. The inequality on the right follows from inequality (2.10), which tells us that

$$\log M - H = \sum_{j} p_j (\log M + \log p_j)$$

$$= \sum_{j} p_j \log(M p_j) \ge K \sum_{j} p_j (1 - \frac{1}{M p_j}) \tag{2.15}$$

where $K = \log e$ and equality holds if and only if $p_j = M^{-1}$ for all j. Thus,

$$\log M - H \ge K \left(\sum_{j} p_j - \sum_{j} M^{-1} \right) = K(1 - 1) = 0 \tag{2.16}$$

with equality if and only if $p_j = M^{-1}$ for all j.

2.9.3   Entropy Lower Bounds Achievable Compression

Now suppose we have a D-ary UD code for a source with letter probabilities $\{p_j\}$. Using base D logs, we deduce that

$$\bar{l} - H = \sum_{j} p_j (l_j + \log_D p_j)$$

$$= \sum_{j} p_j \log_D (p_j D^{l_j}) \ge \log_D e \sum_{j} p_j (1 - \frac{D^{-l_j}}{p_j}) \tag{2.17}$$

where we have used inequality (2.12). Continuing, we have

$$\bar{l} - H \geq \log_D e \sum_j (p_j - D^{-l_j}) = (\log_D e)(1 - \sum_j D^{-l_j}) \geq$$

$$(2.18)$$

$$(\log_D e)(1 - 1) = 0$$

with the final inequality being a consequence of the fact that the word lengths $\{l_j\}$ of a UD code must satisfy the Kraft inequality. We have established the following key result:

The average codeword length of any D-ary UD code is always at least as great as the source entropy calculated using base D logs.

In symbols, $\bar{l} \geq H$. If each of the source letter probabilities is a negative integer power of D, then the Huffman code achieves equality here. Otherwise the inequality is strict.

For example, suppose $M = 7$ and the source letters all are negative powers of three, namely $p_1 = p_2 = \frac{1}{3}$, $p_3 = p_4 = \frac{1}{9}$, and $p_5 = p_6 = p_7 = \frac{1}{27}$. Then $\bar{l}$ for the ternary Huffman code shown in Figure 2.10 is $\frac{2}{3} \cdot 1 + \frac{2}{9} \cdot 2 + \frac{3}{27} \cdot 3 = \frac{13}{9}$, which equals H calculated with base 3 logs. However, since the source letters are not negative powers of two, $\bar{l}$ for the binary Huffman code shown in Figure 2.11 is $(\frac{2}{3}) \cdot 2 + (\frac{2}{9} + \frac{1}{27}) \cdot 3 + \frac{2}{27} \cdot 4 = \frac{65}{27} = 2.\overline{407}$, but H calculated with base 2 logs is only $(\frac{13}{9})\log_2 3 = 2.289$ bits. The optimum binary code's $\bar{l}$ is some 5% bigger than entropy.

The gap between $\bar{l}$ and H is known as the *redundancy* of the coding scheme. Hence, another way to express the optimality of Huffman codes is to say that they achieve the lowest possible redundancy among all UD instantaneous codes. If we are willing to forego the requirement that each source symbol be coded instantaneously upon its arrival, we often can achieve lower redundancy by grouping the source symbols into pairs and then constructing a Huffman code for these pairs. In the previous example, there are $7^2 = 49$ such pairs. The pairs (1, 1), (1, 2), (2, 1) and (2, 2) each have probability $\frac{1}{3} \cdot \frac{1}{3} = \frac{1}{9}$. There are 11 pairs that each have probability $\frac{1}{27}$, 16 that have probability $\frac{1}{81}$, 12 that have probability $\frac{1}{243}$, and 9 that have probability $\frac{1}{729}$. One of the binary Huffman codes for this alphabet of size 49 has 4 words of length 3, 8 of length 5, 8 of length 6, 8 of length 7, 12 of length 8, 7 of length 9, and 2 of length 10. Calculations show that the $\bar{l}$ common to the Huffman codes for this 49-ary source is 4.608. Since there are two of the original 7-ary symbols per pair, the Huffman code for the pairs has an $\bar{l}$ of 2.304 binary code digits per source symbol. This exceeds the entropy of 2.289 bits/symbol by less than 1%, so coding pairs instead of single symbols has closed most of the 5% redundancy associated with the binary Huffman code for single symbols.

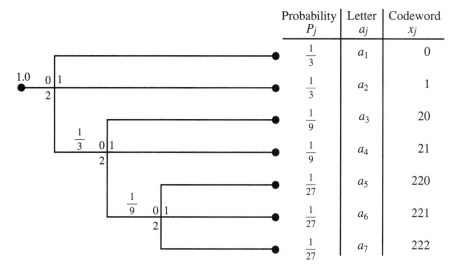

Probability P_j	Letter a_j	Codeword x_j
$\frac{1}{3}$	a_1	0
$\frac{1}{3}$	a_2	1
$\frac{1}{9}$	a_3	20
$\frac{1}{9}$	a_4	21
$\frac{1}{27}$	a_5	220
$\frac{1}{27}$	a_6	221
$\frac{1}{27}$	a_7	222

$$\bar{l} = H = \left(\frac{1}{3} + \frac{1}{3}\right) \cdot 1 + \left(\frac{1}{9} + \frac{1}{9}\right) \cdot 2 + \left(\frac{1}{27} + \frac{1}{27} + \frac{1}{27}\right) \cdot 3 = \frac{13}{9}$$

FIGURE

2.10   Ternary Huffman Code for a Triadic Source

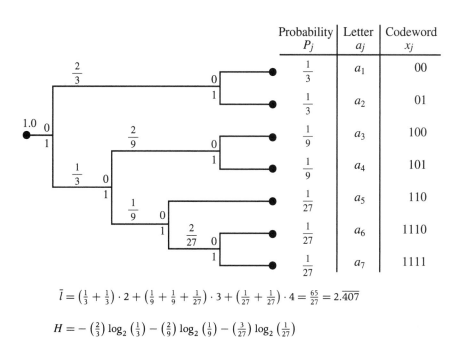

Probability P_j	Letter a_j	Codeword x_j
$\frac{1}{3}$	a_1	00
$\frac{1}{3}$	a_2	01
$\frac{1}{9}$	a_3	100
$\frac{1}{9}$	a_4	101
$\frac{1}{27}$	a_5	110
$\frac{1}{27}$	a_6	1110
$\frac{1}{27}$	a_7	1111

$$\bar{l} = \left(\frac{1}{3} + \frac{1}{3}\right) \cdot 2 + \left(\frac{1}{9} + \frac{1}{9} + \frac{1}{27}\right) \cdot 3 + \left(\frac{1}{27} + \frac{1}{27}\right) \cdot 4 = \frac{65}{27} = 2.\overline{407}$$

$$H = -\left(\frac{2}{3}\right) \log_2 \left(\frac{1}{3}\right) - \left(\frac{2}{9}\right) \log_2 \left(\frac{1}{9}\right) - \left(\frac{3}{27}\right) \log_2 \left(\frac{1}{27}\right)$$

$$= \left(\frac{2}{3} + \frac{4}{9} + \frac{9}{27}\right) \log_2 3 = \left(\frac{13}{9}\right) \log_2 3 = 2.289$$

FIGURE

2.11   Binary Huffman Code for a Triadic Source

Unfortunately, we pay a price both in complexity and in delay for this improvement in compression. There are more and longer codewords to store and to look up. Moreover, we have to wait until the second symbol of each pair arrives before we can produce the full codeword for the pair. The basic code for single symbols is said to be *instantaneous* in the sense that the codeword for each source symbol can be produced the instant that symbol is observed, and the codeword can be decoded the instant all its symbols have been received. Single-symbol Huffman codes achieve the maximum possible compression among all instantaneous UD codes, but in the likely instance that the p_j's don't all equal a negative power of D, noninstantaneous codes exist that achieve better compression.

In the limit as $n \to \infty$, Huffman codes for n-tuples of symbols from the source compress to the optimum value of H binary digits per source symbol (see Section 2.11.3). However, the approach to H is not necessarily monotonic in n. Consider, for example, an i.i.d. binary source whose more likely letter has probability 0.8. A Huffman code for 3-tuples from this source uses 0.728 binary digits per source letter, only slightly greater than $H = 0.8\log_2 0.8 + 0.2\log_2 0.2 = 0.722$. However, a Huffman code for 4-tuples from this source requires 0.741 binary digits per source letter. The reason is that the more likely among the 3-tuples all have probabilities that are close to negative powers of two, but the more likely among the 4-tuples do not. For the equiprobable ternary source $\{p_1 = p_2 = p_3 = \frac{1}{3}\}$, there are infinitely many values of n for which the binary Huffman code for n-tuples is less compressive than that for $(n-1)$-tuples.

2.10   Conditional Entropy and Mutual Information

Let $\mathcal{U} = \{a_1, \dots, a_M\}$ be an M-ary alphabet, and let U be a random variable that is distributed according to the probability distribution $\{p_U(u), u \in \mathcal{U}\}$. The entropy

$$H(\{p_U(u)\}) = -\sum_{u \in \mathcal{U}} p_U(u)\log p_U(u) \tag{2.19}$$

of this distribution is also called the entropy of the random variable U and denoted $H(U)$. (This is an abuse of preferred notation in probability theory, but it is a time-honored, universally accepted abuse.) We showed in Section 2.9.3 the key result that $H(U)$ is a lower bound on the average number of symbols from the coding alphabet one must receive in order to remove the a priori uncertainty about which value $u \in \mathcal{U}$ has been assumed by the random variable U. We shall see in Section 2.11 that it is possible to provide an average of only slightly more than $H(U)$ symbols in order to specify that value assumed by U, so there is strong justification for considering $H(U)$ to be a measure of the *uncertainty* one has a priori about which value the random variable U will assume.

Now let U and V be two random variables. Suppose we are allowed to observe the value assumed by V. Intuition correctly suggests that, on average, this observation can only reduce our uncertainty about U. The reason is that the best way to make use of knowledge of V to reduce uncertainty about U certainly does so at least as well as does simply ignoring the observed value of V and thereby leaving our uncertainty about U unchanged. Let's see how we can quantify this intuition.

Suppose we are told that V has assumed the value v. Then the distribution for U changes from the a priori, or unconditional, distribution $\{p_U(u), u \in \mathcal{U}\}$ to the a posteriori, or conditional, distribution $\{p_{U|V}(u|v), u \in \mathcal{U}\}$. Our a posteriori uncertainty about U therefore is

$$-\sum_{u \in \mathcal{U}} p_{U|V}(u|v) \log p_{U|V}(u|v) \tag{2.20}$$

Since observation of V results in v with probability $p_V(v)$, our *average* uncertainty about U after observing V, which we shall denote by $H(U|V)$ and refer to as the *conditional entropy* of U given V, is

$$H(U|V) = -\sum_{v \in \mathcal{V}} p_V(v) \sum_{u \in \mathcal{U}} p_{U|V}(u|v) \log p_{U|V}(u|v)$$

$$= -\sum_{(u,v)} p(u,v) \log p(u|v) \tag{2.21}$$

In the final step we have suppressed the U and V subscripts on the distributions and used the fact that $p(v)p(u|v) = p(u,v)$.

The difference $H(U) - H(U|V)$ between the unconditional and conditional entropies (i.e., between our prior and posterior uncertainties) is called the *average mutual information* between U and V. It is customarily denoted by $I(U; V)$; that is,

$$I(U; V) = H(U) - H(U|V) \tag{2.22}$$

Therefore, to establish our claim that observing V can, on average, only reduce our uncertainty about U, it will suffice to show the following: $I(U; V) \geq 0$ with equality if and only if U and V are statistically independent.

Here's how to derive this result. Since $\sum_v p(u, v) = p(u)$, we may write

$$I(U; V) = H(U) - H(U|V) = -\sum_u p(u) \ln p(u) + \sum_{u,v} p(u, v) \ln p(u|v)$$

$$= \sum_{u,v} p(u, v) \ln[p(u|v)/p(u)]$$

(2.23)

where we have used natural logs for convenience. Therefore, using the basic inequality $\ln z \geq 1 - (1/z)$, we see that

$$I(U; V) \geq \sum_{u,v} p(u, v)[1 - \frac{p(u)p(v)}{p(u, v)}]$$

$$= \sum_{u,v} p(u, v) - \sum_{u,v} p(u)p(v) = 1 - 1 = 0$$

(2.24)

with equality if and only if $p(u, v) = p(u)p(v)$ for every $(u, v) \in \mathcal{U} \times \mathcal{V}$, that is, if and only if U and V are statistically independent.

The result we've just established, namely, that conditioning can only decrease uncertainty in the case of two random variables U and V, can be extended to more general contexts. In this regard, suppose W is some third random variable. If after observing V we go on to observe W, our uncertainty about U will change again from $H(U|V)$ to $H(U|(V, W))$. The difference $H(U|V) - H(U|(V, W))$ is called the *conditional average mutual information* between U and W given V and is denoted by $I(U; W|V)$. $I(U; W|V)$ is readily proven to be nonnegative by the same argument as above with $p(u|v)$ in the role previously played by $p(u)$, and $p(u|v, w)$ in the role previously played by $p(u|v)$. It equals zero if and only if U and W are conditionally independent given V; that is, if and only if

$$p(u, w|v) = p(u|v)p(w|v) \text{ for all } (u, v)$$

(2.25)

We use the fact that conditioning can only reduce uncertainty when we study the entropy rate of stationary sources in Appendix D.

The conditional independence condition $p(u, w|v) = p(u|v)p(w|v)$ often is expressed by saying that U, V, and W form a *Markov chain*, or *Markov string*, and is symbolized by the suggestive notation $U \rightarrow V \rightarrow W$. It is easy to show that $U \rightarrow V \rightarrow W$ if and only if $W \rightarrow V \rightarrow U$. The extension to more than three random variables is immediate.

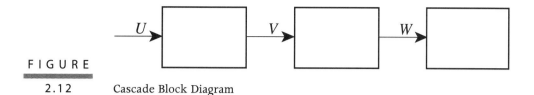

2.12   Cascade Block Diagram

In block diagrams, system designers implicitly assume conditional indepen-
dence when they draw cascades such as the one shown in Figure 2.12. This
cascade implicitly states that there is no hidden feedback or feedforward around
any or all of the blocks, as a consequence of which $U \rightarrow V \rightarrow W$.

2.11   Entropy Rate of a Stationary Source

Data compression is used in practice principally for sources whose successive
output letters exhibit substantial statistical interdependencies. By capitalizing
on the natural redundancy inherent in the memory structure of such sources, we
often can improve the compression ratio significantly relative to that achievable
by encoding each source symbol individually. It is important to keep in mind,
however, that the more we compress the data from a source, the more vulnerable the reconstituted version becomes to errors that may corrupt the compressed
representation. The discipline that deals with the trade-off between compression ratio and error rate is known as *joint source-channel coding;* we do not treat
it here.

Our objective in this section is to extend the concept of the entropy of a
memoryless source to that of the entropy rate of a source that possesses memory.
This can be done in a fully satisfactory manner for sources whose memory
structure is stationary in the sense of the definition given in the next paragraph.

Let the vector $\mathbf{U} = (U_{m+1}, \ldots, U_{m+n})$ be comprised of the n source outputs
produced between times $m + 1$ and $m + n$ inclusive, and let $p_{m,n}(\mathbf{u})$ denote
the probability that said $\mathbf{U}$ assumes the specific value $\mathbf{u} = (u_1, \ldots, u_n) \in \mathcal{U}^n$;
here, m is an integer and $\mathcal{U}$ continues to represent the instantaneous source
alphabet. If for all n and all $\mathbf{u}$, $p_{m,n}(\mathbf{u})$ does not depend on m, we say the source
is *stationary.* The physical significance of a source being stationary is that its
joint statistics are invariant to the choice of the time origin. Equivalently, the
probabilistic fluctuations exhibited by a stationary source are governed by a
steady-state as opposed to a time-varying mechanism.

We seek to define the entropy rate of a stationary source in such a way that it represents the per symbol rate at which the source generates information over the long haul. That is, we need to be able to show both (1) that a stationary source's entropy rate lower bounds the rate of any lossless encoding of its outputs, and (2) that any stationary source can be losslessly encoded using an average number of code symbols per source symbol that barely exceeds its entropy rate.

2.11.1 Joint Entropy and the Chain Rule

The *joint entropy* of the random variables $U_1, \ldots, U_n$ is denoted either by $H(U_1, \ldots, U_n)$ or, more compactly, by $H(\mathbf{U})$, where $\mathbf{U} = (U_1, \ldots, U_n)$. It is computed according to the prescription

$$H(\mathbf{U}) = -\sum_{\mathbf{u}} p_{\mathbf{U}}(\mathbf{u}) \log p_{\mathbf{U}}(\mathbf{u}) \tag{2.26}$$

The index of summation $\mathbf{u}$ in this equation ranges over the cross product $\mathcal{U}_1 \times \cdots \times \mathcal{U}_n$ of the alphabets of the random variables $U_1, \ldots, U_n$. When the components of $\mathbf{U}$ represent successive outputs of an information source, their alphabets are all the same; then we sum $\mathbf{u}$ over $\mathcal{U}^n$ in order to compute $H(\mathbf{U})$.

We introduced the conditional entropy $H(U|V)$ of a random variable U given another random variable V in Section 2.10 and showed that the formula for computing it is

$$H(U|V) = -\sum_{(u,v)} p(u, v) \log p(u|v) \tag{2.27}$$

Conditional entropy has a natural extension to random vectors. Namely, the conditional entropy of the random vector $\mathbf{U}$ given the random vector $\mathbf{V}$ is

$$H(\mathbf{U}|\mathbf{V}) = -\sum_{(\mathbf{u},\mathbf{v})} p(\mathbf{u}, \mathbf{v}) \log p(\mathbf{u}|\mathbf{v}) \tag{2.28}$$

It quantifies how uncertain we remain on the average about the value of $\mathbf{U}$ after being told what value $\mathbf{V}$ has assumed.

As is common in the literature of probability, we let the operator E denote joint statistical expectation with respect to all random entities in the expression that appears immediately to the right of E. With this convention we see that

$$H(\mathbf{U}) = -E \log \, p(\mathbf{U}) \tag{2.29}$$

and

$$H(\mathbf{U}|\mathbf{V}) = -E \log \ p(\mathbf{U}|\mathbf{V}) \tag{2.30}$$

where we have *intentionally* used capital letters as the arguments of $p(\cdot)$ and $p(\cdot|\cdot)$. (Think about this until you are sure you have it straight!)

The *chain rule* for entropy reads

$$H(U_1, \ldots, U_n) = H(U_1) + H(U_2|U_1) + \cdots + H(U_n|U_{n-1}, \ldots, U_1) \tag{2.31}$$

It expresses the idea that we can remove all the uncertainty about a random vector by first specifying its initial component, then removing the conditional uncertainty that remains about the second component after the first component has been specified, and so on. The chain rule is easily derived with the aid of the operator E as follows:

$$H(\mathbf{U}) = -E \log \ p(\mathbf{U}) = -E \log \ p(U_1)p(U_2|U_1) \ldots p(U_n|U_{n-1}, \ldots, U_1)$$

$$= -E[\log \ p(U_1) + \log \ p(U_2|U_1) + \cdots + \log \ p(U_n|U_{n-1}, \ldots, U_1)]$$

$$= -E \log \ p(U_1) - E \log \ p(U_2|U_1)$$

$$- \cdots - E \log \ p(U_n|U_{n-1}, \ldots, U_1)$$

$$= H(U_1) + H(U_2|U_1) + \cdots + H(U_n|U_{n-1}, \ldots, U_1) \tag{2.32}$$

2.11.2   Definitions of Entropy Rate

There are two natural ways of thinking about the entropy rate of a stationary source. With the volumetric approach, we calculate the limit as $n \to \infty$ of $1/n$ times the joint entropy of a random vector $\mathbf{U} = (U_1, \ldots, U_n)$ comprised of n successive source outputs. This suggests the mathematical definition

$$H_{\text{volume}} = \lim_{n \to \infty} n^{-1} H(U_1, \ldots, U_n) \tag{2.33}$$

With the incremental, or innovations, approach we seek to ascertain how much new information the next source symbol will convey, on the average, when it is conditioned on our already having observed an effectively infinite number of symbols immediately preceding it. This suggests an alternative mathematical definition of the form

$$H_{\text{increm}} = \lim_{n \to \infty} H(U_n|U_{n-1}, \ldots, U_1) \tag{2.34}$$

If we can show that H_{volume} and H_{increm} are equal, then their common value will emerge as the prime candidate for the source's entropy rate. The following results, which we establish in Appendix D, assure among other things that H_{volume} and H_{increm} are indeed equal for stationary sources:

Let $\{U_k, k = 1, 2, \ldots\}$ be a stationary source, let $H_n = n^{-1}H(U_1, \ldots, U_n)$, and let $h_n = H(U_n|U_{n-1}, \ldots, U_1)$. Then

1. h_n approaches a limit, call it h, in a monotonic nonincreasing manner.
2. $h_n \le H_n$ for all n.
3. H_n also approaches a limit, call it H, in a monotonic nonincreasing manner.
4. h and H are equal.

(Note that, in this notation, the chain rule reads $nH_n = h_1 + \cdots + h_n$, so H_n is the arithmetic average of h_1 through h_n.)

Figure 2.13 shows the typical relationship that prevails between $\{H_n\}$ and $\{h_n\}$ for a stationary source. Their common limit $H = h$ is called the *entropy rate* of the source and is denoted by $H(\{U_k\})$; this notation usually is contracted simply to H whenever there is no ambiguity about which source's entropy rate is intended.

In the case of an i.i.d. source, the entropy rate $H(\{U_k\})$ equals the entropy of any lone letter from the source, say, $H(U_1)$. To see this, note that

$$H_n = -n^{-1}E\log\, p(U_1, \ldots, U_n) = -n^{-1}E\log\prod_{k=1}^{n} p(U_k) \tag{2.35}$$

where $p(\cdot)$ in the right-hand side is the distribution that is common to the individual letters of the i.i.d. source. Continuing,

$$H_n = -n^{-1}\sum_{k=1}^{n} E\log\, p(U_k) = -n^{-1}\sum_{k=1}^{n} H(U_k)$$

$$= -n^{-1}\sum_{k=1}^{n} H(U_1) = H(U_1) \tag{2.36}$$

Since H_n equals $H(U_1)$ for all n, the entropy rate equals $H(U_1)$.

Another important class of sources are the *Markov sources*. These are characterized by the fact that, conditional on observation of the value u_n assumed by the random source symbol U_n at some particular time n, the past of the data sequence, namely, $\{U_{n-1}, U_{n-2}, \ldots\}$, becomes statistically independent of the future data $\{U_{n+1}, U_{n+2}, \ldots\}$. Loosely put, a source is Markov if "given the present, the future becomes conditionally independent of the past." The mathematical embodiment of Markovianness is that for all integers n, all positive inte-

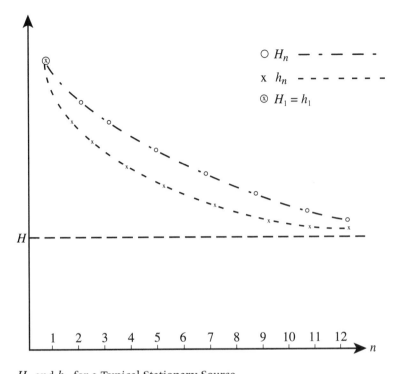

FIGURE

2.13
H_n and h_n for a Typical Stationary Source

gers N and M, and all source vectors $(u_{n-N}, u_{n-N+1}, \ldots, u_{n-1}, u_n, u_{n+1}, \ldots, u_{n+M-1}, u_{n+M})$ of dimension $M + N + 1$,

$$P(U_{n+1} = u_{n+1}, \ldots, U_{n+M} = u_{n+M}|$$

$$U_n = u_n, U_{n-1} = u_{n-1}, \ldots, U_{n-M} = u_{n-M}) \qquad (2.37)$$

$$= P(U_{n+1} = u_{n+1}, \ldots, U_{n+M} = u_{n+M}|U_n = u_n)$$

An rth-order Markov source is one in which, whenever the source output values are observed at r successive time instants, all source outputs that occur later in time than these r then become conditionally statistically independent of all those that occur earlier in time than these r; $r = 1$ corresponds to ordinary, or simple, Markovianness. The mathematical embodiment of rth-order Markovianness is obtained by replacing $U_n = u_n$ to the right of the conditioning bar in the last term of the preceding equation by $U_n = u_n$, $U_{n-1} = u_{n-1}, \ldots, U_n - r + 1 = u_{n-r+1}$. Markovianness is widely used to model phenomena of interest in many applications involving probabilistic systems, including many data compression operations. An example is provided by the sequence of line segments L_k discussed in conjunction with FMH coding of line drawings in Section 2.8.

For a stationary Markov source, $h_n = h_2$ for all $n \geq 2$ because

$$h_n = -E\log\, p(U_n|U_{n-1}, \ldots, U_1) = -E\log\, p(U_n|U_{n-1})$$
$$= -E\log\, p(U_2|U_1) = h_2 \tag{2.38}$$

where the first and last equalities are definitions of h_n and h_2, and the second and third equalities are consequences of Markovianness and stationariness, respectively. Accordingly, the entropy rate of a stationary Markov source is

$$\lim_{n\to\infty} h_n = h_2 = H(U_2|U_1) \tag{2.39}$$

This is easily generalized to show that an rth-order stationary Markov source's entropy rate equals $h_{r+1} = H(U_{r+1}|U_r, \ldots, U_1)$.

2.11.3 Shannon-Fano Codes

The following asymptotically optimum technique for losslessly encoding stationary sources was discovered independently in the 1940s by Claude Shannon (1948), the founder of information theory, and by Robert Fano (1961).

Let $\underline{u} = (u_1, u_2, \ldots, u_n)$ be an n-word from a source, and let $p(\underline{u})$ denote its probability. (Other names used instead of n-word are n-tuple, n-block, n-vector, and super-letter.) The *self-information* of $\underline{u}$ is denoted $i(\underline{u})$ and defined by

$$i(\underline{u}) = -\log_D p(\underline{u}) \tag{2.40}$$

Shannon-Fano coding assigns to each $\underline{u}$ a codeword whose length is the integer ceiling of $i(\underline{u})$, namely,

$$l(\underline{u}) = \lceil -\log_D p(\underline{u}) \rceil \tag{2.41}$$

These are allowable codeword lengths for a UD code because they satisfy the Kraft inequality, since

$$\sum_{\underline{u}} D^{-l(\underline{u})} = \sum_{\underline{u}} D^{-\lceil -\log_D p(\underline{u}) \rceil} \leq \sum_{\underline{u}} D^{\log_D p(\underline{u})} = \sum_{\underline{u}} p(\underline{u}) = 1 \tag{2.42}$$

the inequality following from removal of the ceiling function making the exponent less negative. The average codeword length per source letter for a Shannon-Fano code satisfies

$$n^{-1}\bar{l}_{SF} = n^{-1} \sum_{\underline{u}} p(\underline{u})l(\underline{u}) < n^{-1} \sum_{\underline{u}} p(\underline{u})(-\log_D p(\underline{u}) + 1)$$

(2.43)

$$= H_n + n^{-1}$$

Since n^{-1} vanishes and $H_n \to H$ as $n \to \infty$, we see that the compression factor of a Shannon-Fano code converges to the entropy rate of the stationary source as n grows. That is, Shannon-Fano codes are asymptotically optimum. It follows that a lossless data compression ratio of H can be approached arbitrarily closely if one is willing to work hard enough. Conversely, replacing single source letters by source n-tuples (super-letters) in Section 2.9.3 leads to the conclusion that no UD code for n-tuples can compress to fewer than H_n code symbols per source symbol. Since for every n, H_n is at least as great as H for a stationary source (see Appendix D), we have reached the following key conclusion:

H is the fundamental limit on the efficiency of lossless compression schemes for a stationary source.

That is, no UD code can use fewer than H code symbols per source symbol, and there exist lossless codes that come as close as desired to this limit. The problem is that, in order to approach H code letters per source letter, it usually is necessary to build a code for n-words with n large. Such codes not only tend to be highly complex but also introduce end-to-end latency that may be intolerable in certain applications. In practice, therefore, people usually don't implement lossless source codes that compress all the way down to the entropy rate. Rather, they settle for slightly suboptimum compression in order to achieve ease of implementability and/or low latency. The Group 3 and Group 4 facsimile standards that we discussed in Section 2.7 are examples of practical lossless compression schemes that sacrifice a modicum of compression efficiency in order to enhance implementability and robustness.

3 Universal Lossless Source Coding

3.1 Adaptivity and Universality

The lossless coding techniques described in Chapter 2 can be applied effectively only when the statistics of the data source are known completely. In practice, we do not possess this knowledge; we are not clairvoyant.

It can be argued that if the encoder does not know the statistics of the data source a priori, it can estimate them empirically with increasing accuracy as the data stream unfolds; that is, the encoder can *adapt* to the statistics of the source. This is true, but several conditions must be satisfied for it to be useful. One is that the application must be such that the delay and the complexity associated with the encoder's adaptation scheme are tolerable. Another is that the source statistics must be close enough to stationary that the encoder can adapt faster than the statistics change. Finally, it is best for the encoder and the decoder to have decided a priori on the adaptation scheme that will be used; this permits the decoder to adapt in step with the encoder as its losslessly decoded data unfolds without the need for the encoder to send side information continually describing how it has adapted.

The natural first step in adapting to a discrete-alphabet source is to form ongoing estimates of the source letter probabilities, $\{p(x), x \in \mathcal{X}\}$. Indeed, this is precisely what the adaptive Huffman coding scheme used in the Unix Compact utility does. However, this step alone enables the encoder to compress a stationary source only down to H_1, the first-order approximation to the entropy rate H. We have seen in Chapter 2 that H is strictly less than H_1 unless the source is memoryless. We rarely encounter memoryless sources in practice, and H_1 often is several times larger than H. Accordingly, we need adaptive compression schemes that are more robust than this. By working harder, the encoder can estimate the joint probability distribution of pairs of successive source letters, $p(x_k, x_{k+1})$. Since $p(x_k, x_{k+1}) = p(x_k)p(x_{k+1}|x_k)$, this is equivalent to estimating the one-step transition probabilities $p(x_{k+1}|x_k)$ because the single-letter distribution $p(x_k)$ already has been estimated. In other words, it is equivalent to estimating the parameters of a first-order Markov approximation to the actual source statistics. This, in turn, will enable the encoder to achieve compression approaching h_2, but h_2 also often is significantly larger than H.

Speaking temporarily from a purely theoretical standpoint, we can provide whatever degree of robustness in adaptation is desired by empirically estimating joint distributions of sufficiently high order. A good approximation to the rth-order joint distribution would support data compression performance approaching h_r. Finally, making r large enough would permit data compression approaching H because $\lim_{r \to \infty} h_r = H$. In practice, however, this approach is fraught with insurmountable difficulties.

Consider, for example, approximating text from a language such as English that uses 35 symbols at a bare minimum—namely, 26 lowercase letters, comma, period, space, open and close parentheses, question mark, apostrophe, colon, and semicolon. For just a second-order Markov approximation, we would need to estimate the probabilities of all 3-tuples from this alphabet. There are $35^3 = 42{,}875$ of these, so we would need access to mountains of text and would consume lots of computational and storage resources. When you consider that most computers use an alphabet of 8-bit bytes to code successive letters of a language like English, the number of conceivable 3-tuples balloons to $256^3 = 16{,}777{,}216$. It is apparent that this approach is wholly unworkable. To make matters worse, there are 3-tuple patterns that never occur in English text, such as *jxq*, but we wouldn't know of similar exclusions for a language we are encountering for the first time. (Actually, no pattern can be guaranteed never to appear. For example, *jxq* did in fact appear in the previous sentence, and since the current sentence also counts, *jxq* already has appeared twice—oops, three times!) Hence, even after we looked at many millions of symbols, we still would have empirical probabilities of zero for many of the 3-tuples yet would have no guarantee that they never will appear in the future.

We say that a coding scheme is *universal* if, in the limit of a large amount of data from any (stationary) source with a given alphabet, it succeeds in compressing that data down to the entropy rate of the source despite having no a priori knowledge of the source statistics.

A scheme that "learns" the rth-order joint distribution is not truly universal in the above sense because it can achieve H only for Markov sources of order $s < r$, yet there exist Markov sources of all orders. There even exist stationary sources that are not Markovian of any finite order. Therefore, in order to produce a truly universal coding scheme via estimation of rth-order distributions, it is necessary to estimate these distributions for ever-increasing values of r as more data pours in. Given the above-cited complexity of such estimates even for $r = 3$ in cases of considerable practical interest, the quest for a universal lossless coding scheme might seem altogether hopeless.

Remarkably, universal data compression schemes have been discovered in recent years. Even more remarkably, strong approximations to these universal schemes have been implemented that require only modest computational and storage resources. Lempel-Ziv (LZ) coding and arithmetic (with the accent on the syllable *met,* not the syllable *rith*) coding are the two most commonly used universal lossless coding techniques. Variants of the LZ algorithm form the basis of Unix Compress, gzip, pkzip, Stacker, and other computer file compression utilities. Also, most modems operating at or above 14.4 kbps implement LZ data compression as a matter of course in their default configuration. Arithmetic coding has been adopted by JBIG as the preferred method of data compression for the next generation of facsimile equipment. We shall examine the theory and application of these universal lossless coding schemes in this chapter.

3.2   Parsing

Many robust lossless coding schemes *parse* the source symbol string into a sequence of *phrases* and then generate compressed code to represent these phrases. For illustrative purposes, in this section we present several parsings of the same data string, each associated with a different universal scheme. Since the rules that generated these parsings are described cursorily if at all in this section and some of them are moderately sophisticated, you ought not try to intuit them from the short data sequence and brief discussion here. The parsing rules will be explicated in detail when the coding techniques themselves are treated in Section 3.3.

The classical runlength scheme for binary sequences parses by specifying the lengths of runs of 0s between successive 1s. For example, it parses the sequence

0 0 0 1 0 1 1 0 0 0 0 0 1 0 1 0 0 1 0 0 1 0 0 0 1 0 0 1 1 . . .

into the phrases shown below, each of which consists of a run of 0s and the associated terminal 1; imaginary commas separate the phrases for display purposes:

0 0 0 1, 0 1, 1, 0 0 0 0 0 1, 0 1, 0 0 1, 0 0 1, 0 0 0 1, 0 0 1, 1, . . .

There are a total of 10 phrases so far. The 3rd and 10th phrases correspond to a run of 0s of length 0, while the other phrases correspond to runs of 0s of positive length.

There are many variants of the Lempel-Ziv algorithm, and they don't all use the same parsing. The two principal versions—LZ77 and LZ78—derive their names from having first appeared in papers coauthored by Abraham Lempel and Jacob Ziv in the *IEEE Transactions on Information Theory* in 1977 and 1978 (Ziv and Lempel 1977, 1978). Unlike runlength schemes, both LZ77 and LZ78 parse the data into unique phrases in the sense that no two phrases in the LZ parsing of a sequence are identical.

LZ77 serves as the compression engine in the Stacker, zip, gzip, pkzip, and winzip compression utilities, among others. It has become commonplace to bundle such utilities into computer platform operating systems. The compressing, or "zipping," routine is invoked before storage or download/ftp of files, and the associated "unzipping" routine is used to expand (some say "explode") them during file recall or installation of downloaded executables. The Lempel-Ziv-Welch (LZW) algorithm (Welch 1984), a variant of LZ78 that we shall discuss, serves as the core of the widely deployed Unix Compress utility.

Here is the LZ77 parsing of the above data sequence:

0, 0 0, 1, 0 1 1, 0 0 0 0, 0 1 0 1 0, 0 1 0 0, 1 0 0 0 1, 0 0 1 1, . . .

LZ77 maintains a growing window that contains the entirety of the data sequence it has parsed thus far. Specifically, after the first five phrases have been parsed in the above example, this window contains their concatenation, 00010110000, with no commas. The main step in forming the sixth phrase is to search this window for a long match to the front end 0101001001. . . of the future of the data (i.e., the as-yet-unparsed portion of the data). In this instance the longest match is 0101, starting at position 3 in the window. The sixth phrase is this longest match extended one source symbol deeper into the future, which in this case means appending a 0 and thereby obtaining 01010, as shown in the parsing.

Next, we look at the LZ78 parsing of the same data sequence:

0, 0 0, 1, 0 1, 1 0, 0 0 0, 0 1 0, 1 0 0, 1 0 0 1, 0 0 0 1, 0 0 1, 1 · · ·, . . .

LZ78 maintains a structure, usually a stack or a tree, containing all the phrases into which it has divided the portion of the data sequence it has parsed thus far. The next phrase is formed by concatenating two items: (1) that phrase in the structure that achieves the longest match with the beginning of the as-yet-unparsed portion of the data and (2) the next source datum beyond the end of this maximal match. For example, when it comes time to form the eighth phrase in the LZ78 parsing for our sample data sequence, the as-yet-unparsed portion of the data reads 100100100. . . . The longest match to the beginning of this among the seven phrases already parsed is achieved by the fifth phrase, 10; hence, the eighth phrase is 100 (i.e., 10 concatenated with 0).

LZ77 parses most data sequences into longer (hence, fewer) phrases than does LZ78. For example, LZ77 parses our sample sequence into 9 phrases; LZ78 requires 11 phrases, with the final 1 lapping over into phrase 12. However, the matching portion of an LZ78 phrase can be described by giving only the number of the appropriate phrase that appeared earlier in the parsing; describing an LZ77 phrase requires specifying not only a pointer to where to start copying but also what length to copy. Moreover, the number of possible locations for the pointer in LZ77 is considerably larger than the number of prior phrases in LZ78, so we need to use more bits to point to it. Hence, it is not clear which method is "better."

It turns out—and this is the major result of LZ theory—that in the limit of long data sequences, neither LZ77 nor LZ78 is better than the other because they both are *universally asymptotically optimum;* that is, they each require a limiting number of code letters per source letter that converges to the entropy rate, H, of whatever stationary source actually happens to be generating the data! The same universality also is exhibited by other variants of the LZ algorithm that we shall discuss.

Why bother, then, to discuss several variants of LZ coding when they are all universally asymptotically optimum? The reason is that LZ convergence to H is slow (see Section 3.3.6); this allows some variants to outperform others significantly for intermediate-sized data sequences (say, 10 KB to 10 MB) such as those commonly encountered in downloading and/or storage of computer files. Moreover, many practical data sources are nonstationary, so it actually turns out to be better to purge the data structure (stack, tree, window) of old data that is no longer statistically pertinent. Accordingly, asymptotic optimality never gets to kick in fully anyway.

There is a *tail-biting* version of LZ77 parsing that produces still longer phrases (Ziv and Lempel 1977). Tail-biting LZ77 also points to a location in the window at which to start copying the present phrase, but it allows the phrase's length to be *longer* than the remainder of the window content beyond the pointer. This is achieved by considering appending the symbols of each candidate for the current phrase to the window as they are produced and, in the event that the current match reaches the end of the original window, permitting the leading appended symbols to be copied if this correctly extends the match. For example, the tail-biting parsing of our sample sequence is

0, 001, 011, 0000, 01010, 01001000, 10011,...

Tail-biting LZ77 uses only seven phrases for our data string as opposed to the nine phrases used by ordinary LZ77. Tail-biting is invoked when parsing the second and sixth phrases. The second phrase is formed by copying a phrase of length 2 starting at the lone 0 then in the window and then adding a terminal 1; we slide the first digit copied (a 0 in this case) into the window and then immediately copy it to get the second digit of the current phrase. Similarly, the sixth phrase is formed by copying a string of length 7 starting at the third position before the end of the window and then adding a terminal 0; a four-symbol tail is bitten in this case. (It can be argued that the tail actually grasps the head rather than the head biting the tail.) The spot to point to at which to begin the copying need not be unique; for example, there are two different places in the window to which we could point to start copying the 1001 portion of the seventh phrase.

The Lempel-Ziv-Welch (LZW) algorithm is a variant of LZ78. LZW is the core of the widely deployed Unix Compress utility. It parses our sample sequence as follows:

0, 00, 1, 0, 1, 10, 00, 001, 01, 0010, 010, 00100, 11···, ...

Note that the phrases of an LZW parsing are not unique and tend to be shorter than those of the other parsings we have considered so far. The advantages that account for LZW's popularity will be detailed in Section 3.3 when we analyze system performance.

Finally, the Lempel-Ziv-Yokoo (LZY) algorithm (Yokoo 1992; Kiyohara and Kawabata 1996) parses our sample sequence as follows:

0, 00, 1, 01, 10, 000, 01, 010, 0100, 100, 01001, 1...

LZY uses only 11 nonunique phrases to parse one more symbol of our sample sequence than LZW is able to parse using 13 phrases. We argue in Section 3.3 that LZY provides a desirable mix of properties from LZ77 (with tail-biting), LZ78, and LZW. Since LZY usually outperforms LZW in practical examples, it would have provided a better foundation for Unix Compress than does LZW. However, LZW already was too firmly entrenched to be displaced and also is computationally less intensive than LZY.

3.3   LZ Compression

The easiest way to understand how an LZ algorithm compresses is to apply it step by step to an example. We shall do this now for the 29-symbol sequence we parsed in the previous section, first for LZ78, then for LZW, then for LZY, and finally for LZ77. We treat LZ77 last even though it was first chronologically because analyzing its compression efficiency involves additional subtleties.

The 29-symbol sequence of our example is too short to allow the LZ algorithms to achieve compression; they have just begun to warm up to the job when we truncate the input. Also, we have no knowledge of the mechanism that generated this sequence, so we don't even know if it should be possible to compress it much. Although it has only 10 ones as opposed to 19 zeros, we should not deduce from this that it's highly compressible. Indeed, if (this may be a big "if") the digits were produced i.i.d. by a binary source having probability precisely $\frac{10}{29}$ of emitting 1 as opposed to 0 at any instant, its entropy would be $-(\frac{10}{29}) \log_2(\frac{10}{29})$ $-(\frac{19}{29}) \log_2(\frac{19}{29}) = 0.929$ bits/symbol. This would imply that only 7.1% compression is possible even when given an unlimited amount of data and when fully informed of the source's probability structure. Nonetheless, the example fulfills our objective of elucidating how to quantify LZ compression performance. In Section 3.3.5 we give results for sequences comprised of several thousand symbols, including some generated by a known probabilistic model whose entropy rate we can compute. This lets us compare the compression performances of the algorithms not only against one another but also against an absolute standard.

The difference between the compression ratio an algorithm achieves and the ultimate limit set by the entropy rate is called the algorithm's *redundancy rate*. Since LZ algorithms have been proven to be universal, their redundancy rates vanish in the limit as the amount of source data compressed grows without bound. The speed with which the redundancy rate decays as the length of the data sequence increases is of considerable interest; in Section 3.3.6 we study it graphically and comment on its analytical behavior. In addition, we discuss techniques for enhancing the compression ratio in the short and intermediate term at the expense of increases in execution time, program size, and temporary memory allocation.

3.3.1 LZ78

LZ78's parsing of the first 28 symbols of the sequence into 11 phrases is repeated below:

0, 00, 1, 01, 10, 000, 010, 100, 1001, 0001, 001, 1···, ...

Associated with this parsing is the LZ78 tree shown in Figure 3.1; the left branch (if any) out of a node always is labeled 0 and the right branch (if any) always

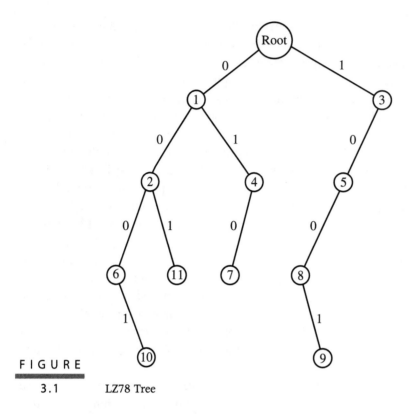

FIGURE

3.1   LZ78 Tree

is labeled 1. The tree is grown one node at a time. Initially, only the root is present. Since the first phrase in the LZ78 parsing is 0, we branch out of the root to the left. The node reached is denoted as node 1 because it corresponds to phrase 1. Returning to the root, we now use phrase 2 to designate the path to node 2. Phrase 2 is 00; its first 0 brings us to node 1, and its final 0 tells us to branch left. Accordingly, node 2 is the left descendant of node 1 in this case, as shown. Nodes 3 through 11 are appended similarly. Thus, the concatenation of the binary digits on successive branches of the path from the root to node k in the LZ78 tree is phrase k of the LZ78 parsing. It follows that phrase k can be described by specifying which node is its immediate ancestor and then saying whether it is the left or the right descendant of its ancestor. This is precisely how the LZ78 encoder specifies the next phrase to the LZ78 decoder. The decoder then is able to build the LZ78 tree in step with the encoder. It is important to appreciate that no side information needs to be conveyed to the decoder to allow it to construct the LZ78 tree. All the information needed for the decoder to update the tree incrementally is by design inherent in LZ78's representations of the successive phrases.

T A B L E	Performance of LZ78 Variants					
3.1						
		Phrase	$\lceil \log_2 k \rceil + 1$		$\lceil \log_2 L(k) \rceil + 1$	E[LAI] +1
	Phrase	Number, k	LZ78	$L(k)$	LZ78E	LZ78EP	LZ78SEP

Phrase	Number, k	LZ78	$L(k)$	LZ78E	LZ78EP	LZ78SEP
0	1	1	1	1	1	1
00	2	2	2	2	2	2
1	3	3	3	3	$\frac{8}{3}$	$\frac{5}{3}$
01	4	3	3	3	$\frac{8}{3}$	$\frac{5}{3}$
10	5	4	3	3	$\frac{8}{3}$	$\frac{8}{3}$
000	6	4	4	3	3	3
010	7	4	5	4	$\frac{17}{5}$	$\frac{17}{5}$
100	8	4	6	4	$\frac{11}{3}$	$\frac{11}{3}$
1001	9	5	7	4	$\frac{27}{7}$	$\frac{27}{7}$
0001	10	5	8	4	4	4
001	11	5	9	5	$\frac{38}{9}$	$\frac{29}{9}$
Total	—	40	—	36	33.146	30.146
Total/28	—	1.43	—	1.29	1.18	1.077

Vanilla LZ78

Let's see how many binary digits the LZ78 encoder requires to specify phrase k. At the moment that the encoder embarks upon parsing phrase k, there are already k nodes in the tree—namely, the root and nodes 1 through $k - 1$. Hence, $\lceil \log_2 k \rceil$ binary digits suffice to describe the ancestor node for phrase k using classic brute-force binary encoding. One more digit then is appended in order to specify whether phrase k is the left descendant or the right descendant of its ancestor; an equivalent way of saying this is that the final digit of each phrase is sent uncompressed.

The first three columns in Table 3.1 contain, respectively, the phrases, their phrase numbers, and the lengths $\lceil \log_2 k \rceil + 1$ of their LZ78 descriptions. Note that a total of 40 binary digits is required to encode the first 11 phrases. Since these phrases comprise 28 source symbols, LZ78 has *expanded* the data by a factor of 1.43 so far instead of compressing it! (You were warned to expect that in this brief example.) We now describe some modifications of LZ78 encoding that substantially improve its short-term performance.

LZ78S

We can improve compression performance by making the following observation. In LZ parsing of binary data, the second time that a node is specified as being the ancestor node for the current phrase, everyone immediately knows that this phrase must end with the remaining descendant of that node rather than the descendant we appended earlier. (If its next digit were the one on the branch to the descendant we appended earlier, we would have continued copying to, and perhaps beyond, that descendant in search of the ancestor of the current phrase rather than stopping where we did.) Accordingly, it is not necessary to send the decoder the terminal digit of such a phrase. The variant of LZ78 that suppresses the terminal digit of any phrase that is the final descendant of its ancestor is called LZ78S, where S stands for "suppress." In the current example, phrase 3 is the second and final descendant of the root, phrase 4 is the final descendant of node 1, and phrase 11 is the final descendant of node 2. Accordingly, LZ78S uses an average of only $40 - 3 = 37$ binary digits to encode the first 28 source symbols. This reduces the expansion to $37/28 = 1.32$ (i.e., 32% instead of 40%).

LZ78E and LZ78SE

Observe that after phrase 3 has been parsed, the LZ78 tree consists only of the root and nodes 1, 2, and 3 of Figure 3.1. From this point on, we will never again use the root as the ancestor node of a phrase because both of its immediate descendants are already in the tree. Likewise, after we parse phrase 4, we will never again use node 1 as the ancestor node because both of its descendants now are in the tree. The root and node 1 now are "dead," but nodes 2, 3, and 4 are still alive. We are free to expurgate, or excise, dead nodes from the tree and then push down the indices of the live nodes accordingly. The algorithm that does this is called LZ78E, where E stands either for "expurgation" or "excision." Column 4 of Table 3.1 shows the number $L(k)$ of live nodes in the tree when it comes time to parse phrase k, and column 5 shows the number $\lceil \log_2 L(k) \rceil + 1$ of binary digits that LZ78E needs to describe phrase k. Since the LZ78E decoder knows when each node in the tree dies and knows how to push down the node indices, it is not necessary to send any additional information to keep the encoder's and decoder's bookkeeping identical. We see that LZ78E reduces the number of binary digits needed to describe the 11 phrases from 40 to 36.

We can combine both suppression and excision. We call the algorithm that does this LZ78SE. LZ78SE requires only $36 - 3 = 33$ code digits to encode the first 28 source symbols, thereby reducing the expansion factor to $33/28 = 1.18$, or 18%.

LZ78EP and LZ78SEP

We now show how to describe the LZ78 parsing still more efficiently by replacing $\lceil L(k) \rceil$ with something smaller. When $L(k) = 3$, as it does when $k = 3$,

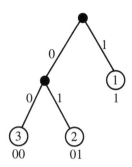

F I G U R E
3.2   Prefix Code for $L(k) = 3$

$k = 4$, and $k = 5$ (see Table 3.1), we can use the three-leaf binary tree of Figure 3.2 to prefix encode which of the three live nodes in the original tree
will serve as the ancestor node for phrase k. This permits us to encode one
of the three possible ancestors with only one digit and the other two with two
digits each. We don't know the probability distribution that governs which
of the three possible ancestors will be selected. However, regardless of what
that distribution is, we sometimes succeed in using only $1 = \lfloor \log_2 L(k) \rfloor$ binary digit instead of $2 = \lceil \log_2 L(k) \rceil$. With this scheme the average number of
binary digits we need to encode the immediate-ancestor portion of a phrase
when all three possible immediate ancestors are assumed a priori equally likely
is $\text{E[LAI]} = \frac{1}{3} \cdot 1 + \frac{2}{3} \cdot 2 = \frac{5}{3}$, where LAI stands for Level of the Ancestor's
Index.

Column 6 of Table 3.1 lists the average number of binary digits we need to
encode a phrase when we use this scheme, namely, E[LAI] plus one more for
the phrase's terminal symbol. This is why $\frac{8}{3} = \frac{5}{3} + 1$ appears in rows 3, 4, and
5 of column 6. Figure 3.3 shows the nine-leaf tree that one uses to prefix code
the ancestor node for phrase 11; it has seven nodes at depth 3 and two at depth
4. It follows that, in this instance, $\text{E[LAI]} = \frac{7}{9} \cdot 3 + \frac{2}{9} \cdot 4 = \frac{29}{9}$, which is why
the entry in row 11 of column 6 is $\frac{29}{9} + 1 = \frac{38}{9}$. The other entries in column
6 are analogously obtained. (You may wish to verify that, if the number L of
live nodes satisfies $2^{m-1} \le L < 2^m$, then the prefix code for the ancestor indices
has $2^m - L$ nodes on level $m - 1$ and $2L - 2^m$ nodes on level m, resulting in
$\text{E[LAI]} = m + 1 - \frac{2^m}{L}$.) Summing the entries in column 6 yields 33.146, or 1.18
code digits per source digit. Since a prefix coding technique has been used
to reduce the mean number of code digits needed to specify the pushed-down
index of each phrase's ancestor node, we call this coding scheme LZ78EP, where
P stands for "prefix." Finally, column 7 details the performance of LZ78SEP,
which improves upon LZ78EP by suppressing the terminal digit of phrases 3, 4,

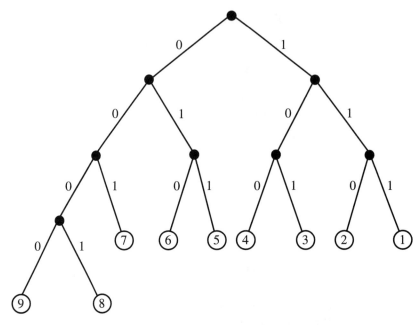

FIGURE

3.3   Prefix Code for $L(k) = 9$

and 11. LZ78SEP requires an average of $(33.146 - 3)/28 = 30.146/28 = 1.077$ code symbols per source symbol, an expansion of only 7.7%.

A lesson to be learned here is that a parsing is less important than the coding algorithm that is used to describe it. All the algorithms we have described here in Section 3.3.1 use the same 11-phrase parsing of the first 28 source symbols in our example. However, the most sophisticated of them, LZ78SEP, is 33% more compressive than vanilla LZ78. Of course, improved compression does not come for free. The source code for a more sophisticated algorithm usually fills more storage space, and the execution time of compression and decompression usually increases.

3.3.2   LZW

The LZW algorithm parses our 29-symbol sample sequence into exactly 13 phrases as follows:

0, 00, 1, 0, 1, 10, 00, 001, 01, 0010, 010, 00100, 11,...

The distinguishing feature of LZW is the "Welch modification" (Welch 1984), which seeks to overcome the inefficiency inherent in sending the last symbol of

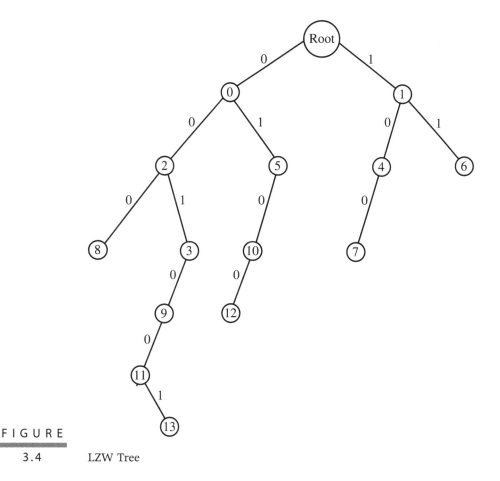

FIGURE

3.4   LZW Tree

each phrase uncompressed. This is particularly important for sources that are highly compressible in the sense that their entropy rates are much smaller than the log of the cardinality of the source alphabet. Such sources are commonly encountered in practice and are natural targets for data compression.

The initial LZW tree consists of the root node and all its one-symbol extensions. In the case of binary data, then, the initial LZW tree consists of the root, its 0-descendant, and its 1-descendant; these are depicted as nodes "root," 0, and 1, respectively, in Figure 3.4. The kth LZW phrase, ϕ_k, equals the longest match the encoder can find in the current LZW tree to the beginning of the portion of the data not already parsed by the first $k - 1$ phrases. After parsing ϕ_k, the encoder recursively updates its LZW tree by adding the node that corresponds to the one-digit extension of ϕ_k that agrees with the source data yet one more symbol into the future. The encoder does this despite the fact that this additional symbol is not part of ϕ_k and hence will not be described to the decoder at this time. However, the decoder always is able to deduce this "mystery symbol" one time step later because the mystery symbol also is the first symbol of the next phrase, ϕ_{k+1}. Now, once the decoder is told the number of the node to which to copy in order to obtain ϕ_{k+1}, it then knows which branch out of the root is the first branch on the path to that node; the symbol on that branch is the mystery symbol. Thus, the decoder can update the tree recursively, too. The fact that decoder updates lag one step behind encoder updates is another feature that distinguishes LZW from LZ78 and its variants.

Let's see how LZW encoding works in the case of our sample sequence. The first symbol is 0, so the 0-descendant of the root (i.e., node 0) is designated as the description of the first LZW phrase. The second source digit also is a 0, so the encoder updates its tree by inserting the 0-descendant of node 0 and gives it the next node number, 2. When the decoder receives the first phrase, $\phi_1 = 0$, it knows that node 2 is a descendant of node 0, but does not yet know whether it is the 0-descendant or the 1-descendant. The encoder now parses $\phi_2 = 00$, since this is the longest match to the as-yet-unparsed future of the data that can be found in the encoder's current tree. The node corresponding to 00 is node 2, the one the encoder most recently inserted, the exact position of which is still unknown to the decoder. However, as soon as the decoder learns that node 2 has been designated as the one to which to copy to produce ϕ_2, the decoder can deduce that the first digit of ϕ_2 is a 0 by reasoning that, as a descendant of node 0, node 2 lies in the left subtree of the LZW tree of Figure 3.4, where *all* paths begin with a 0. The decoder knows, moreover, that the first digit of ϕ_2 also served as the terminal digit the encoder used when it constructed the path to node 2. Thus, the decoder now knows that the path to node 2 is 00, not 01. Accordingly, the decoder can place node 2 into its version of the LZW tree at this juncture. Finally, since the decoder was told to use the path to node 2 as ϕ_2, the decoder correctly decodes $\phi_2 = 00$.

The preceding paragraph illustrates the concept of the Welch extension, including the fact that it is permissible for the encoder to designate the path to the node it has just inserted into the tree as the description of the next phrase in the parsing, even though the decoder does not yet know the last digit of that path! It also illustrates why all the singletons must be in the initial LZW tree.

Continuing, the encoder next updates its tree by inserting node 3 as the 1-descendant of node 2; then it parses $\phi_3 = 1$. LZW encoding and decoding proceed in this manner. The LZW tree that the encoder uses to parse $\phi_{13} = 11$ is shown in Figure 3.4. At that moment the decoder does not yet know whether node 13 is the 0-descendant or the 1-descendant of node 11; it will be able to

TABLE 3.2 Performance of LZW Variants

Phrase, ϕ_k	Phrase Number, k	$\lceil \log_2(k+2) \rceil$ LZW	$L(k)$	$\lceil \log_2 L(k) \rceil$ LZWE	E[LAI] LZWEP
0	1	2	2	1	1
00	2	2	3	2	$\frac{5}{3}$
1	3	3	4	2	2
0	4	3	5	3	$\frac{12}{5}$
1	5	3	5	3	$\frac{12}{5}$
10	6	3	5	3	$\frac{12}{5}$
00	7	4	6	3	$\frac{8}{3}$
001	8	4	6	3	$\frac{8}{3}$
01	9	4	7	3	$\frac{20}{7}$
0010	10	4	8	4	3
010	11	4	9	4	$\frac{29}{9}$
00100	12	4	10	4	$\frac{17}{5}$
11	13	4	11	4	$\frac{39}{11}$
Total	—	44	—	39	33.22
Total/29	—	1.52	—	1.34	1.15

deduce that it's the 1-descendant as soon as the encoder tells it that node 6 is the one to which to copy to produce ϕ_{13} because it knows node 6 is in the right subtree, where every path starts with a 1.

Table 3.2 contains the same sort of information for LZW that Table 3.1 did for LZ78. Columns 1 and 2 show the LZW phrases and their phrase numbers. Column 3 shows the bit count for vanilla LZW; $\lceil \log_2(k+2) \rceil$ binary digits are required to describe ϕ_k because there are $k+2$ total nodes in the LZW tree at the moment that ϕ_k is parsed. Vanilla LZW requires a total of 44 code digits to describe our length-29 sequence, an expansion of 52%. Column 4 shows the number $L(k)$ of live nodes in the LZW tree at the moment ϕ_k gets parsed, and column 5 shows the bit counts $\lceil \log_2 L(k) \rceil$ for the algorithm LZWE that excises dead nodes in a manner analogous to that described for LZ78E. The total bit count falls to 39, a 34% expansion. The final column, labeled LZWEP, shows the expected bit count if we enhance LZWE by using prefix coding to describe the phrase indices. The total expected bit count for this is 33.22, an expansion of 15%. However, if we limit our attention to the back end of the sequence, we can see that LZWEP already has begun to achieve compression. The last four

LZW phrases—0010, 010, 00100, and 11—have a total of 14 source digits, but the last four numbers in the LZWEP column sum to only 13.17, a compression of 5.9%. Finally! (In fact, if we limit our attention only to phrases 10, 11, and 12, then LZWEP achieves 19.8% compression. Of course, it is not good science to single out the most favorable place to look after the fact.)

Because LZW does not send the final digit of each phrase uncompressed the way LZ78 does, there is no suppress option for LZW. Nonetheless, we can improve LZW compression performance by using the fact that sometimes the final branch to the new node the encoder inserts into the LZW tree is predetermined. To do so, however, necessitates employing a modified LZW parsing we have chosen not to describe here.

3.3.3 LZY

The LZY parsing of our sample sequence is

$$0, \ 00, \ 1, \ 01, \ 10, \ 000, \ 01, \ 010, \ 0100, \ 100, \ 01001, \ 1\cdots, \ldots$$

The first 11 LZY phrases comprise the first 28 source symbols. Phrase 4 and phrase 7 both equal 01, illustrating that the phrases of an LZY parsing are not necessarily distinct. LZY parsing and coding has to be preceded by constructing the sequence $\{D_n\}$ of LZY dictionaries via the process described below. The encoder either can form the entire D_n-sequence first and then do all the parsing and coding, or can alternate between dictionary updating and parsing/coding.

Here is the procedure for constructing the sequence D_n of LZY dictionaries. D_0 is comprised of the empty string Λ and singletons (single-symbol words) for each letter in the source alphabet. (In tree parlance, D_0 is the root node and its full fan.) The recursive rule for updating the dictionary is

$$D_n = D_{n-1} \cup W_n \tag{3.1}$$

where the new word W_n equals whichever word in D_{n-1} is the longest match to the source data starting at position n, extended to match yet one more symbol. This assures, among other things, that all the words in D_n are distinct from one another.

By way of example, here's D_{24} for our sample sequence:

$$D_{24} = \{\Lambda, 0, 1, 00, 001, 01, 10, 011, 11, 100, 000, 0000, 0001, 0010, 010,$$
$$101, 0100, 1001, 00100, 01001, 10010, 001000, 01000, 1000,$$
$$00010, 001001, 010011\}$$

```
0  0
   0  0  1
      0  1
         1  0
            0  1  1
               1  1
                  1  0  0
                     0  0  0
                        0  0  0  0
                           0  0  0  1
                              0  0  1  0
                                 0  1  0
                                    1  0  1
                                       0  1  0  0
                                          1  0  0  1
                                             0  0  1  0  0
                                                0  1  0  0  1
                                                   1  0  0  1  0
                                                      0  0  1  0  0  0
                                                         0  1  0  0  0
                                                            1  0  0  0
                                                               0  0  0  1  0
                                                                  0  0  1  0  0  1
                                                                     0  1  0  0  1  1
```

FIGURE

3.5   Illustration of the Forward March Property

All the earlier dictionaries, $D_0, \ldots, D_{23}$, also appear here: $D_0 = \{\Lambda, 0, 1\}$, $D_1 = \{\Lambda, 0, 1, 00\}$, $D_2 = \{\Lambda, 0, 1, 00, 001\}$, and so forth.

Each word added into the LZY dictionary always penetrates at least as deeply into the data sequence as does any word already in the dictionary, a phenomenon we shall call the *forward march property*. Figure 3.5 shows the successive dictionary entries in D_{24} projecting into the data stream in keeping with the forward march property. (The initial entries Λ, 0, and 1 are not displayed.) We prove the forward march property of LZY in Appendix E.

Here is how the LZY parsing is constructed: Suppose the next LZY phrase starts at position n of the data sequence. Then that phrase will be the longest word in dictionary D_{n-1} that matches the data starting at position n.

(Equivalently, it will consist of all but the final digit of the word W_n that is added to D_{n-1} to form D_n.) Since we have noted that the entries in any LZY dictionary are distinct, there is never a tie for this longest match.

For example, the 11th phrase in the LZY parsing of the example starts at position 24 of the source sequence. Accordingly, it is the longest word in D_{23} that matches the data sequence starting at position 24, namely, 01001; it also equals all but the final digit of the word $W_{24} = 010011$ that we add to D_{23} in order to form D_{24}.

As with the other LZ algorithms we have studied thus far, LZY has a basic version and various enhanced forms. We shall content ourselves with exploring only vanilla LZY, LZYE, and LZYEP. In order to encode a newly parsed phrase, the LZY encoder has to specify the index of the appropriate word in the dictionary used to parse that phrase. If the phrase starts at position n, then the dictionary in question is D_{n-1}, which has $3 + (n - 1)$ entries, namely Λ, 0, 1, and W_k for $1 \leq k \leq n - 1$. Λ never gets selected, so there are a total of $n + 1$ entries from which to choose. Hence, it takes $\lceil \log_2(n + 1) \rceil$ bits for vanilla LZY to encode a phrase that starts at position n. In our example, there are 11 phrases, which start at positions 1, 2, 4, 5, 7, 9, 12, 14, 17, 21, and 24. Vanilla LZY therefore needs 1 bit for the first phrase, 2 for the second phrase, 3 for each of the next three phrases, 4 for each of the next three, and finally 5 for each of the last three. This is a total of 39 code bits to encode the first 28 source digits, a 39% expansion. This can be improved upon by using excision. For example, since $W_1 = 00$ and $W_3 = 01$, the singleton 0 in the initial dictionary will never be designated by the encoder for any phrase starting in position 4 or beyond. Similarly, 1 can be excised for positions 7 and beyond, 00 starting with position 9, 000 starting with position 11, 01 starting with position 13, 10 starting with position 14, 0100 starting with position 21, 100 starting with position 22, and 00100 starting with position 24. It follows that LZYE needs only 34 bits to describe the same 11 phrases, which drops the expansion to 21%. If we use prefix coding as well, we find that the E[LAI] numbers for the 11 phrases are 1, $\frac{5}{3}$, 2, $\frac{12}{5}$, $\frac{8}{3}$, $\frac{20}{7}$, $\frac{29}{9}$, $\frac{29}{9}$ again, $\frac{11}{3}$, $\frac{59}{15}$, and 4. These sum to 30.63, so LZYEP expands by only 9.4%. If, as we did with LZW, we consider only the last four phrases, we see that they consist of $3 + 4 + 3 + 5 = 15$ source symbols but are encoded by LZYEP using an average of only $\frac{29}{9} + \frac{11}{3} + \frac{59}{15} + 4 = 14.82$ digits, a compression of 1.2%. LZYEP has already begun to show its colors.

LZY shares certain properties with LZW (see Section 3.3.2). For one, the initial LZY dictionary consists of the empty string, Λ, and all the singletons. For another, the LZY encoder sends only the index of the longest match to the future that resides in the dictionary at the moment of parsing; it does not send the one-symbol, uncompressed extension the way LZ77 and LZ78 do (see Sections 3.3.4 and 3.3.1), though it does add it to its next dictionary. Finally, LZY exhibits a generalized version of LZW's ability for the decoder to be able to cope with the encoder sending as the descriptor of the next phrase an index for which the decoder does not yet know the entirety of the word associated with it; the very fact that this index is designated, coupled with other knowledge the decoder already possesses, allows the decoder to deduce the entirety of the designated phrase. As an example of this, consider the eighth LZY phrase, 010, which starts at position 14. It is encoded by specifying that we should copy $W_{12} = 010$, the next-to-most-recent entry in the dictionary D_{13} used for encoding starting at position 14 (assuming no excision). At that moment the decoder knows only the first seven phrases of the LZY parsing, which cover only positions 1 through 13. When the encoder earlier determined that W_{12} should be 010, however, it used the fact that this matched the source data not only in positions 12 and 13 but also in position 14! (Note that $x_{12}x_{13}x_{14} = 010$.) However, by virtue of being informed that W_{12} is the word to copy starting at position 14, the decoder immediately knows that $x_{14} = x_{12} = 0$ and $x_{15} = x_{13} = 1$, whereupon it can then further deduce that $x_{16} = x_{14} = 0$. This, in turn, is enough information for the decoder to be able to determine from the rules of LZY dictionary formation that $W_{12} = 010$ and hence to decode phrase 8. Often the LZY decoder has to iterate this bootstrapping procedure in order to deduce several of the digits at the end of a designated phrase, not just one digit as in this instance.

3.3.4   LZ77

The nine-phrase LZ77 parsing of our 29-symbol sample sequence is

$$0,\ 0\,0,\ 1,\ 0\,1\,1,\ 0\,0\,0\,0,\ 0\,1\,0\,1\,0,\ 0\,1\,0\,0,\ 1\,0\,0\,0\,1,\ 0\,0\,1\,1, \ldots$$

Recall that LZ77 must send three items to describe the kth phrase, ϕ_k, in its parsing. Where $\mathcal{W}_{k-1}$ denotes the window of previously encoded phrases that the LZ77 coder searches for matches to the future, these three items are

- S_k, the index of the datum in $\mathcal{W}_{k-1}$ at which to start copying ϕ_k
- L_k, the length to copy
- T_k, the terminal symbol of ϕ_k

Note that S_k and L_k are interdependent because, unless we are using the tail-biting variant, we must have $S_k + L_k - 1 \le W_{k-1}$, where W_{k-1} denotes the width of the window $\mathcal{W}_{k-1}$.

An LZ77 coder devotes most of its output to encoding S_k values as opposed to L_k values and T_k values. There usually is a slight bias in favor of values in the more recent, as opposed to the more distant, portions of the window, but most practical algorithms do not try to capitalize on this. Therefore, it requires about $\log_2 W_{k-1}$ binary digits to encode S_k. By contrast, the length L of the maximum match within a window of width W to the future of the data sequence typically is of order $\log_2 W$. (More precisely, in the case of a stationary source of entropy rate H bits/symbol, this match length is confined, in certain satisfying senses of probabilistic convergence, to a snug interval around $H^{-1} \log_2 W$. See Wyner and Ziv 1994; Wyner 1997; Shields 1993.) Accordingly, it usually should take only approximately $\log_2(\log_2 W_{k-1})$ symbols to encode L_k. We must use cleverness, however, in order to achieve such $\log(\log W)$ representations of the match length. The catch is that it is always possible for a match as long as the whole window to occur (even longer when tail-biting is permitted) because nothing rules out the possibility that the source data suddenly might start repeating itself from the beginning. Thus, even without tail-biting, the range of L has cardinality W, suggesting that $\log W$ symbols may be needed to specify the value of L after all, not just $\log(\log W)$. In Appendix F we describe a scheme for encoding L_k that uses only $\lceil \log_2(\log_2 W_{k-1}) \rceil + \lceil \log_2 L_k \rceil$ binary digits. As desired, this is $O(\log_2(\log_2 W_{k-1}))$ when L_k assumes a typical value near $\log_2 W_{k-1}$ and is larger only on those rare occasions when the match length L_k is inordinately large. Since on such occasions LZ77 is copying a long phrase and hence achieving a strong local compression factor, it tolerates a small penalty in the form of a longer-than-usual description of L_k. Although the encoding scheme of Appendix F is not *exactly* what is used by commercial versions of LZ77 such as gzip, Stacker, pkzip, and winzip to produce compressed representations of phrase lengths, it captures the essence of it.

It requires $\lceil \log_2(W_{k-1} + 1) \rceil$ digits to encode S_k. The "+1" appears here because we need to provide an additional code index to handle cases in which ϕ_k starts with a symbol that has yet to appear in the window, as in the case of ϕ_3 of the example. Once each of the M distinct symbols in the source alphabet has appeared at least once, it is no longer necessary to include this "+1." In the case of a binary source, this usually happens early on. Hence, in the calculations below for our example, only $\lceil \log_2 W_{k-1} \rceil$ binary digits were allotted for encoding S_k once both 0 and 1 are in the window.

It requires at most $\lceil \log_2 M \rceil$ binary digits to encode the terminal symbol T_k. However, when compressing a binary source, we usually don't need to use any digits at all to encode T_k! This is because, once S_k and L_k have been specified, the LZ77 decoder knows that the match extends from window position S_k through position $S_k + L_k - 1$ but not through position $S_k + L_k$. Thus, it knows that the terminal digit of ϕ_k must be the complement of the binary digit in position $S_k + L_k$. The only exception to this occurs when we are not using tail-biting and the match extends all the way to the end of the window (i.e.,

T A B L E	Performance of LZ77							
3.3	k	ϕ_k	W_{k-1}	L_k	$\lceil\log_2(W_{k-1}+1^*)\rceil$	$\lceil\log_2(\log_2 W_{k-1})\rceil$	$\lceil\log_2(L_k/2)\rceil$	$\lceil\log_2 M\rceil^*$	N_k

k	ϕ_k	W_{k-1}	L_k	$\lceil\log_2(W_{k-1}+1^*)\rceil$	$\lceil\log_2(\log_2 W_{k-1})\rceil$	$\lceil\log_2(L_k/2)\rceil$	$\lceil\log_2 M\rceil^*$	N_k
1	0	0	0	0	—	—	1	1
2	00	1	1	1	0	0	1	2
3	1	3	0	2	1	—	0*	3
4	011	4	2	2*	1	0	1	4
5	0000	7	3	3	2	1	0*	6
6	01010	11	4	4	2	1	0*	7
7	0100	16	3	4*	2	1	0*	7
8	10001	20	4	5	3	1	0*	9
9	0011	25	3	5	3	1	0*	9
Total				26	14	5	3	48

when $S_k + L_k - 1 = W_{k-1}$). Hence, in the calculations below, a binary digit was assessed for the terminal symbol only in such cases. The total number of binary digits to encode ϕ_k thus is

$$N_k = \lceil\log_2(W_{k-1}+1^*)\rceil + \lceil\log_2(\log_2 W_{k-1})\rceil + \lceil\log_2 L_k\rceil + \lceil\log_2 M\rceil^* \quad (3.2)$$

where the asterisk means that often this contribution can be omitted in accordance with the considerations discussed above. Table 3.3 uses the above formula to quantify LZ77 compression performance in the case of the 29-digit binary sequence of our example. Entries in this table marked with an asterisk are smaller than they otherwise would be if the asterisks did not appear in the above formula.

Since 48 code symbols are used to encode 29 source symbols, there is a 65.5% expansion. However, we can improve upon this. For starters, we can reduce some of the entries in the $\lceil\log_2(\log_2 W_{k-1})\rceil$ column. For example, although the entry in this column for $k = 3$ is $\lceil\log_2(\log_2 3)\rceil = 1$, we do not need to send this bit because the entry in column 5 already has informed the decoder that the symbol that starts this phrase has yet to appear in the window, so the phrase length must be 1 and there is no need to waste bits describing it. Also, we don't need to send any length information for $k = 4$ either. The reason for this is that the column 5 entry has told the decoder that copying starts in position 3, so the first digit of the future, and hence of ϕ_4, is a 0. This means that the future must start with either 01 or 001 or 0001 or 0000. If it started with 001, the column 5 entry would have designated position 2 as the starting point S_4 for copying of the front end of ϕ_4. Similarly, if the future started with 0001, column 5 would have stood for $S_4 = 1$. Finally, if the future started with 0000, the column 5 entry also would have stood for $S_4 = 1$. Since it actually designated $S_4 = 3$, the decoder can deduce that the copied portion of ϕ_4 must be 01 and hence needs no length information about it. No savings of this sort are possible in rows 5, 6, or 8. In row 7, however, the phrase to be copied is 010, which can be found starting either at position 3, position 12, or position 14; if the encoder is smart enough to designate $S_7 = 14$ rather than 3 or 12, then the decoder will know immediately that 010 is to be copied and also that 0 is the terminal digit. That's because 0101 could be copied starting either at 3 or at 12, so one of those would have been designated if the future indeed started with 0101; they were not, so ϕ_7 must be 0100. This saves both the 2 in column 6 and the 1 in column 7. Similarly, in row 9 we can save both the 3 in column 6 and the 1 in column 7 by designating $S_9 = 23$ as opposed to any of the four other smaller alternatives. In all, the above observations reduce the bit count by 9 from 48 to 39, dropping the expansion factor to 34.5%. If, in addition, prefix coding were used to represent the entries in column 5, the sum there would drop from 26 to 24.2, and the expansion factor to 28.3%. A modicum more could be saved by prefix coding the nonzero entries in columns 6 and 7. In order to make a significant further improvement, it is necessary to capitalize on the fact that the $W_{k-1} + 1^*$ possibilities for S_k are not equiprobable in practice. Rather, they have a natural bias in favor of the more recent values, and we have seen that it pays to exaggerate this bias by choosing the most recent value whenever there is more than one possibility for S_k because this saves bits in columns 6 and 7. The more aggressive commercial versions of LZ77 do this when they are striving for maximum compression.

Commercial implementations of LZ77 do not necessarily strive for maximum compression. As we have seen, milking maximum compression out of the LZ77 approach requires sophisticated data processing that consumes time and temporary memory. Requiring more RAM during the compressing phase is less significant nowadays than it was before 1990, say, because storage has become relatively cheap. But time is always a factor and sometimes is of the essence. Therefore, the better commercial realizations of LZ77 let the user trade compression time and temporary memory requirements off against compression efficiency. The principal way time can be saved is to relax the requirement that the algorithm do an exhaustive search to find the longest possible match in the window. Rather, a structured hierarchical search is employed that attempts to find a long enough match fast. Since the expected match length is $H^{-1} \log W$, the algorithm can be allowed to stop searching if and when it finds a match about this long; since it doesn't know the entropy rate H of the source it is compressing, it uses an empirical estimate of H derived from calculating the running compression ratio achieved to date. Alternatively, it can be programmed to stop searching for a longer match once it finds that it hasn't been able to improve (significantly) on its best candidate match in a while. The speed, flexibility, and general cleverness of the search algorithm are the main things that differentiate one implementation of LZ77 from another. We shall not embark upon discussions of the hashing strategies and search heuristics that have been used in these algorithms. As evidence that they are indeed considered important, multimillion dollar lawsuits have been tried in which LZ77 search algorithms were the intellectual property at issue.

In the practical comparisons for intermediate-size files given in Section 3.3.5, algorithms based on LZ77 outperform those based on LZ78. Let's see why that is not the case for our 29-symbol example. As noted, the chief task for LZ77-based algorithms is to encode the point S in a past of duration W from which to start copying each phrase. This requires approximately $\log_2 W$ binary digits. LZ78-based algorithms, by contrast, need to point only to which previous phrase to copy. When W is large (which it never gets to be in the example), the number of past phrases is to a first approximation $W/(H^{-1}\log_2 W)$. Hence, it requires approximately $\log_2 W + \log_2 H - \log_2(\log_2 W)$ to specify the desired one. For large W, the term $\log_2 H$ here will be negligible, so LZ78 needs about $\log_2(\log_2 W)$ fewer bits to say where to start copying than LZ77 does. On top of that, LZ78 doesn't need to say how many bits to copy; LZ77 has to spend approximately $\log_2(\log_2 W)$ more bits to describe the phrase length. Thus, LZ77 has a handicap of about $2\log_2(\log_2 W)$ bits per phrase. It overcomes this by producing longer phrases than LZ78 because it possesses a greater number of options for where to start copying. Asymptotically, the distinction balances out, and they both compress to H bits/symbol. But in the intermediate run that characterizes practical applications, the advantage usually leans toward LZ77. Even in our short example, LZ77 already uses fewer phrases than LZ78; the problem is that W is too small to create enough of a difference between $\log_2 W$ and $\log_2(\log_2 W)$ for this phrase-saving ability to pay off adequately. LZY occupies an intermediate ground. Like LZ77 it needs $\log_2(\log_2 W)$ more bits than LZ78 to say where to start copying, but unlike LZ77 it does not need to expend any bits specifying a copying length. Naturally, it gets phrase lengths that are longer on the average that those of LZ78 but shorter than those of LZ77; LZY has LZ77's flexibility about where to start copying but LZ78's restriction of having a prescribed length to copy associated with each starting point, thereby reducing the chances for meaningfully longer-than-normal matches.

T A B L E	Compression Performance of LZW (Unix Compress)	
3.4	Data Type	Compression Ratio
	English text	1.8
	Cobol files	2–6
	Floating-point arrays	1.0
	Formatted scientific data	2.1
	System log data	2.6
	Program source code	2.3
	Object code	1.5

3.3.5 Comparative Performance of LZ77, LZW, and LZY

Table 3.4 (from Welch 1984) shows the compression performance achieved by LZW for some common types of computer files. Since the widely adopted Unix Compress utility is, in essence, Welch's implementation of LZW, you may interpret these results as relevant for Unix Compress. In each case the source alphabet consists of 8-bit bytes.

Here are some comments on these results:

1. The results for English text are fairly good. Experimentation has revealed that, if people fluent in English are provided with truthful answers to binary questions they are allowed to ask about a typical English text, then between 1.3 and 2.5 questions per letter of text suffice for them to deduce the sample English text losslessly, depending on whether or not we distinguish between upper and lower case letters, use punctuation marks, and/or allow numbers. Hence, it should be possible to compress a file that uses 8-bit byte representations of English characters (e.g., an ASCII English text file) by a factor of $8/2.5 = 3.2$, but LZW achieved only 1.8. It must be appreciated, however, that LZW does not know that it is confronting English text (as opposed to French, Spanish, or Fortran), does not know the rules of English grammar, possesses no a priori knowledge of English vocabulary and spelling, and most of all possesses no semantic knowledge or life experience. Nonetheless, it is true that if an LZ algorithm that is allowed to keep growing its data structure were given a long enough text (which it never will be given in practice), it would "learn" all these things. Asymptotically, it would achieve compression comparable to that of skilled humans and better than that of average humans!

2. Apparently, not all Cobol files are comparably redundant.

3. Floating-point arrays consist of the characters 0 thru 9, decimal point, plus, minus, and space. Since there are no more than 16 possibilities for a floating-point character, it should be possible to pack two of them into an 8-bit byte. It would appear that this is what has been done here. If there were truly one character per 8-bit byte as opposed to per 4-bit nibble, LZW should have been able to compress the floating-point array by about 2:1 even if it contained random numbers, as indeed could many far less sophisticated compression schemes. It appears the data set was packed two characters to a byte.

4. The results for formatted scientific data seem correct. Formatted scientific data has the same character set as floating point, with the addition of an E for exponentiation. When formatted, it also tends to have a fixed interval between the decimal points, which the algorithm eventually should get good at predicting. Accordingly, with one character per byte (it is less likely that data in scientific notation would get packed into nibbles), a compression ratio of slightly over 2 is to be expected.

5. System log data is likely to be more redundant than other "texts."

6. Object code gets compiled directly from program source code via deterministic transformation. Therefore, the lengths of compressed files that result from applying LZ(W) to the source code and the object code should be about the same in any specific instance (and, hence, also when averaged over several instances). The fact that the compression ratio is bigger for source code than for object code, therefore, is not a consequence of the compressed version being shorter for the source code; rather, it is attributable to the compiler, in the process of converting the source code into object code, also tending to remove enough of the inherent redundancy in source code that the object code file that results takes up only about half as much disk space as the source code file did even before the application of LZ techniques to compress it still further.

Table 3.5 shows the compression performance achieved by LZW/Compress for some TeXfiles and PSfiles. File sizes, both compressed and uncompressed, are in 8-bit bytes. TeXfiles were compressed by factors that cluster tightly around 2.2. PSfiles were compressed by factors that cluster tightly around 2.6; `fat.ps`, the exception that compressed by a factor of three, differs from the others in that it consisted almost entirely of LARGE font. This causes PostScript to include certain formatting instructions repeatedly—a fact that LZW apparently succeeded in recognizing and capitalizing upon.

As their names suggest, `fat.ps` is the PostScript file that resulted from applying `dvips` to `fat.dvi`, the file that was produced when LaTeX was applied

T A B L E   TeXfile and PSfile Performance of Unix Compress

3.5

File Name	Input Length	Output Length	Compression Ratio
file1.tex	75,053	33,797	2.22
file2.tex	64,957	30,786	2.16
fat.tex	107,697	49,533	2.17
file1.ps	209,746	80,413	2.61
file2.ps	315,921	119,683	2.64
file3.ps	244,686	94,975	2.58
file4.ps	222,201	185,827	2.59
cat.ps	992,554	378,233	2.62
fat.tex	107,697	49,533	2.17
fat.ps	693,713	230,491	3.01

to fat.tex. Note that fat.ps is a factor of 6.44 bigger than fat.tex. This is representative; the expansion factors for the conversion from TeX to PS of some 50 files were observed to run from just above 2 to as much as 12.

The comparative verbosity of PSfiles accounts for why it is more desirable to communicate a technical paper to someone as a TeXfile than as a PSfile. Nonetheless, PSfiles often get sent by email or by ftp because they are easier for recipients (especially non-LaTeX recipients) to print. Also, they are less vulnerable to incompatibilities between the sender's and the receiver's versions of LaTeX (what style files and fonts are mounted, storage and floating of encapsulated PostScript figures, and such).

When a PSfile is sent via a modem that uses data compression, it might seem that its verbosity shouldn't cause a problem. Indeed, the data compression routine in the modem (an LZ77 variant in most of today's commercial products) not only should eliminate the factor of 6.44 expansion that occurred when fat.ps was produced from fat.tex but should go on to achieve further compression by eliminating redundancy lurking in fat.tex. But Table 3.5 shows that this did not happen! (True, Unix Compress's version of LZW, not LZ77, was used to get the figures in Table 3.5. However, LZ77 achieves only moderately better results; see Table 3.6.) Rather, fat.ps was compressed only to 230,491 bytes, which is still 2.14 times as big as fat.tex and $2.14 \cdot 2.17 = 4.65$ times bigger than the compressed version of fat.tex. Although Compress saved us almost half a megabyte in the storing and/or transmitting of fat.ps, it might seem that it should have been able to save us another factor of 4.65 (even more, for surely it is possible to compress losslessly beyond what Compress achieved when it was

T A B L E	Performance Comparisons of LZW, LZY, LZYEP, and LZ77				
3.6	File	Bytes	LZW	LZY	LZYEP	LZ77
	A	1250	1.054	1.042	0.993	0.774
	B	46,976	0.480	0.439	0.425	0.360
	C	179,021	0.394	0.361	0.351	0.301

applied to `fat.tex`). Here are two reasons why our supposedly "universal" LZW algorithm did not accomplish this; no doubt, there are other reasons as well.

Reason 1 is that neither a TeX nor a PostScript file fully describes the desired hard copy unassisted. Rather, they refer to extensive code stored in the `/tex` directory in one case and in the PS-compatible printer memory in the other; the LZ compression algorithm in the above examples never sees this auxiliary information. In the limit of an extremely long file, this stored code would become a negligible consideration because there is only a finite amount of it. However, in practice we do not operate in this limit; indeed, the stored code is several times larger in the above examples than are the TeXfiles and PSfiles that LZ is being asked to compress. Although most of what's stored in the TeX utility and most of the bitmaps stored in the PostScript cartridge are not consulted when processing any particular target file, their presence makes it difficult to assess the extent to which PSfiles truly deserve to be accused of being verbose. To put it another way, TeX usually consumes many more megabytes of computer disk than PostScript does of printer memory, so a PSfile "deserves" to be longer than the corresponding TeXfile.

Reason 2 is that universality is an asymptotic property. To possess true universality, LZW must continue to grow the tree, or stack, of past phrases that can be copied, but practical LZW implementations do not do this for a variety of good reasons. In this regard, consider the entry for `cat.ps`, which was produced by concatenating `file1.ps` through `file4.ps` and thus has a length equal exactly to the sum of their lengths. Even though this file is almost a megabyte, the compression ratio achieved for it effectively equals the weighted mixtures of those achieved for the files that were concatenated to produce it. This is because each of the component files is already several times longer than the maximum number of entries Unix Compress is willing to hold in its LZW data structure. If we were to keep growing the data structure, slightly better performance would result. However, even with a growing data structure, a megabyte file is not nearly long enough to make the leading term in the redundancy analysis of (LZ) universal algorithms negligible (see Section 3.3.6).

Although people should be unhappy with performance such as that shown for `fat.ps` in the last line of Table 3.5, most people are thrilled! They have saved two-thirds of the disk space or transmission time that would have been needed without compression. They tend not to concern themselves with the fact that, at least in theory, most of the remaining one-third could have been saved as well. (One of the perquisites of being a data compression engineer is that, even if you do only a half-baked job, many people are likely to consider you a mini-hero worthy of lavish praise.)

Table 3.6 shows the results of using LZW, LZY, LZYEP, and LZ77 on files A, B, and C described below. The LZW and LZ77 results were obtained by applying Unix Compress and gzip, respectively. File A is a binary sequence of length 10,000 bits produced by a homogenous Markov chain characterized by the one-step transition probabilities $P(0|1) = 1$ (so the source never produces two 1s in a row), $P(1|0) = p$, and $P(0|0) = 1 - p$; p was set to the value 0.382, which results in the maximum entropy rate, namely 0.694 bits/symbol. The 10,000 bits were packed into 1250 bytes, as indicated in Table 3.6. File B, approximately 40 KB long, is the LaTeX file for approximately half of Chapter 2 of this book. Let's call it fileb.tex. File C is the PostScript file corresponding to file B; that is, file C was created by the Unix command latex fileb.tex; dvips fileb.dvi > fileb.ps.

LZW and LZY failed to compress file A. (The Unix Compress version of LZW was kind enough to provide a warning message to that effect.) LZYEP achieved a modicum of compression. On the other hand, the LZ77-based utility, gzip, compressed file A to 0.774, an impressive performance, especially when we consider that source A has an entropy rate of 0.694. Another LZ77-based compressor, pkzip, achieved a compression of only 0.84 for file A. Why would one LZ77-based compression program do better in this instance than another one? Actually, it didn't; the compressed code is effectively identical in both instances. The difference is that pkzip is an archiver as well as a compressor; gzip is not. The archival file that pkzip creates has additional bytes devoted to the time and date, the version of pkzip used, the filename, the compression ratio achieved, and so forth, with the extent of the archival information being under user control. For file B and file C, gzip again is the clear winner; in these instances we cannot quantify how it outperformed LZW and LZY because we do not know the sources' entropy rates.

In Table 3.7 we show LZY performance for files A, B, and C, now considered to be a sequence of binary characters rather than a sequence of characters from an alphabet of size 2^8. Of course, this is the "natural" representation of file A, and we see a corresponding improvement in the performance of the LZY-based algorithms. Nonetheless, even LZYEP does not do quite as well as gzip did in Table 3.6. For files B and C, however, it is less natural: stringing together the bits of the successive bytes that comprise these files results in LZY phrases that

T A B L E	Performance of Bit-Based LZY, LZYE, and LZYEP			
3.7	File	Bits	LZY	LZYE	LZYEP
	A	10,000	0.866	0.828	0.796
	B	375,808	0.703	0.689	0.671
	C	1,432,168	0.542	0.533	0.521

bridge what had been the byte boundaries, in general starting inside one byte and ending inside a later byte. The bit-based phrases will be longer on average because as soon as you reach what had been the beginning of a byte, you can copy as much as the byte-based algorithm could have plus perhaps a few more bits. It might seem that this should lead to better performance for the bit-based than for the byte-based algorithm even when the input file's natural alphabet is 8-bit bytes, but comparison of the performances on files B and C in Tables 3.6 and 3.7 reveals that this is not the case.

The reason is that the bit-based phrases being longer on average does not compensate sufficiently for the fact that there are eight times as many entries in the bit-based LZY dictionary than there are in the byte-based one; this necessitates providing about 3 more code bits per phrase in the bit-based as opposed to the byte-based algorithm. Thus, converting bytes to bits before compressing worsens the compression ratio that LZY achieves. The same is true for all LZ77-based compression schemes, too. LZ78-based schemes profit from this bytes-to-bits ruse because the entries in the data structure are indexed by phrase number rather than input symbol number. However, the improvement is modest and, of course, disappears asymptotically in the size of the file being compressed, so practical LZ78 algorithms have tended not to incorporate it.

3.3.6   Redundancy Decay

A proof of the universality of LZ78, due mainly to A. D. Wyner, appears in the textbook by Cover and Thomas (1991). Wyner and Ziv (1994) provide a careful proof that LZ77 is universal that overcomes additional subtle obstacles. The redundancy of these algorithms therefore tends to zero as data continues to pour in from a (stationary) source. It is of considerable theoretical interest to study the rate at which the redundancy (i.e., the difference between the compression ratio achieved on the first n source symbols and the source entropy) decays to zero. However, the theory of LZ redundancy decay is of only limited interest in practice because practical algorithms have to truncate the database (tree, stack, window, and so on), which prevents them from achieving the asymptotic redundancy decay predicted by the mathematical theory for the ideal version.

The obvious argument for justifying mathematical analysis of asymptotic LZ theory is that it gives insight into what may and what may not be gained by extending the database and/or search routine of a practical algorithm. Another perhaps more compelling reason is that it reveals what it is that we sacrifice to be assured of (near) universality. Specifically, although a universal algorithm will drive the redundancy to zero, it may not do so as rapidly as will an algorithm that is specifically designed with knowledge of the correct statistical model of the source.

A. J. Wyner (1997) has shown that if the LZ77 database is held fixed at size n, then the redundancy ρ_n will behave according to

$$\rho_n = H \frac{\log \log n}{\log n} + o(\frac{\log \log n}{\log n}) \tag{3.3}$$

Contrastingly, we saw in Section 2.11 that if a Shannon-Fano code for n-tuples perfectly matched to the nth-order source statistics is employed, its redundancy will decay like $1/n$. Since $1/n$ is much smaller than $\log \log n/\log n$, perhaps we have a handle on the price paid for assurance of universality. However, the above comparison is flawed because the meaning of n is not the same in the LZ and Shannon-Fano cases. In the latter, we actually encode n source symbols at a time; in the former, we consult n past source symbols at a time, but we encode a phrase that usually comprises on the order of $\log n/H$ source symbols. Therefore, it may be more appropriate to compare the performance of LZ with a database of length n to that of a Shannon-Fano code for k-tuples where $k = k(n) = \log n/H$. If so, then the penalty paid for LZ's universality is just the $\log \log n$ factor in the numerator of the above equation, which grows so slowly as to be negligible in practice. Moreover, Wyner and Wyner (1997) have analyzed a finite-memory version of an LZ77 variant suggested by Bender and Wolf (1991) that eliminates this $\log \log n$ factor from the expression for the redundancy. Savari (1997) has shown that the asymptotic redundancy of LZ78 also is $H/(\log n)$. These results suggest that it may not be necessary to pay any penalty after all in the asymptotic behavior of the redundancy in order to be assured of robustness in the sense of universality.

Although the long-run LZ compression ratio approaches the entropy if the database is not truncated, the *local compression ratio* behaves much more erratically. Specifically, let us define the local compression ratio for the nth LZ phrase to be the ratio of the number of source symbols $L(n)$ in this phrase to the number of LZ code bits it takes to describe the phrase. Figure 3.6 shows a plot of $L(n)/\log n$ for a Bernoulli source with $P(1) = 0.8$ and $P(0) = 0.2$;

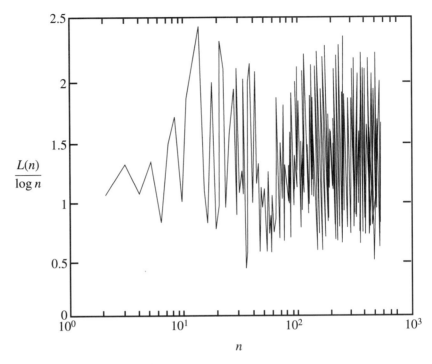

3.6   Local LZ Compression Ratio

here $\log n$ serves as a first-order approximation to the number of code bits an LZ algorithm needs to describe the nth phrase. For large n, the ratio $L(n)$ to $\log n$ will cluster around the reciprocal of the entropy, which in this case is $1/0.722 = 1.385$. Indeed, after some fluctuations for small n, this is what we see in the figure. However, we also see that the local compression ratio exhibits occasional "spikes" that are much higher and much lower than this average. A natural question to ask is, Will these spikes eventually become so rare as to effectively disappear? The answer is "No!" In an attempt to provide insight into this phenomenon, let us consider LZ topiary, that is, the shape of LZ trees. LZ compression may be attributed to the fact that LZ trees are heavily skewed; they have long paths in directions corresponding to "likely" phrases and considerably shorter ones in directions corresponding to "unlikely" phrases. However, every so often the source is cantankerous and produces a local pattern that is "unlikely," resulting in a downward spike in Figure 3.6. Likewise, when the source produces local data that happen to be more repetitive of the past than one would expect, an upward spike results. It turns out that this spiking behavior does not dissipate; the lim sup (limit of the upper envelope) and lim inf (limit of the lower envelope) in Figure 3.6 (and in all others like it for stationary sources and all LZ algorithms) are not equal. Jacquet and Szpankowski (1995) have provided formulas for these inferior and superior limits for i.i.d. sources and certain Markov sources.

LZ parsings are "greedy"—they do not look ahead in the data sequence to see if there is a better way to parse the entire sequence. As such, they can be used without substantial modification in low-latency applications such as digital speech compression, video telephony, and videoconferencing. In applications where the entire file is available a priori, it is possible to achieve a modicum of improvement by using lookahead parsings. DeAgostino and Storer (1996) have studied lookahead versions of LZ. Also, Burrows and Wheeler (1994) have developed a "block sorting" approach to lookahead data compression. For applications in which the latency associated with the combination of look-ahead and increased algorithm complexity can be tolerated, such approaches yield improvements over the usual LZ algorithms in tests with the Carleton corpus, a collection of files that serves as a yardstick for comparing lossless data compression schemes (see also Nelson and Gailly 1995). Since LZ algorithms are universal, lookahead algorithms cannot provide any improvement in the limit of infinite file length.

Because LZ algorithms and other universal compression schemes compress any (stationary) source to its entropy rate, the asymptotic compression ratio they achieve serves as a consistent estimate of the entropy of the source. For finite n, bias can be removed from such estimates, at the expense of increased variability, by correcting for the $H/\log n$ or $H \log(\log n)/\log n$ redundancy term, using the estimage of H in place of H in this procedure to achieve unbiasedness. It is also advisable to smooth the estimate in order to overcome the spiking phenomena discussed in conjunction with Figure 3.6. Finally, we remark that universal compression algorithms can be used as random number generators since, at least asymptotically, their output is a sequence of i.i.d. symbols.

3.4   Elias Coding, Arithmetic Coding, and JBIG Fax

Elias coding is a theoretical data compression scheme that supplies the underpinnings for arithmetic coding, a popular universal coding scheme. Arithmetic coding is well suited to the task of lossless image and volume compression, provided the alphabet is small—preferably 2 or fewer bits per pixel or per voxel. The inherent nature of the medium might provide the small alphabet, as in the case of facsimile. This partially explains why arithmetic coding has been adopted as the basic compression engine in the JBIG fax standard. However, many applications that require lossless compression of images and volumes—for example, medical imaging applications—do not have an inherently small alphabet. In such instances JBIG specifies a parameter that provides the bit depth and then deals with the image one or two bit planes at a time. The more significant bits usually can be substantially compressed. The least significant bit or two often is random noise anyway and hence not amenable to compression by any technique. JBIG tends not to be as efficient as certain competing techniques for gray-level images that are more than 8 bits deep at each pixel.

In Section 3.4.1 we describe how Elias coding can *in theory* compress any source with known statistics down to its entropy rate. Then we discuss the following obstacles that make Elias coding difficult to implement:

1. Elias coding is parametric. It requires knowledge of the source's probabilistic structure.

2. Elias coding is precision-hungry. It requires that computations be performed to an unbounded and hence unattainable level of precision.

3. Elias coding is retentive. Code symbols sometimes are hoarded and released highly asynchronously in variable-length bursts.

In Section 3.4.2 we explain how arithmetic coding overcomes each of these obstacles. Section 3.4.3 is devoted to a discussion of the JBIG fax standard, with emphasis on its use of arithmetic coding.

3.4.1 Elias Coding

Peter Elias invented a general scheme for compressing data from any (stationary) source as closely as desired to its entropy rate (Jelinek 1968). Elias was aware that, although the scheme was mathematically sound, it possessed shortcomings that rendered it totally impractical. Perhaps this explains why he never published his findings; nonetheless, they became widely known in the international research community, which always has referred to the technique as "Elias coding."

We discuss Elias coding of a binary source first and then generalize. An Elias coder treats any binary sequence as if it were a binary word in the interval [0,1]. It maps the value of the source binary word to a second binary word that is also in the interval [0,1] but usually requires fewer bits to express. It does this by capitalizing cleverly on its knowledge of the joint probability distribution of the source data.

Every binary sequence corresponds to a point in the unit interval [0,1] obtained by putting a "binary point" in front of it. For example, 011010011 is associated with $.011010011 = 0 \cdot 2^{-1} + 1 \cdot 2^{-2} + \cdots + 1 \cdot 2^{-9} = 0 + 0.25 + 0.125 + \cdots + 0.001953125 = 0.412109375$. So far this is only a finite sequence, so we don't know yet exactly where it will end up in $[0,1]$. But we do know that, regardless of how the rest of the places get filled with 0s and 1s, its decimal representation will lie somewhere between 0.412109375 and $0.412109375 + \sum_{k=10}^{\infty} 2^{-k} = 0.412109375 + 2^{-9} = 0.4140625$. That is, after a finite amount of data has been observed, we can associate it with the subinterval of $[0,1]$ that contains all the binary decimals whose leading digits equal this data. Elias coding begins by assigning to each finite binary source sequence not the usual subinterval of $[0,1]$ as illustrated above but rather a *different* one that depends on the source's statistics as described below.[1]

For definitiveness, temporarily assume we have a Bernoulli-p source with $p = \frac{3}{4}$, that is, a source that produces independent binary random variables, each of which equals 1 with probability $p = \frac{3}{4}$ and equals 0 with probability $\frac{1}{4}$. In this case the Elias coder assigns to the length-1 string, 0, the interval $I_0 = [0, \frac{1}{4})$, and to the length-1 string, 1, the interval $I_1 = [\frac{1}{4}, 1)$. The intervals it assigns to the length-2 sequences 00 and 01 are, respectively, the lower quarter and the upper three quarters of I_0, namely, $I_{00} = [0, \frac{1}{16})$ and $I_{01} = [\frac{1}{16}, \frac{1}{4})$. Similarly, the intervals assigned to 10 and 11 are the lower quarter and the upper three quarters of I_1, namely, $I_{10} = [\frac{1}{4}, \frac{1}{4} + \frac{3}{16}) = [\frac{1}{4}, \frac{7}{16})$ and $I_{11} = [\frac{7}{16}, 1)$. The intervals assigned to length-3 sequences are the lower quarter and upper three quarters of the intervals assigned to their length-2 prefixes, and so on. In the case of a Bernoulli-p source with general p, intervals are assigned by replacing "upper three quarters" in the above description by "upper pth" and "lower quarter" by "lower qth," where $q = 1 - p$. Observe that every time the next source digit is a 0, the length of the associated interval shrinks by a factor of q, and every time it is a 1, the length of the associated interval shrinks by a factor of p. The intervals assigned to the 2^n source sequences of length n do not overlap, and their union is $[0,1)$.

Given any interval I, let $|I|$ denote its length. It follows that the length of the interval $I_{\mathbf{u}}$ assigned to source sequence $\mathbf{u} = u_1 u_2 \ldots u_n$ is

$$|I_{\mathbf{u}}| = q^{N(0|\mathbf{u})} p^{N(1|\mathbf{u})} \tag{3.4}$$

---

1. If you are probabilistically inclined, you may wish to know that the interval assigned to $\underline{b} = 0.b_1 b_2 \ldots b_n$ is $[F(\underline{b}000\ldots), F(\underline{b}111\ldots))$, where $F(\cdot)$ is the cumulative distribution of the infinite binary decimal representation $0.B_1 B_2 \ldots$ of the random source sequence. Fortunately, you don't need to know that in order to understand the ensuing description of Elias compression, much less to build an Elias coder.

where $N(0|\mathbf{u})$ is the number of 0s in $\mathbf{u}$, and $N(1|\mathbf{u})$ is the number of 1s in $\mathbf{u}$. We know, however, that for large n we will have $N(0|\mathbf{u}) \sim nq$ and $N(1|\mathbf{u}) \sim np$ with overwhelming probability for a Bernoulli-p source. Therefore,

$$- \log |I_{\mathbf{u}}| \sim -nq \log q - np \log p = nh(p) \tag{3.5}$$

or equivalently,

$$|I_{\mathbf{u}}| \sim 2^{-nh(p)} \tag{3.6}$$

Next observe that, given any interval I and any integer L such that $2^{-L} \le |I|/2$, I must fully contain at least one interval of the form $[(k-1)2^{-L}, k2^{-L}]$, where k is an integer. Moreover, if I is a subset of $[0,1]$, then $1 \le k \le 2^L$. Accordingly, for any fixed n we can describe the n-sequence $\mathbf{u}$ by specifying an integer k associated in this sense with the corresponding interval $I_{\mathbf{u}}$. Said integer k lies between 1 and $2/|I_{\mathbf{u}}| \sim 2^{[nh(p)+1]}$, so it requires only $nh(p) + 1$ binary digits to specify it. Accordingly, Elias coding compresses the representation of the n-sequence $\mathbf{u}$ to $h(p) + 1/n$ binary digits per source letter, which approaches the source's entropy rate $h(p)$ as $n \to \infty$.

The above analysis readily extends to a general binary source as follows. After $U_1 U_2 \ldots U_{n-1}$ has been observed to have assumed a particular value $u_1 u_2 \ldots u_{n-1}$, we define

$$p_n = P[U_n = 1 | u_1 u_2 \ldots u_{n-1}] \tag{3.7}$$

and

$$q_n = P[U_n = 0 | u_1 u_2 \ldots u_{n-1}] \tag{3.8}$$

We then divide each of the 2^{n-1} subintervals of $[0,1]$ associated with the various binary $(n-1)$-sequences into its lower q_nth and its upper p_nth. This yields

$$|I_{\mathbf{u}}| = \prod_{k=1}^{n} p(u_k | u_1 u_2 \ldots u_{k-1}) = p(\mathbf{u}) \tag{3.9}$$

where $p(\mathbf{u})$ is the joint distribution of $U_1, \ldots, U_n$ evaluated at the observed data $\mathbf{u} = u_1, \ldots, u_n$. It follows that $\mathbf{u}$ can be specified by means of a number of binary digits per source symbol that does not exceed

$$-\frac{1}{n} \log |I_{\mathbf{u}}| + \frac{1}{n} \sim -n^{-1} \log p(\mathbf{u}) \tag{3.10}$$

Powerful results from information theory (see, for example, Cover and Thomas 1991, Chapter 3) assure us that, as $n \to \infty$, $-n^{-1} \log p(\mathbf{U})$ approaches the entropy rate of the source in several strong senses of stochastic convergence that need not concern us here.

Elias coding works for any finite-alphabet source. For a ternary source, for example, the Elias coder divides each subinterval into its lower rth, its middle pth, and its upper qth, where p, q, and r are the conditional probabilities of the three possible values of the current source symbol given the past of the data sequence. Thus, Elias coding can be used to compress any finite-alphabet (stationary) source with known statistics to its entropy rate!

We turn now to the previously cited shortcomings of Elias coding—parametricity, precision hunger, and retentivity. Parametricity appears to be a serious deficiency because the way in which the interval [0,1] has to be subdivided at every step depends intimately on the conditional probability distribution of the next symbol given the past, and this distribution usually is not known. In actuality, compression performance usually is relatively insensitive to errors in estimation of the source's distribution; any reasonable algorithm for adaptively estimating the source's possibly time-varying statistics suffices. (Many good algorithms for such dynamic modeling are available in this age of adaptive signal processing; see in this regard the discussion of arithmetic coding in the next subsection.)

The following discussion provides a quantitative appreciation for the relative insensitivity of an Elias code's compression performance to a moderate mismatch in the source statistics. Suppose an i.i.d. source with distribution $\{p(u)\}$ is producing the data, but the Elias coder is designed under the assumption that the data comes from an i.i.d. source with distribution $\{p^*(u)\}$. For large n and each $u \in \mathcal{U}$, a block of n source digits almost always will contain approximately $np(u)$ occurrences of the letter u. Each time the letter u appears, the Elias coder will select for its next subinterval one whose length is a fraction $p^*(u)$ of that of the current interval. Accordingly, after processing n letters, the Elias coder will have its attention focused on an interval of length approximately

$$\prod_{u \in \mathcal{U}} p^*(u)^{np(u)} \tag{3.11}$$

This interval fully contains a subinterval of the form $[(k-1)2^{-L}, k2^{-L}]$, where L is any integer such that

$$2^{-L} \leq 0.5 \prod_{u \in \mathcal{U}} p^*(u)^{np(u)} \tag{3.12}$$

Therefore, which subinterval of [0,1] in the nth Elias partition is the one that corresponds to the source string can be specified by a binary sequence whose length is the smallest length L that satisfies the above inequality. In this way n source letters get specified by only L binary digits, where, upon taking logs in the previous equation, we see that L is any integer that satisfies

$$-L \le -1 + \sum_{u \in \mathcal{U}} n p(u) \log_2 p^*(u) \tag{3.13}$$

The compressed data rate L/n therefore is given by

$$L/n \sim 1/n - \sum_u p(u) \log_2 p^*(u) \xrightarrow[n \to \infty]{} - \sum_u p(u) \log_2 p^*(u) \tag{3.14}$$

The mismatched coder cannot compress the data to less than the source entropy because its coding is lossless, and we know that lossless compression is not possible using fewer than H code letters per source letter (see Chapter 2). To establish this fact rigorously, note that the discrepancy between the coding rate of the mismatched Elias code and the entropy rate is

$$-\sum_u p(u) \log p^*(u) - H = \sum_u p(u) \log(p(u)/p^*(u))$$

$$\ge \sum_u p(u)(1 - p^*(u)/p(u)) = \sum_u p(u) - \sum_u p^*(u) = 1 - 1 = 0$$

with equality if and only if $p^*(u) = p(u)$ for all $u \in \mathcal{U}$, where we have used inequality (equation 2.10).

In Figure 3.7 we have graphed the effect of mismatch for the basic case of a Bernoulli-p source. The mismatched compression performance, $-p \log_2 p^* - (1-p) \log_2(1-p^*)$, is a linear function of p that is tangent to the convex entropy curve $h(p) = -p \log_2 p - (1-p) \log_2(1-p)$ at the point $p = p^*$, at which there is no mismatch. It is readily seen that, except near 0 and 1, the effect of a mild mismatch is negligible.

The other two shortcomings of Elias coding—retentivity and hunger for precision—are so tightly intertwined that we will treat them jointly. Let's return to our example of a Bernoulli-$\frac{3}{4}$ source. Suppose the source sequence is $\mathbf{u} = 1101100. \ldots$ Upon seeing the leadoff 1, the Elias coder knows that the point in [0,1], let us call it x, into which it will encode $\mathbf{u}$ satisfies $\frac{1}{4} \le x \le 1$. When the second 1 arrives, the encoder eliminates the lower quarter of that interval and thereby deduces that $\frac{7}{16} \le x \le 1$. The arrival of the third source digit, 0, allows the encoder to eliminate the upper three quarters of $[\frac{7}{16}, 1]$ and

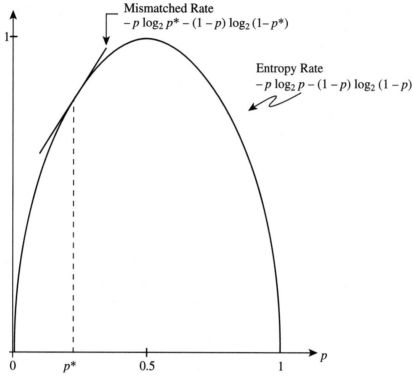

FIGURE

3.7 Mismatched Encoder Performance for a Bernoulli Source

conclude that $\frac{7}{16} \leq x \leq \frac{37}{64}$, or, in decimals, $0.4375 \leq x \leq 0.578125$. Note that, after processing the leading three digits 110, the Elias encoder still doesn't know whether x will be less than or greater than 0.5. As a consequence, it is unable to release any code digits yet!

Temporarily suppose the fourth source digit had been a 0 instead of a 1. Then x would have been confined to the lower quarter of $[0.4375, 0.578125]$, that is, $[0.4375, 0.47265625]$. Now the Elias coder finally would have been able to release some code digits. Specifically, it would now be known that x is going to lie in $[\frac{3}{8}, \frac{4}{8}]$, where all binary decimals start with .011, so the Elias coder would have been able to release 011. (It would not necessarily have to release all three of these digits at this time; it might release only 0 or only 01.)

But, the source's fourth digit was a 1, not a 0 (which, by the way, is more in line with what we expect from a Bernoulli-$\frac{3}{4}$ source—three out of the first four source digits are 1s). As a result, x gets confined instead to the upper three quarters of $[0.4375, 0.578125]$, that is, $[0.47265625, 0.578125]$. Since this contains $\frac{1}{2}$, the Elias coder can't emit anything yet. When the fifth source digit also is seen to be a 1, the new interval becomes [0.499023437, 0.578125], so still nothing emerges. Then a 0 arrives and the new interval becomes the lower quarter of its predecessor, namely [0.499023437, 0.518798827]—still no output. The seventh digit, another 0, leaves us with [0.499023437, 0.503967284] and still no code digits!

The retentivity problem should now be obvious. Indeed, it is easy to keep extending the source sequence in such a way that nothing ever comes out of the Elias coder! Also, hand in hand with this retentivity problem comes a requirement for uncanny accuracy. The calculations above were done only to nine significant decimal digits at each stage, which already resulted in some inaccuracy in the endpoints in the last two intervals calculated. Small inaccuracies of this sort can conspire to produce a code sequence that is entirely wrong and that results in many errors upon decoding. In addition, source letter probabilities never would be known precisely enough to justify calculation even to nine significant decimal digits. Strict-sense Elias coding is manifestly unimplementable, as Elias knew from the outset.

3.4.2 Arithmetic Coding

Arithmetic coding is a variant of Elias's data compression scheme that is both implementable and universal. Pioneering work on arithmetic coding can be found in the thesis by Pasco (1976) and in papers by Rissanen (1976, 1984). Aficionados of arithmetic coding like to say that two steps are involved—modeling and compression. The modeling step is what yields the universality; the coding step uses the probability estimates from the modeling step in a modification of Elias coding that avoids the retentivity and precision pitfalls cited above.

If we somehow eradicate the Elias coder's tendency to be retentive, then its precision-hungriness also will vanish. This is because the emission of code digits permits the picture to be *rescaled* in the following sense. Recall the above discussion of Elias coding for a Bernoulli-$\frac{3}{4}$ source. There we saw that if the first three symbols out of the source are 110, then the Elias coder has focused its attention on the interval $[\frac{7}{16}, \frac{37}{64}] = [0.4375, 0.578125]$ but has not yet been able to emit any code digits. We also saw that, were the next source symbol a 0, the Elias coder would further focus in on $[\frac{7}{16}, \frac{121}{256}] = [0.4375, 0.47265625]$ and finally would be able to emit three code digits—011. The fact that the first code digit is a 0 signals that the Elias coder is operating in an interval contained entirely in the left half of [0,1]. This allows both the encoder and the decoder to eliminate [0.5,1] and then scale everything in the left half up by a factor of two so that it fills the entirety of $[0,1]$. In particular, this rescaling changes the current interval of interest from $[\frac{7}{16}, \frac{121}{256}] = [0.4375, 0.47265625]$ to $[\frac{7}{8}, \frac{121}{128}] = [0.875, 0.9453125]$. Note that there is one fewer significant figure to the endpoints after the rescaling than there was before it. Continuing, the fact that the second code digit is a 1 signals that the Elias coder is operating in an interval contained entirely in the right half of what has been rescaled to fill $[0,1]$. This allows both the encoder and the decoder to eliminate $[0, 0.5]$ and then scale everything in $[0.5, 1]$ up by a factor of two. It is more convenient to shift $[0.5, 1]$ down to $[0, 0.5]$ before upscaling it by two so that the resulting interval again becomes $[0, 1]$. Doing this converts the current interval of interest from $[\frac{7}{8}, \frac{121}{128}]$ to $[2(\frac{7}{8} - 0.5), 2(\frac{121}{128} - 0.5)]$ $= [\frac{3}{4}, \frac{57}{64}] = [0.75, 0.890625]$. Note that again one fewer significant digit is needed for the endpoints after this upscaling. Similarly, the third emitted digit being a 1 allows a similar shifting and scaling, which converts the interval of interest to $[\frac{1}{2}, \frac{25}{32}] = [0.5, 0.78125]$. It now should be apparent that the precision problem becomes tractable provided we somehow force the Elias encoder never to be overly retentive.

A simple fix for retentivity is to set a limit on the maximum precision that will be permitted in the computation of interval endpoints; then, whenever a situation is encountered where that limit will be exceeded if the next symbol should happen to be one that prolongs retention, simply stuff into the data stream a fictional data symbol that ends rather than prolongs retention. Here is one way for the decoder to figure out when this symbol-stuffing has happened; it is not exactly the way it is done in practice, but it is similar in flavor and much easier to explain. The decoder performs Elias encoding on the sequence it decodes and simply drops the next symbol from its decoded string each time it sees that the encoder was obliged to insert a fictional datum at that point. The penalty for this retentivity fix is, to a first approximation, that the encoding string is a fraction s longer than the actual source string, where s is the expected number of stuffed symbols per source symbol. Willingness to provide a reasonable degree of precision in calculations, which is not difficult with today's 32-bit-word and 64-bit-word digital circuitry, assures that $s \ll 1$, and hence that the penalty in compression performance is negligible.

3.4.3   The JBIG Fax Standard

Our treatment of JBIG is divided into subsections: the first provides an overview, the second describes resolution reduction, the third treats the deterministic portion of progressive transmission, and the last describes the arithmetic coding implementation that JBIG uses as its probabilistic compression engine.

T A B L E	JBIG Improvement Factors	
3.8	Document Type	Improvement Factor
	Scanned images of printed characters	1.1–1.5
	Computer-generated images (bitmaps)	up to 5
	Dithered gray-scale images	2–30

Overview and Performance Improvements

JBIG is an advanced facsimile standard that achieves performance improvements over the Group 3 and Group 4 standards we discussed in Section 2.7. The improvement is moderate for some kinds of documents but dramatic for others (see Table 3.8). JBIG also incorporates a progressive transmission mode that makes it well suited for browsing (digital information search and retrieval), a popular practice in modern libraries and networked databases such as the Internet's World Wide Web. Progressive transmission also jibes well with networks such as broadband ISDN and ATM that support prioritization; lower-resolution information usually is sent with higher priority to facilitate a speedy search process.

JBIG is a good example of a state-of-the-art blending of predictive modeling, adaptation, and lossless coding. By virtue of selecting a form of arithmetic coding as its compression engine, the JBIG design is well matched to fax data's binary alphabet. By contrast, we saw in Chapter 2 that small-alphabet situations are precisely those for which instantaneous Huffman coding offers little, if any, compression. Of course, the Group 3 and Group 4 coding schemes apply Huffman codes not directly to the 0s and 1s (white and black pixels) themselves but to other variables such as runlengths and runlength offsets; hence, the improvement that JBIG offers is less dramatic than the preceding sentence might suggest. Rather, JBIG's advantage over Group 3 and Group 4 is principally attributable to its arithmetic coder's ability to adapt to the statistics of the image types it encounters. This ability is especially important in the case of half-toned images because the JBIG encoder can "learn" about the "dithering" patterns that a particular half-toning scheme uses to represent gray levels via configurations having appropriate densities of black pixels on a fine grid. The human visual system smoothes over the edges of the small pixels because of its limited resolution capabilities, causing the 1-bit image to look from a distance as if it were a gray-level image. The pseudorandom dithering patterns result in many short runs of white and black pixels instead of the longer runs (white runs, especially) that Group 3 expects to see. Moreover, the runs don't tend to align well from one line to the next, so Group 4 also is ill suited to compressing half-tones. In the case of computer-generated images, JBIG adapts to the clean nature of the image edges to achieve improved performance. Table 3.8 lists performance gains over G3/G4 performance claimed in a JBIG working document. These figures represent behavior observed over an ensemble of documents of each indicated type; the actual degree of improvement realized varies markedly from one individual document to another.

Given the substantial compression improvement factors reported in Table 3.8 and the additional advantages provided by support of a browsing mode, you may wonder why JBIG fax machines have not taken the world by storm, since the standard has been in place since the early 1990s. One possible explanation is that JBIG fax machines are more complicated and hence more expensive. A second is that compliance with the JBIG standard does not necessitate back compatibility to G3/G4. Neither of these explanations is compelling, however. Although the cost of JBIG equipment versus G3/G4 equipment might be daunting to the average homeowner or small business, the theory was that big businesses would be willing to foot the bill in order to achieve great reductions in transmission cost and low-latency transport for their large traffic volumes. Sales to big business would bring the cost of JBIG equipment down, whereupon a mass market would follow. Also, G3/G4 back compatibility could be provided at a negligible marginal cost, so that's not the explanation. What went wrong? Did JBIG, the Joint Bi-level Image Experts Group, commit a technological blunder or make a miscalculation?

There was no technological blunder. Indeed, JBIG is a technologically sophisticated standard that was generated with thorough professionalism jointly by a telecommunications standards body and a computer standards body. But there was a miscalculation of sorts that had nothing whatsover to do with telecommunications or computers. It consisted of not anticipating the meteoric rise of national and international express mail! In this high-tech age, it was counterintuitive that a new transportation service would outdo a new communications service. Indeed, all indicators were pointing strongly in the opposite direction; communication was expected to replace transportation as the preferred solution in more and more scenarios. So far, however, it turns out that there simply are not that many applications in which it is necessary to get a large document somewhere in a few minutes to an hour's time when it can be sent overnight for much the same price and contain such things as genuine inked signatures, photographic color prints, and 3-D accompaniments. In addition, the popularity of the World Wide Web and the rise of JPEG and MPEG standards (see Chapters 9 and 11) have shifted the emphasis in information retrieval from black-and-white texts and gray-level images and graphics, to color graphics,

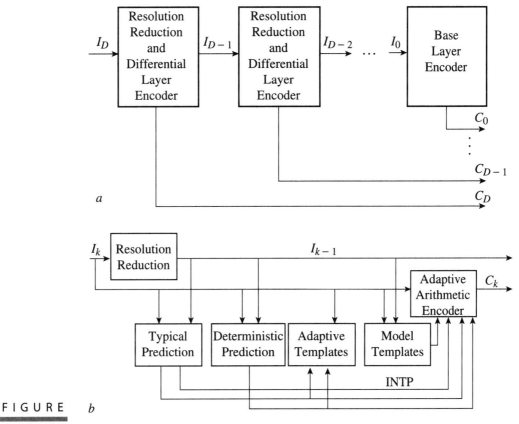

FIGURE

3.8

(*a*) Overall JBIG Block Diagram; (*b*) Expansion of a Resolution Reduction and Differential Layer Encoder Box

color images, and color videos, leaving JBIG with a far smaller fraction of the browsing market than was anticipated. Most people, and even most organizations, still find G3/G4 fax adequate for their facsimile needs. The marketplace always has and always will be characterized by major surprises!

Block Diagram, Progressive Mode, and Resolution Reduction

The JBIG block diagram is shown in Figure 3.8. The progressive transmission mode is the default, but it can be overridden. In the progressive mode, the full-resolution image I_D enters at the left. (Advanced JBIG hardware may be capable of ingesting the entire image in parallel by means of electro-optic sensors not dissimilar to those used in photocopying machines, as opposed to having to scan it in line by line the way G3/G4 machines do.) The image is successively reduced

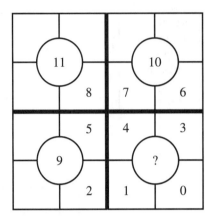

FIGURE

3.9   Resolution Reduction Template

in resolution to $I_{D-1}, \ldots, I_0$ by a process we shall describe in conjunction with Figure 3.9. The lowest-resolution level is called the *base layer;* all the finer-resolution levels are called *differential layers.* Information describing the base layer is sent first, followed by information that specifies the differential layer immediately above, and so on through full resolution, unless the recipient signals to put a stop to the process sooner.

Each resolution reduction stage halves the number of lines and the number of pixels per line. Figure 3.9 shows how this is done. All the pixels from the immediately preceding higher level of resolution have already been calculated to be either black or white; they are represented by the small squares, nine of which are numbered 0 through 8. The reduced-resolution pixels are calculated in standard raster scan order (left to right, top to bottom).

In the progressive mode, the full-resolution image I_D enters with one reduced-resolution pixel computed per nonoverlapping 2 × 2 square of pixels from the immediately higher level of resolution; they are represented by the circles. Three are numbered 9, 10, and 11 and the remaining one is our current target pixel, labeled "?". We compute either a white or a black value for "?" by consulting its 12 neighbors numbered 0 through 11, 9 from the next higher level of resolution and 3 reduced-resolution pixels that have already been calculated earlier in the current scan. Since each of these 12 neighbors can have either of two values, there are $2^{12} = 4096$ possible configurations stored in a resolution reduction table. The appropriate line in this table is consulted, and it returns a decision either of "white" or of "black" for the target pixel.

Classic resolution reduction would calculate "?" by majority vote of its four nearest higher-resolution neighbors—0, 1, 3, and 4 in this instance. Unless

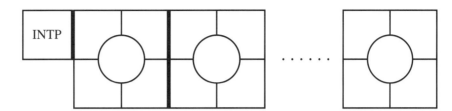

F I G U R E

3.10   Line-Pair for Differential Layer Typical Prediction

there is a tie—two white and two black—"?" is assigned the color of the majority. Usually, "?" is made black if there is a tie; otherwise, since most fax documents have much more light than dark area, there would be a tendency for the document to wash out as it progresses toward successively coarser resolutions. The 4096-entry table agrees often, but not always, with the majority of the nearest neighbors when there is such a majority. Also, it breaks all the two-two ties in a more sophisticated fashion than does classical resolution reduction. In the main, the default resolution reduction algorithm corresponds to thresholding a weighted average of pixels 0 through 11, but it gives preference to preserving edges and thin lines in hopes of retaining as much as possible of the character of the document despite dropping down a resolution level. A JBIG encoder does not have to use the default resolution reduction algorithm; it is free to specify any algorithm of its choosing.

Deterministic Prediction Techniques

As progressive JBIG encoding proceeds up the resolution chain, it usually is possible to save a considerable amount of data rate by capitalizing on the fact that many of the pixels in I_{k+1} are heavily dependent on neighboring pixels in I_k that have already been sent to the decoder. Indeed, the box labeled "Typical Prediction" in Figure 3.8 allows us to avoid having to resort to arithmetic coding at approximately 95% of the pixel locations in text or line art images by capitalizing on the fact that such documents usually contain large areas of solid color. Here's how it works.

By a "line-pair" we shall mean a pair of neighboring lines in I_{k+1} that constitute the upper and lower nearest neighbors of a line of pixels in I_k (see Figure 3.10).

Let us call a pixel in I_k "solid" if it and all eight of its nearest neighbors in I_k have the same color. Furthermore, let's call a pixel in I_k "nontypical" if it is solid but at least one of its four nearest neighbors in I_{k+1} does not have the same color that it has. A line-pair in I_{k+1} is said to be nontypical if one

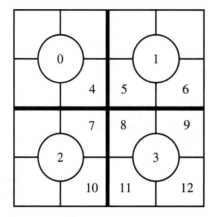

3.11   Template for Deterministic Prediction

or more of the pixels in I_k that it brackets is nontypical; otherwise, it is said to be typical. By definition, all the pixels in a typical line-pair in I_{k+1} that are immediate neighbors of a solid pixel in I_k have the same color as that solid pixel. Differential layer typical prediction consists of determining for each line-pair in I_{k+1} whether or not it is typical and then sending a 0 if it is and a 1 if it isn't before proceeding to code that line-pair. In clean documents most line-pairs are typical and most pixels are solid, so differential layer prediction saves much effort and many code bits.

Each pixel in I_{k+1} is assigned a "phase" as follows: phase 0 pixels are located immediately above and to the left of their nearest neighbor in I_k, phase 1 pixels above and to the right, phase 2 below and left, and phase 3 below and right (see Figure 3.11, where pixels 8, 9, 11, and 12, for example, have respective phases 0, 1, 2, and 3). Sometimes we can infer high-resolution pixels from low- and high-resolution pixels already received. This ability is a consequence of the "sometimes invertible" nature of the resolution reduction algorithm. The box labeled "Deterministic Prediction" in the system block diagram capitalizes on this fact. When it is time to try to predict a phase 3 pixel, such as pixel 12 in Figure 3.11, pixels 0 through 11 shown there all have already arrived. It turns out that for 1024 of the $2^{12} = 4096$ different values that this 12-bit pattern can assume, the rules of the default resolution reduction algorithm deterministically specify pixel 12. Hence, for 25% of the possible patterns, a phase 4 pixel does not have to be coded. For phase 2 pixels, such as pixel 11, there are only 11 reference pixels because pixel 12 hasn't been communicated to the decoder yet; 26% of the corresponding 2048 bit patterns turn out to deterministically predict pixel 11. Similarly, 21% of phase 1 patterns and 8% of phase 0 patterns yield deterministic predictions. If the possible contexts for each phase were to occur equally likely, then $(8 + 21 + 26 + 25)/4 = 20\%$ of all pixels would be deterministically predictable in this sense.

However, the patterns do not occur anywhere near equally likely, especially when attention is restricted only to those pixels not already determined by differential layer typical prediction. Experiment reveals that, on average over a representative class of facsimile documents, the Deterministic Prediction box can perfectly predict only approximately 7% of the pixels it gets to process. Nonetheless, this constitutes a worthwhile savings in computational effort and bit rate. The above description of deterministic prediction explains why an encoder that does not use the default resolution reduction table either has to send the decoder a corresponding deterministic prediction table or has to abandon deterministic prediction altogether.

Arithmetic Q-Coder and JBIG Validation

Pixels that cannot be determined by either the Typical Prediction module or the Deterministic Prediction module in Figure 3.8 are handled in the box labeled Adaptive Arithmetic Encoder. Figure 3.12 shows the 12-bit model templates that JBIG's arithmetic coder uses to predict such pixels in each of phases 0, 1, 2, and 3. Each template consists of a target pixel labeled "?" that has the phase in question plus ten other pixels. Four of these ten, indicated by circles labeled X, come from I_k; of the other six, all of which come from earlier in the current scan for I_{k+1}, five are labeled X and one is labeled A. The one labeled A is called the *adaptive* pixel; its canonical position is as indicated in Figure 3.12, but the JBIG encoder has the option to specify a different location for it that it can adapt from document to document in order to better cope with such things as dithering patterns in half-toning schemes.

A *context* is a particular configuration of 0s and 1s (i.e., whites and blacks) assigned to each pixel in a template except for the target pixel. Since there are four phases and 2^{10} contexts for each phase's template, there are 4096 differential layer contexts.

For the base layer, which has no coarser level of resolution to provide the circled pixels, the entire template comes from earlier in the base layer scan, and there is no concept of phase. The JBIG encoder has two base layer templates available to it, each of which consists of 11 fixed pixels and 1 adaptive one. In one, the 11 fixed pixels are confined to the current and previous line; in the other template, some of the pixels reside in the line above that. The encoder gets to designate for each document which base layer template it is using and

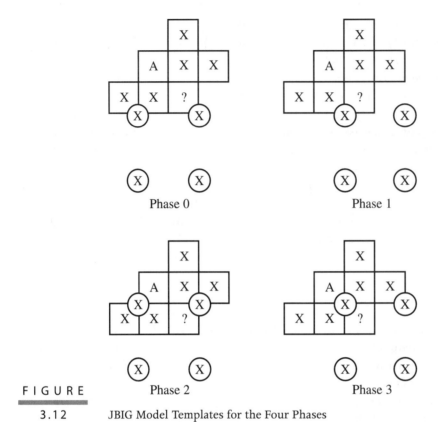

FIGURE

3.12 JBIG Model Templates for the Four Phases

where its adaptive pixel is located. Once that has been done, there are $2^{12} = 4096$ distinct contexts for the base layer, too.

The arithmetic coder stores and updates quantized probability estimates for each of its 4096 base layer templates and each of its 4096 differential layer templates. For some contexts, the two possible values of the target pixel each occur with probability close to $\frac{1}{2}$; such contexts do not provide much opportunity for data compression for the document in question. By contrast, adaptation drives the estimate of the less probable symbol (LPS) for other contexts to a value that is considerably smaller than that for the more probable symbol (MPS). These are the contexts that afford us the chance for meaningful data compression for the document in question. Fortunately, contexts for which the probability estimates are highly skewed in this sense are plentiful in practice; as a result, the JBIG arithmetic coder usually achieves strong compression performance.

T A B L E	Two Rows of the Q-coder Update Table			
3.9	State	LSZ	Up State	Down State
	73	0.0027	71	74
	74	0.0021	72	76

The JBIG arithmetic coder quantizes its estimates of the probability of the LPS for the contexts into a set of 128 values $\{Q_k, k = 1, 2, \ldots, 128\}$. The Q_k closely track a geometric progression,

$$\log Q_k \approx -k\alpha + \beta \qquad (3.15)$$

where $\alpha > 0$ and β are constants. Indeed, JBIG's arithmetic coder is nicknamed the Q-coder (Pennebaker et al. 1988). JBIG adapts to the probabilistic structure of the document being encoded by updating its estimate of the probability of the LPS for the current context each time that the target pixel observed when in that context results in a renormalization of the Elias interval length. Table 3.9 shows two rows of this updating table. The "state" in the far left column is the index k of the quantized probability estimate Q_k for the LPS, so the full table has 128 rows. The quantity "LSZ" in the second column is a number related to Q_k but not equal to it; specifically, it is close to $0.75 Q_k$ for a reason that will be explained shortly. If a context currently assigned state 73 appears, then row 73 of the update table is consulted. If the target pixel is observed to be the MPS, then the LSZ entry is subtracted from the length, A, of the current coding interval (in the sense of Elias coding). If the resulting new A is less than $\frac{1}{2}$, then renormalization occurs. Specifically, A is doubled along with the position within the current coding interval that represents the Elias representation of the observed data sequence. Finally, because the MPS was observed, we adjust the estimate of the LPS downward for the context in question in accordance with the entry in the Down State column; specifically, the next time this context appears, the state pointer stored with it will say to consult row 74 of the update table rather than row 73. If the target pixel is observed to be the LPS, then A temporarily is replaced by LSZ, but then doubled enough times to get it back over $\frac{1}{2}$; a concomitant small burst of code symbols usually can be emitted at this juncture. The appearance of the unexpected LPS occasions revising the LPS probability estimate for the context in question upward, in this case from that of state 73 to that of state 71.

The Q-coder does not follow the optimum adjustments of the current interval prescribed by Elias coding as described in Section 3.4.1. Specifically, whenever the MPS is observed, Elias says to replace A by $A - \text{P(LPS)} \times A$, where P(LPS) preferably is the "true" probability of the LPS for the context in question; in practice, of course, we use instead our present estimate of that probability. The problem with this adjustment procedure is that it requires a multiplication of two quantities; moreover, the first quantity often is quite small and the second also may be in the case of pure Elias coding. Such multiplications, and the high-precision computational requirements they occasion, are undesirable. The Q-coder avoids them by approximating them by additions as follows. Recall that the Q-coder keeps A in the range $[\frac{1}{2}, 1]$ by forcing frequent renormalizations that pure Elias coding would not consider warranted yet. Indeed, these renormalizations do occasion a penalty (usually small) in the achieved compression ratio, but they confine the interval length adjustment, P(LPS)$\times A$, between 0.5P(LPS) and P(LPS). Since 0.75P(LPS) is in the center of this interval, it is never off by much, especially when the Q-coder's estimate for P(LPS) is small, which is the case for all the contexts in which meaningful data compression is possible when they occur. By these means, the Q-coder significantly lowers computational effort and computational precision demands over those of the Elias algorithm while incurring only a minor penalty in compression efficiency. From the above discussion, we see that it is necessary to keep one 8-bit byte of information tagged to each of the 4096 contexts associated with the current resolution layer. One bit indicates whether the LPS for this context is a 0 or a 1; the other 7 bits specify which of the 128 states to consult in the update table in order to see whether or not a renormalization is in order and to return the new state index.

We conclude with some comments about JBIG validation. Section 7 of the JBIG standard gives two tests. One is a small (256-bit) input and the resulting valid 200-bit code stream. The other is a 1951×1960 algorithmically generated test image and a table of trace parameters that result when this image is encoded correctly (e.g., number of typically and deterministically predicted pixels, encoded pixels, total bytes produced at each resolution layer, etc.). Agreement with the reported results is a good indication of compliance but, of course, not a guarantee. Although this cannot be considered an altogether satisfying validation check, it instills better confidence than what can be obtained for many of the lossy standards such as JPEG and MPEG that will be considered in later chapters. ITU-T speech coding standards, by contrast, provide bit-exact specifications together with test vectors. The status of JBIG validation lies somewhere between these two extremes.

4 Quantization

4.1 Introduction

Every signal or parameter that is to be transmitted or stored in digital form must be quantized. Quantization is a many-to-one mapping, and as such, there is an inherent loss of fidelity. However, if the number of quantization levels, or number of bits per sample, is large enough, the loss in quality may be insignificant. The information inherent in a truly continuous-amplitude random variable is infinite, and hence the quantization operation, no matter how fine, is sometimes called *entropy reduction*. This implies, therefore, that any quantization step is also data compression; however, most data compression systems start with a high-quality digital representation of a signal or parameter, and for most intents and purposes, this high-quality digital version is considered to be the "original."

Whether the quantization is fine or coarse, the principles are the same. In this chapter, we develop the basic principles and techniques for the design and analysis of uniform, nonuniform, and adaptive scalar and vector quantizers. You are probably familiar with the analog-to-digital conversion of a continuous-time, continuous-amplitude signal like speech, where after filtering and sampling at or above the Nyquist rate, the continuous-amplitude time samples are discretized in amplitude. Direct quantization of time samples of signals, such as speech, still images, or video, is an important operation, and our development is applicable to this type of problem. However, many important compression methods implement a *redundancy removal* step prior to quantization. Redundancy removal may consist of a linear prediction operation or a discrete transform of some type on the original source data. One output of the redundancy removal step may thus be a set of linear prediction coefficients or a set of transform coefficients. To be able to reinsert the redundancy, and hence, reconstruct the source using these coefficients, the coefficients must be stored or transmitted. This implies that these coefficients must be quantized. Therefore, many of the applications of quantization that we will be interested in require the quantization of coefficients or parameters of some type rather than direct quantization of the original spatio-temporal samples. The quantization principles presented in this chapter are applicable in these situations as well.

Quantization is a fundamental building block of any data compression method, and although it does not seem like a very exotic operation, inventive quantization methods and the parameters chosen to be quantized play a primary role in high-performance data compression systems. This fact is clearly evident in later chapters, but our goal here is to lay the groundwork for what will be discovered in later chapters and to provide the insights needed in future designs.

4.2   Scalar Quantization

Quantization is the process of converting a continuous-amplitude signal or other parameter into one of a finite number of discrete amplitudes. We assume throughout this discussion that any time domain signal being quantized has been appropriately sampled at or above the Nyquist rate. However, it should be evident that the quantizers developed in this chapter are applicable to the quantization of parameters and coefficients, as well as to space/time samples of a signal. Scalar quantization is the quantization of the amplitude of a single parameter or a single sample; the adjective "scalar" refers to the dimension of the variable being quantized, namely, one-dimensional (Jayant 1976; Jayant and Noll 1984; Gersho and Gray 1992).

4.2.1   Uniform Quantization

The input/output characteristic of an eight-level uniform quantizer is shown in Figure 4.1, where the horizontal axis is the input and the vertical axis is the quantized output value. The hash marks along the horizontal axis are called *step points* or *decision points,* except for the most positive and most negative hash marks, which are called *overload points.* The hash marks on the vertical axis are *output levels* or *output points.* To find the quantized output value corresponding to a given input, the input value is found along the horizontal axis and then projected vertically until the staircase input/output

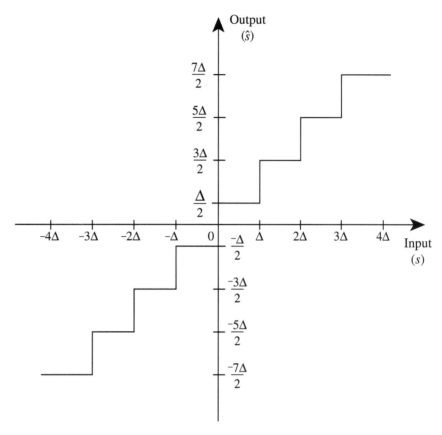

FIGURE

4.1   Uniform Symmetric Midriser Eight-Level Quantizer with Step Size Δ

function is encountered. The horizontal projection onto the vertical axis yields the corresponding quantized value along the vertical axis.

The quantizer in Figure 4.1 is said to be *uniform,* or sometimes *linear,* because the spacing between step points on the horizontal axis and between the output levels on the vertical axis is always the same, denoted here by Δ and called the *quantizer step size.* For an n-bit quantizer, there are $L = 2^n$ output levels, so the quantizer in Figure 4.1 is a 3-bit quantizer. The total range of the input values (maximum negative to maximum positive) is often called the *dynamic range* of the input. For a chosen number of output levels and a given input dynamic range, say $2V$, the step size of a uniform quantizer is given by the simple formula $\Delta = 2V/L$.

Defining the quantization error as $\hat{s} - s = q$, the quantization error can be plotted as a function of input value, as shown in Figure 4.2. Whenever the input

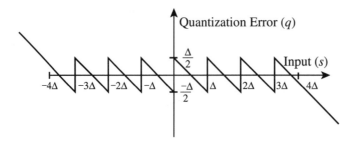

4.2   Quantization Error versus Input Value

exceeds the most negative and most positive hash marks, which means the input falls outside the designed dynamic range, the quantizer is said to be in *overload* and the range of values outside the dynamic range is called the *overload region*. In the overload region, the quantization error increases linearly with increasing magnitude of the input. However, within the designed–for dynamic range, the magnitude of the quantization error is always bounded by $\Delta/2$. This is called the *granular region,* and the quantization error in this region is called *granular noise*.

The performance of a quantizer is often represented as the mean squared quantization error or as the output signal-to-noise ratio (SNR), defined as

$$\text{SNR} = 10 \ \log_{10} \frac{\sigma^2}{D} \tag{4.1}$$

where σ^2 is the variance of the input and D is the mean squared quantization error. A classical result (and rule of thumb) is obtained if we assume that the input is uniformly distributed between the overload points, so that the input variance is $\sigma^2 = L^2\Delta^2/12$, and it follows that the quantization error is uniformly distributed between $\pm\Delta/2$. In this case, the mean squared quantization error is $\Delta^2/12$, and the quantizer SNR is $20 \log_{10} L$. Letting $L = 2^n$, the SNR is $6.02n$ dB. Thus, the performance of an n-bit quantizer increases linearly with the number of bits at a rate of 6 dB/bit. It turns out that for just about any input, as long as we assume uniformly distributed quantization noise and no overload, this rule of thumb holds. Perhaps unfortunately, even in many cases when the quantization error is not uniform, this rule of thumb is used as a rough performance estimate.

If we model the source as a random variable and we are given the probability density function (pdf) of the source to be quantized, we can design a uniform quantizer to minimize a chosen distortion measure. For instance, letting $g(\hat{s} - s)$ be the chosen distortion measure that here depends on the difference between

TABLE
4.1
Optimum Step Sizes for Uniform Quantization of a Gaussian pdf

Number of Levels (L)	Step Size (Δ_{opt})	Minimum Mean Squared Error (D)	SNR (dB)
4	0.9957	0.1188	9.25
8	0.5860	0.03744	14.27
16	0.3352	0.01154	19.38

Source: Max, J. Quantizing for minimum distortion. *IRE Trans. Inf. Theory.* © 1960 IEEE.

the input s and the quantized output $\hat{s}$, we can write the average distortion as

$$D = \int_{-\infty}^{\infty} g[\hat{s} - s] f_s(s) ds \tag{4.2}$$

where $f_s(s)$ is the pdf of the input. For a uniform quantizer, the output $\hat{s}$ is $(2i - 1)\Delta/2$ when $(i - 1)\Delta \leq s < i\Delta$, so for a symmetric quantizer with an even number of levels, the distortion in equation (4.2) can be expressed as

$$D = 2 \sum_{i=1}^{L/2-1} \int_{(i-1)\Delta}^{i\Delta} g\left[\frac{(2i - 1)\Delta}{2} - s\right] f_s(s) ds$$

$$+ 2 \int_{(L/2-1)\Delta}^{\infty} g\left[\frac{(L - 1)\Delta}{2} - s\right] f_s(s) ds \tag{4.3}$$

where Δ is the step size to be chosen. Minimizing D with respect to Δ yields

$$\sum_{i=1}^{L/2-1} (2i - 1) \int_{(i-1)\Delta}^{i\Delta} g'\left[\frac{(2i - 1)\Delta}{2} - s\right] f_s(s) ds$$

$$+ (L - 1) \int_{(L/2-1)\Delta}^{\infty} g'\left[\frac{(L - 1)\Delta}{2} - s\right] f_s(s) ds = 0 \tag{4.4}$$

to be solved for Δ_{opt}, where $g'(x) = \frac{d}{dx} g(x)$. For the squared error distortion measure $g[\hat{s} - s] = (\hat{s} - s)^2$ and a zero mean, unit variance Gaussian input pdf, the optimum step sizes (Δ_{opt}), the minimum distortion, and the SNR for $L = 4$, 8, and 16 levels are presented in Table 4.1 (these must be computed numerically). We see from the table that for this type of quantization, we are obtaining about 5 dB improvement for each additional bit devoted to quantization.

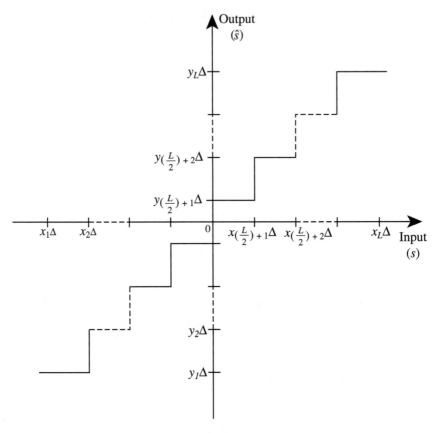

FIGURE
4.3   Symmetric Nonuniform Midriser Quantizer with Parameter Δ

4.2.2 Nonuniform Quantization

While uniform quantizers offer the advantage of simplicity, today it is quite easy to implement nonuniform quantizers, and many signals and parameters are much better matched by a nonuniform quantizer. A general nonuniform quantizer characteristic is shown in Figure 4.3, where the step points ($x_0 = -\infty, x_1, x_2, \ldots, x_{L-1}, x_L = +\infty$) and the output levels ($y_1, y_2, \ldots, y_L$) are constants that can be selected to minimize some function of the quantization error for a known or assumed input pdf. The parameter Δ is simply used for scaling, but it is still often called the step size, even though it cannot be strictly interpreted as such. For the quantizer in Figure 4.3 with $\Delta = 1$, equation (4.2) becomes

$$D = \sum_{i=1}^{L} \int_{x_{i-1}}^{x_i} g[y_i - s] f_s(s) ds \qquad (4.5)$$

For fixed L, we minimize D with respect to both the x_i and y_i, so the necessary conditions to be satisfied are

$$g[y_i - x_j] = g[y_{j+1} - x_j] \qquad (4.6)$$

for $j = 1, 2, \ldots, L - 1$, and

$$\int_{x_{j-1}}^{x_j} g'[y_j - s] f_s(s) ds = 0 \qquad (4.7)$$

for $j = 1, 2, \ldots, L$. Letting $g[\hat{s} - s] = [\hat{s} - s]^2$, we obtain

$$x_j = \frac{y_{j+1} + y_j}{2} \qquad (4.8)$$

and

$$y_j = \int_{x_{j-1}}^{x_j} s f_s(s) ds \bigg/ \int_{x_{j-1}}^{x_j} f_s(s) ds \qquad (4.9)$$

Equations (4.8) and (4.9) define the minimum mean squared error (MMSE) optimal quantizer or Lloyd-Max quantizer (Max 1960; Lloyd 1957). Because of the complicated functional relationships, these equations must be solved numerically. Max (1960) tabulates the x_i and y_i for a Gaussian pdf and 1 to 36 output levels. His results for 4-, 8-, and 16-level quantizers are collected in Tables 4.2 through 4.4. The values shown are normalized and must be multiplied by the input standard deviation (Δ in Figure 4.3) to get the correct step points and output levels. Similarly, the MSE is normalized and must be multiplied by the input variance to obtain the actual mean squared error.

Comparing the minimum mean squared errors and SNRs between the uniform quantizers in Table 4.1 and the nonuniform quantizers in Tables 4.2 through 4.4, it is evident that the nonuniform quantizers generally provide a smaller D (larger SNR) for the same number of output levels L. Moreover, if some form of lossless compression is to be used on the quantizer outputs, the rate versus distortion comparison is different.

4.2.3 Logarithmic Companding

The most familiar form of nonuniform quantization is the logarithmic companding characteristic used for speech coding in the telephone network since the

T A B L E 4.2	MMSE Four-Level Gaussian Quantizer	
i	x_i	y_i
1	−0.9816	−1.510
2	0.0	−0.4528
3	0.9816	0.4528
4	∞	1.510

$D = 0.1175$

SNR = 9.30 dB

Source: Max, J. Quantizing for minimum distortion. *IRE Trans. Inf. Theory.* © 1960 IEEE.

T A B L E 4.3	MMSE Eight-Level Gaussian Quantizer	
i	x_i	y_i
1	−0.748	−2.152
2	−1.050	−1.344
3	−0.5006	−0.7560
4	0.0	−0.2451
5	0.5006	0.2451
6	1.050	0.7560
7	1.748	1.344
8	∞	2.152

$D = 0.03454$

SNR = 14.62 dB

Source: Max, J. Quantizing for minimum distortion. *IRE Trans. Inf. Theory.* © 1960 IEEE.

1960s. The principal motivation behind logarithmic companding is that low-amplitude signals in speech can be very important perceptually, and thus should be quantized as accurately as possible, while still preventing large-amplitude signals from experiencing overload. Since uniform quantizers designed for a given dynamic range and no overload have an output SNR that decreases linearly with decreasing input signal power, the SNR for low-amplitude signals with linear quantization will be poor. Thus, the idea behind log companding, and the direct method used in early implementations, is to boost the amplitude of the low-amplitude signals before linear quantization, then quantize, and then pass the decoded quantized value through the inverse of the characteristic used

T A B L E	MMSE 16-Level Gaussian Quantizer		
4.4	i	x_i	y_i
	1	−2.404	−2.733
	2	−1.844	−2.069
	3	−1.437	−1.618
	4	−1.099	−1.256
	5	−0.7996	−0.9424
	6	−0.5224	−0.6568
	7	−0.2582	−0.3881
	8	0.0	−0.1284
	9	0.2582	0.1284
	10	0.5224	0.3881
	11	0.7996	0.6568
	12	1.099	0.9424
	13	1.437	1.256
	14	1.844	1.618
	15	2.401	2.069
	16	∞	2.733

$D = 0.009497$

SNR = 20.22 dB

Source: Max, J. Quantizing for minimum distortion. *IRE Trans. Inf. Theory.* © 1960 IEEE.

to boost the input. If it were not for the quantization, this inverse operation would restore the input value exactly. However, even with the quantization, the inverse restores the original scale of each input value. Most importantly, the inverse operation also scales the quantization error in the same proportion that it scales the overall quantized value. This is what keeps the mean squared error relatively small or, equivalently, the SNR at an acceptable level. Specifically, this scheme was implemented initially by passing the analog speech signal through a characteristic of the form

$$F_\mu(s) = \frac{\ln[1 + \mu|s|]}{\ln[1 + \mu]} \mathrm{sgn}(s) \qquad (4.10)$$

where s is the normalized speech signal ($-1 \leq s \leq 1$) and μ is a parameter usually selected to be $\mu = 255$. The function $F_\mu(s)$ is shown in Figure 4.4. Notice that $F_\mu(s)$ tends to amplify small amplitudes more than larger amplitudes

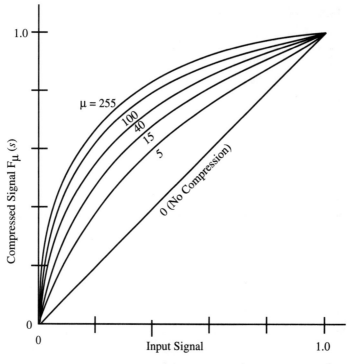

FIGURE

4.4 μ-Law Companding Characteristic

whenever $\mu > 0$. The output of $F_\mu(s)$ then serves as input to a uniform n-bit quantizer. To resynthesize the speech signal, the quantizer output $\hat{s}$ was passed through the inverse function of equation (4.10), given by

$$F_\mu^{-1}(\hat{s}) = \frac{1}{\mu}[(1+\mu)^{|\hat{s}|} - 1]\mathrm{sgn}(\hat{s}) \qquad (4.11)$$

where, of course, $-1 \le \hat{s} \le 1$.

The performance in SNR of this system for $\mu = 255$ and $n = 8$ bits is shown in Figure 4.5. It is evident from this figure that SNR is relatively flat over a wide dynamic range of input signal power (amplitudes), and hence, low-amplitude signals are reproduced almost as well as higher-amplitude signals.

The μ-law quantization characteristic given by equation (4.4) is used in the United States, Japan, and Canada. However, an alternative to the μ-law characteristic is the A-law characteristic, given by

$$F_A(s) = \begin{cases} \left[\frac{A|s|}{1+\ln A}\right]\mathrm{sgn}(s), & 0 \le |s| \le 1/A \\ \left[\frac{1+\ln|As|}{1+\ln A}\right]\mathrm{sgn}(s), & 1/A \le |s| \le 1 \end{cases} \qquad (4.12)$$

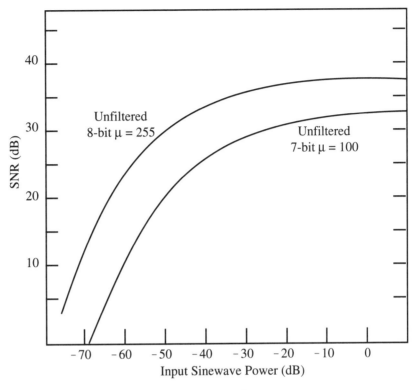

FIGURE

4.5 SNR versus Input Power for μ-Law Companding

where $0 \leq |s| \leq 1$ and $A = 87.6$. The inverse to this characteristic is

$$
F_A^{-1}(\hat{s}) = \begin{cases} \frac{|\hat{s}|[1+\ln A]}{A}\text{sgn}(\hat{s}), & 0 \leq |\hat{s}| \leq 1/(1+\ln A) \\ \frac{\exp\{|\hat{s}|[1+\ln A]-1\}}{A}\text{sgn}(\hat{s}), & 1/(1+\ln A) \leq |\hat{s}| \leq 1 \end{cases} \tag{4.13}
$$

where, if there is no quantization involved, $\hat{s} = F_A(s)$. The primary differences between the A-law and μ-law characteristics are that the A-law has a slightly wider dynamic range, but the μ-law has a little better (less) idle channel noise (noise during silent intervals). The A-law quantizing characteristic is implemented in Europe, Africa, Australia, and South America.

4.2.4 Adaptive Quantization

A solution to the problem of minimizing overload while maintaining good quantizer performance for low amplitudes is to adapt the quantizer step size or, equivalently, the dynamic range. All of the quantizer characteristics discussed thus far are normalized, so the step points and output levels can be scaled by a parameter, Δ, that we have called the step size.

There are two broad classes of quantizer step size adaptation approaches, called forward adaptation and backward adaptation. *Forward adaptive* (FA or AQF) quantizers extract step size information from the input, while *backward adaptive* (BA or AQB) quantizers adapt the step size based on the quantized output signal only (Jayant and Noll 1984). Both methods have their advantages and disadvantages.

For FA quantizers, the step size is not changed for every input value, but rather it is calculated for a block of data and then held constant over that block. Thus, the procedure for FA quantization is to (1) buffer a set (block) of input values, (2) calculate $\Delta(k)$ for this block, (3) supply the calculated $\Delta(k)$ to the quantizer, and (4) release the block of values to be quantized by the fixed quantizer with step size $\Delta(k)$. The multipliers of Δ in Figure 4.3 are not usually changed with time, but are fixed to some preselected values such as those in Tables 4.2 through 4.4. For forward adaptation in communications applications, not only must the quantizer output levels be coded and transmitted to the receiver, but the quantizer step size for the block must be coded and transmitted. Forward adaptive quantizers insert a delay at least as large as the block length used to calculate the step size, which is usually on the order of 10–25 ms. This delay alone is not noticeable to the user; however, for long-distance speech transmission over the telephone network, this delay can aggravate existing echo problems, and if FA quantizers are included in several series-connected communication links, the cumulative delay could be objectionable.

The major factor in FA quantizer performance is how often the step size is updated. Generally, the more often $\Delta(k)$ is recalculated, the better the performance. However, for communications applications, the more often $\Delta(k)$ is calculated, the higher the required transmission rate. This implies a design trade-off.

There are numerous algorithms that have been proposed for adapting the FA quantizer step size. We present only the most generic one, given by

$$\Delta(k) = \alpha \sqrt{\frac{1}{N} \sum_{i=1}^{N} s^2[(k-1)N + i]} \qquad (4.14)$$

where α is a parameter to be selected, N is the number of samples in a block, and $k = 1, 2, \ldots$, denotes the kth block of data. Thus, from equation (4.14), for the first block,

$$\Delta(1) = \alpha \sqrt{\frac{1}{N} \sum_{i=1}^{N} s^2(i)} \tag{4.15}$$

for the second block,

$$\Delta(2) = \alpha \sqrt{\frac{1}{N} \sum_{i=1}^{N} s^2(N+i)} \tag{4.16}$$

and so on.

Backward adaptive quantizers calculate the step size based upon the quantizer output only, and the step size is adapted after every input value. This gives BA quantization an advantage over FA quantizers since no delay is inserted by the BA quantizer adaptation. The sample-by-sample update may also seem to give BA quantization a performance advantage over FA quantizers; however, this increased update rate is more than compensated for by the "lookahead" capability of FA quantizers. The choice between FA and BA quantizers is not an easy one, and it involves many factors that are affected by the specific application of interest.

The backward adaptive quantizer configuration that has attracted the most attention is the "one-word memory" or "instantaneously" adaptive quantizer developed by Jayant (1973), in which the step size evolves according to

$$\Delta(k+1) = M(|I(k)|)\Delta^{\beta}(k) \tag{4.17}$$

where the time index k denotes a sampling time instant rather than a block number and $M(\cdot)$ is a time-invariant multiplier function that depends upon the magnitude of the transmitted codeword at time k, denoted $|I(k)|$, which corresponds to the particular transmitted quantizer output level, and $0 < \beta < 1$ is included to dissipate error effects. A representative eight-level backward adaptive quantizer with code assignments and multipliers is shown in Figure 4.6. The binary codes are written above the output level, and the corresponding multiplier is shown below the output level. Thus, if a code corresponding to an outer (larger-magnitude) quantizer level is received, a multiplier greater than 1 is used in equation (4.17), while if a code denoting an inner level is received, a multiplier less than 1 is used. If an intermediate level occurs, such as $y_2\Delta(k)$ or $y_5\Delta(k)$, then the multiplier is 1.0. Thus, an outer level causes an expansion, an inner level a contraction, and an intermediate level leaves the quantizer unchanged. There is nothing magic about the multipliers shown except that they

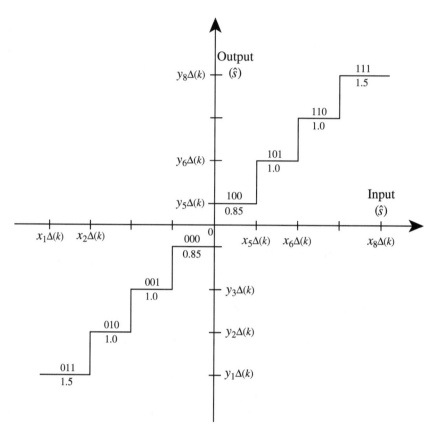

FIGURE

4.6   Backward Adaptive Quantizer

are typical, and other multipliers can also be used. As an example, some workers have found it advantageous to expand faster than they contract for speech
sources.

β is a design parameter, and the smaller β is, the less channel errors affect
the adaptation. However, a small β yields a short quantizer memory, a narrow
dynamic range for the step size, and, as a result, poor quantizer performance in
the absence of errors. We therefore are presented with yet another design trade-
off, since a larger β is preferred for relatively noise-free channels. For speech,
usually $\frac{31}{32} < \beta < \frac{255}{256}$, depending upon the specific application.

The effects of channel errors on forward adaptive quantizers can be greatly
reduced or eliminated by using forward error protection on the few bits per
block representing the step size. This is quite different from the BA quantizer,
which uses the entire bit sequence for step size adaptation. Furthermore, even

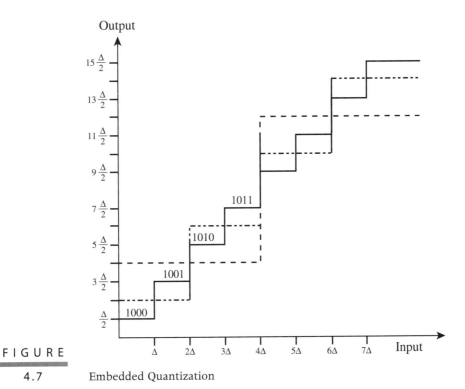

FIGURE

4.7   Embedded Quantization

if an erroneous step size is received for one block in FA quantization, the step size for the next block is not affected, since a new step size is sent for each block of data.

4.2.5 Embedded Quantization

In some applications, it would be desirable if we had a code representing a quantized value with the property that the least significant bits could be simply discarded should we need to reduce the data rate or storage requirements. All quantization and compression methods do not have this property, but embedded quantizers or embedded codes are examples of such codes (Goodman 1980). An input/output characteristic for a 16-level embedded quantizer is shown in Figure 4.7. Note that the key property here is that the 8- and 4-level quantizers have quantizer step points that are a subset of the 16-level quantizer step points. Thus, we see that with the 4-bit code, say 1010, if we delete the least significant bit to obtain 101, we have a unique output point. Similarly, if we continue and delete the least significant bit again to obtain 10, we have a unique 4-level output value.

Embedded quantizers can be combined with predictive coding to obtain an embedded differential encoder (discussed in Chapters 5 and 6). Other embedded coders are being developed and find applications in a variety of transmission environments.

4.3 Vector Quantization

We begin by carefully defining what is meant by *vector quantization*. For simplicity, we abbreviate both vector quantization and vector quantizer by VQ. Whether VQ stands for vector quantization or vector quantizer should be evident from the context (Gersho and Gray 1992).

4.3.1 VQ Structure, Design, and Performance

Let $\mathbf{X}$ be an N-component source vector with joint pdf $f(\mathbf{X}) = f(x_1, x_2, \ldots, x_N)$. An N-dimensional VQ is a function $\mathbf{Q}(\mathbf{X})$ that maps $\mathbf{X} \in \Re^N$ into one of L points with each output point corresponding to an output vector $\mathbf{Y}_1, \mathbf{Y}_2, \ldots, \mathbf{Y}_L$, belonging to $\Re^N$. The quantizer is completely specified by listing the L output vectors and their corresponding partitions of $\Re^N$ into L disjoint and exhaustive regions denoted by $\mathcal{P}_1, \mathcal{P}_2, \ldots, \mathcal{P}_L$, so that $\mathbf{Q}(\mathbf{X}) = \mathbf{Y}_i$ if $\mathbf{X} \in \mathcal{P}_i$ for $i = 1, 2, \ldots, L$. An N-dimensional VQ is sometimes called a block quantizer with block length N. Throughout this section, we emphasize (for simplicity) the mean squared error (MSE) per component distortion measure, given by

$$D = \frac{1}{N} E\{d(\mathbf{X} - \mathbf{Y})\}$$

$$= \frac{1}{N} E\|\mathbf{X} - \mathbf{Q}(\mathbf{X})\|^2$$

$$= \frac{1}{N} \sum_{i=1}^{L} \int_{\mathbf{X} \in \mathcal{P}_i} \|\mathbf{X} - \mathbf{Y}_i\|^2 f(\mathbf{X}) d\mathbf{X} \qquad (4.18)$$

where $\|\cdot\|$ denotes the usual ℓ_2 norm.

For purposes of transmission or storage, the output vectors $\mathbf{Y}_i$ are assigned a binary codeword c_i of length b_i bits. The average codeword length is thus

4.8   Nonuniform Scalar Quantizer

$$\bar{b} = \sum_{i=1}^{L} b_i P(\mathbf{X} \in \mathcal{P}_i) \text{bits/vector} \tag{4.19}$$

so the average rate in bits/component is

$$R = \frac{\bar{b}}{N} \tag{4.20}$$

and hence

$$\frac{1}{N} H(\mathbf{Y}) \le R \le \frac{1}{N} \log_2 L \tag{4.21}$$

The design of a VQ for a given distortion measure and input vector pdf requires the selection of the partitions $\mathcal{P}_i$ and the output vectors $\mathbf{Y}_i$, $i = 1, 2, \ldots, L$, often called the *VQ codebook*, such that the partitions are nonoverlapping and cover $\Re^N$. In the scalar case $(N = 1)$, the problem is relatively simple since partitioning of $\Re^1$ consists of choosing nonoverlapping intervals along the real line, as shown in Figure 4.8. Note that this figure is a redrawn version of the nonuniform scalar quantizer input/output characteristic shown in Figure 4.3 with $\Delta = 1$, where the step points are shown in Figure 4.8 as hash marks and the output values are shown as dots. Thus, partitions for a scalar quantizer are nonoverlapping intervals.

For $N > 1$, the partitions $\mathcal{P}_i$ can take on any shape, and hence, there are infinitely many candidates for the set of optimum partitions. Even when the N-dimensional VQ is uniform, which implies that the $\mathcal{P}_i$ are just translates of the same shape, there are many different kinds of partitions that cover $\Re^N$. For example, triangles, quadrilaterals, and hexagons all can be used to partition $\Re^2$ (Gersho 1979); a hexagonal partition is shown in Figure 4.9. This availability of many possible shapes for the partition makes the design procedure more complicated for $N > 1$, but it also provides a possible performance advantage over scalar quantization.

The performance of a VQ is completely determined by two quantities, the average distortion D in equation (4.18) and the required rate R in equation (4.20). If we wish to find the optimum performance possible using an N-dimensional

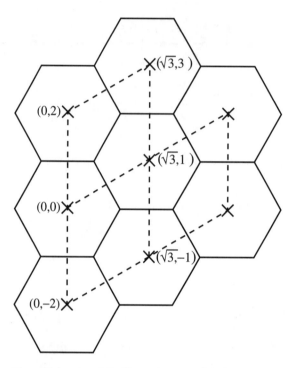

FIGURE

4.9   Two-Dimensional Uniform Hexagonal VQ

VQ, we could take either one of two possible approaches (Gray and Davisson 1974). We could fix the acceptable distortion D and find the VQ that requires the minimum rate R for a distortion less than or equal to D, or we could fix the maximum rate R and find the VQ that achieves the smallest distortion D with rate less than or equal to R. However, both of these approaches, as described, imply that we must design an optimum N-dimensional VQ.

The ultimate bound on the performance of vector quantizers—indeed, on any data compression system—is provided by rate distortion theory as originally developed by Shannon (1948, 1959). The utility of rate distortion theory stems from the fact that the optimum performance theoretically attainable for any data compression system can be computed without actually designing such a system; in fact, all that is needed is a characterization of the source and a specification of the distortion measure. A slightly closer connection with VQ can be made if we avoid the definitions involving mutual information and consider the average distortion of an N-dimensional VQ as specified in equation (4.18). The distortion rate approach to designing a VQ is to choose $\mathbf{Q}(\mathbf{X})$ to minimize the average distortion in equation (4.18) subject to the rate constraint in equation (4.21). Specifically, we seek

$$
\begin{aligned}
D_N(R) &= \min_{Q(X)} \frac{1}{N} E\{d(X - Y)\} \\
&= \min_{Q(X)} \frac{1}{N} E\|X - Q(X)\|^2
\end{aligned}
$$

(4.22)

over all $Q(X)$ that satisfy

$$
\frac{1}{N} H(Q(X)) = \frac{1}{N} H(Y) \le R
$$

(4.23)

The distortion rate function can be obtained from equation (4.22) as

$$
D(R) = \lim_{N \to \infty} D_N(R)
$$

(4.24)

Equation (4.24) implies that as the vector length becomes large, the performance of a VQ can be made to approach the best performance attainable by any data compression system. Thus, in theory at least, we have a coder, namely vector quantization, that can achieve the performance promised by rate distortion theory.

4.3.2   Optimal VQ

Now that we have defined vector quantization, we are ready to see how optimal vector quantizers can be found (Linde, Buzo, and Gray 1980; Gray 1984; Gersho and Gray 1992). As noted previously, an N-dimensional VQ is completely determined by specifying the partitions $\mathcal{P}_i$ and the output vectors Y_i, $i = 1, 2, \ldots, L$, such that the $\mathcal{P}_i$ are nonoverlapping and completely cover $\Re^N$. Two necessary conditions that must be satisfied for an optimal N-dimensional minimum MSE quantizer are that (1) the partition of $\Re^N$ must be a Dirichlet partition (also called a Voronoi region), that is,

$$
\mathcal{P}_i = \{X : \|X - Y_i\| \le \|X - Y_j\| \text{ for each } j \ne i\}
$$

(4.25)

and (2) the output points must be centroids of their respective regions, so

$$
Y_i = \{Y : \int_{\mathcal{P}_i} \|X - Y\|^2 f(X) dX \text{ is minimum}\}
$$

(4.26)

One important approach for VQ design is based upon using training sequences representative of the vectors to be quantized and the LBG algorithm, which is a version of the K-means algorithm in the pattern recognition literature (Linde, Buzo, and Gray 1980; MacQueen 1967). This iterative algorithm can be shown to converge to at least a local optimum, and global optimality can be approximated by repeatedly running the algorithm with different initialization vectors. This algorithm (in general) produces a nonuniform partition of $\Re^N$ and a nonuniform distribution of VQ output points. This design procedure is performed totally offline, but the computational and storage requirements of this process are still not insignificant. In fact, for M training vectors and I iterations of the algorithm, the computational cost is about $NLMI = NMI2^{RN}$ operations, and the storage cost is $N(L + M)$. Since M must be at least $10L$, these quantities are large and grow exponentially with an increase in R and N (Makhoul, Roucos, and Gish 1985).

Once we have obtained a VQ codebook offline, the online quantization process consists of calculating the distortion between the current input vector and each output vector and choosing that output vector that produces minimum distortion. If each distortion calculation requires N operations, then the quantization process requires $NL = N2^{RN}$ operations. The storage cost is also $N2^{RN}$. Since these operations must be accomplished in real time, this computational burden is quite significant. For example, if $R = 2$ bits/component and $N = 10$, the number of operations is $10 \cdot 2^{20} \cong 10$ million! These computational and storage requirements are for a full-search VQ, and much research effort is going into reducing these numbers with some loss in performance.

4.3.3 Structured VQ

Vector quantizer codebooks designed using the LBG algorithm generally have no discernible structure, and this "random" codebook distribution is what complicates the quantization or encoding process. On the other hand, it is this random structure that offers the near-optimal performance of vector quantizers.

Considerable effort has been expended in the past 15 years searching for structured VQs that achieve good performance. In this section, we briefly describe four VQ structures that have been useful in a number of practical compression problems: tree-structured VQ, gain/shape VQ, multistage or cascaded VQ, and lattice VQ. Each of these structures has its own set of advantages and disadvantages, and each is appropriate for different types of problems (Gersho and Gray 1992; Abut 1990).

The idea behind tree-structured VQ (TSVQ) is that for a VQ with $L = K^d$ output points, it may be possible to break the search for the best output vector

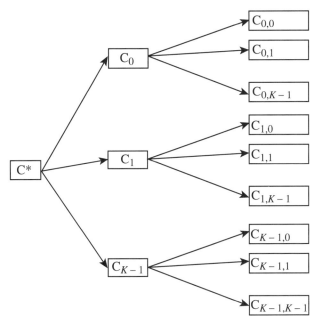

FIGURE

4.10 Basic Structure of Tree-Structured VQ Encoding

for a given input down to a series of K searches in a tree structure, as indicated in Figure 4.10. Therefore, we need at each stage in the tree a set of K vectors, each of which can be considered representative of a set of vectors at the next level in the tree. The encoded search is simplified because at any level in the tree only K comparisons are performed, and the total number of comparisons required to determine the best output vector is Kd. When contrasted with the $L = K^d$ comparisons needed for a full search, the reduction in complexity is evident.

Another important structured VQ is the gain/shape VQ. Here the idea is to split an RN-bit codebook into two codebooks, an R_1N_1-bit codebook and an R_2N_2-bit codebook, such that $RN = R_1N_1 + R_2N_2$ bits. However, the simplification comes because the search for the best output level is broken into two separate searches, one over $L_1 = 2^{R_1N_1}$ levels and the other over $L_2 = 2^{R_2N_2}$ levels. The reduction in the number of calculations can be illustrated by considering the example of $RN = 10$ bits and letting $R_1N_1 = 3$ bits and $R_2N_2 = 7$ bits, so that one search is over $L_1 = 8$ output points and the other is over $L_2 = 128$ output points, which can be constrasted to a single full search over $L = 2^{RN} = 1024$ points.

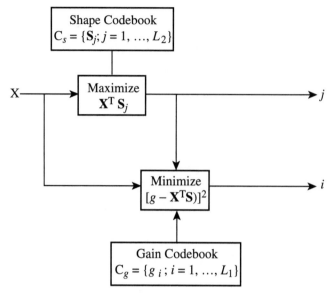

FIGURE

4.11   Gain/Shape VQ Encoder

This is a general example of a product VQ, but we are interested here in the special case of a gain/shape VQ, illustrated by Figure 4.11. In this figure, the gain codebook is represented by C_g and the shape codebook by C_s. The online encoding is accomplished by choosing the shape vector from the codebook that maximizes the inner product between the input vector $\mathbf{X}$ and all possible shape vectors in the codebook C_s. Then, using the selected shape codevector, $\mathbf{S}$, the scalar gain is chosen to minimize the squared error indicated in the figure.

Clearly, the gain/shape method is most suitable for those physical problems where the input vector naturally separates into such quantities. One example where gain/shape VQs have been applied is to the quantization of speech spectra represented as linear prediction (autoregressive) models.

An important VQ structure, not only because it reduces complexity, is the multistage VQ, often called a cascaded VQ or residual VQ (Barnes and Rizui 1996). There are several observations to be made about multistage VQs as represented in Figure 4.12. First, from this figure, the origin of each of these several names is evident. Second, the search is reduced because the best output vector is found by three lower dimensional subsearches that occur in stages. Third, and perhaps different from our previous discussions, the multistage VQ

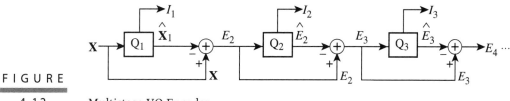

FIGURE

4.12   Multistage VQ Encoder

shown is an example of an embedded code (also a successively refinable code). More explicitly, the vector $\mathbf{X}$ can be represented coarsely by the index I_1, and the representation can be improved (or refined) by sending the index I_2 and refined still further by sending index I_3. If E_4 is losslessly compressed, $\mathbf{X}$ can be reconstructed exactly by proceeding from output to input and adding in the quantized vector values.

Alternatively, this code can be viewed as an embedded code if it is imagined that the error E_4 is discarded and the overall code is taken as the indices $I_1I_2I_3$. Thus, during transmission, I_3 can be removed and an approximation to the input vector $\mathbf{X}$ can be achieved without reencoding. Similarly, I_2 can be discarded and a coarse reconstruction of $\mathbf{X}$ obtained. Successively refinable and embedded codes provide a rate scaling mechanism that can be extremely helpful in many applications.

Another way to simplify the encoding step of an N-dimensional VQ is to partition the N-dimensional vector into two (or more) subvectors with dimensions l and m, where $l + m = N$. The N-vector search is thus broken into two separate l-vector and m-vector searches, each of dimension smaller than N. For an MSE distortion measure,

$$\|\mathbf{X}\|_N^2 = \|\mathbf{X}\|_l^2 + \|\mathbf{X}\|_m^2 \tag{4.27}$$

where the subscripts indicate the vector dimension. The selection of the sub-optimally encoded vector thus proceeds by choosing the encoded vector as the combination of the l-vector and m-vector that minimizes each of the components, as previously noted, yielding a total number of searches equal to $2^l + 2^m$. This is clearly a reduction in complexity compared to the full search requiring 2^N searches.

The success of the partitioned VQ approach is very much dependent on the physical problem.

Each of these preceding VQs still represents a nonuniform quantizer, and they are still usually designed by a training mode procedure. We could alternatively consider uniform VQs, thus obtaining additional structure to simplify the encoding step. As noted before, N-dimensional space can be covered with many different regular partitions, so the design of an N-dimensional uniform VQ is nontrivial. To obtain uniform VQ designs, researchers have turned to N-dimensional structures called *lattices*.

Lattices in $\Re^N$ have considerable structure, and hence, lattice-based quantizers offer the promise of design simplicity and reduced complexity encoding, providing that lattices can be found in high dimensions that yield good quantization performance (Gibson and Sayood 1988). A lattice is defined as a set of vectors

$$\Lambda = \{\mathbf{x} : \mathbf{x} = u_1 \mathbf{a}_1 + u_2 \mathbf{a}_2 + \cdots + u_N \mathbf{a}_N\} \tag{4.28}$$

where $\mathbf{a}_i$, $i = 1, 2, \ldots, N$, are the basis vectors of the lattice and the u_i are integers. We form a VQ from a lattice by selecting L of the lattice points $\mathbf{x}$ to be the output points $\mathbf{Y}_i$ and forming Voronoi regions about these output points so that if a source vector $\mathbf{X} \in \mathscr{P}_i$, then $\mathbf{Y}_i = \mathbf{Q}(\mathbf{X})$.

A good example of a uniform VQ in two dimensions is the hexagonal VQ in Figure 4.9. This lattice is designated as A_2 (to prevent digressions, we will not describe the origins of these lattices nor their designations and leave these details to the references), and it is the best lattice in two dimensions for a uniform source input distribution and the MSE distortion criterion. A simple two-dimensional lattice—and perhaps the simplest—is the Z^2 lattice, which is the cross product of two scalar integer lattices, each designated as Z.

To design an N-dimensional uniform VQ, it is necessary to select the lattice, choose the desired number of output points (by setting the rate in bits/component), and truncate the lattice (since lattices are infinite structures). Figure 4.13 shows examples of two-dimensional lattices for Gaussian and Laplacian input sources, based upon the Z^2 lattice, where the number of output levels has been truncated to 37 and 41 points, respectively (Jeong and Gibson 1993). There are fast quantizing methods for various lattices (Conway and Sloane 1982, 1983) but as you get near or outside the boundary, some point-by-point comparisons are necessary. Further, note that quantizing and encoding in N dimensions are not exactly the same, since once the best output point is found, the code for the point must be obtained, perhaps by table lookup. So, fast encoding structures are also of importance.

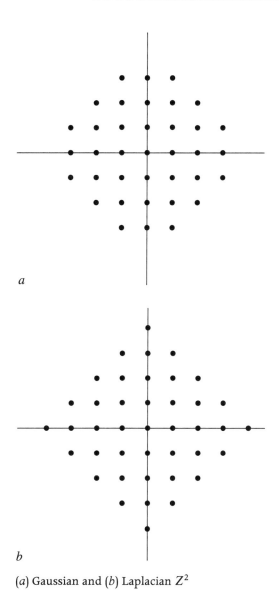

b

(*a*) Gaussian and (*b*) Laplacian Z^2

An interesting two-dimensional piecewise-uniform lattice VQ based upon Z^2 is shown in Figure 4.14. This is reminiscent of one-dimensional companding. There is considerable theory, design, and implementation information in the literature concerning lattice VQs, and we do not delve into these ideas in more detail here (for this information, see Conway and Sloane 1988; Gibson and Sayood 1988).

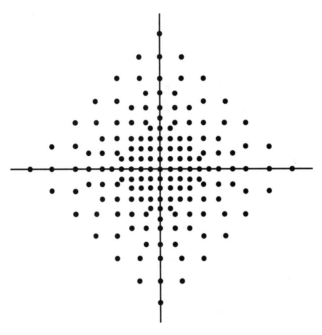

FIGURE
4.14   Laplacian Piecewise-Uniform Z^2 Lattice Codebook

4.4   Summary

The principal motivating idea behind this chapter is that everything to be transmitted or stored in digital form must be quantized. This includes temporal or spatial samples, coefficients, parameters, scale factors, or any other quantity. Well-designed quantization techniques must incorporate knowledge of the signal or parameter to be quantized as well as employ the appropriate quantization methods.

To prepare for subsequent chapters and for data compression system design and analysis, we have presented the fundamental ideas behind scalar and vector quantization and have outlined typical design procedures. Our designs and performance evaluations have emphasized mean squared error as a distortion measure, but it is just as likely today that the quantizers used in a data compression system will be chosen based upon offline perceptual experiments. Thus, quantizer designs incorporate elements of the source (parameter to be quantized) and the user (perceptual performance). As we saw in Section 4.3, complexity is also a factor, especially when one considers using vector quantization. Finally, we have not emphasized channel effects in this chapter, but as later chapters will show, channel errors can also impact quantizer design and codeword assignments.

5 | Predictive Coding

5.1 Introduction

Speech coding is the process of representing speech in digital form with as few bits as possible while maintaining the quality and intelligibility required for a particular application (Gibson 1993). The first really successful speech coders were called *vocoders* because they were thought of as coding the vocal tract. Many of these early vocoders used filters to break the input speech into narrow frequency bands, measured the energy in each of these bands, and coded and sent this information to the receiver. At the receiver, each filter was excited with the appropriate energy level to resynthesize the speech. These coders produced intelligible speech, but the speech lacked naturalness and often lost the quality needed to identify the speaker (Flanagan 1972). These coders are properly classified as *frequency domain coders* and are discussed in Chapter 7. Today the term *vocoder* is used most often to include speech coders that digitize speech by explicitly modeling the vocal tract. Linear predictive coding (discussed in Section 5.2) is an example of this type of vocoder.

The next speech coders to be useful were delta modulation (DM) and differential pulse code modulation (DPCM), which fall into the class of coders called *waveform coders*. Delta modulation and DPCM not only tend to maintain good intelligibility but also retain speaker identity. Their distortions are usually granular sounding in character at their effective data rates. At lower rates, increased granular noise or hissing occurs, but spectral distortions not previously present also begin to appear. Delta modulation and DPCM are both *predictive coders* and were the first predictive coders to achieve widespread use in applications (Jayant 1976).

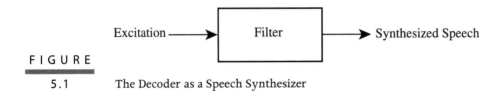

FIGURE
5.1   The Decoder as a Speech Synthesizer

In the past 25 years, both vocoders and waveform coders have been improved dramatically, and new classes of speech coders have been invented. Perhaps the best approach to understanding and classifying all of these speech coders is to view them as speech synthesizers, as represented in block diagram form in Figure 5.1. Thus, to synthesize speech, speech coders need parameters to model the synthesis filter and an appropriate excitation for the filter. The better the filter models the speech production process, the fewer bits must be allocated to the excitation. This is the basic idea behind LPC. Conversely, some of the pressure on getting the vocal tract model right is removed if there are sufficient bits available to transmit a highly accurate version of the excitation. Delta modulation and DPCM utilize this concept.

In the past 10 to 15 years, not only have vocoders and waveform coders been substantially refined, but a truly innovative new method of speech coding has become popular. This class of coders is called *analysis-by-synthesis coders*, since these coders choose the best coded version of the input speech by synthesizing at the transmitter all possibilities for the given coder structure, finding the best perceptual match to the input speech from these possibilities, and then sending the bits representing this best perceptual match to the receiver. Predictive coders currently constitute the preeminent examples of analysis-by-synthesis coders. Analysis-by-synthesis coders require substantial complexity at the encoder but allow *perceptual distortion measures* to be used in finding the best match. Perceptual distortion measures are critical to their success and constitute their primary advantage over previous coders.

Analysis-by-synthesis techniques have a long history in speech processing; earlier they served as important methods in speech analysis for applications other than coding, such as speech modeling and speech synthesis (Flanagan 1972). The analysis-by-synthesis idea for source compression is inherent in the disciplines of information theory and rate distortion theory, and the theory predates the application to speech coding, but the implied complexity and lack of source and perceptual models delayed their introduction into speech coding applications (Berger 1971; Stewart 1981).

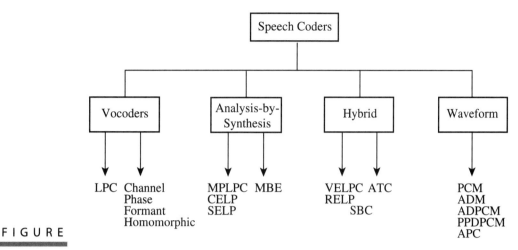

5.2   Speech Coding Taxonomy According to Coding Method and Domain

Figure 5.2 shows a taxonomy of speech coding that includes vocoders, waveform coders, and analysis-by-synthesis coders (Kondoz 1994). Another class of coders, called *hybrid coders,* is also shown. These coders were developed after vocoders and waveform coders and are an intermediate step between the former two approaches. Hybrid coders still find important applications today and will be discussed as appropriate in this chapter and in Chapter 6. In Figure 5.2, reading left to right, the four classifications correspond roughly to increasing bit rate. Under each classification, the left downward arrow corresponds to time domain approaches, while the right arrow corresponds to coding methods that primarily have a frequency domain interpretation. All of the waveform coders are time domain methods since they all attempt to reproduce the time domain waveform. Figure 5.2 should be helpful in classifying the several speech coding techniques.

This chapter begins with a development of the linear prediction model that is common to all predictive coders currently in use.

5.2   The Linear Prediction Model and Linear Predictive Coding

Linear predictive coding (LPC) of speech is based on classical least-squares estimation methods and a fortuitous perceptual match between a mathematical

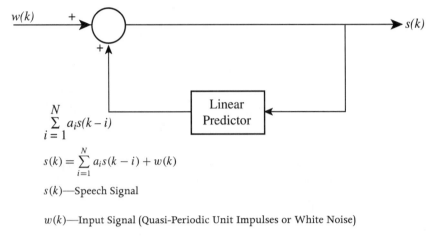

$$s(k) = \sum_{i=1}^{N} a_i s(k-i) + w(k)$$

$s(k)$—Speech Signal

$w(k)$—Input Signal (Quasi-Periodic Unit Impulses or White Noise)

a_i—Predictor Coefficients

FIGURE

5.3   Linear Prediction Model

idealization, called the *linear prediction model,* and human speech characteristics (Atal and Hanauer 1971; Makhoul 1975; Markel and Gray 1976). Linear predictive coding achieves intelligible speech at a data rate of 2.4 to 4.8 kbps or so (under ideal conditions), and the synthesis portion of LPC has found widespread application in consumer and military products. The complete LPC system (analysis and synthesis) is also an important, real-time digital voice coder. Furthermore, many aspects of linear prediction modeling as discussed here are incorporated in more recent, higher-quality speech coders.

LPC can be viewed as a modification of waveform encoding in which the prediction error is not transmitted, or it can considered to be a vocoder that models the human vocal tract mechanism. Both viewpoints lead to insights and generalizations. In this section, LPC is developed by starting with the linear prediction model, with as few appeals as possible to waveform encoders or speech physiology.

The linear prediction model shown in Figure 5.3 simply assumes that the current speech sample can be represented by a weighted linear combination of past speech samples plus a driving term (Atal and Hanauer 1971),

$$s(k) = \sum_{i=1}^{N} a_i s(k-i) + Gw(k) \tag{5.1}$$

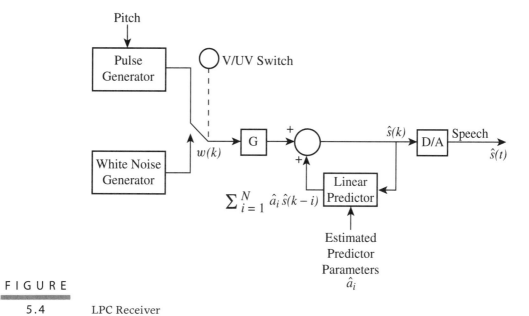

F I G U R E

5.4   LPC Receiver

where $s(\cdot)$ represents the speech samples, the set $\{a_i : i = 1, 2, \ldots, N\}$ are called *predictor coefficients*, N is the *predictor order*, and $Gw(k)$ is the *driving term* or *input* at the kth time instant. The driving term is either white noise for unvoiced speech or quasi-periodic impulses for voiced speech.

For a chosen N, linear predictive coding consists of computing the predictor coefficients and the driving term gain G, classifying the speech as voiced or unvoiced, and then transmitting this information to the receiver, where the speech can be resynthesized by a structure as shown in Figure 5.4. Although this all may sound very simple, it is not, and the following sections develop each of the LPC components in more detail.

5.2.1   Coefficient Calculation

The predictor coefficients are selected to minimize the mean squared error between the speech signal at time k and the predicted value given by

$$s(k|k-1) = \sum_{i=1}^{N} a_i s(k-i) \qquad (5.2)$$

Thus, it is desired to minimize

$$\varepsilon = \frac{1}{M} \sum_{k=1}^{M} [s(k) - s(k|k-1)]^2$$

$$= \frac{1}{M} \sum_{k=1}^{M} \left[s(k) - \sum_{i=1}^{N} a_i s(k-i) \right]^2 \tag{5.3}$$

where M is the block of speech samples over which the minimization is performed (called a *frame*). Taking partial derivatives of (5.3) with respect to each a_j and equating to zero yields

$$\sum_{i=1}^{N} a_i \left\{ \frac{1}{M} \sum_{k=1}^{M} s(k-i)s(k-j) \right\} = \frac{1}{M} \sum_{k=1}^{M} s(k)s(k-j) \tag{5.4}$$

for $j = 1, 2, \ldots, N$.

Letting

$$\phi_{ij} = \frac{1}{M} \sum_{k=1}^{M} s(k-i)s(k-j) \tag{5.5}$$

(5.4) can be written as

$$\sum_{i=1}^{N} a_i \phi_{ij} = \phi_{j0}, \quad j = 1, 2, \ldots, N \tag{5.6}$$

Using matrix notation, (5.6) becomes

$$\Phi A = \psi \tag{5.7}$$

where Φ is an $N \times N$ nonnegative definite symmetric matrix, A is an $N \times 1$ column vector of predictor coefficients, and ψ is an $N \times 1$ column vector. The matrix Φ is usually called the *covariance matrix* by speech researchers, and the method in (5.7) has been called the *covariance method* (Makhoul 1975; Markel and Gray 1976).

The optimum linear predictor coefficients are obtained by solving the N simultaneous equations represented by (5.7). Note that the relationship in (5.7) was obtained by minimizing the mean squared error over a block of M samples, but the covariance terms require $M + N$ samples, with N samples taken from an adjacent block. This is one of the differences between the covariance method and the autocorrelation method (to be described next). In calculating the predictor coefficients from (5.6) or (5.7), there is nothing to guarantee the stability of the resulting synthesis filter at the receiver. Since an unstable set of predictor coefficients can produce unacceptable quality speech, some method for checking and correcting the stability of the covariance method coefficients must be employed.

An alternative method for calculating the predictor coefficients still minimizes the prediction error in (5.3), but the speech is windowed so that all samples outside the current frame of M samples are zeroed. As a result, (5.4) can be rewritten as

$$\frac{1}{M}\sum_{i=1}^{N} a_i \sum_{k=-\infty}^{\infty} s(k-j)s(k-i) = \frac{1}{M}\sum_{k=-\infty}^{\infty} s(k)s(k-j) \tag{5.8}$$

which after letting $m = k - i$, becomes

$$\frac{1}{M}\sum_{i=1}^{N} a_i \sum_{m=-\infty}^{\infty} s(m)s(m+j-i) = \frac{1}{M}\sum_{m=-\infty}^{\infty} s(m)s(m+j) \tag{5.9}$$

for $j = 1, 2, \ldots, N$.

Because of the infinite limits on the summations, (5.9) can be expressed in terms of autocorrelation terms as

$$\sum_{i=1}^{N} a_i R(|j-i|) = R(j) \tag{5.10}$$

for $j = 1, \ldots, N$, where

$$R(j) = \frac{1}{M}\sum_{m=-\infty}^{\infty} s(m)s(m+|j|) \tag{5.11}$$

and hence

$$R(j) = R(-j) \tag{5.12}$$

In matrix notation, (5.10) becomes

$$RA = C \tag{5.13}$$

where R is an $N \times N$ Toeplitz matrix, A is a column vector of predictor coefficients, and C is a column vector of terms $C_j = R(j)$. Using the windowing assumption, the infinite sum in (5.11) can be reduced to

$$R(j) = \frac{1}{M} \sum_{k=0}^{M-|j|-1} s(k)s(k+|j|)$$ (5.14)

The linear simultaneous equations in (5.10) define what is called the *autocorrelation method* for calculating the predictor coefficients.

The predictor coefficients calculated from the autocorrelation method are guaranteed to yield a stable speech synthesis filter. Further, only $N+1$ autocorrelation terms need to be calculated, as opposed to $N(N+1)/2$ terms for the covariance method. Equally important is the fact that the special form of the equations in (5.10) allows them to be solved very efficiently.

The most efficient method for solving the set of linear simultaneous equations in (5.10) is due to Durbin (1960) and consists of the following recursive procedure (Makhoul 1975; Markel and Gray 1976):

1. Let

$$E^{(0)} = R(0)$$ (5.15)

2. Compute

$$k_i = \left\{ R(i) - \sum_{j=1}^{i-1} a_j^{(i-1)} R(i-j) \right\} \bigg/ E^{(i-1)}, \quad 1 \leq i \leq N$$ (5.16)

3. Then

$$a_i^{(i)} = k_i$$ (5.17)

$$a_j^{(i)} = a_j^{(i-1)} - k_i a_{i-j}^{(i-1)}, 1 \leq j \leq i-1$$ (5.18)

4. Next calculate

$$E^{(i)} = (1 - k_i^2) E^{(i-1)}$$ (5.19)

5. Go to step 2.

Equations (5.16) through (5.19) are solved starting with $i = 1$. The parenthetical exponents on the a's indicate the predictor order. The quantity $E^{(i)}$ is the mean squared prediction error for the ith-order predictor.

The parameters $\{k_i, i = 1, 2, \ldots, N\}$ that show up in the recursion are also very special coefficients. They are sometimes called *partial correlation (PARCOR) coefficients* due to their statistical interpretation or *reflection coefficients* due to their vocal tract modeling interpretation, and they have the

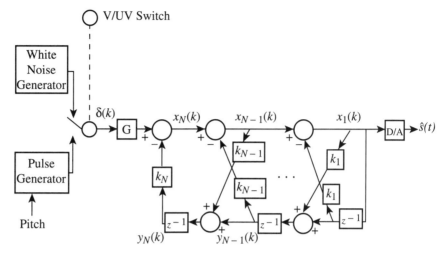

FIGURE 5.5   LPC Lattice Receiver Using PARCOR Coefficients

property that if $|k_i| \leq 1$ for all $i = 1, \ldots, N$, the speech synthesis filter is stable. This is a particularly important property since even a stable set of predictor coefficients can be made unstable by the quantization and coding required for transmission. To check stability, the PARCORs can be generated from the a's by the following recursion (Makhoul 1975; Markel and Gray 1976):

$$k_i = a_i^{(i)} \tag{5.20}$$

$$a_j^{(i-1)} = \frac{a_j^{(i)} + a_i^{(i)} a_{i-j}^{(i)}}{1 - k_i^2}, \quad 1 \leq j \leq i - 1 \tag{5.21}$$

where $i = N$, then $N - 1, \ldots$, and so on, with $a_i^{(N)} = a_i$, $i = 1, \ldots, N$.

Of course, rather than transmit the $\{a_i\}$, we can instead transmit the $\{k_i\}$, and, in fact, there is a receiver structure for the $\{k_i\}$, shown in Figure 5.5. The advantages of transmitting the PARCORs are the check on stability and their relative insensitivity to quantization. The lattice receiver in Figure 5.5 is also a very stable structure for hardware implementation.

There are numerous subtleties in LPC analysis. The analysis frame is typically 10–25 ms long, and the windowing for the autocorrelation method is generally nonrectangular of the Hamming or Hanning type. Preemphasis of frequencies above 500 Hz can substantially improve LPC speech quality since higher-frequency peaks in the spectrum are better identified. Also, interpolation of coefficients between transmission frames can improve the synthesized speech and is often used in CELP coders.

5.2.2 Other Parameters

There are also other parameters that are well suited to quantization and coding. One such set is the log-area ratios (LARs) related to the PARCORs by

$$g_i = \log \left[\frac{A_{i+1}}{A_i} \right] = \log \left[\frac{1 - k_i}{1 + k_i} \right] \tag{5.22}$$

The inverse sine function of the PARCORs, given by

$$\lambda_i = \sin^{-1}(k_i) \tag{5.23}$$

is also a useful parameter for quantization purposes. Viswanathan and Makhoul (1975) and Gray and Markel (1976) give analyses and experiments on LPC using these parameters for quantization and transmission.

More recently, spectral representations of the LPC coefficients have been introduced (Itakura 1975a) and studied (Soong and Juang 1984) that are claimed to reduce the bit rate required to transmit the LPC filter parameters by 25% over other techniques while maintaining the quality and intelligibility of the higher-rate LPC. These new spectral representations are called *line spectrum pairs* (LSP) or *line spectrum frequencies* (LSF).

For a given predictor order M, the LPC coefficients a_i, $i = 1, 2, \ldots, M$, can be used to form a z–domain polynomial representing the LPC inverse filter,

$$A_M(z) = 1 + a_1 z^{-1} + a_2 z^{-2} + \cdots + a_M z^{-M} \tag{5.24}$$

Using (5.24) we can write two additional polynomials, given by

$$P(z) = A_M(z) + z^{-(M+1)} A_M(z^{-1}) \tag{5.25}$$

and

$$Q(z) = A_M(z) - z^{-(M+1)} A_M(z^{-1}) \tag{5.26}$$

Note that the definitions of $P(z)$ and $Q(z)$ are sometimes reversed in the literature. $P(z)$ in (5.25) is an even symmetric polynomial with one root at $z = +1$, and $Q(z)$ is an odd symmetric polynomial with one root at $z = -1$. All remaining roots of $P(z)$ and $Q(z)$ lie on the unit circle, are interlaced with each other, and occur in complex conjugate pairs. Thus, the locations of these roots can be represented by M real numbers that are the angles of the roots ω_i, $i = 1, 2, \ldots, M$, called the line spectrum pairs (LSP). If the roots of the LPC inverse filter $A_M(z)$ are located inside the unit circle, then the roots of $P(z)$ and $Q(z)$ lie on the unit circle.

There are many useful properties of the LSP. The LSP frequencies are related to the spectral content of a signal, where roots of $P(z)$ and $Q(z)$ tend to be close together near formants (spectral peaks). The inverse filter is stable as long as the neighboring roots of $P(z)$ and $Q(z)$ are not the same, and the closer the LSP frequencies are, the nearer the corresponding root of $A_M(z)$ is to the unit circle. Soong and Juang (1984) studied the LSP frequencies by calculating the LPC coefficients and the LSP frequencies for 37,000 20-ms frames of male and female speech data. From histograms of the LSP frequencies, they note that as one moves along the unit circle, the LSP frequencies increase in an orderly fashion and are quite localized. LSP frequency differences only cover the range of 0 to 0.1 in normalized frequency (normalized by the folding frequency), so that a quantizer need only be matched to this dynamic range.

5.2.3   Voiced/Unvoiced Decision and Excitation Signal

The voiced/unvoiced decision is used to control the type of excitation function at the receiver. Broadly, voiced speech is fairly well behaved, while unvoiced speech is random in nature. Because of this characteristic, counting zero crossings of the time domain speech signal can be very helpful in the voiced/unvoiced classification. Mixed voiced and unvoiced excitation (across the full band) has been studied with some success, but recently multiple band mixed voicing has been developed. The impulse excitation commonly employed for voiced speech also has the problem of placing too much energy in the first part of the pitch period, thus producing what is called a high peak-to-rms ratio that (among other things) reduces output speech quality for a fixed b-bit output D-to-A.

The voicing decision is the most problematical part of an LPC system. Determining whether speech is voiced or unvoiced is difficult, and inaccurate voicing can substantially degrade speech quality. If speech is classified as unvoiced too often, the reconstructed speech sounds "breathy"; if speech is declared voiced too often, the reconstructed speech is "buzzy." In fact, even voiced speech is not all voiced across the frequency band. Usually, voiced speech segments have a periodic spectrum up to 2–3 kHz, but the higher frequencies do not exhibit periodicity. As a result, voiced excitation speech in LPC always tends to be somewhat buzzy because of the unnatural periodicity at higher frequencies.

As previously noted, the classical impulse excitation for voiced speech results in a much larger dynamic range for the synthesized speech as compared to the input (original) speech when both have the same energy. Speech researchers call this a high peak-to-rms ratio. Since for any real communications configuration and for digital-to-analog conversion, both signals must have the same dynamic range, the synthesized speech must be scaled down. The result of this scaling is a loss in detail of lower-amplitude values of the time domain waveform and a concomitant degradation in output speech quality. This problem can be avoided by spreading the excitation signal energy over a larger portion of the pitch period. One approach involves applying the impulse excitation first to an all-pass filter and then using the output of the all-pass filter as the excitation to the speech synthesizer. The all-pass filter may have two to eight poles, and it has a constant magnitude response and a nonlinear, nonminimum phase. The energy in the impulse is therefore spread out over several samples (20–60) without distorting the speech synthesizer magnitude response that is known to be perceptually important. Experimental results indicate a significant reduction in peak-to-rms ratio with the all-pass filter as compared to the straight impulse and a noticeable improvement in synthesized speech quality.

A second possibility for spreading out the excitation energy is to develop a fixed generic excitation function. This is done in the U.S. Government Standard LPC-10 (see Section 6.3 and Papamichalis 1987).

5.2.4 Pitch Period Estimation

Pitch period estimation is one of the two thorniest problems inherent in LPC analysis and synthesis. Accurate, real-time pitch extraction is critical to the synthesis of high-quality, highly intelligible speech because, for voiced speech, the pitch period length determines at what intervals the excitation is applied to the speech synthesis filter at the receiver. The general approach to pitch period extraction is to find that value of M_1 that minimizes

$$\varepsilon_1^2 = \langle [s(k) - s(k - M_1)]^2 \rangle \tag{5.27}$$

The M_1 that minimizes (5.27) is the M_1 that maximizes the normalized correlation coefficient

$$\rho = \left[\frac{\langle s(k)s(k - M_1) \rangle^2}{\langle s^2(k) \rangle \langle s^2(k - M_1) \rangle} \right]^{1/2} \tag{5.28}$$

Numerous extensive studies of pitch extraction have been performed, but no single technique has been generally accepted. Those involved in LPC analysis usually develop their own unique approach to extract pitch. Details of a few successful pitch extraction methods could easily fill several volumes, and hence we mention two relatively simple, but commonly used, approaches here.

A block diagram of the simplified inverse filter tracking (SIFT) pitch detector, based on the SIFT algorithm developed by Markel (1972), is shown in Figure 5.6 (Rabiner and Schafer 1978). The figure shows that the speech is low-pass filtered to 900 Hz since only the fundamental pitch frequency is being sought. The low-pass-filtered speech is then decimated and a low-order (often four) inverse filtering operation is performed. The periodicity is then found by searching for peaks in the autocorrelation of the inverse filter output. The desired pitch frequency is then obtained by a 1:5 interpolation of samples. A voiced/unvoiced decision is also generated.

The average magnitude difference function (AMDF) pitch extractor, developed by Ross et al. (1974), has the block diagram shown in Figure 5.7 (Rabiner and Schafer 1978). The basic motivation behind the AMDF algorithm is to achieve reduced complexity compared to autocorrelation-based methods. The AMDF function just computes the sum of the absolute value of the differences between speech samples in two shifted frames of speech data. At shifts where the speech is highly correlated, there will be a null in the AMDF function. As can be seen in Figure 5.7, the speech is also low-pass filtered prior to this calculation. A voiced/unvoiced decision is also produced by examining zero crossings, energy, and AMDF value.

These are but two examples of pitch detectors. Obtaining reliable, automatic, real-time pitch and voicing information for a wide range of speakers is a very difficult problem. If delays of several frames are admissible, comparisons of various indicators in successive frames can be performed to improve the reliability of the estimate. This approach is used in the U.S. Government Standard LPC-10.

5.2.5 Excitation Gain

The computation of the gain at the receiver can be accomplished in two ways, depending on whether energy from previous periods is carried over into the new pitch period or the energy from previous pitch periods is quenched. Atal and Hanauer (1971) carry forward the energy from the previous pitch period into the new pitch period. The gain G of the receiver input amplifier is recomputed every pitch period from the new rms value and new predictor coefficients such that the output speech power equals the input speech power for the same speech segment.

If the remaining energy from the previous pitch period is squelched, then, for voiced speech,

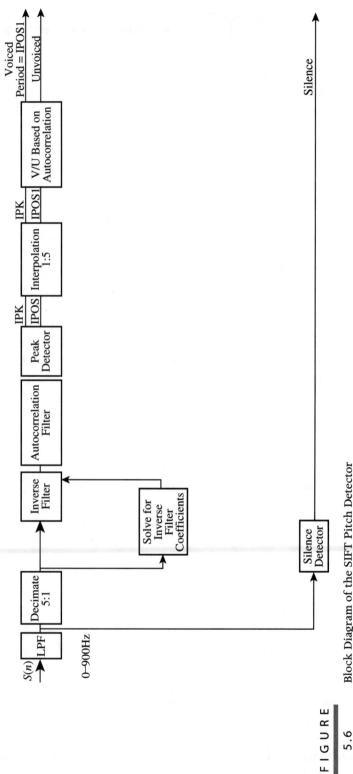

FIGURE

5.6   Block Diagram of the SIFT Pitch Detector

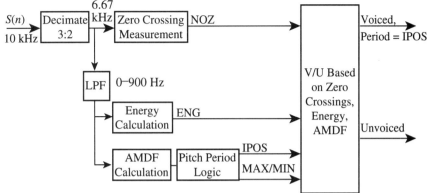

5.7   Block Diagram of the AMDF Pitch Detector

$$G = \sqrt{P} \left[R(0) - \sum_{i=1}^{N} a_i R(i) \right]^{1/2} \tag{5.29}$$

while for unvoiced speech,

$$G = \left[R(0) - \sum_{i=1}^{N} a_i R(i) \right]^{1/2} \tag{5.30}$$

where $P =$ number of samples in the pitch period.

5.2.6   LPC Performance

In the final evaluation, linear predictive coding as in Figure 5.4, when used in a real-time speech coding environment, is not limited by the accuracy of any of the computations but by the fundamentally flawed idea that the linear prediction synthesizer has an excitation that can be classified as either voiced or unvoiced and represented, respectively, by an impulse sequence or white noise. Even if the LPC coefficients, pitch period, and gain are sent perfectly (unquantized), which implies the highest bit rate possible for a given frame rate, the reconstructed speech quality cannot exceed the characteristic synthetic sound imposed by the voiced/unvoiced representation of the excitation.

5.3   Delta Modulation and Differential PCM

A class of speech digitization techniques called waveform-following coders, or simply waveform coders, attempts to reproduce the actual amplitude versus time variation of the input analog signal. Log-PCM (pulse code modulation) is the most straightforward waveform-following approach for speech, but by incorporating more of what is known about the source into the waveform coder, reductions in data rate below PCM can be achieved while still maintaining the required fidelity. An important subclass of waveform coders is designated as either differential encoders, predictive coders, or predictive quantizers. This subclass of coders includes delta modulation (DM) and differential pulse code modulation (DPCM), among others. The principles involved in the operation of differential encoders are *redundancy removal* and *entropy reduction*. Redundancy removal is accomplished by subtracting a predicted value from each input speech sample; entropy reduction is achieved by quantizing the difference between the input sample and the predicted value to a limited number of amplitude levels. Thus, two important components of a differential encoder are the *predictor* and the *quantizer*.

The block diagram of a classic DPCM system is shown in Figure 5.8. The system operates as follows. The predicted value at time instant k based on output values through time $k - 1$, denoted by $\hat{s}(k|k - 1)$, is subtracted from the input signal at time k, designated by $s(k)$, to produce the prediction error signal $e(k)$. The prediction error is then quantized, and the quantized prediction error, $e_q(k)$, is coded (represented as a binary number) for transmission to the receiver. Simultaneously with the coding, $e_q(k)$ is summed with $\hat{s}(k|k - 1)$ to yield a reconstructed version of the input sample, $\hat{s}(k)$. Assuming no channel errors, an identical reconstruction is accomplished at the receiver. At both the transmitter and receiver, the predicted value at time instant $k + 1$ is derived using reconstructed values up through time k, and the procedure is repeated. The terms "forward adaptation" and "backward adaptation" in the figure are defined shortly.

The principal components of the DPCM system are the quantizer, the binary encoder/decoder pair, and the predictor. A symmetric, $2L$-level quantizer with adaptive step size $\Delta(k)$ is shown in Figure 5.9. For $\eta_i \Delta(k) \leq e(k) < \eta_{i+1} \Delta(k)$, $i = 0, 1, 2, \ldots, L - 1$, (with $\eta_0 \triangleq 0$ and $\eta_L \triangleq \infty$), the output is given by $e_q(k) = \xi_{i+1} \Delta(k)$. The normalized step points $\{\eta_i, i = 0, 1, \ldots, L\}$ and output levels $\{\xi_j, j = 1, 2, \ldots, L\}$ can be chosen to produce a uniform or a nonuniform quantizer characteristic. There exist many algorithms for updating the step size $\Delta(k)$, the details of which have been discussed previously.

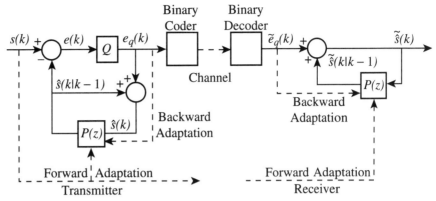

FIGURE

5.8   Classic Differential Pulse Code Modulation (DPCM)

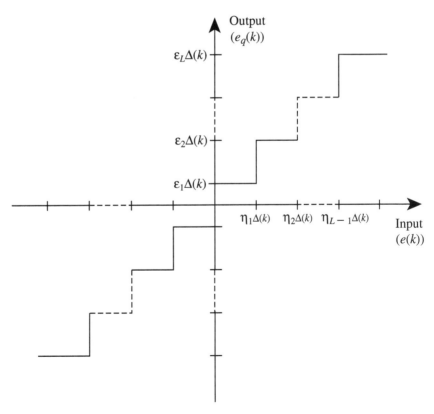

FIGURE

5.9   Symmetric Quantizer with Adaptive Step Size $\Delta(k)$

The binary coder block in Figure 5.8 performs what is called *noiseless or lossless source coding,* which is so named because the coding process is invertible. In its simplest form for a $2L$-level quantizer, $L = 1, 2, \ldots$, the coder assigns a binary word of length $\log_2(2L)$ to each quantization level on a sample-by-sample basis. If there are an odd number of quantization levels, this sample-by-sample encoding may prove inefficient, and the quantized samples may be grouped before coding. For example, if we consider a three-level quantizer, we could assign a two-digit binary word to each of the three quantization levels, thus leaving one two-digit binary word unused, or we could group the quantizer output words into blocks of three ternary symbols, which we then map into five-digit binary words. The former approach requires $1\frac{1}{3}$ bits/quantization symbol, while the latter technique uses $\frac{32}{27} \cong 1.185$ bits/quantization symbol, which is slightly more efficient.

If the probabilities of the quantizer output levels are known or can be estimated, a technique popularly called *entropy coding*, described in Chapter 2, can be employed. This method assigns short codewords to highly probable levels and longer codewords to less probable levels, thus yielding a short *average* codeword length. Since this procedure maps fixed-length blocks into variable-length binary words, buffering is necessary at both the transmitter and receiver.

Other parameters that affect DPCM system performance, and adaptive predictors in particular, are the input signal bandwidth and sampling rate and whether the input signal is low pass or bandpass. Low-pass signals are, on the average, more highly correlated than bandpass signals, and hence, in general, adaptive prediction offers a greater performance improvement for low-pass signals than for bandpass signals. For many applications it may be necessary to adjust the input signal bandwidth and/or sampling rate to achieve an acceptable DPCM system design. More specifically, reducing the input signal bandwidth while holding the sampling rate fixed may yield a perceptually more pleasing reconstructed signal, and for a given input bandwidth, lowering the sampling rate (but not below the Nyquist limit!) can "free up" bits for allocation to transmitting side information or to channel coding. However, decreasing the sampling rate for a fixed bandwidth can reduce the utility of an adaptive predictor since the average sample-to-sample correlation is smaller.

5.3.1 Delta Modulation

The simplest speech differential encoder used today is the delta modulator. Delta modulators employ a first-order predictor,

$$\hat{s}(k|k-1) = a\hat{s}(k-1) \tag{5.31}$$

so that $P(z) = az^{-1}$, where z^{-1} represents a unit delay. Further, the quantizer has only two levels, and the input speech is oversampled so that the waveform variations from sample to sample can be followed accurately by the two-level quantizer. The delta modulator sampling rate is often two to four times the Nyquist rate. For delta modulators to be effective, the quantizer step size, $\Delta(k)$, must be adaptive.

The describing equations for the DM system can be developed with reference to Figures 5.8 and 5.9 as follows. The input to the quantizer is the *prediction error signal*, given by

$$e(k) = s(k) - a\hat{s}(k-1) \tag{5.32}$$

The quantizer output is

$$e_q(k) = \Delta(k) \, \text{sgn}[e(k)] = \begin{cases} +\Delta(k), & e(k) \geq 0 \\ -\Delta(k), & e(k) < 0 \end{cases} \tag{5.33}$$

Denoting the transmitted bit sequence by $b(k)$ and letting $b(k) = +1$ if $e_q(k) = +\Delta(k)$ and $b(k) = -1$ if $e_q(k) = -\Delta(k)$, then equation (5.33) can be rewritten as

$$e_q(k) = \Delta(k)b(k) \tag{5.34}$$

The reconstructed signal from Figures 5.8 and 5.9 (assuming no channel errors) is

$$\hat{s}(k) = a\hat{s}(k-1) + e_q(k) \tag{5.35}$$

The quantization error or noise is defined to be

$$\begin{aligned} n_q(k) &= e_q(k) - e(k) \\ &= \hat{s}(k) - s(k) \end{aligned} \tag{5.36}$$

by using equations (5.32) and (5.35). Note from equation (5.36) that the total reconstruction error is simply the quantization noise, that is, $\hat{s}(k) = s(k) + n_q(k)$.

The primary difference among all existing delta modulators are the *type of implementation* (analog or digital) and the *quantizer step size adaptation rule*. Thus far, we have been describing a digital implementation, and we will continue to emphasize this implementation.

Because of the vast number of step size adaptation algorithms, we describe only a rather general approach here that allows the several trade-offs involved to be highlighted. Most delta modulator step size adaptation algorithms are backward adaptive, so that the step size is adapted based on the transmitted data sequence $\{b(k)\}$. For a typical algorithm, the step size evolves according to the rule

$$\Delta(k) = \beta \Delta(k-1) + (1-\beta)\Delta_{\min} + f(k) \tag{5.37}$$

where $\Delta_{\min}$ is the minimum quantizer step size, $0 < \beta < 1$ is a parameter to be selected, and

$$f(k) = \begin{cases} (1-\beta)[\Delta_{\max} - \Delta_{\min}], & \text{if } b(k) = b(k-1) = b(k-2) \\ 0, & \text{otherwise} \end{cases} \tag{5.38}$$

with $\Delta_{\max} \triangleq$ maximum step size. One of the parameters often used to characterize a delta modulator is the *compression ratio* (CR), defined as

$$\text{CR} \triangleq \Delta_{\max}/\Delta_{\min} \tag{5.39}$$

Equation (5.37) can be rewritten in the more instructive form

$$[\Delta(k) - \Delta_{\min}] = \beta[\Delta(k-1) - \Delta_{\min}] + f(k) \tag{5.40}$$

From equation (5.40), it can be shown that for $\beta < 1$ and $f(k) = 0$, the latter of which occurs during the *idle channel condition* (input speech is zero), $\Delta(k)$ approaches $\Delta_{\min}$. Similarly, if many consecutive positive or many consecutive negative values of $b(k)$ occur, $\Delta(k)$ approaches $\Delta_{\max}$. The parameter β controls how fast $\Delta(k)$ decays to $\Delta_{\min}$ under idle channel conditions, and it is a very important design parameter. The closer β is to one, the better the reconstructed speech quality and intelligibility, but under noisy channel conditions, the closer β is to one, the longer it takes for the transmitter and receiver to resynchronize, and hence the poorer the output speech quality. Clearly, a compromise between ideal and noisy channel conditions must be made. For 16,000 bps, a typical value of β is $\frac{31}{32}$, which causes past step size values to be quickly forgotten. Finally, the fixed predictor coefficient is usually chosen such that $0.95 \le a \le 0.99$ for 16 kbps, with a tendency toward the high end.

Figure 5.10 illustrates the two principal types of distortion in a delta modulated signal, called *granular noise* and *slope overload*. In the figure, T is the sampling interval, $s(t)$ is the input speech, and $\hat{s}(t)$ is the staircase version of $\hat{s}(k)$ prior to filtering. Note that, for simplicity, only a fixed step size is assumed. From time 0 to $t = 6T$, the distortion is classified as granular noise since the output is oscillating somewhat about the input signal. For $t = 7T$ to $t = 14T$, the distortion is called slope overload distortion, and the delta modulator is said

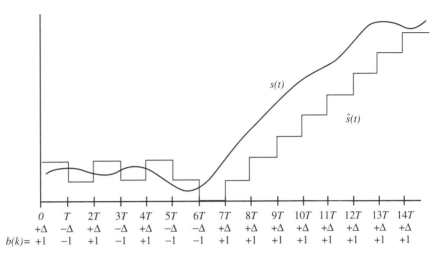

	0	T	2T	3T	4T	5T	6T	7T	8T	9T	10T	11T	12T	13T	14T
	+Δ	−Δ	+Δ	−Δ	+Δ	−Δ	−Δ	+Δ	+Δ	+Δ	+Δ	+Δ	+Δ	+Δ	+Δ
$b(k)=$	+1	−1	+1	−1	+1	−1	−1	+1	+1	+1	+1	+1	+1	+1	+1

5.10   Input Waveform and Typical Fixed DM Output

to be in a condition of slope overload since the output is increasing at its maximum possible rate. It has been claimed that granular noise is more objectionable perceptually, although this conclusion would seem to be application and system (coder) dependent. Although the illustration is only for a fixed step size, both types of distortion are also evident in the output of adaptive DM systems.

A second widely studied delta modulator uses the step size adaptation rule

$$\Delta(k) = M \cdot \Delta^{\beta}(k - 1) \tag{5.41}$$

where $M > 1$ if $b(k) = b(k - 1)$ and $M < 1$ if $b(k) \neq b(k - 1)$. This scheme is usually called *adaptive delta modulation* (ADM). ADM uses only 2 bits to make an adaptation decision, which can yield better ideal channel (storage) performance; however, increased responsiveness may not be advisable for noisy channel communications applications. Again, the parameter β serves to limit the memory of the adaptation logic.

Of course, other adaptation logic variations are possible. One could expand slowly if $b(k) = b(k - 1)$, expand rapidly if $b(k) = b(k - 1) = b(k - 2)$, and contract if $b(k) \neq b(k - 1)$. More bits could also be used. The choice is application dependent.

The choice of the input sampling rate fixes the transmitted data rate. CVSD and ADM produce intelligible, good-quality speech at 32 kbps and have been studied down to 7.2 and 9.6 kbps. However, they are generally applied for data compression at 16–40 kbps.

5.3.2 Nyquist-Sampled Predictive Coders

While a classical differential pulse code modulation (DPCM) system has the same block diagram as a delta modulator, namely that in Figures 5.8 and 5.9, there are some substantive differences. First, the input to the DPCM system transmitter is sampled at or slightly above the Nyquist rate (but much less than twice). Second, the quantizer has more than two levels and may be forward or backward adaptive. Third, the predictor may be higher order, and the predictor coefficients may be fixed or adaptive. A fourth difference is that while partially analog implementations of delta modulators are common, DPCM implementations use discrete-time, discrete-amplitude signals throughout.

The structure of the predictors in differential encoders is usually chosen to mimic an assumed model of the input signal process. For example, for the DPCM system in Figure 5.8 with a speech input, $P(z)$ is usually chosen to be a weighted linear combination of past output values, that is,

$$P(z) = \sum_{i=1}^{N} a_i z^{-i} \tag{5.42}$$

based on the assumption that speech is well modeled by the familiar linear prediction model. However, the early DPCM systems did not rely explicitly on the linear prediction speech model but simply used a single ($N = 1$) fixed coefficient to generate the predicted value, that is,

$$P(z) = a_1 z^{-1} \tag{5.43}$$

Differential encoding systems have the advantage that even if the assumed model is incorrect, the performance degradation is not catastrophic, since a quantized version of the prediction error is transmitted to the receiver. In fact, if the quantization process is ideal, that is, $e_q(k) = e(k)$, then the reconstructed speech at the receiver is identical to the transmitter input speech ($\hat{s}(k) = s(k)$). Of course, this last system is impractical, since it would take an unacceptably high transmission rate to achieve $e_q(k) = e(k)$!

We begin by briefly describing a classical DPCM system for speech inputs with an L-level quantizer and an N-tap predictor. The equations describing the workings of a DPCM system look very similar to those for DM and can be discerned with the aid of Figures 5.8 and 5.9. The analog input speech is low-pass or bandpass filtered to some frequency band within 0 to 4 kHz, and the filtered speech is sampled 8000 times/second and digitized to 12-bit (or higher) accuracy to produce the sequence $\{s(k)\}$. The predicted value given by

$$\hat{s}(k|k-1) = \sum_{i=1}^{N} a_i \hat{s}(k-i) \tag{5.44}$$

where N is the *predictor order*, the coefficients $\{a_i, i = 1, 2, \ldots, N\}$ are called *predictor coefficients* or *tap gains*, and the $\{\hat{s}(\cdot)\}$ sequence consists of past output values, is subtracted from the input sample at time instant k to form the prediction error signal

$$e(k) = s(k) - \hat{s}(k|k-1) \tag{5.45}$$

This prediction error is then quantized to one of L levels by the quantizer to yield

$$e_q(k) = e(k) + n_q(k) \tag{5.46}$$

where $\{n_q(k)\}$ denotes a quantization noise sequence that is not necessarily spectrally white and not necessarily uncorrelated with $\{e(k)\}$. Now, from the block diagrams

$$\begin{aligned} \hat{s}(k) &= \hat{s}(k|k-1) + e_q(k) \\ &= s(k) + n_q(k) \end{aligned} \tag{5.47}$$

where the last equality follows from equations (5.45) and (5.46). It is evident that in the absence of channel errors, the receiver output signal $\hat{s}(k)$ differs from $s(k)$ by an amount exactly equal to the quantization noise and that $\hat{s}(k)$ at the transmitter and $\hat{s}(k)$ at the receiver are the same. Thus, the transmitter contains a duplicate of the receiver, and the $\hat{s}(\cdot)$ values are used in equation (5.44) at the transmitter and receiver to form the predicted value for the next incoming sample. The values of $\hat{s}(k)$ are then converted to analog by filtering and presented to the user. When lossless coding is not employed, the transmitted bit rate is given by the formula

$$R = f_s \log_2 L \text{ bps} \tag{5.48}$$

where f_s is the sampling rate (8000 here) and L is the number of quantizer levels. Of course, the quantization levels must be represented in terms of a binary code for transmission to the receiver.

The classic DPCM structure in Figure 5.8 is motivated by the linear prediction model for speech, which is an all-pole model. Of course, it is well known

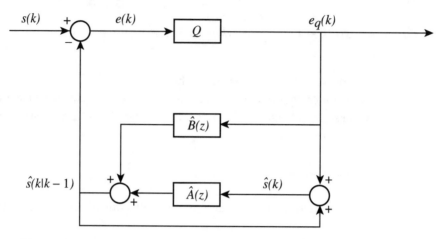

FIGURE

F I G U R E

5.11   Differential Encoder Transmitter with a Pole-Zero Predictor

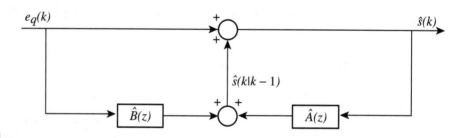

F I G U R E

5.12   Receiver for a Differential Encoder Transmitter with a Pole-Zero Predictor

that an accurate model of the vocal tract should contain zeros as well as poles, and a DPCM system transmitter based on a pole-zero model is illustrated in Figure 5.11.

In comparing the predictors in Figures 5.8 and 5.11, we note that the predictor transfer function, which is the transfer function from $e_q(k)$ to $\hat{s}(k|k-1)$, is $P(z)/[1 - P(z)]$ for Figure 5.8 and $[\hat{A}(z) + \hat{B}(z)]/[1 - \hat{A}(z)]$ for Figure 5.11. Thus, both predictors have zeros in addition to poles. However, the predictor zeros are fixed by the pole locations in Figure 5.8, while for Figure 5.11, the zeros and poles can be specified independently. We will use the term "pole-zero predictor" to denote a predictor of the form in Figure 5.11, but not the more restrictive form in Figure 5.8. The receiver for a differential encoder transmitter with a pole-zero predictor is shown in Figure 5.12.

Although the pole-zero predictor in Figures 5.11 and 5.12 can be motivated by an assumed pole-zero model for speech, the original impetus for its use came from a need to obtain good prediction performance in the presence of transmission errors. To understand this motivation for employing a pole-zero predictor as in Figures 5.11 and 5.12, we must examine in more detail the way the various predictor structures influence the system memory. In particular, we must determine how long a single value of $e_q(k)$ or $\tilde{e}_q(k)$ in Figures 5.8, 5.11, and 5.12 can influence the reconstructed output speech. This is especially important for noisy channel applications where $e_q(k) \neq \tilde{e}_q(k)$. Since the receivers in Figures 5.8 and 5.12 involve recursions on past $\hat{s}(k)$, these receivers are said to have an infinite impulse response (IIR), or to be IIR systems. The fact that the receivers in Figures 5.8 and 5.12 have an infinite impulse response follows from using synthetic division on the $e_q(k)$-to-$\hat{s}(k)$ transfer function to show that $\hat{s}(k)$ can be represented as an infinite sum of weighted past values of $e_q(k)$. This weighted sum is the receiver impulse response. The number of significant terms in this infinite sum depends on the weights, which, in turn, depend on the predictor coefficients. By properly selecting the predictor coefficients, the receiver memory, or the number of reconstructed values, $\hat{s}(k)$, affected by a single value of $e_q(k)$, can be made quite small or very large. Usually, for good predictor performance, a relatively long memory of, say, 30 or more samples is desirable. However, in the presence of transmission errors, a long memory can be a disadvantage since a single transmission error can affect the reconstructed output for many samples. This dichotomy highlights an important differential encoding system design trade-off.

A finite impulse response (FIR) receiver can be obtained by setting $\hat{A}(z) \equiv 0$ in Figure 5.12. In this situation, the number of past values of $e_q(k)$ used to synthesize $\hat{s}(k)$ is equal to the order of the polynomial $\hat{B}(z)$. When we let $\tilde{A}(z) = 0$ in Figures 5.11 and 5.12, we are approximating the usual IIR linear prediction model for speech by the first few terms in its impulse response. As a result, past $e_q(k)$ values affect $\hat{s}(k)$ only over a relatively short period of time and then are shifted out of the predictor. This is an important property in the presence of transmission errors, since erroneous $e_q(k)$ at the receiver only affect the output for a few samples.

With this short discussion of receiver memory in mind, we now reconsider the motivation for using a pole-zero predictor to obtain good prediction performance in the presence of transmission errors. Again, we must strike a compromise between good predictor performance, which implies a long memory, and the deleterious effects of channel errors, which suggest a shorter memory. The general approach to satisfying these contradictory requirements has been to use very few poles (2–4) with restricted coefficient values and several zeros (6–10).

5.3.3   Short-Term Predictor Adaptation

To extract the maximum possible performance from differential encoding systems for a wide variety of inputs, including different speakers and perhaps data signals, it is necessary to adapt the predictor parameters to the changing input signals. There are two quite different approaches to parameter adaptation in differential encoding systems (see Figure 5.8). One approach, called *forward adaptive prediction*, uses various algorithms to compute the desired parameters based on the actual input signal. Of course, the transmitter and receiver must use the same predictor, and since the input signal is not available at the receiver, the computed parameters must be quantized, coded, and transmitted to the receiver to allow the output signal to be generated. For a fixed total transmitted date rate, this approach reduces the rate available to transmit the quantized prediction error sequence $\{e_q(k)\}$. The second approach adapts the predictor parameters on a sample-by-sample basis using past values of the reconstructed sequence $\{\hat{s}(k)\}$, which is available at both the transmitter and receiver. This approach has been designated as *backward adaptive* since it does not require additional information to be transmitted to the receiver. Thus, for backward adaptive schemes, all of the total transmitted data rate is allocated to $\{e_q(k)\}$.

Forward adaptive predictors have been studied often in conjunction with both transversal and lattice predictor structures. The forward adaptation is usually accomplished by collecting several milliseconds of the input speech data into a frame or block and using the standard autocorrelation linear predictive analysis technique described in Section 5.2 to calculate either the transversal filter parameters or the reflection coefficients. No matter which predictor structure is used, the parameters to be transmitted are usually represented as reflection coefficients or LSFs for transmission because of their desirable sensitivity properties. The types of windows (such as rectangular or Hamming), the amount of preemphasis, the amount of frame overlap, the number of coefficients, and other details vary with different implementations, but the philosophy of making these various selections is similar to that used for low-bit-rate LPC systems.

Specifically, forward adaptive predictors calculate the predictor coefficients that minimize

$$\varepsilon^2 = \sum_{k=0}^{K} \left[s(k) - \sum_{i=1}^{N} a_i s(k - i) \right]^2 \tag{5.49}$$

where K is chosen such that 5–20 ms of speech data are used in the calculation. Since equation (5.49) uses the transmitter input $s(k)$ (see Figure 5.8), which is not available at the receiver, the set of coefficients must be transmitted to the receiver if the two predictors are to be identical, hence the name *forward prediction*. The details of forward adaptive prediction in waveform coders are the same as for computing and transmitting the LPC coefficients as discussed in Section 5.2.

Numerous algorithms have been proposed for the backward adaptation of predictor parameters. Backward adaptive algorithms may operate on a sample-by-sample basis, in contrast to the block update of forward adaptation, and a new set of predictor parameters is calculated immediately after each new output value is generated. Clearly, predictor parameters to be used to predict the input at time instant k, $s(k)$, can only use output values through time instant $k - 1$. Alternatively, backward adaptation can be performed on a block basis using only past reconstructed output values. This approach is taken in LD-CELP as used in G.728 (see Section 6.8). We emphasize the sample-by-sample algorithms here.

For the direct form predictor in Figure 5.8, mostly gradient and Kalman-type algorithms, which attempt to minimize the mean squared prediction error, have been employed for coefficient adaptation. These algorithms typically compute the predictor coefficient estimates in a recursive fashion by adding to the coefficient estimates at the preceding time instant an incremental change that is a weighted version of the quantized prediction error at the most recently available time instant. The differences among the various algorithms center on the methods for computing the weight given the quantized prediction error as a function of time. Because they are recursive, these algorithms are IIR systems themselves. Hence, to limit the memory of these algorithms, it is common, when computing a new coefficient estimate, to multiply the immediately preceding estimate by a positive scalar less than one (but near one) to cause past estimates to be forgotten over an acceptable period of time. Multiplying the past coefficient estimate by this damping factor causes the coefficient estimates to decay toward zero over a long period of time. Better performance is usually obtained if the coefficients are caused to decay to some fixed average set by adding in the chosen fixed value weighted by one minus the damping factor.

Backward adaptive prediction algorithms run the gamut from quite simple to relatively complex. One of the simpler algorithms, often called a *gradient algorithm*, updates the predictor coefficients $\{a_i(k), i = 1, 2, \ldots, N\}$ in Figure 5.8 according to

$$a_i(k+1) = \alpha a_i(k) + G(k+1)e_q(k+1) \qquad (5.50)$$

where $a_i(k)$ is the ith coefficient at time k, α is a parameter to be selected ($0 < \alpha < 1$ and usually α is near 1), $e_q(k+1)$ is the quantized prediction error at time $k+1$, and $G(k+1)$ is a vector gain defined as

$$G^T(k+1) = g[\hat{s}(k)\hat{s}(k-1)\ldots\hat{s}(k-N+1)]/ \left\{ \delta + \sum_{j=0}^{N-1} \hat{s}^2(k-j) \right\}$$

$$(5.51)$$

where g and δ are scalar parameters selected by experiment.

Gradient algorithms can also be defined for the pole-zero structure in Figures 5.11 and 5.12. Specifically, letting $\hat{\mathbf{a}}^T(k) = [\hat{a}_1(k)\hat{a}_2(k)\ldots\hat{a}_N(k)]$, the coefficients corresponding to the poles are adapted according to

$$\hat{\mathbf{a}}(k+1) = \alpha_a \hat{\mathbf{a}}(k) + K_a(k+1)e_q(k+1) \qquad (5.52)$$

where α_a is a parameter and

$$K_a(k+1) = \frac{g_a \hat{S}_N(k)}{100 + \hat{S}_N^T(k)\hat{S}_N(k)} \qquad (5.53)$$

with $\hat{S}_N^T(k) = [\hat{s}(k)\hat{s}(k-1)\ldots\hat{s}(k-N+1)]$ and g_a an experimentally selected gain. The coefficients corresponding to the zeros, denoted by the vector $\hat{\mathbf{b}}^T(k) = [\hat{b}_1(k)\hat{b}_2(k)\ldots\hat{b}_M(k)]$, are adapted via the algorithm

$$\hat{\mathbf{b}}(k+1) = \alpha_b \hat{\mathbf{b}}(k) + K_b(k+1)e_q(k+1) \qquad (5.54)$$

with

$$K_b(k+1) = \frac{g_b E_{qM}(k)}{100 + E_{qM}^T(k)E_{qM}(k)} \qquad (5.55)$$

where α_b and g_b are parameters and $E_{qM}^T(k) = [e_q(k)e_q(k-1)\ldots e_q(k-M+1)]$.

Simplified versions of these algorithms are employed in ITU-T Recommedation G.726.

5.4 Embedded DPCM

In communications and computer networks, it is sometimes advantageous to allow the network to "shed load" whenever traffic gets too high. This can be accomplished if the network switches were allowed to simply drop least significant bits in a transmitted data word, without the source being reencoded. Interestingly, not all digital representations of sources admit this possibility without substantial distortion in the reconstructed source. In fact, without special care, most compressed sequences cannot withstand dropped bits. Compression methods called *embedded codes* were developed to be used in these situations (Goodman 1980).

DPCM systems can be particularly sensitive to dropping even the least significant bit. To see this, consider the curves in Figure 5.13, where the top line represents DPCM systems that are designed to operate at 8, 7, 6, 5, 4, 3, and 2 bits/sample (without lossless coding), called *adjusted DPCM*. Thus, this curve represents the best possible performance of this DPCM system at these bit rates. The bottom solid line is the performance of a DPCM system that transmits 8 bits/sample, but lower rates are attained by dropping one or more of the least significant bits. For example, dropping only 1 bit yields the point on the solid line at 7 bits, which is about 6 dB worse than the adjusted DPCM result. Clearly, the performance loss is undesirable.

A block diagram of an embedded DPCM system is shown in Figure 5.14. Comparing the encoder to a standard DPCM encoder, it is evident that there is a second quantizer inside the prediction loop. Quantizers Q_1 and Q_2 are embedded quantizers, as discussed in Chapter 4, where Q_2 has fewer levels than Q_1. The result is that the prediction loop always uses the coarsely quantized prediction error signal so that dropping bits does not change the operation of the IIR feedback loop. This is also true at the receiver or decoder, and so dropping least significant bits only affects the accuracy of the prediction error signal added in to reconstruct the speech at the decoder. This points out another difference between embedded DPCM and standard DPCM—namely, the encoder does not have an explicit replica of the decoder.

The performance of embedded DPCM is also shown in Figure 5.13 where the performance line falls almost exactly on top of the adjusted DPCM system. The result shown is an experimental result for one speech sentence, but it agrees well with Goodman's theoretical result. One caveat is that this low loss is for a first-order predictor, and the gap between embedded DPCM and adjusted DPCM increases for higher-order predictors. However, the loss by dropping bits in regular DPCM can be more substantive for higher-order prediction as well.

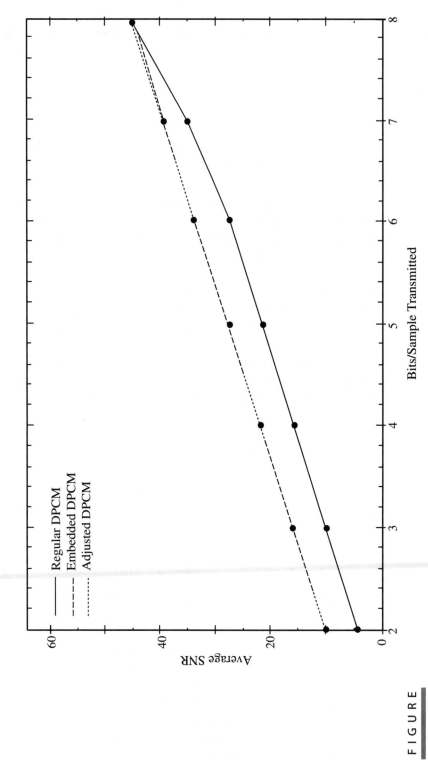

Average SNR

Bits/Sample Transmitted

Regular DPCM
Embedded DPCM
Adjusted DPCM

Comparison of Embedded DPCM to Regular DPCM

F I G U R E

5.13

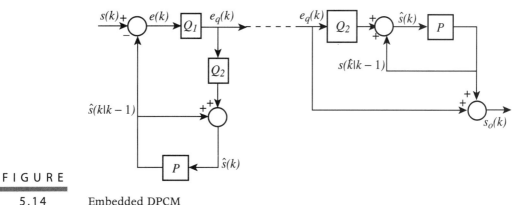

FIGURE

5.14   Embedded DPCM

5.5   Multipulse Linear Predictive Coding (MPLPC)

Multipulse linear predictive coding (MPLPC) still has the predictive coding structure of LPC and ADPCM, but it is a significant departure from these systems in that it is an analysis-by-synthesis coder that employs perceptual weighting. MPLPC tries to improve on LPC by doing a better job in modeling the excitation, but without directly quantizing and transmitting the prediction residual as in ADPCM and related waveform coders. To accomplish this, MPLPC allows several (multiple) impulses to be used as the synthesis filter excitation over a frame of speech. The number of pulses is usually selected in advance and is affected by a trade-off between complexity and speech quality. It was originally felt that multipulse LPC might obviate the need for pitch extraction, but for high-quality speech at 16 kbps and below, where the excitation search complexity is justifiable, a pitch prediction loop is required (Atal and Remde 1982; Singhal and Atal 1984).

MPLPC has produced good-quality speech at 6.4 kbps. A block diagram representing a typical MPLPC system is shown in Figure 5.15. It is evident from this figure that there are many steps in a high-quality speech coder, but the previously unseen analysis-by-synthesis step is represented by the "Pulse Search" block. The analysis-by-synthesis search procedure is shown diagrammatically by Figure 5.16. To elaborate on this figure, consider a typical input frame of, say, 80 samples. In MPLPC, all excitation samples are set to zero except for eight impulses, whose amplitude, polarity, and location in the frame are to be determined. If there are no constraints on location, amplitude, or polarity, there are an infinite number of possibilities, so the usual procedure in MPLPC is to place each of the eight pulses and determine their amplitude and polarity one pulse at a time. This approach is suboptimal, but necessary to keep the complexity

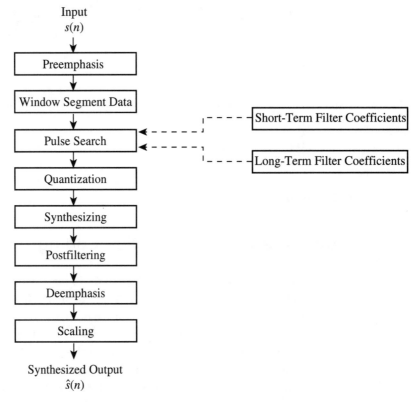

Input
$s(n)$

Preemphasis

Window Segment Data

Short-Term Filter Coefficients

Pulse Search

Long-Term Filter Coefficients

Quantization

Synthesizing

Postfiltering

Deemphasis

Scaling

Synthesized Output
$\hat{s}(n)$

FIGURE

5.15   A Block Diagram of MPLPC

manageable. The sequential procedure is shown in Figure 5.16 and is described in the following. Suppose that the analysis frame size is N samples, that m_i and g_i are the ith pulse location and the ith pulse amplitude, respectively, and that the amplitudes and positions of $I - 1$ pulses have been determined. The search for the Ith pulse location and amplitude proceeds as follows.

The excitation input is

$$u(n) = \sum_{i=1}^{I} g_i \delta(n - m_i) \tag{5.56}$$

so the synthesized output is

$$\hat{s}(n) = u(n) * h(n)$$

$$= \sum_{i=1}^{I} g_i h(n - m_i) \tag{5.57}$$

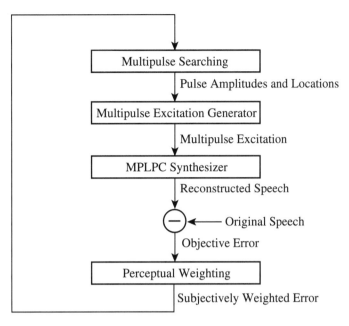

5.16   Block Diagram of Analysis-by-Synthesis Pulse Search Method

The error weighting has the transfer function

$$W(z) = \frac{1 + \sum_{i=1}^{p} a_i z^{-i}}{1 + \sum_{i=1}^{p} a_i \gamma^i z^{-i}} \tag{5.58}$$

with time domain response $w(n)$, and hence the perceptually weighted error is

$$e_w(n) = (s(n) - \hat{s}(n)) * w(n)$$

$$= s_w(n) - \hat{s}_w(n)$$

$$= s_w(n) - \sum_{i=1}^{I} g_i h_w(n - m_i) \tag{5.59}$$

where $s_w(n)$, $\hat{s}_w(n)$, and $h_w(n)$ are weighted signals of $s(n)$, $\hat{s}(n)$, and $h(n)$, respectively. We can now write the total weighted squared error as

$$E_w(n) = \sum_{n=1}^{N} e_w^2(n)$$

$$= \sum_{n=1}^{N} \left[s_w(n) - \sum_{i=1}^{I} g_i h_w(n - m_i) \right]^2 \tag{5.60}$$

which upon minimizing with respect to g_I yields

$$g_I = \frac{\sum_{n=1}^{N} s_w(n)h_w(n - m_I) - \sum_{i=1}^{I-1} g_i \sum_{n=1}^{N} h_w(n - m_i)h_w(n - m_I)}{\sum_{n=1}^{N} h_w(n - m_I)h_w(n - m_I)}$$

(5.61)

Under the assumptions of the autocorrelation method, (5.61) can be rewritten as

$$g_I = \frac{R_{hs}(m_I) - \sum_{i=1}^{I-1} g_i R_{hh}(m_i - m_I)}{R_{hh}(0)}$$

(5.62)

where $R_{hh}(\cdot)$ is the autocorrelation of $h_w(n)$, and $R_{hs}(\cdot)$ is the crosscorrelation between $h_w(n)$ and $s_w(n)$. The optimum pulse location $1 \leq m_I \leq N$ is that position that maximizes g_I in (5.61) and (5.62). Since $R_{hh}(0)$ is fixed in an analysis frame, $R_{hh}(0)$ can be removed from the iterative search routine. After a pulse is allocated to a location, this location is excluded from future searches within the present frame. If the search frame size is equal to the error minimization frame size, the contributions of the pulses at the end of the search frame are small, thus generating a disproportionate number of pulses at the beginning of the frame. To partially compensate for this effect, the error minimization frame size may be selected to be slightly longer than the search frame size.

To simplify the search procedure in MPLPC, Kroon developed a variation, called *regular pulse excitation* (RPE) coding, where the nonzero pulse locations are preset at a chosen spacing (Kroon, Deprettere, and Sluyter 1986). This eliminates the need to search all possible pulse locations; one need only search over a very few shifts of the sequence since it is periodic. For example, if we allow eight nonzero pulses in a 40-sample frame, there will be four zero amplitude values between each pair of nonzero pulses, so only five sets of pulse locations need to be searched. The pulse amplitudes still have to be selected and are usually selected one at a time.

5.6   Code Excited Linear Predictive Coding

Code excited linear predictive coding (CELP) is currently the most popular method for speech coding at rates below 9.6 kbps. It is an attempt, and a successful one we might add, to extend the analysis-by-synthesis approach used in multipulse LPC to lower bit rates. The general idea is to replace the multipulse excitation with a finite number of stored sequences called a *codebook*. The codebook encoding scheme in CELP relies on two facts:

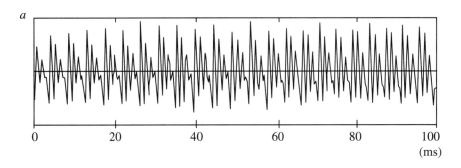

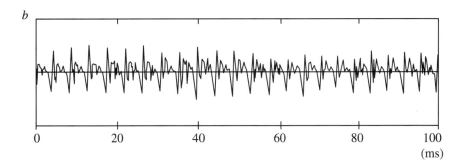

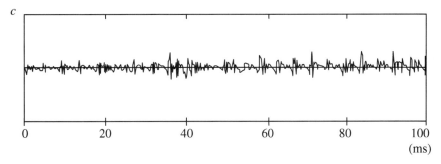

FIGURE

5.17   Redundancy Removal from Speech Signals: (*a*) Speech Waveform; (*b*) Short-Term Removed Signal; (*c*) Long- and Short-Term Removed Signal

1. After all of the redundancy has been removed from a speech signal using long- and short-term predictors, the remaining signal can often be accurately modeled by a sequence of independent, identically distributed random variables, called an *innovation* or *excitation sequence* (illustrated by Figure 5.17).

2. A finite number of possible sequences can be found that, for the purposes of encoding, accurately approximate the totality of perceptually important

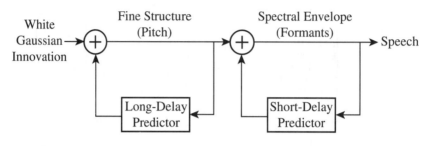

5.18   Speech Production Model

excitation sequences that can occur in any speech segment. It is this set of excitation sequences that is called the codebook.

As result of these two facts, speech coding of a given block consists of finding the best long- and short-term linear predictors, driving them with all possible excitations, and then finding the sequence in the codebook that produces a synthetic speech signal that best approximates the input speech in the sense of the sum of the squared perceptually weighted reconstruction errors. The long- and short-term predictor information and the binary word corresponding to the chosen excitation sequence from the codebook are all sent to the receiver for synthesis.

Atal and Schroeder (1984) were the first to successfully demonstrate the promise of the code excited approach, and since the basic principles of CELP coding are exemplified in their work, we describe it in more detail here.

In general, the speech process can be modeled by a long-term predictor that accounts for the spectral fine structure or pitch followed by a short-term predictor that accounts for the spectral envelope or formants (see Figure 5.18). In the original studies of stochastic coding, the excitation of this cascade of predictors was a white Gaussian noise sequence (Atal and Schroeder 1984). To encode speech using this structure, the long- and short-term predictors are computed every 5–25 ms using techniques virtually identical to those used in LPC. However, the similarity with LPC ends here, since the goal of stochastic coding or CELP is to improve on the quality of LPC and to provide an approach less sensitive to pitch extraction and not dependent on a voicing decision, as is LPC.

The long-term predictor in multipulse LPC and code excited LPC, sometimes replaced with a parallel form called an *adaptive codebook,* usually has one or three taps and is chosen to minimize the sum of the squared prediction errors (Atal 1982):

$$\varepsilon_p^2 = \left\langle \left[s(k) - \sum_{i=1}^{3} \beta_i s(k - M_1 - i + 2) \right]^2 \right\rangle \tag{5.63}$$

where $s(k)$ is the input speech sequence and $< \cdot >$ denotes time averaging over a frame length. The pitch lag M_1 is selected as that value of m that maximizes

$$\rho = \left[\frac{\langle s(k)s(k - m) \rangle}{\langle s^2(k) \rangle \langle s^2(k - m) \rangle} \right]^{1/2} \tag{5.64}$$

After M_1 is found, the coefficients $\{\beta_1, \beta_2, \beta_3\}$ are selected to minimize (5.63), which yields the set of linear simultaneous equations

$$\begin{bmatrix} \phi(M_1 - 1, M_1 - 1) & \phi(M_1 - 1, M_1) & \phi(M_1 - 1, M_1 + 1) \\ \phi(M_1, M_1 - 1) & \phi(M_1, M_1) & \phi(M_1, M_1 + 1) \\ \phi(M_1 + 1, M_1 - 1) & \phi(M_1 + 1, M_1) & \phi(M_1 + 1, M_1 + 1 \end{bmatrix} \begin{bmatrix} \beta_1 \\ \beta_2 \\ \beta_3 \end{bmatrix}$$

$$= \begin{bmatrix} \phi(0, M_1 - 1) \\ \phi(0, M_1) \\ \phi(0, M_1 + 1) \end{bmatrix} \tag{5.65}$$

with

$$\phi(i, j) = \langle s(k - i)s(k - j) \rangle \tag{5.66}$$

where $< \cdot >$ indicates averaging over all k in the frame. In order to guarantee the stability of this predictor while still maintaining a high prediction gain, it is necessary to use the stability tests and scaling procedures developed by Ramachandran and Kabal (1989).

If we allocate 2 kbps for the excitation and we assume 5-ms frames or blocks at a sampling rate of 8000 samples/second, then we are allowed to transmit only 10 bits/block, which is an average rate of 0.25 bits/sample. Since a 10-bit word can represent a maximum of 1024 possible sequences, we can have 1024 possible excitation sequences for each 5-ms block. These 1024 sequences are called the *codebook*, and once a codebook is chosen (offline), it is fixed for all speech utterances to be coded. In Atal and Schroeder (1984), the 1024 possible excitation sequences are just 1024 output sequences of a zero mean, unit variance Gaussian random number generator.

The actual encoding then consists of applying each of these 1024 random sequences to the speech model in Figure 5.18 and comparing each of the 1024 synthesized output sequences with the input speech in the current block. The synthesized output that gives the best fit to the input speech is chosen to represent the block. Atal and Schroeder (1984) use a perceptual weighting

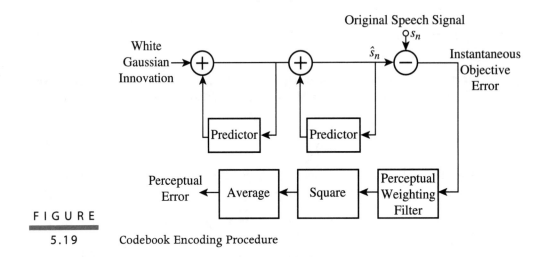

5.19   Codebook Encoding Procedure

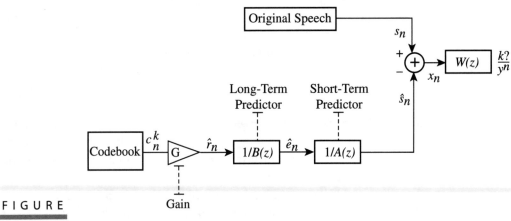

FIGURE

5.20   Codebook Search in Code-Excited LPC

criterion to determine the best fit (see Figure 5.19). The best output can be sent to the receiver or stored by using 10 bits to indicate the chosen excitation and by whatever coding methods are selected to encode the long- and short-term predictors. The search for the best excitation sequence in a given codebook is more clearly illustrated by Figure 5.20. In this figure, $W(z)$ represents the perceptual weighting function.

The complexity of this encoding method is also high, however, since for each block, all 1024 synthesized utterances must be compared to the input for each block. In Atal and Schroeder (1984), this required 125 times real-time operation on a Cray-1 computer. However, this requirement has been significantly reduced.

The surprising thing about random codebooks is that a relatively small number of codes are required to yield good performance. In Atal and Schroeder (1984), 1024 codes were used to represent 40 samples. Although 1024 seems like a large number, note that if we allowed only a single, independent binary digit for each of the 40 speech samples, we would have $2^{40} = 10^{12}$ possible sequences. Viewed from this perspective, 1024 is relatively small. Perhaps even more surprising is the fact that some systems use codebooks as small as 256.

In addition to random codebooks, researchers have investigated convolutional codes, vector quantization, permutation codes, and experimentally designed codebooks. As is often true in speech coding, some codebooks work better for some speakers and utterances than for others. Of course, including more sequences in the codebook improves performance but also leads to higher complexity and increased data rate.

The offline training of excitation codebooks can produce important perceptual improvements in synthesized speech quality, and this seems to be the rule rather than the exception. However, the most recent breakthrough is that all of the pulses in a codebook can have the same amplitude level and the synthesized speech quality is not affected. Thus, if an efficient way to search for good excitation pulse locations can be found, the code excited analysis-by-synthesis search is greatly simplified. As is developed in Chapter 6, this is the essence of algebraic CELP (ACELP).

The research on code excited linear prediction in recent years has emphasized investigations into finding better codebook excitation sequences, simpler implementation procedures, new methods for modeling the long-term pitch excitation, and techniques for efficiently encoding the short-term coefficients and other side information. Future work is likely to include new approaches to modeling and to including perceptual weighting.

Further discussions of code excited approaches are deferred to Chapter 6, where several of the current standards utilize this coding paradigm.

5.7   Perceptual Weighting and Postfiltering

Perceptual weighting is absolutely essential to the success of the analysis-by-synthesis coders such as MPLPC and CELP. Using the unweighted sum of the squared errors in the search for the best excitation in the analysis-by-synthesis approach does not yield acceptable quality speech. Additionally, most of the

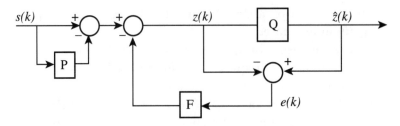

FIGURE

5.21   Equivalent DPCM Structure

CELP coders, when pushed to the limit of ever lower rates, exhibit granular-sounding noise in the reconstructed speech even when perceptual weighting is used in the excitation codebook search. The effects of this noise on the reconstructed speech can be reduced by placing a postfilter at the decoder output. The form of the perceptual weighting used in the analysis-by-synthesis codebook search and the form of the transfer functions used in postfiltering both have their origins in the noise spectral shaping technique employed in adaptive predictive coders in the late 1970s (Atal and Schroeder 1979).

Figure 5.21 illustrates how noise spectral shaping is implemented in predictive waveform coders. The quantization noise is fed back through a digital filter that shapes the noise spectrum in such a way that it is more pleasing perceptually. The total noise power within the passband remains the same as without shaping, but the noise power is relocated in the frequency domain such that the speech signal components mask, or cover up, the presence of the noise. The form of the noise spectral shaping filter is chosen to be related to the calculated linear prediction model for the current frame of the input speech. Using this information, the shaping filter, $F(z)$, attempts to push more noise power into bands where there is significant speech signal power, that is, where the formants are located. Generally, speech quality is enhanced if the signal spectrum is above the noise spectrum at all frequencies and if the signal-to-noise ratio is relatively constant across the frequency band of interest.

To illustrate these ideas, consider the predictive coder in Figure 5.21. The power spectrum of the noise in the reconstructed output is proportional to

$$S_n(f) = \left| \frac{1 - F(e^{j2\pi ft})}{1 - P(e^{j2\pi ft})} \right|^2 \tag{5.67}$$

Atal and Schroeder propose that the noise shaping filter be chosen as $F(z) = P(\alpha z^{-1})$, where α is between 0 and 1. With $\alpha = 0$, $F(z) = 0$, and there is no noise shaping, just an open loop predictive coder. When α is chosen to be 1, the shaping filter cancels out the effect of the decoder synthesis filter on the noise spectrum, and we have DPCM. These ideas are made more specific in Figure 5.22. (Note that we do not assume a flat reconstruction error spectrum for DPCM as the early references do in order to clarify their point. What is shown in Figure 5.22 is the actual reconstruction error spectrum for the chosen frame.) The input speech spectrum and the noise spectrum in the reconstructed output for one frame are plotted in Figure 5.22(a) for $\alpha = 0$ and for $\alpha = 1$ in Figure 5.22(b). The output speech corresponding to (a) can have a rumbling sound due to the closeness of the speech and noise spectra at the lowest formant, while that for (b) has a granular-sounding distortion because of the low signal-to-noise ratio in between formants. For $\alpha = 0.9$, the result in Figure 5.22(c) is obtained, which gives a much more pleasing sound than the other two. By inspection of (a) through (c), the reason for this result is clear—the noise spectrum is much more uniformly below the speech spectrum across the band in (c) when compared to (a) and (b).

By drawing on these prior results, researchers incorporated perceptual weighting filters of the form

$$H(z) = \frac{1 - P(z/\beta)}{1 - P(z/\alpha)}, \quad 0 < \beta < \alpha < 1 \tag{5.68}$$

in analysis-by-synthesis coders. Appropriately selecting the parameters in the numerator and denominator polynomials gives substantially improved speech over straight squared error analysis-by-synthesis encoding. Performance is not too sensitive to the actual parameter values.

Postfilters also employ a short-term filter similar to that used for perceptual weighting inside the codebook search loop; however, this filter has a downward spectral tilt, as illustrated in Figure 5.23 for various α, that can muffle the output speech while reducing the noise. To counteract this, a high-frequency emphasis filter is included in postfilters, which yields the result shown in Figure 5.24. In general, a postfilter to enhance the spectral fine structure is also employed. Finally, after all of this postdecoder spectral shaping, the gains in successive frames of speech may exhibit discontinuities, and hence a gain correction must also be part of a postfilter. A general form for a postfilter, taken from Chen and Gersho (1995), is shown in Figure 5.25. All of the components are present, and their paper gives a clear discussion of both the motivating factors and the performance that can be expected from postfiltering.

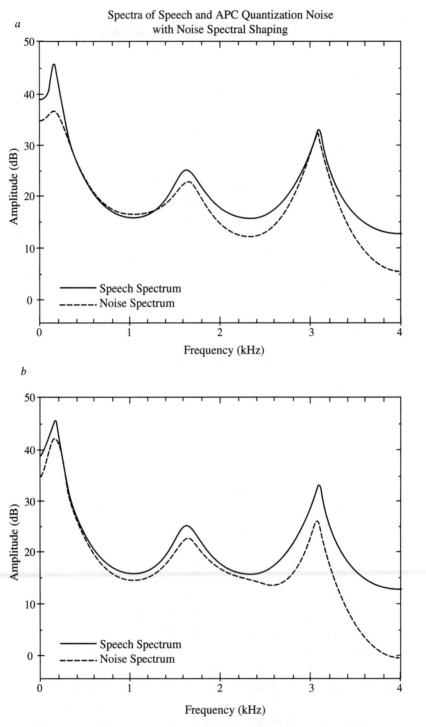

FIGURE

5.22

Noise Spectral Shaping in Waveform Coders: (a) No Noise Spectral Shaping ($\alpha = 0$);
(b) Maximum Noise Spectral Shaping ($\alpha = 1$); (c) Perceptually Best Noise Spectral
Shaping ($\alpha = 0.9$)

c

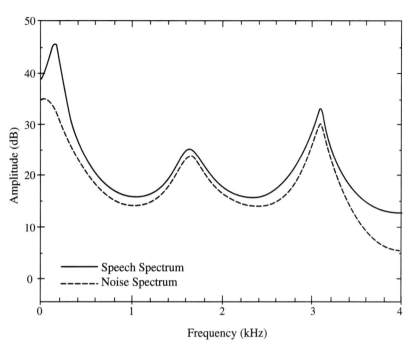

5.22   *(continued)*

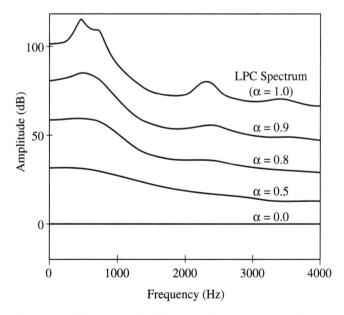

F I G U R E

5.23   Spectrum of Speech and All Pole Postfilter Frequency Responses

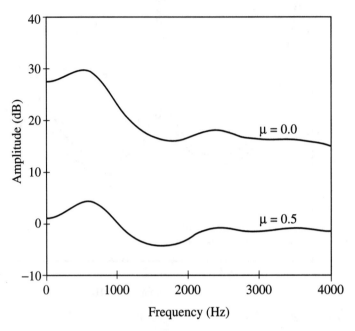

5.24   Frequency Response of Pole-Zero Postfilters

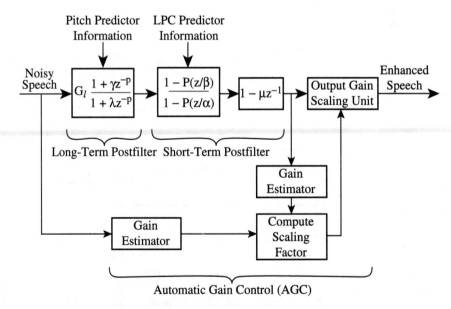

5.25   General Form for a Postfilter

5.8   Summary

This chapter has laid the foundations for predictive coding of speech as implemented in many of the existing and evolving speech coding standards. Note how the predictive coders discussed here have a decoder structure as shown in Figure 5.1, and much effort is put into finding a good synthesis filter and a proper excitation sequence. There are other "bells and whistles" that appear in standards specifications that are important to achieving the performance required in the numerous applications of speech coding, and these additional techniques are discussed in the sections on standards as they are needed. With the information in this chapter, you should be prepared to understand the basic operation of speech predictive coders and have enough details to know where to start in developing your own applications.

6   Linear Predictive Speech Coding Standards

6.1   Introduction

There has been enormous activity recently in establishing speech coding standards both nationally and internationally. These standards have a substantial impact on telecommunications systems, industry, and consumers. For many years, about the only speech coding standard around was G.711, log-PCM. The U.S. federal government then began to develop its own standards for voice coding with the broader goal of having secure voice communications. While this effort has continued, the ITU-T (formerly the CCITT) has accelerated its efforts in establishing digital voice standards, and simultaneously, digital cellular mobile radio has become important throughout the world. Today speech coding standards are seemingly being set for every imaginable application, and even when a standard has not been set for a particular application, established standards still have an impact because of a need for compatibility or a desire to use a "known" approach.

Table 6.1 lists most of the established speech coding standards. In this chapter we discuss those standards that are based upon some form of predictive coding. Other than G.711, we classify the remaining (nonpredictive) speech coding approaches in the table as frequency domain coders; their description is deferred until Chapter 8, after the basic principles are developed in Chapter 7. Of course, other speech coder classifications are possible; some examples are given in Gersho (1994), Spanias (1994), and Kondoz (1994). As to the predictive coding standards covered in this chapter, the treatment here is descriptive at the system level, with an emphasis on performance, complexity, particular quirks, and critical components. This chapter is meant to be read after Chapter 5, so if

	Speech Coder Standards			
TABLE 6.1	Year of Introduction	Bit Rates (kbps)	Description	MOS
	1972	64	PCM (for PSTN)	4.4
	1976	2.4	LPC-10 (U.S. Federal Standard 1015)	2.7
	1984	32	G.721 ADPCM (for PSTN)	4.1
	1990	4.15	INMARSAT (satellite)	≈3.2
	1991	13	GSM (European cellular)	3.6
	1991	4.8	CELP (U.S. Federal Standard 1016)	3.2
	1992	16	G.728 (low-delay CELP)	4.0
	1992	8	VSELP (NA cellular)	3.5
	1993	1–8	QCELP (NA CDMA)	≈3.4
	1993	6.8	VSELP (Japanese cellular)	≈3.3
	1995	8	G.729 (new toll-quality)	≈4.2
	1995	6.3	G.723.1 (in H.323 and H.324)	3.98
	1995	5–6	Half-rate GSM	≈3.4
	1996	2.4	New low-rate U.S. Federal Standard	≈3.3

some details seem to be missing, first consult Chapter 5 and the references there. Standards are usually written as concisely as possible, with the background for many of the choices of approaches and parameters left entirely to the literature, so you will need to have considerable background to fully digest most standards documents. Our goal here is to provide that background—and more.

Developing future standards in telephony, digital cellular, and personal communications systems are outlined at the end of this chapter, with a comparative view of the performance and complexity of all of the predictive coding standards.

6.2 ITU G.721/G.726/G.727

Were the problem only to achieve high-quality, highly intelligible speech at 32 kbps, the development of the standard would have been relatively simple. However, the G.721 standard had to accommodate a number of other network-imposed conditions. In fact, the evolution of G.721 into G.726 reflects these requirements as well. The 32-kbps G.721 standard was developed to offer the possibility of doubling the number of speech conversations carried over existing

64-kbps channels with other requirements that there be low delay through the coder (less than 2 ms), independent bit error rates up to 10^{-2}, coding of some voiceband data modem signals, and acceptable transmission performance through several synchronous or asynchronous tandems (Petr 1982). From G.721, an ADPCM-based standard for 24 kbps and 40 kbps, designated G.723, was established to allow flexibility in DCME and to address the encoding of 9.6-kbps modem signals, which required 40 kbps. Since G.721 and G.723 both used the same ADPCM algorithm, they were combined to yield the G.726 standard that also includes a 16-kbps option (to be used only for overload conditions). All of these standards rely on the following algorithm.

The predictor in G.726 has two poles and six zeros and is expressible as

$$\hat{s}(k|k-1) = \sum_{i=1}^{2} a_i \hat{s}(k-i) + \sum_{j=1}^{6} b_j e_q(k-j) \tag{6.1}$$

The use of six zeros and only two poles allows the predictor to be robust to transmission errors while still achieving good prediction performance. The predictor coefficients are adapted according to the gradient algorithms

$$b_j(k+1) = \left(\frac{255}{256}\right) b_j(k) + \frac{1}{128} \operatorname{sgn} e_q(k) \operatorname{sgn} e_q(k-j), \quad j = 1, 2, \ldots, 6 \tag{6.2}$$

$$a_1(k+1) = \left(\frac{255}{256}\right) a_1(k) + \left(\frac{3}{256}\right) \operatorname{sgn} \tilde{s}(k) \operatorname{sgn} \tilde{s}(k-1) \tag{6.3}$$

$$a_2(k+1) = \left(\frac{127}{128}\right) a_2(k) + \left(\frac{1}{128}\right) \operatorname{sgn} \hat{s}(k) \operatorname{sgn} \hat{s}(k-2)$$

$$- \left(\frac{1}{128}\right) f[a_1(k)] \operatorname{sgn} \tilde{s}(k) \operatorname{sgn} \tilde{s}(k-1) \tag{6.4}$$

where

$$\tilde{s}(k) = e_q(k) + \sum_{j=1}^{6} b_j(k) e_q(k-j) \tag{6.5}$$

and

$$f[a_1(k)] = \begin{cases} 4a_1(k) & \text{if } |a_1(k)| \le \frac{1}{2} \\ 2 \operatorname{sgn} a_1(k) & \text{if } |a_1(k)| > \frac{1}{2} \end{cases} \tag{6.6}$$

To guarantee stability, the following constraints are placed on the coefficients for the two poles:

$$-0.75 \le a_2 \le 0.75$$

$$|a_1| \le \frac{15}{16} - a_2 \tag{6.7}$$

These are conservative constraints obtained from the usual triangular stability region in the a_1, a_2 plane.

The algorithms in equations (6.2) through (6.4) are particularly simple since they use only polarities of the adaptation signals. Robustness to errors is also enhanced by using the FIR signal $\tilde{s}(k)$ as part of the adaptation driving terms in equations (6.3) and (6.4).

The adaptive quantizer in the G.726 standard for 32 kbps is a 15-level, midtread quantizer with the step points and output levels chosen to minimize the mean squared encoding error for a Gaussian input (Max 1960). To track the dynamic range of the prediction error signal, the quantizer is expanded and contracted according to a scale factor called the step size. Two scale factors are updated at every sampling instant. One scale factor, called the unlocked step size $\Delta_u(n)$, adapts according to

$$\Delta_u(n) = \Delta^\beta (n-1) M(|I(n-1)|) \tag{6.8}$$

where $\beta = \frac{31}{32}$ and the $M(\cdot)$ parameters are the multipliers shown in Table 6.2. Generally, for quantizers that adapt according to (6.8), we would expect that inner levels contract and outer levels expand, and further, if the levels are equally likely to occur, the product of the multipliers should be less than or equal to one for stability (Jayant 1973). However, it has been found that in ADPCM coding of speech, the quantizer should expand more often and faster than it contracts. The quantity $\beta = \frac{31}{32}$ is chosen to dissipate mistracking between the transmitter and receiver due to channel errors. This is actually a relatively small number, so the coder is very robust.

In addition to the instantaneously adaptive step size in (6.8), there is a more slowly varying step size denoted by $\Delta_\ell(n)$, where ℓ represents "locked." This step size adapts according to the logarithm of its value, so letting $\nabla_\ell(n) = \log \Delta_\ell(n)$, we have

$$\nabla_\ell(n) = \frac{63}{64} \nabla_\ell(n-1) + \frac{1}{64} \nabla_u(n), \tag{6.9}$$

T A B L E	Quantizer Step Size Multipliers for G.726	
6.2	$|I(\cdot)|$	$M(|I(\cdot)|)$
	1	0.984
	2	1.006
	3	1.037
	4	1.070
	5	1.142
	6	1.283
	7	1.585
	8	4.482

$\nabla_u(n) = \log \Delta_u(n)$. Since it can be shown that a fixed step size gives better performance for relatively stationary signals such as voiceband data, it is desirable to use $\Delta_\ell(n)$ for these situations.

The final step size is a combination of the unlocked and locked step sizes according to

$$\nabla(n) = w\nabla_u(n) + (1 - w)\nabla_\ell(n) \tag{6.10}$$

where w is selected using several rules. Other parameters of the quantizer are $|\text{input}| = 4096$, $\Delta_{\min} = \Delta(0)$ for log-PCM, and $\Delta_{\max}/\Delta_{\min} = 1024$. This last quantity is sometimes called the compression ratio, and this large a value indicates a very responsive coder. However, $\beta = \frac{31}{32}$ moderates this somewhat.

Although the slowly varying quantizer is advantageous for stationary signals, there is an interaction with the adaptive predictor that can occur that results in poor performance. FSK modem signals consist of stationary, or partial band, signals and transitions between these signals. If the prediction gain is high and the quantizer is in the locked mode, problems can result. To avoid these conditions, two tests are performed. One test monitors a_2 to detect the presence of a partial band signal, and the other monitors a_2 and the quantized prediction error to detect transitions between partial band signals. When these conditions are detected, the quantizer is switched to the unlocked mode, and the predictor coefficients are set to zero.

The G.726 ADPCM system at 32 kbps produces highly intelligible, high-quality speech, has low delay, maintains good performance for up to four asynchronous tandems, passes V.26 2400-bps and V.27 4800-bps voiceband data, and is robust to noisy channels.

An alternative standard using ADPCM, which has the same bit rates as G.726, is called G.727 and is an embedded coder. This standard has 2-, 3-, 4-, and 5-bit uniform quantizers that are designed as embedded quantizers. This structure allows the least significant bits of a data stream to be discarded within the network, without reencoding, and yet the reconstructed speech quality suffers only slight degradation at the lower rate compared to ADPCM actually encoded at that rate.

6.3   U.S. Federal Standard 1015

The U.S. Federal Standard 1015 speech coder is LPC-10 at 2.4 kbps. Figures 6.1 and 6.2 show block diagrams of the transmitter and receiver, respectively. Table 6.3 lists the main features of the coder, and Table 6.4 shows the bit allocations for the various parameters. Two slight differences between LPC-10 and most other LPCs are that LPC-10 uses the average magnitude difference function (AMDF) pitch extractor and that the covariance method is used to calculate the short-term predictor coefficients rather than the autocorrelation method.

There are two other distinctive differences. One is that the excitation signal is not an impulse but a standardized excitation, as shown in Table 6.5. Non-impulse excitations spread the energy more evenly throughout a pitch period, thus reducing the peak-to-rms ratio and improving the synthesized speech for a fixed D-to-A converter accuracy. A second important difference is the pitch and voicing correction block in Figure 6.1, which is used to smooth pitch and voicing over several frames. The primary limit to LPC performance is good pitch and voicing extraction. In LPC-10, a dynamic programming algorithm allows adjacent frame information to be used to obtain more reasonable pitch and voicing contours. However, while this improves pitch and voicing determination, the coder delay is greatly increased as well.

LPC-10 was a true breakthrough in its time, the early 1970s, but it suffers from the limitation that the excitation must fall into one of two classes—voiced or unvoiced. Since all speech cannot be classified in this way, the quality of the synthesized speech is often unnatural. Since for voiced speech the excitation is quasi-periodic and for unvoiced speech the excitation is random noise, the speech can be too "buzzy" if the excitation is too periodic, or it can be too "breathy" if a partially voiced segment is classified as unvoiced. This is simply a limitation of the LPC model. There have been numerous attempts over the years to correct this deficiency; one method is allowing mixed voicing, that is, allowing a speech segment to have an excitation that combines quasi

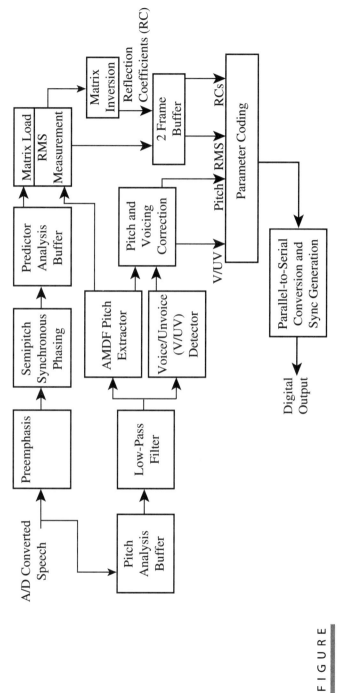

F I G U R E
6.1

Transmitter of the LPC-10 Algorithm

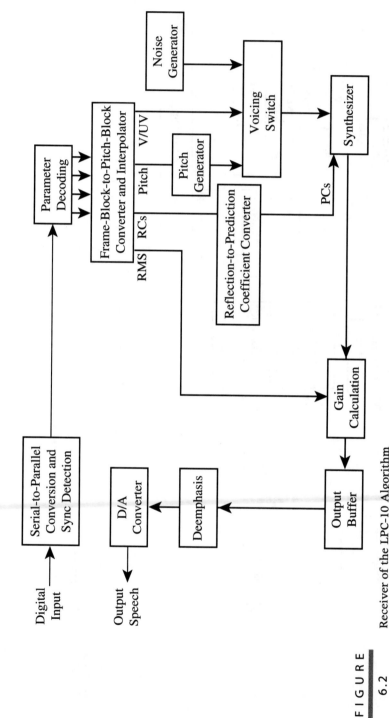

FIGURE
6.2

Receiver of the LPC-10 Algorithm

TABLE
6.3

Main Features of the Government Standard LPC-10 Algorithm

Sampling rate	8 kHz
LPC predictor order	10 for voiced speech 4 for unvoiced speech
Data rate	2400 bps
Frame length	22.5 ms
Assigned bits/frame	54
Pitch	AMDF method Range: 51.3–400 Hz Coding: Semilog, 60 values
Gain	RMS value Coding: Semilog, 32 values
LPC analysis	Semipitch synchronous
Analysis method	Covariance
LPC parameter coding	Log-area ratios for K_1–K_2 Linear for K_3–K_{10}
Synthesis	Pitch synchronous
Excitation	Stored waveform for voiced frame

TABLE
6.4

Bit Assignment for the LPC-10 Government Standard

Parameter	Voiced	Unvoiced	Comments
Pitch	7	7	6 bits pitch, 1 voicing 60 values, semilog
Energy	5	5	32 values, semilog
K_1	5	5	LAR
K_2	5	5	LAR
K_3	5	5	linear
K_4	5	5	linear
K_5	4	—	linear
K_6	4	—	linear
K_7	4	—	linear
K_8	4	—	linear
K_9	3	—	linear
K_{10}	2	—	linear
Synchronous	1	1	alternating 1s and 0s
Error protection	—	21	
TOTAL	54	54	

T A B L E	Excitation Sequence for Federal Standard 1015 LPC-10		
6.5	Sample	Amplitude	Sample	Amplitude

Sample	Amplitude	Sample	Amplitude
1	249	21	−82
2	−262	22	−123
3	363	23	−39
4	−362	24	65
5	100	25	64
6	367	26	19
7	79	27	16
8	78	28	32
9	10	29	19
10	−277	30	−15
11	−82	31	−29
12	376	32	−21
13	288	33	−18
14	−65	34	−27
15	−20	35	−31
16	138	36	−22
17	−62	37	−12
18	−315	38	−10
19	−247	39	−10
20	−78	40	−4

periodicity and random noise. The result was only partially successful. The accurate designation of voicing and then pitch extraction for a voiced segment is also very difficult, and the dynamic programming technique used by LPC-10 is a definite innovation.

A new 2400-bps federal standard has been selected to replace Federal Standard 1015. This coder has much less synthetic, much higher quality output speech than LPC-10.

6.4   U.S. Federal Standard 1016

The U.S. Federal Standard 1016 voice coder is a forward adaptive CELP coder with a short-term predictor, an adaptive codebook, and a stochastic codebook

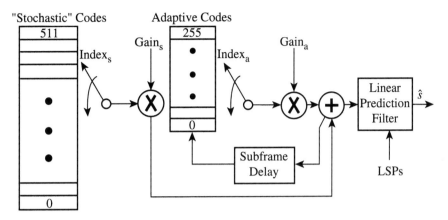

FIGURE
6.3

Federal Standard CELP Decoder

Parameters for the Federal Standard 1016 CELP Coder

	Linear Predictor	Adaptive CB	Stochastic CB
Update	30 ms	$30/4 = 7.5$ ms	$30/4 = 7.5$ ms
Parameters	10 LSPs (independent)	1 gain, 1 delay 256 codewords	1 gain, 1 index 512 codewords
Analysis	open loop 10th-order autocorrelation 30-ms Hamming window no preemphasis 15-Hz expansion interpolated by 4	closed loop 60-dimensional mod MSPE VQ weighting $= 0.8$ delta search range: 20–147 noninteger delays	closed loop 60-dimensional mod MSPE VQ weighting $= 0.8$ shift by -2 77% sparsity ternary samples
Bits per frame	34 (3, 4, 4, 4, 4, 3, 3, 3, 3, 3)	index: $8 + 6 + 8 + 6$ $\pm$gain: 5×4	index: 9×4 $\pm$gain: 5×4
Rate	1133.33 bps	1600 bps	1866.67 bps
Miscellaneous	The remaining 200 bps are used as follows: 1 bit per frame for synchronization, 4 bits per frame for forward error correction, and 1 bit per frame for future expansion.		

(Campbell, Welch, and Tremain 1989). The adaptive codebook accounts for the long-term or pitch prediction. The synthesizer or decoder is shown in block diagram form in Figure 6.3, and the principal coder parameters are summarized in Table 6.6. The input speech is filtered to a passband of 200–3400 Hz, and the

TABLE	Weighted Averaging for Subframe LSPs		
6.7	Present Subframe	Previous Frame LSPs	Present Frame LSPs
	1	$\frac{7}{8}$	$\frac{1}{8}$
	2	$\frac{5}{8}$	$\frac{3}{8}$
	3	$\frac{3}{8}$	$\frac{5}{8}$
	4	$\frac{1}{8}$	$\frac{7}{8}$

speech is sampled at 8000 samples per second with at least a 12-bit dynamic range. The short-term predictor analysis frame is 30 ms, and the 10 coefficients are calculated using Hamming windows (nonoverlapped), no preemphasis, and the autocorrelation method with 15-Hz bandwidth expansion. The analysis frame includes the last two subframes of the present frame and the first two subframes of the next frame. The linear prediction coefficients are transformed into line spectrum pairs (LSPs) for coding and transmission, and the LSPs corresponding to each of the four subframes in a frame are determined by a weighted average of the LSPs in the previous and current frames. Table 6.7 shows the weights used for each subframe.

The adaptive codebook combines a 128-element integer delay codebook and a 128-element noninteger delay codebook, which is interpolated from the nearest lower value of the integer delay code. The stochastic codebook has 512 excitation sequences, whose samples are $+1$, 0, or -1, and the relative number of zeros is about 75%. This reduces codebook search complexity.

Of course, it is essential to use perceptual weighting in the codebook search, and the recommended weighting is a cascade of the linear prediction whitening filter and a bandwidth expanded synthesis filter with recommended radial scaling of 0.8, which gives the weighting filter

$$W(z) = \frac{1 - \sum_{i=1}^{N} a_i z^{-i}}{1 - \sum_{i=1}^{N} a_i (0.8)^i z^{-i}} \tag{6.11}$$

The importance of the excitation is clear from the fact that 3466.7 bps out of 4800 are allocated to the transmission of excitation codewords from the adaptive and stochastic codebooks.

6.5   GSM 13-kbps Coder

The Global Systeme Mobile (GSM) selected a simplified regular pulse excitation code excited LPC system with a long-term predictor as its standardized
speech coder for use in the Pan-European digital mobile radio system. This coder
is designated as RPE-LTP and operates at a bit rate of 13 kbps. Block diagrams
showing the encoder and decoder are given in Figures 6.4 and 6.5 (Vary et al.
1988). Rather than use the full analysis-by-synthesis RPE approach from Kroon,
Deprettere, and Sluyter (1986), the GSM employs a modification, also discussed
in Kroon, Deprettere, and Sluyter (1986), that greatly simplifies the search for
the best excitation.

Eight short-term predictor (actually reflection) coefficients are calculated
every 20 ms (160 samples). The reflection coefficients are transformed into log-
area ratios (LARs) and quantized to the following accuracies:

i	1 and 2	3 and 4	5 and 6	7 and 8
LAR(i)	6 bits each	5	4	3

When generating the short-term prediction error signal, the coefficients from
two adjacent 20-ms frames are linearly interpolated during the first 5 ms after the
reception of a new set. This is done to avoid transients at the frame boundaries.

The long-term predictor has a single coefficient at a single lag that is found
to maximize the autocorrelation of the short-term prediction error sequence
over the range of 40–120 samples. Since lags below 40 are not searched, for
short-pitch-period speakers, the long-term predictor will use a multiple of the
pitch period. This presents no difficulty for coders that do a relatively good job
of approximating the excitation. The long-term predictor is recalculated every
5 ms, four times more often than the short-term coefficients. The long-term
coefficient is coded using 2 bits, and the lag using 7 bits.

The regular excitation of interest here is determined by passing the prediction residual after short-term and long-term filtering through a fixed FIR filter,
downsampling by a factor of three, and finding the energy in the 20-ms frame for
each of four shifted pulse excitation sequences. The excitation with the largest
energy is chosen. This approximately solves the analysis-by-synthesis problem
under fixed perceptual weighting filter assumptions. The pulse sequence phase
is encoded using 2 bits, the normalized pulse amplitudes by 3 bits, and the
normalization factor quantized logarithmically with 6 bits.

The overall speech coder data rate can be calculated by referring to the bit allocations in Table 6.8 for a 20-ms frame. At 260 bits/frame and 50 frames/second,
we have a data rate of 13 kbps.

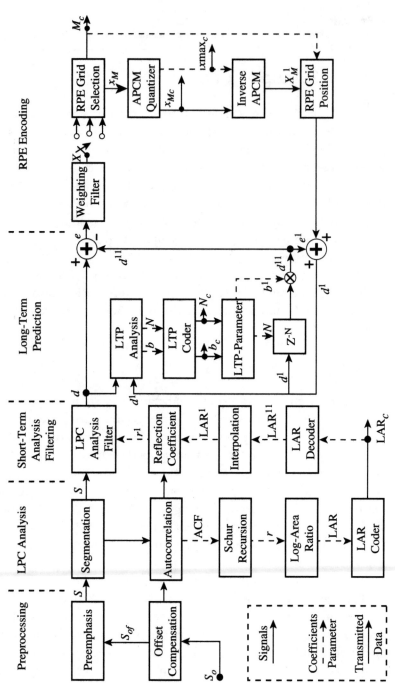

FIGURE
6.4

Block Diagram of the RPE-LTP Encoder

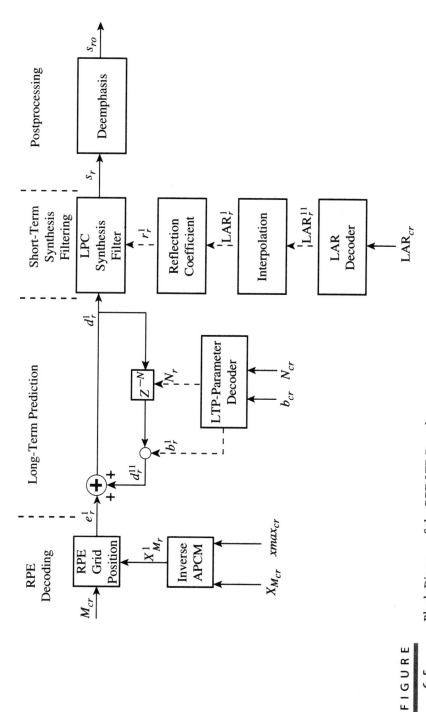

Block Diagram of the RPE-LTP Decoder

T A B L E	Bit Assignments for the GSM RPE-LTP Coder	
6.8	Parameter	Number of Bits
	8 LARs	36
	4 LTP coefficients	8
	4 LTP delays	28
	4 phase values	8
	4 block normalizations	24
	52 RPE pulses	<u>156</u>
	TOTAL	260 per 20-ms frame

6.6   TIA 8-kbps VSELP

The Telecommunications Industry Association (TIA) has adopted standard IS-54 for use with TDMA in the North American digital cellular mobile radio system. The speech codec for this standard is a version of CELP called *vector sum excited linear prediction* (VSELP), and it has a nominal data rate of 8 kbps (Gerson and Jasiuk 1991). The decoder or synthesizer for VSELP is shown in Figure 6.6. The synthesis filter block is a standard 10th-order LPC all-pole filter. These short-term coefficients are recalculated and transmitted every 20 ms and are interpolated between 5-ms subframes at the receiver. The long-term filter is a single tap pitch predictor with lag L and gain β_q.

Certainly, a noticeable difference between the VSELP block diagram in Figure 6.6 and the usual CELP block diagram is the presence of two codebooks. This dual codebook structure is an approach to generating a sufficient variety of excitation sequences while at the same time keeping the complexity at a reasonable level. The structure of the two codebooks is also unique in VSELP in the sense that the codewords in each codebook are combinations of orthogonal basis vectors rather than Gaussian random variates or a VQ codebook. Letting $v_{k,m}(n)$ be the mth basis vector of the kth codebook and $u_{k,i}(n)$ be the ith codevector in the kth codebook, we can write for $k = 1, 2$,

$$u_{k,i}(n) = \sum_{m=1}^{7} \Theta_{im} v_{k,m}(n) \tag{6.12}$$

$0 \le i \le 127$ and $0 \le n \le 39$ (40 samples in a 5-ms subframe). The Θ_{im} are binary coefficients according to

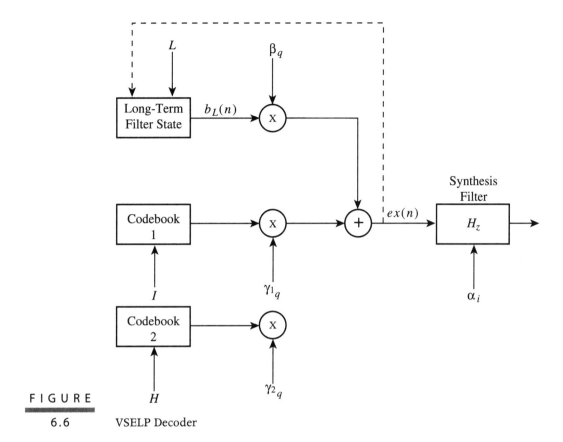

FIGURE

6.6   VSELP Decoder

$$\Theta_{im} = \begin{cases} +1 & \text{if bit } m \text{ of codeword } i = 1 \\ -1 & \text{if bit } m \text{ of codeword } i = 0 \end{cases} \tag{6.13}$$

The basis function description reduces the sensitivity of the codec to channel errors since a single bit error simply flips the sign of one component of the excitation vector.

To establish notation, we first assume that the basis vectors are known and describe the steps in the encoding process. We will then return to the problem of basis vector optimization. Figure 6.7 shows the analysis-by-synthesis block diagram. Starting with the long-term predictor codebook, the codebooks are optimized sequentially by first setting $\gamma_1 = 0 = \gamma_2$. The transfer function $H(z)$ is a bandwidth-expanded version of the LPC synthesis filter, $H(z) = 1/[1 + \Sigma \lambda^i z^{-i}]$, and $p(n)$ in Figure 6.7 is the perceptually weighted input speech (to be coded) after removal of the zero input response. First, β and L are found to minimize

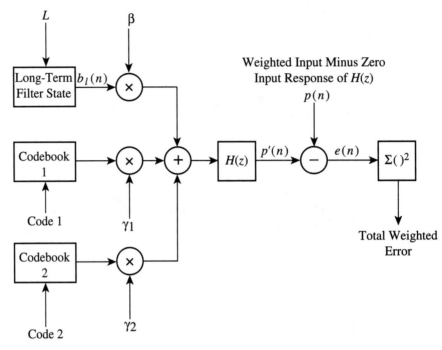

Long-Term Predictor Lag and Code Search

$$E'_L = \sum_{n=0}^{39} [p(n) - \beta^* b'_L(n)]^2 \tag{6.14}$$

where $b'_L(n)$ is the zero state response of $H(z)$ to $b_L(n)$. For codebooks 1 and 2, the codebook search is performed over all codewords, $i = 0, 1, \ldots, 127$, to minimize

$$E'_{k,i} = \sum_{n=0}^{39} [p(n) - \gamma'_k f'_{k,i}(n)]^2 \tag{6.15}$$

where $f'_{k,i}(n)$ represents the orthogonalized versions of the filtered codevectors

$$f_{k,i}(n) = \sum_{m=1}^{7} \Theta_{im} q_{k,m}(n) \tag{6.16}$$

with $q_{k,m}(n)$ the zero state response of $H(z)$ to basis vector $v_{k,m}(n)$. That is,

$$f'_{k,i}(n) = \sum_{m=1}^{7} \Theta_{im} q'_{k,m}(n) \tag{6.17}$$

where $q'_{k,m}(n)$ is $q_{k,m}(n)$ after orthogonalization to $b'_L(n)$. Thus, after calculating the filtered and orthogonalized basis vectors, the codebook search consists of finding that codevector over $i = 0, 1, \ldots, 127$ that maximizes

$$\eta = \frac{(C_i)^2}{G_i} \tag{6.18}$$

where

$$C_i = \sum_{n=0}^{39} f'_i(n) p(n) \tag{6.19}$$

and

$$G_i = \sum_{n=0}^{39} [f'_i(n)]^2 \tag{6.20}$$

The offline optimization of the codebook is an iterative training sequence procedure similar to the LBG vector quantization algorithm. To explain the approach, consider a representative mean squared error expression given by E_j for the jth subframe,

$$E(j) = ||p_j - \gamma_1 \sum_m \Theta_{1m}^j q_{1m}^j - \gamma_2 \sum_m \Theta_{2m}^j q_{2m}^j||^2 \tag{6.21}$$

where the norm is over the 40 component vectors in a subframe. The index j can be taken to correspond to the jth training vector, so averaging over all training vectors gives

$$\sum_j E(j) = \sum_j ||p_j - \gamma_1 \sum_m \Theta_{1m}^j q_{1m}^j - \gamma_2 \sum_m \Theta_{2m}^j q_{2m}^j||^2 \tag{6.22}$$

which is to be minimized by choosing $\{q_{1m}^j, q_{2m}^j, m = 1, 2, \ldots, 7\}$, each of which has 40 components. Thus, we take the partial derivative of $\sum_j E_j$ with respect to $q_{kl}^j(i)$, where $k = 1, 2$; $i = 0, 1, \ldots, 39$; and $l = 1, 2, \ldots, 7$; to get equations of the form

$$\sum_j [p_j - \gamma_1 \sum_m \Theta_{1m}^j q_{1m}^j - \gamma_2 \sum_m \Theta_{2m}^j q_{2m}^j] \gamma_1 \Theta_{kl}^j = 0 \tag{6.23}$$

Bit Allocations for TIA VSELP

LPC coefficients (α_i)		38 bits/frame
Frame energy		5
Lag (L)	7 bits/subframe	28
Codewords	$7 + 7$ bits/subframe	56
Gains (β, γ_1, γ_2)	8 bits/subframe	32
TOTAL		159 bits/frame

There are $2 \times 7 \times 40 = 560$ of these equations to be solved simultaneously for the basis vector components.

Thus, starting with initial basis vectors with components chosen as independent Gaussian variates, the equations in (6.23) are formed and solved for each pass through the training sequence. The resulting basis vectors are then used to form (6.23) in the next pass through the training data. This iterative optimization gives an SNR increase of about 1.5 dB and a noticeable perceptual improvement.

To further improve perceptual quality, the transfer function $H(z)$ in Figure 6.6 may be preceded by a pitch prefilter of the form

$$H_p(z) = \frac{1}{1 - 0.4\xi z^{-L}} \tag{6.24}$$

to emphasize periodicity. Additionally, the output of $H(z)$ is postfiltered by a two-stage filter, one given by

$$\hat{H}(z) = \frac{1 - \sum_{i=1}^{10} \eta_i z^{-i}}{1 - \sum_{i=1}^{10} (0.8)^i \alpha_i z^{-i}} \tag{6.25}$$

and the other by

$$\tilde{H}(z) = 1 - 0.4z^{-1} \tag{6.26}$$

The $\{\alpha_i\}$ are the LPC coefficients, and the η_i are calculated from a modified autocorrelation sequence obtained by passing the original autocorrelation sequence through a binomial window.

There are 159 bits/frame, as shown in Table 6.9. Thus, for a 20-ms frame length, the bit rate is 7950 bps.

6.7   TIA QCELP

A second North American digital cellular standard has been defined that is based on a different multiple access technology called code-division multiple access (CDMA). A characteristic of CDMA is that all mobiles use the entire band for transmission, and each mobile in operation appears as noise to the other users. Thus, when a mobile is not transmitting, it is not interfering with other mobiles. Fixed-rate speech coders are always transmitting at their specified maximum rate even if there is low activity or silence in the current speech frame. Although this is acceptable (but maybe not particularly efficient) for dedicated transmission slots as in TDMA, it only serves to raise interference levels in CDMA. To take full advantage of CDMA, Qualcomm developed a variable-rate version of CELP, popularly called QCELP, that varies the transmitted data rate among four possible rates, 1, 2, 4, and 8 kbps (DeJaco, Gardner, and Lee 1993). The entire CDMA-based approach, including the speech coder, has been designated as IS-95 by the CTIA.

Block diagrams of the QCELP encoder and decoder are shown in Figures 6.8 and 6.9. The encoder in Figure 6.8 has the usual analysis-by-synthesis structure, but exactly what is transmitted and coded depends on the transmitted data rate selected. The automatic rate selection among the four rates is based upon tracking the input energy and comparing to three energy thresholds. In particular, the energy is calculated in a 160-sample frame according to

$$R(0) = \sum_{m=0}^{159} s_w^2(m) \tag{6.27}$$

and the background energy is tracked according to the calculation

$$B_i = \min[R_{i-1}(0), 160{,}000, \max(1.00547 B_{i-1}, B_{i-1} + 1)] \tag{6.28}$$

The input energy in equation (6.27) is compared to a set of thresholds dependent on the B_i according to the expressions

$$T_1(B_i) = -(5.544613 \times 10^{-6}) B_i^2 + 4.047152 B_i + 362 \tag{6.29}$$

$$T_2(B_i) = -(1.529733 \times 10^{-5}) B_i^2 + 8.750045 B_i + 1136 \tag{6.30}$$

$$T_3(B_i) = -(3.957050 \times 10^{-5}) B_i^2 + 18.89962 B_i + 3347 \tag{6.31}$$

If the input energy is below the lowest threshold, the transmitted bit rate is 1 kbps; as the input energy exceeds subsequent thresholds, the rate is increased to the next level. The basic idea is that the thresholds will ride above the

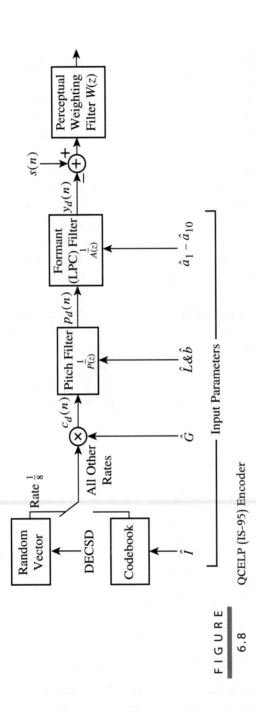

FIGURE
6.8 QCELP (IS-95) Encoder

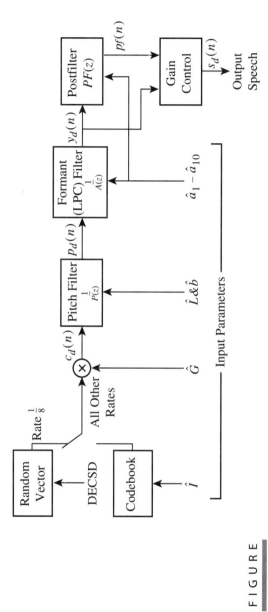

FIGURE
6.9   QCELP (IS-95) Decoder

T A B L E   Parameters Used for Each Rate

6.10

Parameter	Rate 1	Rate $\frac{1}{2}$	Rate $\frac{1}{4}$	Rate $\frac{1}{8}$
Linear predictive coding (LPC) updates per frame	1	1	1	1
Samples per LPC update, L_A	160 (20 ms)	160 (20 ms)	160 (20 ms)	160 (20 ms)
Bits per LPC update	40	20	10	10
Pitch updates (subframes) per frame	4	2	1	0
Samples per pitch subframe, L_P	40 (5 ms)	80 (10 ms)	160 (20 ms)	—
Bits per pitch update	10	10	10	—
Codebook updates (subframes) per frame	8	4	2	1
Samples per codebook subframe, L_C	20 (2.5 ms)	40 (5 ms)	80 (10 ms)	160 (20 ms)
Bits per codebook update	10	10	10	6*

*Rate 1/8 uses 6 bits for pseudorandom excitation, rather than using the codebook.

background noise energy by their dependence on B_i. It is claimed that this technique only allows high energy noise to be coded at the higher rate for a short period of time. Table 6.10 shows the parameter update frame rates and bits/frame for each of the four transmitted bit rates.

From Figures 6.8 and 6.9, we see that there are 10 short-term predictor coefficients and a single lag pitch predictor. The steps in encoding the short-term predictor coefficients are the following:

1. Remove DC from the input samples.
2. Window the input samples using a Hamming window.
3. Compute the autocorrelation function for 11 lags.
4. Determine the LPC coefficients from the autocorrelation values.
5. Bandwidth expand the LPC coefficients.
6. Transform the scaled coefficients to LSP frequencies.
7. Convert the LSP frequencies into LSP codes.

Decoding has the following steps:

1. Convert the LSP codes to LSP frequencies.
2. Check stability.

3. Smooth the LSP frequencies.

4. Interpolate the LSP frequencies for pitch and codebook searches.

5. Convert interpolated LSP frequencies to LPC coefficients.

We note in particular that the LPC coefficients are converted to LSPs for quantization and coding purposes. After subtracting a bias value, each LSP is differentially encoded with a different scalar quantizer. The prediction is zero at full rate, but $P(z) = 0.90625z^{-1}$ for other rates. The codebook gains are also coded differentially. The codebook has 128 center-clipped Gaussian codewords, but is updated more often at the higher rates.

A postfilter is also evident in Figure 6.9. This filter has the form of that shown in Figure 5.25, but without the long-term postfilter. The spectral shaping parameters are chosen as $\beta = 0.5$ and $\alpha = 0.8$, and there is a compensation for spectral tilt that is calculated from an average of the 10 LSPs.

6.8   LD-CELP, ITU G.728

The ITU 16-kbps speech coding standard is AT&T's low-delay code excited linear prediction (LD-CELP) speech coder (Chen et al. 1992). To achieve the ITU low delay of less than or equal to 2 ms, only the excitation sequence is transmitted, and all other coder parameters are calculated in a backward adaptive fashion. There is no side information. Figure 6.10 is a block diagram of the LD-CELP coder (see also Dimolitsas et al. 1993).

This coder does not use a long-term or pitch predictor, but instead the order of the short-term predictor is increased to 50. The short-term predictor is updated every 2.5 ms by calculating the LPC coefficients in a block adaptive manner based upon reconstructed speech samples. In order to guard against ill-conditioning in the 50th-order Toeplitz matrix, the main diagonal is increased by a small amount equivalent to adding white noise at a level 45 dB below the speech power. Further, bandwidth expansion of 15 Hz of the resulting LPC filter is performed by scaling the radial distance from the origin of all poles by a factor of 0.9883.

The excitation vector is five samples long and is encoded using a 10-bit gain/shape VQ, where the gain codebook has 3 bits and the shape codebook has 7 bits. The excitation gain is adapted via a log gain prediction algorithm. That is, if the excitation codevector is denoted by $\mathbf{y}(n)$, and $\mathbf{e}(n)$ is its gain-scaled version, then

$$\mathbf{e}(n) = \sigma(n)\mathbf{y}(n) \tag{6.32}$$

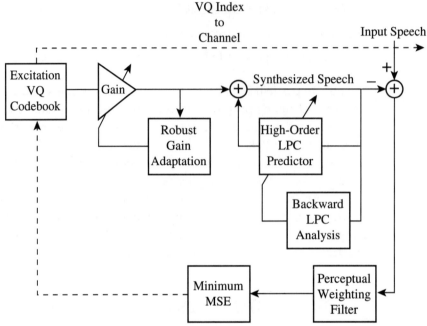

FIGURE

6.10   Low-Delay Backward Adaptive CELP Coder

where $\sigma(n)$ is the backward adaptive excitation gain. From (6.32) we can write

$$\sigma_e(n) = \sigma(n)\sigma_y(n) \qquad (6.33)$$

where $\sigma_e(n)$ and $\sigma_y(n)$ are the rms values of $\mathbf{e}(n)$ and $\mathbf{y}(n)$, respectively, so

$$\log \sigma_e(n) = \log \sigma(n) + \log \sigma_y(n) \qquad (6.34)$$

Given $\log \sigma_e(i)$, $i = n - 1, n - 2, \ldots$, the backward adaptive excitation gain is predicted by

$$\log \sigma(n) = \sum_{i=1}^{10} p_i \log \sigma_e(n - i) \qquad (6.35)$$

The coefficients $\{p_i, i = 1, 2, \ldots, 10\}$ are computed using an autocorrelation method LPC analysis on the previously $\log \sigma_e(i)$ sequence. Note that (6.35) can be rewritten as

$$\log \sigma(n) = \sum_{i=1}^{10} p_i \log \sigma(n - i) + \sum_{i=1}^{10} p_i \log \sigma_y(n - i) \qquad (6.36)$$

Although the stability of (6.36) is guaranteed by the autocorrelation method analysis, robustness is further enhanced by scaling all poles and zeros by a factor of 0.9.

The VQ codebook is designed offline in a manner analogous to the well-known LBG algorithm (Linde, Buzo, and Gray 1980). The design iterations are complicated since the perceptually weighted LD-CELP output must be used as the training sequence. Let $\mathbf{y}_j$ be the jth output vector, $g(n)$ the vector magnitude for the nth training sample, $\eta(n)$ be the corresponding sign bit, and $\mathbf{H}(n)$ the lower triangular matrix with subdiagonals consisting of samples of the impulse response of the cascaded perceptual weighting filter and the LPC filter. If N_j is the set of all training vector indices associated with vector $\mathbf{y}_j$, then the distortion in cell j can be written as

$$D_j = \sum_{n \in N_j} ||\mathbf{x}(n) - \mathbf{H}(n)\eta(n)\sigma(n)g(n)\mathbf{y}_j||^2 \tag{6.37}$$

where $\mathbf{x}(n)$ is the nth training vector. Minimizing (6.37) with respect to $\mathbf{y}_j$ gives the normal equation for the optimal centroid $\mathbf{y}_j^*$,

$$\left[\sum_{n \in N_j} \sigma^2(n)g^2(n)\mathbf{H}^T(n)\mathbf{H}(n) \right] \mathbf{y}_j^* = \sum_{n \in N_j} \eta(n)\sigma(n)g(n)\mathbf{H}^T(n)\mathbf{x}(n) \tag{6.38}$$

$j = 0, 1, \ldots, 127$.

Thus, the procedure is as follows. Begin with an initial codebook of $\mathbf{y}_j$ vectors, and encode the entire training sequence. The summations in (6.38) are then calculated for each j, and the 128 normal equations are solved for new centroids $\mathbf{y}_j$. These new $\mathbf{y}_j$ are then used to encode the entire training set and the iterations repeated until a stopping rule is satisfied. It is reported that this optimization gives a 1–1.5 dB increase in SNR and a substantial perceptual improvement in LD-CELP encoding outside of the training set speech data. A similar minimization can be performed for $g(n)$.

With the optimal gain/shape codebook and the backward adaptive gain adaptation, the actual encoding of speech can be described. For a vector of five speech samples $\mathbf{s}(n)$, the perceptually weighted mean squared error distortion to be minimized with respect to $\mathbf{y}_j$, g_i, and η_k is

$$D = ||\mathbf{s}(n) - \eta_k g_i \mathbf{H}(n)\mathbf{y}_j||^2 \tag{6.39}$$

or equivalently, minimizing

$$\hat{D} = -\eta_k b_i \mathbf{p}^T(n)\mathbf{y}_j + c_i E_j(n) \tag{6.40}$$

where we have defined $b_i = 2g_i$, $c_i = g_i^2$, $\mathbf{p}(n) = \mathbf{H}^T(n)\mathbf{x}(n)$, and $E_j(n) = ||\mathbf{H}(n)\mathbf{y}_j||^2$. Since g_i is fixed, b_i and c_i are fixed. Further $E_j(n)$ is fixed over the 2.5-ms intervals between updates of the LPC coefficients. For each j, the best i and k values that minimize $\hat{D}$ are found. The vector $\mathbf{s}(n)$ is encoded with the η_k, g_i, $\mathbf{y}_j$ combination that yields the smallest $\hat{D}$. The 10-bit representation for this vector is sent to the receiver.

To augment the robustness designed into the various backward adaptation rules, pseudo-Gray coding of the excitation vectors is employed to reduce the effects of bit errors (Zeger and Gersho 1990).

An important addition to G.728 is the postfilter. Since tandem coder connections are unavoidable in telephony, the presence of a postfilter is problematical. This is because the speech will be passed through the postfilter each time the speech is resynthesized for a tandem connection, and the repeated filtering can distort the speech. The inventors of LD-CELP came up with the unique idea of optimizing the postfilter for three tandems with itself, and then checked to see how good the speech was for one encoding/decoding cycle, which is the case most postfilters are optimized for. They found that the single encoding was almost as good as if the postfilter was designed for that case, while greatly enhancing the performance for multiple tandems.

6.9   ITU G.729

A recently established standard for 8-kbps telephony has really "raised the bar" when it comes to speech quality and complexity at this bit rate. This coder is somewhat of a breakthrough because of the rather strict specifications that require performance near or exceeding that of 32-kbps G.726 ADPCM but at the much lower rate of 8 kbps. In particular, the ITU G.729 8-kbps standard achieves performance not worse than G.726, has an algorithmic delay less than 16 ms, has random bit error and background noise performance not worse than G.726, and has an asynchronous tandeming ability with itself such that two tandems are no worse than four asynchronous tandems of the reference G.726. The coder that achieves this performance level is called conjugate structure-algebraic code excited linear prediction (CS-ACELP), and it takes advantage of the special codebook structure to simplify the codebook search. There are other important innovations as well (Adoul et al. 1987; Salami et al. 1994; Salami 1995).

A block diagram showing the CS-ACELP encoding steps is given in Figure 6.11. Of course, this diagram looks almost the same as any other code excited linear predictive coder, but the details yield some special advantages. First, the fixed codebook has an algebraic structure and is called an *interleaved single-*

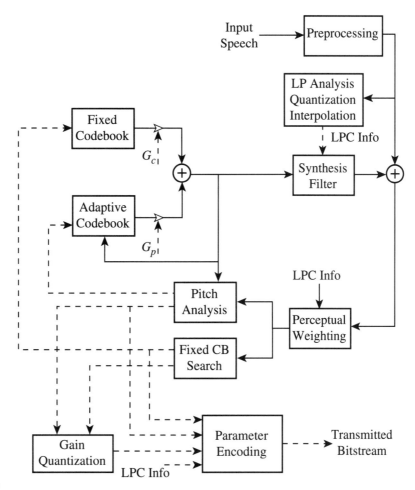

FIGURE

6.11

Encoding Principle of the CS-ACELP Encoder

pulse permutation (ISPP) design. Specifically, each 40-sample excitation vector in the codebook has only four nonzero pulses, designated i_0, i_1, i_2, and i_3, with possible amplitudes and locations as shown in Table 6.11, so that each excitation codeword is of the form

$$c(n) = s_0\delta(n - m_0) + s_1\delta(n - m_1) + s_2\delta(n - m_2) + s_3\delta(n - m_3),$$
$$n = 0, \ldots, 39 \tag{6.41}$$

where $\delta(n)$ is a unit amplitude impulse at time instant n. Note from the table that the possible pulse amplitudes are only +1 or −1, and this limitation, coupled with the sparsity of the codewords, yields great simplifications in codebook searching. The individual pulses also have restricted pulse location possibilities,

TABLE	G.729 Fixed Codebook		
6.11	Pulse	Sign	Positions
	i_0	s_0: ± 1	m_0: 0, 5, 10, 15, 20, 25, 30, 35
	i_1	s_1: ± 1	m_1: 1, 6, 11, 16, 21, 26, 31, 36
	i_2	s_2: ± 1	m_2: 2, 7, 12, 17, 22, 27, 32, 37
	i_3	s_3: ± 1	m_3: 3, 8, 13, 18, 23, 28, 33, 38
			4, 9, 14, 19, 24, 29, 34, 39

as indicated in Table 6.11, where we see that pulse i_1 can only be located at $m_1 = 1, 6, 11, 16, 21, 26, 31$, or 36, and these locations are distinct from those of the other three pulses. To enhance the harmonic structure of these restricted excitations, the codevector is passed through an adaptive pitch filter given by

$$P(z) = \frac{1}{1 - \beta z^{-T}} \tag{6.42}$$

where β is the adaptive gain and T is the pitch delay in the current subframe. The codebook is searched by starting with one pulse in the codevector and performing the search in four nested loops, with each loop corresponding to adding a new pulse. Since the four sets of possible pulse locations are disjoint, we get a conjugate search. There is also a very focused partial codebook search that limits the codebook search effort after the third loop. This search yields speech quality and SNR results close to a full search but with, say, only 5% of the codebook searched. The first three pulse positions are represented by 3 bits each, the fourth by 4 bits, and the pulse amplitudes require 1 bit each, so the number of bits per subframe without the gain is 17 bits.

A fractional pitch delay with $\frac{1}{3}$ sample time resolution is used, which substantially contributes to reconstructed speech quality. The single adaptive codebook gain is determined in a fairly standard fashion, and it is limited to the range of $0 < g_p < 1.2$. The fixed codebook gain is a combination of a predicted gain using a method similar to that used in G.728 and a multiplicative correction factor, γ. These two gains are coded using a two-stage, conjugate-structured codebook, with a 3-bit two-dimensional first stage, followed by a 4-bit two-dimensional second stage.

Figure 6.12 shows the CS-ACELP decoder. Table 6.12 lists the parameters in the figure and how often they are updated, where each subframe is 5 ms long. It is again interesting to note that the bit rate allocated to the excitation is 6200 bps out of the 8 kbps.

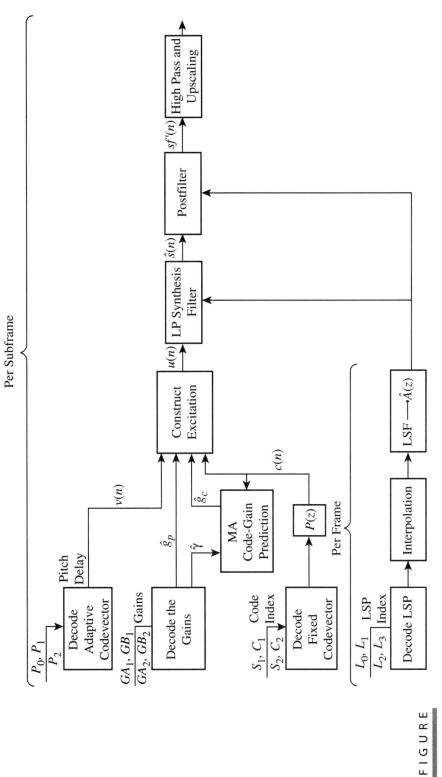

FIGURE

6.12

G.729 CS–ACELP Decoder

T A B L E   Bit Allocation of the 8-kbps CS-ACELP Algorithm (10-ms frame)

6.12

Parameter	Codeword	Subframe 1	Subframe 2	Total per Frame
Line spectrum pairs	L_0, L_1, L_2, L_3			18
Adaptive codebook delay	P_1, P_2	8	5	13
Pitch delay parity	P_0	1		1
Fixed codebook index	C_1, C_2	13	13	26
Fixed codebook sign	S_1, S_2	4	4	8
Codebook gains (stage 1)	GA_1, GA_2	3	3	6
Codebook gains (stage 2)	GB_1, GB_2	4	4	8
Total				80

6.10   ITU G.723.1

One of the current important applications of voice coders—and one of the major future applications—is for visual telephony and videoconferencing. ITU-T standard H.324 for multimedia communications at 28.8 kbps includes two speech coders, one operating at 6.3 kbps and one at 5.3 kbps. The difference in the two coders is the excitation codebook, although both of these coders were heavily influenced by the new G.729 speech coder design. The 6.3-kbps coder has a multipulse excitation with six nonzero pulses for even subframes and five pulses for odd subframes, with the restriction that the pulse positions must be all odd or all even. Motivated by the G.729 coder, there is only a single gain term for all of the excitation pulses.

Block diagrams of the speech encoder and decoder for the dual-rate speech coder are shown in Figures 6.13 and 6.14, respectively. The coders use 30-ms frames and have the bit allocations shown in Tables 6.13 and 6.14. The bit allocation in Table 6.13 for the higher-rate coder actually yields a transmitted bit rate of 6.4 kbps, but the rate can be lowered to 6.3 kbps by combining the coding of the four most significant bits of the pulse positions in the four 7.5-ms subframes into a single 13-bit word by observing that only 9 out of 16 possibilities are really needed. This yields a reduction in rate of 3 bits/frame, or 100 bps. The MP-MLQ excitation gives a multipulse coder so that pulse positions and signs must be estimated, resulting in a complexity of about 18 MIPS, which is 2 MIPS greater than the ACELP design.

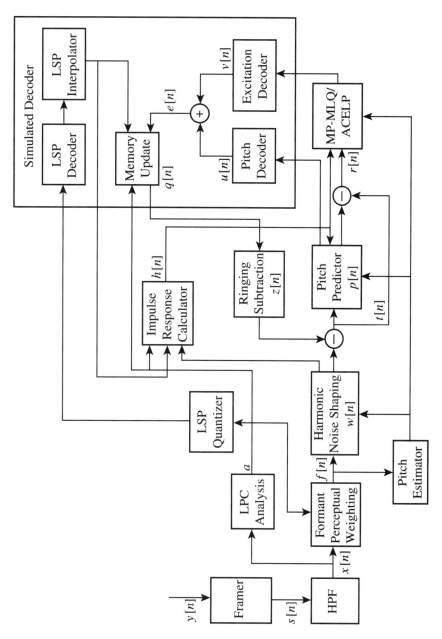

F I G U R E

6.13 G.723.1 Encoder

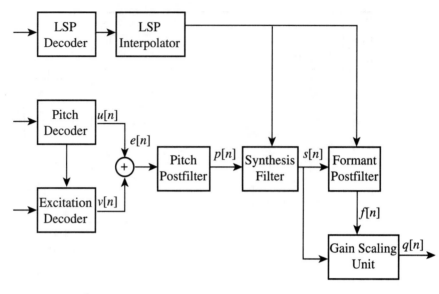

F I G U R E

6.14   G.723.1 Decoder

T A B L E   Bit Allocation of the 6.4- (6.3-) kbps Coding Algorithm

6.13

Parameters Coded	Subframe 0	Subframe 1	Subframe 2	Subframe 3	Total
LPC indices					24
Adaptive codebook lags	7	2	7	2	18
All the gains combined	12	12	12	12	48
Pulse positions	20	18	20	18	76
Pulse signs	6	5	6	5	22
Grid index	1	1	1	1	4
Total					192

The pulse amplitudes and locations for the 5.3-kbps ACELP coder are indicated in Table 6.15. The search methods and coding techniques in this G.723.1 coder are direct adaptations of the G.729 standard, with the differences in rates between 5.3 kbps and 8 kbps coming in terms of number of excitation pulses and frame length. The complexity of the 5.3-kbps coder is about 16 MIPS, and both G.723.1 coders require a little over 2K of RAM.

T A B L E   Bit Allocation of the 5.27-kbps Coding Algorithm

6.14

Parameters Coded	Subframe 0	Subframe 1	Subframe 2	Subframe 3	Total
LPC indices					24
Adaptive codebook lags	7	2	7	2	18
All the gains combined	12	12	12	12	48
Pulse positions	12	12	12	12	48
Pulse signs	4	4	4	4	16
Grid index	1	1	1	1	4
Total					158

T A B L E   ACELP Pulse Position Coding Table

6.15

Pulse	Amplitude	Positions
0	± 1	0, 8, 16, 24, 32, 40, 48, 56
1	± 1	2, 10, 18, 26, 34, 42, 50, 58
2	± 1	4, 12, 20, 28, 36, 44, 52, (60)
3	± 1	6, 14, 22, 30, 38, 46, 54, (62)

6.11   JDC (PDC) Full Rate, GSM Half Rate, and JDC Half Rate

The Japanese Digital Cellular (JDC), more recently designated as Personal Digital Cellular (PDC), full-rate standard is a VSELP coder that operates at 6.7 kbps and has a complexity about the same as the North American standard VSELP with slightly lower quality. The principal difference between the two is that the PDC VSELP has only one excitation codebook.

The half-rate GSM speech coder also uses VSELP, but at a lower rate of 5.6 kbps and with about twice the complexity. Although it seems that the half-rate GSM speech coding rate should be 6.5 kbps, it is not, because more bits are needed to be allocated to channel error correction to account for a reduction in diversity gain. This fact highlights the common issue of having an overall fixed available transmitted bit rate that must be split between source coding and channel coding. The excitation for the GSM/2 VSELP coder depends on the mode selected based upon the open loop pitch prediction gain. In mode 0,

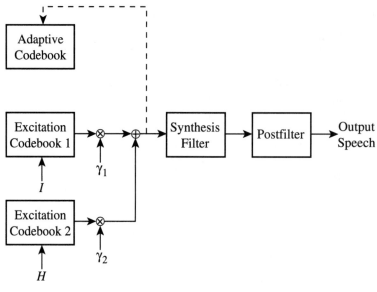

FIGURE
6.15

Basic Structure of the GSM VSELP Decoder: Mode 0

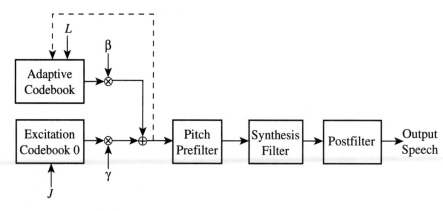

FIGURE
6.16

Basic Structure of the GSM VSELP Decoder: Modes 1, 2, and 3

which is essentially for unvoiced speech, the excitation consists of only the two trained 7-bit codebooks, so that the decoder has the form shown in Figure 6.15. For modes 1, 2, and 3, the excitation is a linear combination of codevectors from an 8-bit adaptive codebook and a 9-bit codebook, as indicated in the decoder block diagram in Figure 6.16. The difference among these modes is that different VQ codebooks are used for the gain.

TABLE 6.16   Bit Allocations for the VSELP Half-Rate GSM Coder

Parameter	Bits/Subframe	Bits/Frame
LP synthesis filter		28
Soft interpolation		1
Frame energy		5
Mode selection		2
Mode 0		
Excitation code I	7	28
Excitation code H	7	28
Gain code G_s, P_0	5	20
Mode 1, 2, and 3		
Pitch lag L (first subframe)		8
Difference lag (subframe 2, 3, 4)	4	12
Excitation code J	9	36
Gain code G_s, P_0	5	20
Total		112

Table 6.16 lists bit allocations for the several coder parameters, where the frame size and subframe size are 20 ms and 5 ms, respectively, as in the North American VSELP. Another innovation is that the pitch lag (adaptive codebook lag) for the four subframes is determined from a list of candidate open loop lag values according to restricted trajectories across the four subframes. The trajectory restrictions are based on the assumptions that the lag cannot change too drastically between adjacent subframes. The lag in the first subframe of a frame is coded with 8 bits, and the following subframes are differentially quantized using 4 bits each. The performance of the GSM/2 is near that of the full-rate GSM, but at the price of greatly increased complexity.

The half-rate PDC speech coder is a code excited predictive coder, and it had the design goal of achieving the same speech quality as the PDC full rate. Since the speech coder rate is only 3.45 kbps, achieving this quality was quite a challenge. The speech coder is called a pitch synchronous innovation CELP (PSI-CELP) coder, and the encoder block diagram is shown in Figure 6.17. The basic frame length is 40 ms, with 10-ms subframes, but the 10th-order linear prediction analysis is performed every 20 ms. Table 6.17 shows

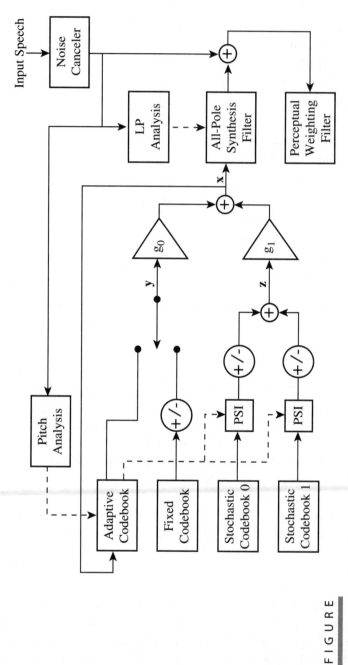

F I G U R E

6.17

Basic Structure of the PSI-CELP Encoder

TABLE 6.17	Bit Allocations for the PSI-CELP Half-Rate JDC Speech Coder	
	Parameter	Bits
	LP synthesis filter	31
	Frame energy	7
	Periodic excitation	8×4
	Stochastic excitation	10×4
	Gain	7×4
	Total	138

the parameter bit allocations. The two sets of 10 linear prediction parameters, LSPs here, are coded using a combined three-way split VQ consisting of 31 bits.

Referring to Figure 6.17, the excitation x is the sum of the y and z components weighted by their gain. The y component uses the periodic adaptive codebook for voiced speech and the fixed codebook for unvoiced speech. The adaptive codebook is constructed of past excitation values, reminiscent of Barnwell's self-excited approach, with the number of previous excitation values included in the codevectors varying as a function of the 192 candidate pitch lags. The fixed codebook is included in the search for the best y excitation for unvoiced speech. The second component z is constructed as the sum of two codevectors chosen from two conjugate codebooks of 4 bits each. The component of z in the direction of y is discarded, thus causing y and z to be orthogonal and justifying independent quantization of their gains. The periodicity of the z component is also enhanced by preprocessing the codevectors to have a period corresponding to the pitch lag. This technique was determined to have a very positive effect on the quality of the reconstructed speech.

6.12 U.S. Federal Standard at 2.4 kbps

In mid-1996, a new U.S. federal standard at 2.4 kbps was adopted to replace the old U.S. Federal Standard 1015 based upon LPC-10e. The selection concluded two years of competition and experimentation. The decision was based upon a host of factors, including intelligibility, quality, complexity,

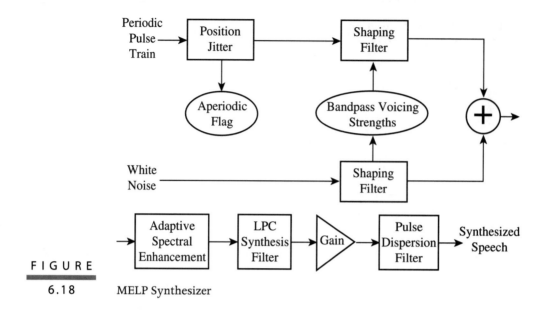

6.18   MELP Synthesizer

tandem performance, and speech coding performance for background impairments. The new 2.4-kbps standard is a predictive coder, but not a code excited analysis-by-synthesis coder. The speech coder is called mixed excitation linear prediction (MELP) and very creatively builds upon known concepts to substantially improve the performance of what is basically an LPC-based approach (McCree and Branwell 1995; McCree et al. 1996). The old idea is that the excitation in LPC should not just be a periodic excitation or a random sequence, but the excitation should be "mixed" even in voiced speech segments. One can also see the emphasis on different excitations in different bands in the IMBE coder and the sinusoidal transform coder (STC), but the MELP method is unique.

A block diagram of the MELP synthesizer is shown in Figure 6.18, where the upper half of the figure illustrates how the excitation is constructed. Generally, the relative mixture of pulse and noise power in each band is determined by an estimate of the voicing strength in each band, and the excitation is a frequency-shaped sum of periodic pulses and a white noise sequence. The excitation quality is improved by transmitting the magnitudes of the 10 lowest frequency harmonics of the LPC residual.

The bit allocation for the 2.4-kbps MELP is shown in Table 6.18. The MOS for this coder is about 3.2, and the complexity is rated at 20 MIPS with 6K of RAM.

T A B L E	MELP Coder Bit Allocation		
6.18	Parameters	Voiced	Unvoiced
	LSFs	25	25
	Fourier magnitudes	8	—
	Gain (2 per frame)	8	8
	Pitch and overall voicing	7	7
	Bandpass voicing	4	—
	Aperiodic flag	1	—
	Error protection	—	13
	Sync bit	1	1
	Total bits/22.5 ms	54	54

6.13 Additional and Forthcoming Standards

There are several other standards and forthcoming standards that implement the predictive coding structures described in Chapter 5. We give a brief overview of these in this section.

The ITU-T has standardized 40-, 32-, 24-, and 16-kbps embedded ADPCM as G.727. The main difference between G.727 and G.726 is that in the embedded standard, the decision levels of the lower-rate quantizers are subsets of the higher-rate quantizers, thus satisfying the embedded requirements outlined in Section 5.4. The bitstream in G.727 is said to contain core bits and enhancement bits, where the enhancement bits are eligible to be dropped by the network without informing the encoder. There are several different pairs of enhancement and core bit allocations depending upon the rate, and they are indicated as (5,4), (5,3), (5,2), (4,4), (4,3), (4,2), (3,3), (3,2), and (2,2), where (5,3) would correspond to enhancement rates of 40 and 32 kbps and a core rate of 24 kbps. Embedded coding works because only the core bits are used in the feedback loops that adapt the quantizers and predictors.

Another existing standard, called Skyphone, was developed by British Telecom International to enable telephone service from widebodied jets throughout the world. The Skyphone implements multipulse LPC (MPLPC) at 9.6 kbps (Boyd and Southcott 1988). This coder achieves an MOS of 3.4 without background noise, has an end-to-end delay of 40 ms, passes DTMF and 300 baud (V.21) modem signals, and is robust to a bit error rate of 10^{-3}. To achieve this quality at this rate, a long-term predictor is required in the MPLPC system.

There are a number of very recent standards. Among these is a new enhanced full-rate GSM coder at 13 kbps; it is an ACELP algorithm and achieves toll-quality speech. There is also an enhanced full-rate coder for North American digital cellular, which will replace IS-54 VSELP, designated IS-641, that operates at 7.4 kbps and adopts many of the features of G.729 ACELP (Cox and Kroon 1996). The variable-rate QCELP IS-96 coder is also being replaced by a variable-rate coder that incorporates generalized analysis-by-synthesis techniques as in RCELP (relaxed CELP) (Kleijn, Kroon, and Nahumi 1994) and that has rates of 8.5, 4, and 0.8 kbps. For simultaneous digital voice and data in the modem industry, the ITU-T has adopted G.729 Annex A, a lower-complexity version of G.729. This coder requires 12 MIPS on a TI DSP320C50 and less than 2K RAM and is bitstream interoperable with G.729 (Salami et al. 1997).

NATO has standardized a version of the U.S. federal standard 1015 at 800 bps that uses vector quantization.

7 Frequency Domain Coding

7.1 Introduction

Frequency domain methods have found applications in voice, wideband audio, CD-quality audio, still-image, and video compression. There are two basic principles involved:

1. By appropriate filtering or transformation, fewer, less correlated components can be obtained in the frequency domain that allow more efficient encoding.

2. Knowledge of the distortion perceived by listeners or viewers in the frequency domain can be used to improve coder subjective performance.

Of course, both of these steps can be aided somewhat if we are able to find "frequency domain" representations, or perhaps more accurately, signal decompositions, that are well matched to the particular source characteristics.

The general concept of frequency domain methods is illustrated in block diagram form by Figure 7.1. The source output that we start with is assumed to be a discrete-time, high-resolution sequence. We then perform the frequency domain decomposition, such as subband filtering or discrete transform, followed by the bit allocation step. Bit allocation determines how many bits should be used to encode each component, and this decision can lead to certain components being discarded completely if they are given 0 bits. Today, bit allocations are often set by offline experimentation to determine which allocation produces the best perceptual results over the class of sources of interest. The quantization step may consist of scalar or vector quantization (Chapter 4), or adaptive versions thereof, and encoding may be the assignment of a fixed-length code

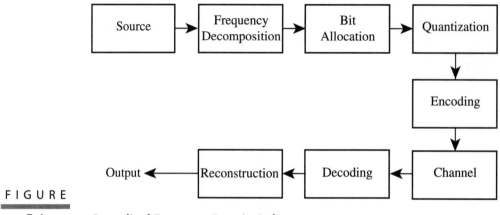

7.1   Generalized Frequency Domain Coding

or some entropy coding procedure such as Huffman, arithmetic, or Lempel-Ziv (Chapters 2 and 3). After passing through the channel, the frequency domain components are decoded and used in the reconstruction process. Reconstruction may be quadrature mirror filtering and summation or an inverse discrete transform. The reconstructed sequence is then made available to the user.

Although the discrete cosine transform (DCT) appears in many image and video coding standards and subband coding with quadrature mirror filters is common, newer decompositions such as wavelets and fractals are receiving substantial attention and consideration today. Wavelet coding is a generalization of both transform and subband coding (see Section 7.5). Although not strictly within the class of frequency domain coding schemes, fractal coding is included in this chapter for want of a better location. In addition to the decomposition methods used, different coding schemes and the incorporation of perceptual distortion measures are of major importance. A concise development of the state of the art in each of these areas is presented in this chapter.

7.2   Subband Coding of Speech

Subband coding of speech was introduced by Crochiere, Webber, and Flanagan (1976) in the form shown by the block diagram in Figure 7.2. The basic operations required by this coder are shown in Figure 7.3. The speech is band-pass filtered into several frequency bands, and each band is separately low-pass translated, decimated, and encoded. At the receiver the coded signals for each band are interpolated back to the original sampling rate and modulated back

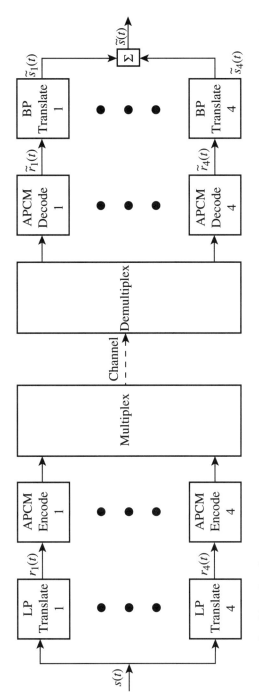

FIGURE

7.2

Four-Band Subband Coder

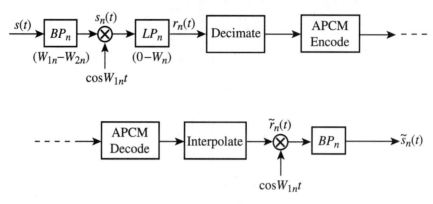

FIGURE

7.3   Basic Operations in Original Subband Coder

to their original frequency band. The components from the several bands are then summed to produce the reconstructed speech signal.

The use of the modulators for frequency translation in Figures 7.2 and 7.3 can be avoided by employing integer-band sampling (Crochiere, Webber, and Flanagan 1976). In this technique, the nth subband with bandwidth W_n has a lower cutoff frequency of mW_n, m an integer, and a higher cutoff frequency of $(m + 1)W_n$. Since the ratio of the lowest frequency in a subband to the subband bandwidth is an integer, that is, $mW_n/W_n = m$, sampling at a rate of $2W_n$ causes no overlap of the replicated spectra, and a copy of the spectrum in subband n appears around zero frequency. Thus, frequency translation is accomplished without modulation.

The three remaining principal operations required in subband coding are filtering into subbands, bit allocation across the subbands, and coding of the subbands. The subbands would ideally cover the entire signal bandwidth with no overlap. However, since physically implementable filters have a finite falloff rate, this ideal situation is not possible. If the subband filter passbands overlap too much, the required bit rate will be increased and the distortion within an individual subband will not be isolated from adjacent bands—there will be aliasing. One possible early solution to reducing the bit rate actually allowed for gaps between some adjacent subbands. However, these gaps can lead to a reverberant quality in the reconstructed speech (Crochiere, Webber, and Flanagan 1976).

The introduction of quadrature mirror filters (QMFs) greatly reduced the difficulties in this area (Esteban and Galand 1977). Generally, quadrature mirror filters allow overlap in the analysis filters at the encoder, which can lead to aliasing, but then the reconstruction filters are appropriately chosen to eliminate

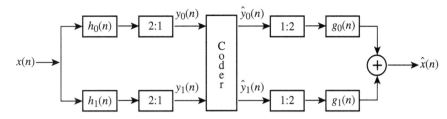

7.4   Two-Band Subband Coder

the aliasing. To demonstrate the technique, we consider the simple two-band subband coder shown in Figure 7.4. The following discussion is a composite of developments by Smith and Barnwell (1986), Vaidyanathan (1987), and Rabbani and Jones (1991). Let z denote $e^{j\omega}$. The outputs of the analysis filters in Figure 7.4 have the transforms

$$Y_0(z) = \frac{1}{2}[H_0(z^{1/2})X(z^{1/2}) + H_0(-z^{1/2})X(-z^{1/2})] \tag{7.1}$$

and

$$Y_1(z) = \frac{1}{2}[H_1(z^{1/2})X(z^{1/2}) + H_1(-z^{1/2})X(-z^{1/2})] \tag{7.2}$$

where the $-z^{1/2}$ terms are due to aliasing. The reconstructed signal is given by

$$\hat{X}(z) = \hat{Y}_0(z^2)G_0(z) + \hat{Y}_1(z^2)G_1(z) \tag{7.3}$$

Neglecting the distortion due to coding, we let $\hat{Y}_0(z^2) = Y_0(z^2)$ and $\hat{Y}_1(z^2) = Y_1(z^2)$, so the reconstructed output becomes

$$\hat{X}(z) = \frac{1}{2}[H_0(z)G_0(z) + H_1(z)G_1(z)]X(z)$$
$$+ \frac{1}{2}[H_0(-z)G_0(z) + H_1(-z)G_1(z)]X(-z) \tag{7.4}$$

The second term in equation (7.4) is due to aliasing, and it can be eliminated by choosing the reconstruction filters as

$$G_0(z) = H_1(-z)$$
$$G_1(z) = -H_0(-z) \tag{7.5}$$

Further, for simplicity of implementation, it is also usually imposed that

$$H_1(z) = H_0(-z) \tag{7.6}$$

which corresponds to

$$h_1(n) = (-1)^n h_0(n) \tag{7.7}$$

The overall transfer function is thus

$$T(z) = \frac{\hat{X}(z)}{X(z)} = \frac{1}{2}[H_0^2(z) - H_0^2(-z)]$$

or

$$T(e^{j\omega}) = \frac{1}{2}[|H_0(e^{j\omega})|^2 - (-1)^{N-1}|H_1(e^{j\omega})|^2] \cdot e^{-j\omega(N-1)} \tag{7.8}$$

The filter length N is chosen to be even since an odd N gives a null at $\omega = \pi/2$. With $H_0(z)$ chosen to be a linear phase FIR filter, the distortion is purely amplitude distortion and is given by

$$|T(e^{j\omega})| = \frac{1}{2}[|H_0(e^{j\omega})|^2 + |H_1(e^{j\omega})|^2] \tag{7.9}$$

Imposing the constraints in (7.5) and (7.6) for all of the analysis and reconstruction filters in M-band subband coding again allows the aliasing terms to be canceled. This is often implemented using a tree structure to split the subbands.

In order to be able to encode certain frequency ranges with greater accuracy than others, the subband bandwidths are usually chosen to be unequal. To obtain these unequal subband splits, it has been common to date to utilize a tree structure consisting of cascaded FIR QMFs that implement 2:1 subband splits. Thus, one might start with a 4-kHz band, say, and use two equal band QMFs to yield subbands covering 0–2 kHz and 2–4 kHz. Often the upper band is left as is, but the lower band at 0–2 kHz is further split into the subbands from 0–1 kHz and from 1–2 kHz. It is also usual to further split the lower band into 0–500 Hz and 500–1000 Hz subbands. Thus, there are four subbands in the final design, with the finer frequency resolution in the lower-frequency range.

The tree-structured implementation of nonuniform subband filters is convenient for having one two-band split design procedure, but it can lead to long delays and excessive complexity if FIR filters are used. This is because the FIR filters need many taps to achieve the magnitude response necessary to minimize adjacent filter band overlap, but this means that the cascaded FIR filters require many multiplications and have an overall delay several times the delay of a single FIR filter. The amount of the delay is proportional to the number of stages in the tree-structured filter bank.

Possible alternatives that remove or reduce these delay and complexity difficulties are to use single-stage nonuniform QMFs or to employ IIR filters in the tree-structured filter bank. The use of filters with nonuniform bands opens the possibility of matching the frequency segmentation of the input signal band with frequency bands corresponding to some perceptually interesting segmentation such as the Articulation Index.

One possible approach to allocating bits to the subbands is to note that the total MSE distortion, say, D, is given by the sum of the MSEs in the subbands, denoted D_i. Further, the distortion in the ith subband is represented by the distortion rate function of a sequence of independent, identically distributed Gaussian random variables, so

$$D_i = \sigma_i^2 2^{-2R_i} \tag{7.10}$$

and

$$D = \sum_{i=1}^{M} \sigma_i^2 2^{-2R_i} \tag{7.11}$$

The distortion in (7.10) is sometimes weighted by a function of R_i, say, $g(R_i)$, that depends on the type of encoding used. Often, $g(R_i)$ is chosen to be a constant. Minimizing D in (7.11) subject to the total rate constraint

$$R = \sum_{i=1}^{M} R_i \tag{7.12}$$

yields the bit (rate) allocation rule

$$R_i = R + \frac{1}{2} \log_2 \frac{\sigma_i^2}{\left[\prod_{l=1}^{M} \sigma_l^2\right]^{1/M}} \tag{7.13}$$

where σ_i^2 is the signal power in the ith subband. The result in (7.13) can yield negative values for one or more of the R_i; in this case, the offending R_i are set to zero and the other rates adjusted to satisfy the total rate constraint.

A newer rate allocation method for subband coding assumes that the rate distortion performance of each available quantizer (or other coder) is known, and it searches for the convex hull of these points in the R-D plane. Westerink, Biemond, and Boekee (1988) give some comparative performance results for images (presented later in this chapter).

To obtain maximum benefit from subband coding, bit allocation for the subbands for speech has generally been accomplished based upon subjective experiments and not using particular bit allocation routines. An adaptive bit allocation rule is always preferred to a fixed bit allocation across subbands, but

T A B L E	Subband Coder Characteristics for Example 1				
7.1		Frequency	Sampling	Bit Allocations	
	Subband	Range (kHz)	Rate (kHz)	16 kbps	24 kbps
	1	0–0.5	1	4	5
	2	0.5–1.0	1	4	5
	3	1.0–2.0	2	2	4
	4	2.0–3.0	2	2	3
	5	3.0–4.0	2	0	0

since the receiver must be informed of the bit allocation for a particular block, the choices for the bit allocation are usually limited to a few possibilities so that a small number of bits per block or frame are needed to transmit this information.

Each subband has its own encoder/decoder pair, and any standard coding scheme can be used, such as adaptive quantization, DPCM, or vector quantization. Backward adaptive methods are often preferred to avoid the requirement of using part of the precious bit rate for side information. We now describe some typical subband coder designs.

7.2.1   Example 1

A subband coder is used in AT&T voice store and forward products (Josenhans et al. 1986). There is both a 16-kbps coder and a 24-kbps coder. Their subbands, sampling rates, and bit allocations are given in Table 7.1. The subband coders use quadrature mirror filters in a tree structure, and the subbands are coded using backward APCM.

7.2.2   Example 2

In this example, we describe two subband coders that were investigated for use in the European mobile radio system (Vary et al. 1988). One coder used block forward adaptive PCM with 14 subbands and operated at a transmitted bit rate of 13 kbps. The other coder employed 6 subbands, each encoded with ADPCM. The total bit rate of this second system was 15 kbps. Extensive listening tests on seven languages over a variety of mobile radio environments yielded MOS scores of 3.14 for the first coder and 2.92 for the second coder.

Of course, one of the major success stories of subband coding has been in the efficient representation of high-quality audio. These systems rely heavily on innovations in signal processing combined with an application of the latest knowledge of human perceptual response and are allocated an entire chapter, Chapter 8.

7.3   Subband Coding of Images

The first application of subband coding to images seems to be due to Woods and O'Neil (1986), and it has proven to be a powerful technique indeed. Generally, the basic idea is the same as subband coding for one-dimensional signals—namely, separate the image into subbands, encode the subbands separately, and then reconstruct. The primary differences are in how to choose the analysis and synthesis filters and that bit allocation is a slightly more important part of the design. We begin with a discussion of QMF filter design for two-dimensional signals, followed by brief discussions of bit allocation and example coding experiments.

The initial part of this section follows the development of Woods and O'Neil (1986). Consider the four-band splitting and reconstruction shown in Figures 7.5 and 7.6, respectively. The filters $H_{ij}(\omega_1, \omega_2)$, $F_{ij}(\omega_1, \omega_2)$, $i, j = 1, 2$, must be designed to cancel the aliasing as in the one-dimensional case. To begin, for real h_{ij} the subband analysis filters are required to satisfy

$$H_{12}(\omega_1, \omega_2) = H_{11}(\omega_1, \omega_2 + \pi) \tag{7.14}$$

$$H_{21}(\omega_1, \omega_2) = H_{11}(\omega_1 + \pi, \omega_2) \tag{7.15}$$

$$H_{22}(\omega_1, \omega_2) = H_{11}(\omega_1 + \pi, \omega_2 + \pi) \tag{7.16}$$

The outputs of the analysis stage in Figure 7.5 after downsampling are

$$Y_{ij}(\omega_1, \omega_2) = \frac{1}{4} \sum_{k=0}^{1} \sum_{l=0}^{1} H_{ij}\left(\frac{\omega_1 + k\pi}{2}, \frac{\omega_2 + l\pi}{2}\right)$$
$$\cdot X\left(\frac{\omega_1 + k\pi}{2}, \frac{\omega_2 + l\pi}{2}\right) \tag{7.17}$$

The components of the reconstruction stage are

$$\hat{X}_{ij}(\omega_1, \omega_2) = Y_{ij}(2\omega_1, 2\omega_2) F_{ij}(\omega_1, \omega_2) \tag{7.18}$$

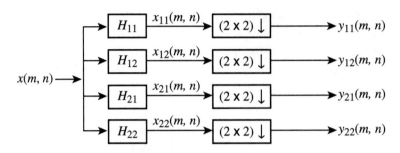

FIGURE

7.5

Four-Band Splitting

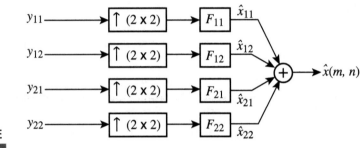

FIGURE

7.6

Four-Band Reconstruction

from which the reconstructed signal can be obtained as

$$\hat{X}(\omega_1, \omega_2) = \frac{1}{4}\sum_k \sum_l X(\omega_1 + k\pi, \omega_2 + l\pi)$$

$$\cdot \left[\sum_i \sum_j H_{ij}(\omega_1 + k\pi, \omega_2 + l\pi) F_{ij}(\omega_1, \omega_2) \right]$$

(7.19)

The desired term in (7.19) is the $k, l = 0, 0$ term, and the remainder is aliasing. The aliasing will be canceled if and only if

$$\sum_i \sum_j H_{ij}(\omega_1 + k\pi, \omega_2 + l\pi) F_{ij}(\omega_1, \omega_2) = 0$$

(7.20)

for $(k, l) \neq (0, 0)$. Thus, the reconstruction filters are chosen as

$$F_{11}(\omega_1, \omega_2) = 4H_{11}(\omega_1, \omega_2)$$

(7.21)

$$F_{12}(\omega_1, \omega_2) = -4H_{12}(\omega_1, \omega_2)$$

(7.22)

$$F_{21}(\omega_1, \omega_2) = -4H_{21}(\omega_1, \omega_2) \qquad (7.23)$$

$$F_{22}(\omega_1, \omega_2) = 4H_{22}(\omega_1, \omega_2) \qquad (7.24)$$

For $(k, l) = (0, 1)$ or $(1,0)$, it can be seen that the aliased terms are zero from (7.14) through (7.16), (7.19), and (7.21) through (7.24). If $(k, l) = (1, 1)$, the aliased term is zero if and only if

$$H_{11}(\omega_1, \omega_2)H_{11}(\omega_1 + \pi, \omega_2 + \pi) = H_{11}(\omega_1, \omega_2 + \pi)H_{11}(\omega_1 + \pi, \omega_2)$$

$$(7.25)$$

Selecting h_{11} to be a symmetric L-by-L FIR filter, the nonaliased term requires

$$|H_{11}^2(\omega_1, \omega_2)| + |H_{11}^2(\omega_1, \omega_2 + \pi)| + |H_{11}^2(\omega_1 + \pi, \omega_2)|$$
$$+ |H_{11}^2(\omega_1 + \pi, \omega_2 + \pi)| = 1 \qquad (7.26)$$

subject to (7.25).

One-dimensional QMF two-band analysis filters satisfy

$$h_1(n) = h_1(L - 1 - n), 0 \leq n \leq \frac{L}{2} - 1 \qquad (7.27)$$

$$h_2(n) = (-1)^n h_1(n) \qquad (7.28)$$

and approximately achieve

$$|H_1(\omega)|^2 + |H_2(\omega)|^2 = 1 \qquad (7.29)$$

A separable two-dimensional filter defined as

$$h_{11}(m, n) = h_1(m)h_1(n) \qquad (7.30)$$

automatically satisfies (7.25). Nonseparable filters yield directional information, while separable filters are computationally simple.

Most two-dimensional subband coding work has used separable filters. A four-band analysis/synthesis structure using separable filters is shown in Figure 7.7. This type of filtering partitions the (ω_1, ω_2) plane approximately as shown in Figure 7.8. Sixteen-band separable filtering is used by Woods and O'Neil (1986) for image coding. Tables 7.2 and 7.3 show subband means and variances of the image LENA for 4-band and 16-band separable filter analysis stages (Rabbani and Jones 1991). Note that only the low-pass subbands have appreciable means and that the variance of the image is very nearly equal to the sum of the subband variances.

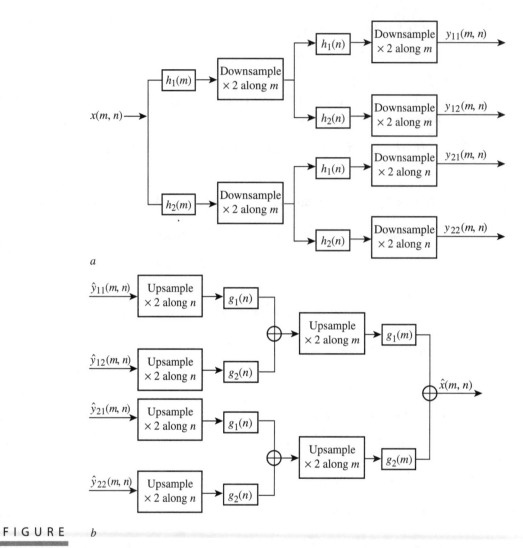

Two-Dimensional Four-Band Separable Filtering: *(a)* Analysis; *(b)* Reconstruction

The most common method of bit allocation is that which relies on distortion rate theory or high-rate quantization theory, as previously discussed for one-dimensional signals. This is the method used by Woods and O'Neil (1986). There is also the approach based upon finding the convex hull of the R-D performance of all available encoders. A comparison of these two methods was performed by Westerink, Biemond, and Boekee (1988), and the two bit allocations are given here in Table 7.4. The difference in SNR for the two methods is less than 1 dB over the range of 0.5 to 1.5 bits/pixel, which, although seemingly small, may prove significant.

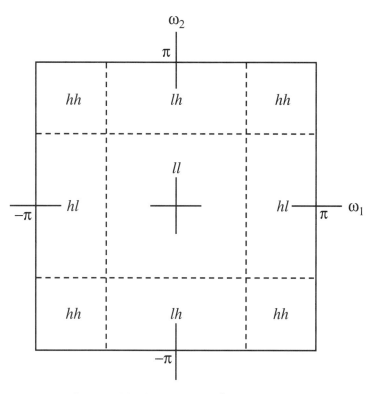

FIGURE

7.8 Frequency Plane Partitioning Corresponding to Figure 7.7

T A B L E Means and Variances for a 4-Band Split

7.2 of LENA (Rabbani and Jones 1991)

Subband	Mean	Variance
$\ell\ell$	123.60	2282.03
ℓh	0.01	4.06
$h\ell$	0.01	10.30
hh	0.00	2.23
Sum	123.62	2298.62
Original	123.61	2298.65

Means and Variances for a 16-Band Split of LENA (Rabbani and Jones 1991)

Subband	Mean	Variance
$\ell\ell$-$\ell\ell$	123.60	2230.78
$\ell\ell$-ℓh	0.01	11.05
$\ell\ell$-$h\ell$	0.01	32.02
$h\ell$-$h\ell$	−0.02	5.41
$\ell\ell$-hh	0.01	8.12
ℓh-ℓh	0.01	1.37
ℓh-$\ell\ell$	0.01	0.65
ℓh-hh	−0.02	1.54
$h\ell$-hh	0.00	2.41
$h\ell$-$\ell\ell$	0.02	1.61
$h\ell$-ℓh	0.01	0.87
hh-hh	−0.01	0.86
ℓh-$h\ell$	0.00	0.49
hh-$h\ell$	0.00	0.47
hh-ℓh	0.00	0.52
hh-$\ell\ell$	0.00	0.37
Sum	123.63	2298.40
Original	123.61	2298.65

Bit Assignments from Two Allocation Algorithms at 0.75 Bits/Pixel (Westerink, Biemond, and Boekee 1988)

Subband	1	2	3	4	5	6	7	8	9	10	11	12	13	14	15	16
	16	8	4	4	1	3	1	1	1	1	1	1	1	1	1	1

(Woods and O'Neil 1986)

	16	4	2	2	3	3	1	3	1	1	1	1	1	1	1	1

(Westerink, Biemond, and Boekee 1991)

T A B L E
7.5

SNR Performance for LENA and Building
(Woods and O'Neil 1986)

Bits/Pixel	LENA (Nonadaptive)	LENA (Adaptive)	BUILDING (Adaptive)
0.67	29.4 dB	30.9 dB	30.6 dB (.57)
1.0	31.4 dB	32.5 dB	33.8 dB
2.0	35.4 dB	36.6 dB	38.0 dB

T A B L E
7.6

Subband Coding with Vector Quantization
(Rabbani and Jones 1991)

Bits/Pixel	SNR LENA	BOOTS
0.38	30.7	26.1
0.56	32.7	27.6
0.75	34.0	28.7
0.94	34.7	29.3

Woods and O'Neil (1986), using 16-band tree-structured separable QMF filters, the approximate scalar bit allocation in (7.13), and DPCM coding of the subbands, achieved the SNR performance shown in Table 7.5. The results of using 16-band subband coding with vector quantization on the LENA and BOOTS images are listed in Table 7.6 (Rabbani and Jones 1991).

Three-dimensional subband coding of video, where time is used as the third dimension, has also been explored. One motivation for considering this approach is the possibility of eliminating the need for motion compensation, which is very susceptible to bit errors and produces serious blocking effects when there is extreme motion. The number of frames employed in the third dimension is a function of complexity and actual "memory" that can be taken advantage of, and often only two frames may be included in the subband decomposition. Research work has revealed that motion compensation is still useful even when three-dimensional subband coding is implemented. As in one- and two-dimensional subband coding, an attraction of three-dimensional subband coding is the possibility of better modeling perceptual effects in the coding process, and this has been the emphasis of much recent work. To date, three-dimensional subband coding has not appeared in any standards nor displaced two-dimensional approaches combined with motion compensation.

7.4   Transform Coding of Speech and Images

The concepts behind transform-based data compression methods are straightforward. First, we find an exact series representation of a given set of input samples. Second, we discard those terms in the series that affect the fidelity of the reconstructed signal the least. Third, we quantize and encode the remaining coefficients (of the basis functions) to produce a digital representation. These bits are then transmitted to the receiver and decoded to yield the truncated (quantized) series coefficients, which are then used to construct an approximation to the input waveform. There is substantial practical interest in these techniques for both speech and image encoding (Rabbani and Jones 1991; Spanias 1994; Vetterli and Kovacevic 1995; Woods 1991).

The steps in transform coding can be represented by the block diagram in Figure 7.9 and can be expressed in matrix notation as follows. We are given a discrete-time, discrete-amplitude sequence, say, $\{s(0), s(1), s(2), \ldots, s(k), \ldots\}$, which we then partition into blocks M samples long. We denote each block of M samples by

$$\mathbf{s} = [s(0)s(1) \ldots s(M-1)] \tag{7.31}$$

Following Figure 7.9, we premultiply the vector $\mathbf{s}$ by the matrix $\mathbf{T}$, representing the transform operation, to generate a vector of transform coefficients

$$\mathbf{c} = \mathbf{Ts} \tag{7.32}$$

The selection matrix $\mathbf{G}$ with components g_{ij}, $j = 1, 2, \ldots, M$, and $i = 1, 2, \ldots, N$, $N \leq M$, has $g_{ij} = 1$ if the jth component of $\mathbf{c}$ is to be retained as the ith element of $\tilde{\mathbf{c}}$. The selection matrix typically would retain the N highest energy components and discard the remaining $M - N$ in order to improve data compression.

The $N \times 1$ vector $\mathbf{c}$ is thus

$$\tilde{\mathbf{c}} = \mathbf{Gc} \tag{7.33}$$

which is then quantized and encoded for transmission over the channel. Assuming no channel errors, the binary data string $\mathbf{b}$ is decoded at the receiver as

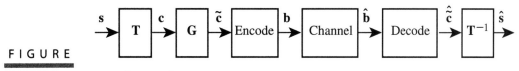

7.9 Transform Coding Operations

$\hat{\mathbf{c}}$. The inverse transform operation yields an approximation to the input vector

$$\hat{\mathbf{s}} = \mathbf{T}^{-1}\hat{\mathbf{c}} \qquad (7.34)$$

In the following, we discuss each of the steps in more detail.

7.4.1 Discrete Transforms

Given this block of M signal (uniformly spaced) samples denoted by $\{s(0), s(1), \ldots, s(M-1)\}$, the *discrete Fourier transform* (DFT) of these samples is given by

$$S(u) = \frac{1}{M} \sum_{k=0}^{M-1} s(k)e^{-j2\pi uk/M} \qquad (7.35)$$

for $u = 0, 1, 2, \ldots, M-1$. The inverse DFT is given by

$$s(k) = \sum_{u=0}^{M-1} S(u)e^{j2\pi uk/M} \qquad (7.36)$$

for $k = 0, 1, 2, \ldots, M-1$. The inverse DFT returns the original sequence exactly if no terms are deleted and no coefficients $\{S(u), u = 0, 1, \ldots, M-1\}$ are modified. Equations (7.35) and (7.36) define the *discrete Fourier transform pair*.

Another important discrete transform is the discrete cosine transform (DCT), which for the sequence $\{s(0), s(1), \ldots, s(M-1)\}$ is represented by

$$C(0) = \frac{1}{\sqrt{M}} \sum_{k=0}^{M-1} s(k) \qquad (7.37)$$

and

$$C(u) = \sqrt{\frac{2}{M}} \sum_{k=0}^{M-1} s(k) \cos\left[\frac{(2k+1)u\pi}{2M}\right] \qquad (7.38)$$

for $u = 1, 2, \ldots, M - 1$. The inverse DCT is defined by

$$s(k) = \frac{1}{\sqrt{M}} C(0) + \sqrt{\frac{2}{M}} \sum_{u=0}^{M-1} C(u) \cos \left[\frac{(2k+1)u\pi}{2M} \right] \tag{7.39}$$

for $k = 0, 1, 2, \ldots, M - 1$.

We have already presented two discrete transforms, and there are in fact many more, so the question arises, "What are the criteria used in selecting a transform?" Two obvious criteria are performance and complexity.

The optimum transform in terms of concentrating the most energy in the fewest transform coefficients is the Karhunen-Loeve transform (KLT), which is also known as the Hotelling transform or the method of principal components. Defining the covariance function of the input vectors as

$$\mathbf{W} = E\{[\mathbf{s} - E(\mathbf{s})][\mathbf{s} - E(\mathbf{s})]^T\} \tag{7.40}$$

the basis functions of the KLT are the eigenvectors of $\mathbf{W}$. Thus, to find the KLT given $\mathbf{W}$, we calculate the eigenvalues of $\mathbf{W}$, $\{\lambda_i, i = 1, 2, \ldots, M\}$ and then solve for the eigenvectors $\{\Psi_i, i = 1, 2, \ldots, M\}$ from

$$\mathbf{W}\Psi_i = \lambda_i \Psi_i \tag{7.41}$$

$i = 1, 2, \ldots, M$. The resulting eigenvectors are orthonormal,

$$\Psi_i^T \Psi_j = \begin{cases} 1, & i = j \\ 0, & i \neq j \end{cases} \tag{7.42}$$

and defining the transform matrix

$$\mathbf{T} = \left[\Psi_1^T \Psi_2^T \ldots \Psi_M^T \right]^T \tag{7.43}$$

we have that

$$\mathbf{T}\mathbf{W}\mathbf{T}^T = \Lambda \tag{7.44}$$

where $\Lambda = \text{diag}(\lambda_1 \lambda_2 \ldots \lambda_M)$.

As an example, consider source vectors of length $M = 2$ with zero mean and

$$\mathbf{W} = \begin{bmatrix} 1 & \rho \\ \rho & 1 \end{bmatrix} \tag{7.45}$$

We find the eigenvalues of $\mathbf{W}$ to be $\lambda_1 = 1 + \rho$ and $\lambda_2 = 1 - \rho$. From (7.41) we then determine the eigenvectors

$$\Psi_1 = \begin{bmatrix} \frac{1}{\sqrt{2}} & \frac{1}{\sqrt{2}} \end{bmatrix} \tag{7.46a}$$

and

$$\Psi_2 = \begin{bmatrix} \frac{1}{\sqrt{2}} & \frac{-1}{\sqrt{2}} \end{bmatrix} \tag{7.46b}$$

so that the transform matrix is

$$\mathbf{T}_{KL} = \frac{1}{\sqrt{2}} \begin{bmatrix} 1 & 1 \\ 1 & -1 \end{bmatrix} \tag{7.47}$$

We will pursue the optimality properties of the KLT a little more shortly, but from the development so far, it is evident that the KLT is not simple to compute. To recapitulate, we need the covariance matrix of the data, and then we must calculate the eigenvalues and eigenvectors. These are not trivial tasks. In contrast, note that the DFT and DCT basis functions are directly available from the given equations—no covariance matrix or eigenvectors are needed.

One of the simplest transforms is the *Walsh-Hadamard transform* (WHT), which is generally drawn from rectangular waves with amplitudes ±1, called *Walsh functions*. It is convenient (and standard) to express the Walsh-Hadamard transform basis functions in terms of the appropriate Hadamard matrices. A Hadamard matrix $\mathbf{H}_k$ of order k is a $k \times k$ matrix of +1s and −1s that satisfies

$$\mathbf{H}_k \mathbf{H}_k^T = k\mathbf{I} \tag{7.48}$$

where $\mathbf{I}$ is the identity matrix. In digital signal processing, it is common to work with a normalized version of $\mathbf{H}_k$, $\frac{1}{\sqrt{k}}\mathbf{H}_k$. From now on, we refer to this normalized matrix as the Hadamard matrix and use $\bar{\mathbf{H}}_k$ as the notation for $\frac{1}{\sqrt{k}}\mathbf{H}_k$. Given a Hadamard matrix of order k, it is possible to express the Hadamard matrix of order $2k$ as

$$\bar{\mathbf{H}}_{2k} = \frac{1}{\sqrt{2}} \begin{bmatrix} \bar{\mathbf{H}}_k & \bar{\mathbf{H}}_k \\ \bar{\mathbf{H}}_k & -\bar{\mathbf{H}}_k \end{bmatrix} \tag{7.49}$$

Thus, starting with $H_1 = 1$, we can generate

$$\bar{\mathbf{H}}_2 = \frac{1}{\sqrt{2}} \begin{bmatrix} 1 & 1 \\ 1 & -1 \end{bmatrix} \tag{7.50}$$

$$\bar{\mathbf{H}}_4 = \frac{1}{\sqrt{4}} \begin{bmatrix} 1 & 1 & 1 & 1 \\ 1 & -1 & 1 & -1 \\ 1 & 1 & -1 & -1 \\ 1 & -1 & -1 & 1 \end{bmatrix} \tag{7.51}$$

and

$$\bar{\mathbf{H}}_8 = \frac{1}{\sqrt{8}} \begin{bmatrix} 1 & 1 & 1 & 1 & 1 & 1 & 1 & 1 \\ 1 & -1 & 1 & -1 & 1 & -1 & 1 & -1 \\ 1 & 1 & -1 & -1 & 1 & 1 & -1 & -1 \\ 1 & -1 & -1 & 1 & 1 & -1 & -1 & 1 \\ 1 & 1 & 1 & 1 & -1 & -1 & -1 & -1 \\ 1 & -1 & 1 & -1 & -1 & 1 & -1 & 1 \\ 1 & 1 & -1 & -1 & -1 & -1 & 1 & 1 \\ 1 & -1 & -1 & 1 & -1 & 1 & 1 & -1 \end{bmatrix} \tag{7.52}$$

and so on. In contrast to error control coding applications, it is more likely in signal processing that the basis functions are written as rows of the matrix in order of increasing number of zero crossings. Therefore, (7.52) is usually rewritten as

$$\bar{\mathbf{H}}_8 = \frac{1}{\sqrt{8}} \begin{bmatrix} 1 & 1 & 1 & 1 & 1 & 1 & 1 & 1 \\ 1 & 1 & 1 & 1 & -1 & -1 & -1 & -1 \\ 1 & 1 & -1 & -1 & -1 & -1 & 1 & 1 \\ 1 & 1 & -1 & -1 & 1 & 1 & -1 & -1 \\ 1 & -1 & -1 & 1 & 1 & -1 & -1 & 1 \\ 1 & -1 & -1 & 1 & -1 & 1 & 1 & -1 \\ 1 & -1 & 1 & -1 & -1 & 1 & -1 & 1 \\ 1 & -1 & 1 & -1 & 1 & -1 & 1 & -1 \end{bmatrix} \tag{7.53}$$

To illustrate the concept of unitary transforms, consider the data vector $\mathbf{s}^T = [10\ 20\ 15\ 5]$. We calculate the WHT as

$$\mathbf{c} = \begin{bmatrix} c_1 \\ c_2 \\ c_3 \\ c_4 \end{bmatrix} = \frac{1}{2} \begin{bmatrix} 1 & 1 & 1 & 1 \\ 1 & 1 & -1 & -1 \\ 1 & -1 & -1 & 1 \\ 1 & -1 & 1 & -1 \end{bmatrix} \begin{bmatrix} 10 \\ 20 \\ 15 \\ 5 \end{bmatrix} = \frac{1}{2} \begin{bmatrix} 50 \\ 10 \\ -20 \\ 0 \end{bmatrix} = \begin{bmatrix} 25 \\ 5 \\ -10 \\ 0 \end{bmatrix} \tag{7.54}$$

Note that $\mathbf{s}^T\mathbf{s} = 10^2 + 20^2 + 15^2 + 5^2 = 750$ and $\mathbf{c}^T\mathbf{c} = 25^2 + 5^2 + (-10)^2 + 0^2 = 750$, so $\mathbf{s}^T\mathbf{s} = \mathbf{c}^T\mathbf{c}$. Transforms that preserve energy in this sense are called *unitary*, and only unitary transforms are considered here.

To choose among the several transforms, we need some performance measure. Clarke (1985) has defined two measures that indicate the performance of transforms in terms of energy packing efficiency and decorrelation efficiency. Letting $\mathbf{W}$ be the covariance matrix of the input data, then the covariance of the transformed data is denoted by $\mathbf{V}$, so

T A B L E	Decorrelation Efficiency Comparison		
7.7		KLT	DCT	WHT
	η_c	1.0000	0.9805	0.9486

T A B L E	Energy Packing Efficiency (Rao and Yip 1990)							
7.8					η_E			
	$N = 1$	2	3	4	5	6	7	8
WHT	0.793	0.893	0.927	0.955	0.967	0.979	0.990	1.000
DCT	0.793	0.909	0.948	0.967	0.979	0.987	0.994	1.000
KLT	0.795	0.911	0.948	0.967	0.979	0.987	0.994	1.000

$$\mathbf{V} = \mathbf{TWT}^T \tag{7.55}$$

Clarke (1985) defines the decorrelation efficiency as

$$\eta_C = 1 - \frac{\Sigma_{j \neq k}|v_{jk}|}{\Sigma_{j \neq k}|w_{jk}|} \tag{7.56}$$

and specifies the energy packing efficiency in the first N components as

$$\eta_E = \frac{\Sigma_{j=1}^{N} v_{jj}}{\Sigma_{j=1}^{M} v_{jj}} \tag{7.57}$$

with $N \leq M$.

For a first-order Markov source sequence of the form

$$s(n) = \alpha s(n-1) + \xi(n) \tag{7.58}$$

we can compare the transforms according to these efficiency measures. The first-order Markov source is of some importance for both speech and image modeling. For $M = 8$ and $\alpha = 0.91$, the values of η_C and η_E for the KLT, DCT, and WHT are shown in Tables 7.7 and 7.8, respectively. The striking agreement in Table 7.8 indicates that, for this source, the DCT has an energy packing efficiency very close to that of the KLT. Table 7.7 shows, however, that the DCT is not as efficient at decorrelating the source as the KLT.

The basis functions for the DCT and the WHT with $M = 8$ are shown in Figures 7.10 and 7.11, respectively. The KLT basis functions for the first-order

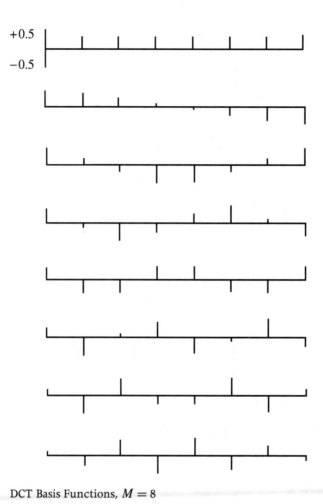

7.10   DCT Basis Functions, $M = 8$

Markov source are given in Figure 7.12. The similarities between the DCT and KLT basis functions in Figures 7.10 and 7.12 are clearly evident and demonstrate further why the DCT is so successful for this source (Clarke 1985). For the first-order Markov source, an asymptotic equivalence between the DCT and the KLT can be established as $M \to \infty$ and/or as $\alpha \to 1$, depending upon the specific DCT algorithm (Rao and Yip 1990).

The transforms defined thus far are called *one-dimensional transforms* since the input data is presented as a function of one variable. One-dimensional transforms have applications to both speech and images, as well as to other physical signals. However, two-dimensional versions of discrete transforms can also be defined that have particular importance for naturally occurring

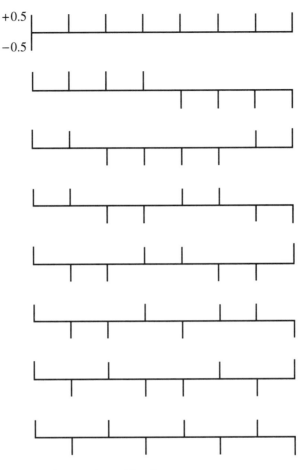

FIGURE

7.11   WHT Basis Functions, $M = 8$

two-dimensional entities such as images. Given a doubly indexed array of samples denoted $\{s(k, \ell), k = 0, 1, \ldots, M - 1, \ell = 0, 1, \ldots, M - 1\}$, the *two-dimensional DFT*, sometimes designated as the 2D-DFT, is defined as

$$S(u, v) = \frac{1}{M^2} \sum_{k=0}^{M-1} \sum_{\ell=0}^{M-1} s(k, \ell) e^{-j2\pi \left[\frac{uk}{M} + \frac{v\ell}{M}\right]} \tag{7.59}$$

for $u, v = 0, 1, \ldots, M - 1$, with the inverse transform

$$s(k, \ell) = \sum_{u=0}^{M-1} \sum_{v=0}^{M-1} S(u, v) e^{j2\pi \left[\frac{uk}{M} + \frac{v\ell}{M}\right]} \tag{7.60}$$

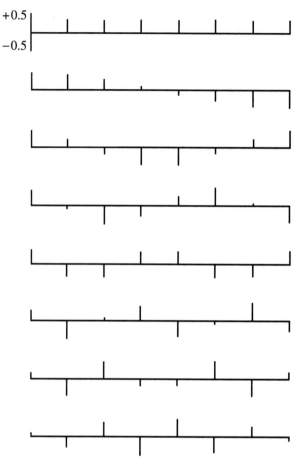

FIGURE

7.12   KLT Basis Functions, Markov Source $\rho = 0.91$, $M = 8$ (Rao and Yip 1990)

for $k, \ell = 0, 1, \ldots, M - 1$. The *two-dimensional DCT* is defined by

$$C(0, 0) = \frac{1}{M} \sum_{k=0}^{M-1} \sum_{\ell=0}^{M-1} s(k, \ell) \tag{7.61}$$

and

$$C(u, v) = \frac{2}{M} \sum_{k=0}^{M-1} \sum_{\ell=0}^{M-1} s(k, \ell) \cos\left[\frac{(2k + 1)u\pi}{2M}\right] \cos\left[\frac{(2\ell + 1)v\pi}{2M}\right] \tag{7.62}$$

$u, v = 0, 1, \ldots, M - 1$, with the inverse transform

$$s(k, \ell) = \frac{2}{M} \left[\frac{C(0, 0)}{2} + \sum_{u=0}^{M-1} \sum_{v=0}^{M-1} C(u, v) \ \cos\left[\frac{(2k + 1)u\pi}{2M}\right] \right.$$

$$\left. \cos\left[\frac{(2\ell + 1)v\pi}{2M}\right] \right] \tag{7.63}$$

for $k, \ell = 0, 1, \ldots, M - 1$.

While these transforms look extremely complicated, it is well known by electrical engineers that a class of "fast" algorithms for implementing the one-dimensional DFT exists, which are all called the *fast Fourier transform* (FFT) *algorithm*. Also, the two-dimensional DFT has a special property, called *separability*, that allows it to be computed using two one-dimensional DFTs, and hence FFTs. Fast algorithms for two-dimensional DCTs and other transforms have been developed, and indeed, the investigation of fast algorithms for important transforms is an active research area.

The separability of the transforms greatly simplifies writing the transform operations in matrix notation. The separability of the 2D-DCT in (7.62) is evident, since we can write the transform first as row, then column, operations,

$$C(u, v) = \frac{2}{M} \Sigma_{k=0}^{M-1} \cos[(2k + 1)u\pi] \Sigma_{l=0}^{M-1} s(k, l) \cos[(2l + 1)v\pi] \tag{7.64}$$

Equation (7.64) implies that we perform the two-dimensional transform by performing separate one-dimensional transforms on the rows and columns. Further, for symmetric kernels, which we have here, we can write that the two-dimensional transform for an $M \times M$ data matrix $\mathbf{S}$ is

$$\mathbf{C} = \mathbf{T S T}^T \tag{7.65}$$

where $\mathbf{T}$ is the $M \times M$ one-dimensional transform matrix.

Transform coding of speech was first studied by Zelinski and Noll (1977), and drawing on their work, transform coding of speech at 16 kbps can achieve communications quality, if not toll quality, and transform coding performance holds up quite nicely until about 12 kbps, where the quality starts to noticeably degrade. Numerous additions have been made to the basic approach, such as incorporating pitch prediction with the subbands and adaptive quantization and adaptive bit allocation. Furthermore, in transform coding, an accurate, efficient representation of the spectrum is important, and several people have investigated parametric models for the spectrum, such as cepstral models.

8	8	5	5	4	4	3	3	2	2	2	1	1	1	1	1
8	5	4	3	3	3	2	2	2	1	1	1	0	0	0	0
6	4	4	3	3	2	2	1	1	1	1	1	1	0	0	0
5	3	3	3	2	2	2	1	1	1	1	0	0	0	0	0
4	3	3	3	2	2	2	1	1	1	1	0	0	0	0	0
4	3	3	2	2	2	1	1	1	1	0	0	0	0	0	0
3	2	2	2	2	1	1	1	1	0	0	0	0	0	0	0
3	2	2	2	2	1	1	1	0	0	0	0	0	0	0	0
2	2	1	2	1	1	1	1	0	0	0	0	0	0	0	0
2	1	2	1	1	1	1	1	0	0	0	0	0	0	0	0
2	1	1	1	1	1	0	1	0	0	0	0	0	0	0	0
2	1	1	1	1	0	0	0	0	0	0	0	0	0	0	0
2	1	1	0	0	0	0	0	0	0	0	0	0	0	0	0
1	0	1	1	0	0	0	0	0	0	0	0	0	0	0	0
1	0	0	0	0	0	0	0	0	0	0	0	0	0	0	0
1	0	0	0	0	0	0	0	0	0	0	0	0	0	0	0

FIGURE 7.13 Example Bit Allocation Map

Transform coding was applied to image compression before it was to speech (Gonzalez and Wintz 1977; Pratt 1978), primarily because of the perceived complexity of the method. Of course, transform coding is the basis of several existing image and video coding standards. Bit allocation methods employed in transform coding are those outlined in Section 7.2; more recently, psychovisual experiments have been used, and the choice among the several methods depends upon the application and the quantization techniques used. As an example, we can use the simple bit allocation method in (7.13) on a monochrome 256 × 256 image. To do this, we use the 2D-DCT on 16 × 16 blocks. To get the variances needed in (7.13) for the coefficients, we compute the variances across the 256 values for each coefficient in the image (there are 256 16 × 16 blocks in the 256 × 256 image). For an average rate of 1 bit/pixel, we get the bit allocation map shown in Figure 7.13, where the number in the upper left-hand corner is for the dc coefficient, the numbers along the horizontal direction are for the harmonic coefficients in the horizontal direction, and the numbers in the columns are the bit allocations for the vertical harmonics. To get the results in Figure 7.13, we limited the maximum number of bits allocated to any coefficient to be 8, and iterated to meet the 256 bits per block rate constraint.

The presentation of the bit allocations as in Figure 7.13 is common in the literature and has no pixel-related interpretation. Note the large number of zero values, which means that these coefficients are being discarded. It is common in standards to use the same type of presentation, but with the bits allocated replaced by the step size. Thus, where the number of bits allocated is large in Figure 7.13, there would be a small step size, and where there is a 0, there would be a large step size. It must also be noted that, although several good algorithms for allocating bits are now available, the bit allocation tables that appear in many of the standards were obtained via actual coding experiments, so that the perceptual effects of the human visual system can be accounted for.

7.5 Wavelet Coding

The discrete transform methods developed in Section 7.4 break the input signal into fixed-length time frames and frequency bands so that the time-frequency plane is covered or tiled by rectangles. Subband coding with uniform bandwidth filters does the same thing. This uniform time-frequency tiling is illustrated in Figure 7.14. Since we know that each of these bands may not have equal perceptual importance, this fact is accounted for by unequal bit allocations. There are limitations to what can be gained by unequal bit allocations, and so engineers have been led to employ nonuniform subband filtering such

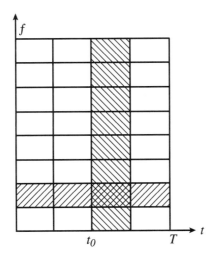

FIGURE

7.14   Uniform Time-Frequency Tiling of the Short-Term Fourier Transform

a 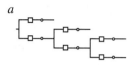   *b*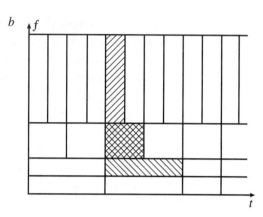

    (a) Octave Band Filtering; *(b)* Time-Frequency Tiling

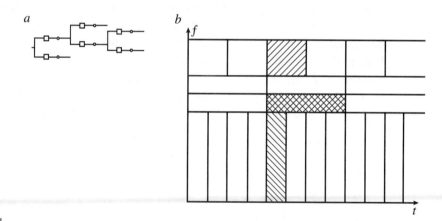

    (a) General Wavelet Filtering; *(b)* Time-Frequency Tiling

as octave band filtering, which has the subband filter configuration shown in Figure 7.15(a) and which yields the time-frequency tiling indicated in Figure 7.15(b). This tiling gives us much more of an opportunity to emphasize various frequency bands, especially at low frequencies.

Even the octave band filtering does not give us complete freedom, and it would be very useful to have even more flexibility in choosing nonuniform time-frequency tilings, as indicated in Figure 7.16. This is one example of a wavelet-based approach. One of the chief challenges in developing wavelet expansions is to find building block signals that completely cover or tile the time-frequency plane and that are easy to generate and work with. The wavelet transform is constructed from a basic function, called a *prototype* or *mother wavelet,* and its scaled (dilated) and shifted (translated) versions. The dilations are often a power of two, which yields a logarithmic frequency scale that corresponds to a constant relative bandwidth (Akansu and Haddad 1992; Vetterli and Kovacevic 1995).

Examples of a mother wavelet and its dilations are shown in Figure 7.17. The corresponding frequency domain representations of these wavelets are shown in Figure 7.18. Thus, a contraction, $a < 1$, in the time domain yields an expansion in the frequency domain; an expansion, $a > 1$, in the time domain produces a contraction in the frequency domain. On a logarithmic frequency scale, these operations give a constant bandwidth, which electrical engineers call a *constant Q response.* The time domain translation by the parameter b produces a frequency shift in the frequency domain.

The Fourier transform pair for a mother wavelet scaled by a and shifted by b is

$$\psi_{ab}(t) = \frac{1}{\sqrt{a}}\psi\left(\frac{t-b}{a}\right) \leftrightarrow \Psi_{ab}(\Omega) = \sqrt{a}\Psi(a\Omega)e^{-jb\Omega} \qquad (7.66)$$

and the continuous wavelet transform of a signal $s(t)$ is

$$W_s(a, b) = \int_{-\infty}^{\infty}\psi_{ab}(t)s(t)dt \qquad (7.67)$$

This transform is invertible if and only if a condition called the resolution of identity holds and the mother wavelet is admissible (Akansu and Haddad 1992).

It is possible to get a discrete wavelet transform by discretizing the parameters a and b. A general discretization is to choose

$$a = a_0^m \qquad b = nb_0a_0^m \qquad (7.68)$$

so that the discrete set of wavelets is

$$\psi_{mn}(t) = a_0^{-m/2}\psi\left(a_0^{-m}t - nb_0\right) \qquad (7.69)$$

and we can express a signal $s(t)$ as

$$s(t) = \sum_m\sum_n d_{m,n}\psi_{mn}(t) \qquad (7.70)$$

We will not go into conditions for admissibility and stable reconstructions, but much of the work on wavelets for compression is involved with finding discrete

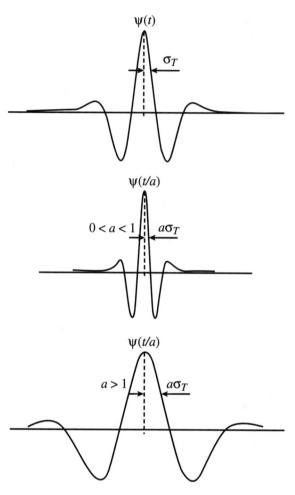

$\psi(t)$

σ_T

$\psi(t/a)$

$0 < a < 1$ $a\sigma_T$

$\psi(t/a)$

$a > 1$ $a\sigma_T$

FIGURE

7.17   Mother Wavelet and Dilations (Scalings)

wavelet transforms with good properties, such as orthogonality and simplicity of implementation.

Many of the wavelet transforms that have been studied impose a filter bank structure on the discrete-time wavelet expansion. This structure is useful to simplify implementations, but it can also have other implications. For example, Daubechies has introduced a wavelet construction in terms of a discrete-time filter bank expansion that under appropriate conditions can be iterated to converge to a continuous-time wavelet basis set (Daubechies 1992). It is also important to note that for any wavelet expansion there is a corresponding discrete-time perfect reconstruction filter bank, and this will often be the

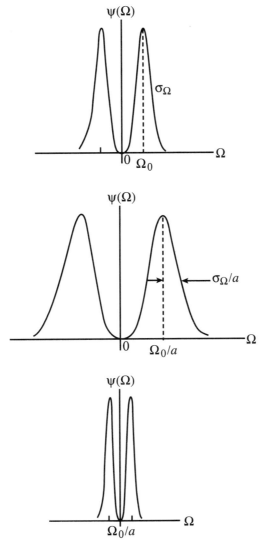

FIGURE

7.18   Fourier Transforms for Wavelets in Figure 7.17

preferred implementation. Of course, this also makes a solid connection with subband methods. Further, it can be shown that transform methods are a special case of subband techniques, where the impulse responses of the subband synthesis filters are the transform basis functions, the impulse responses of the analysis filters are equal to the time-reversed basis functions, and the decimation factor in each band is equal to the transform length. Thus, wavelet expansions are the most general form of frequency domain methods, encompassing both subband coding and transform coding.

For image processing applications, there are several considerations when choosing a wavelet basis. Images can be modeled as generally smooth except for edges, so it is natural to choose a smooth mother wavelet and an orthonormal basis. For computational reasons, it would be nice to have short filters, but short filters are not smooth. Furthermore, we would like to use FIR filters for linear phase, but there are no nontrivial orthonormal linear phase FIR filters that give exact reconstruction.

Some image coding results are presented in Antonini et al. (1992), where they combine wavelet bases and vector quantization. This work uses a perceptual noise weighting to obtain a bit allocation to exploit the masking of the human eye. Additionally, they design multiresolution codebooks with different subcodebooks for the horizontal, vertical, and diagonal directions at each resolution. The image coding results at less than 0.5 bits/pixel is comparable to other subband and VQ coding results reported in the literature, but perhaps with simpler filter designs.

7.6   Fractal Coding

Fractal coding burst onto the scene with claims of 1000:1 compression ratios and caught everyone's attention, even making headlines in the public press. However, to date, fractal coding has not appeared in any standards nor is it currently a focus for establishing a standard. Because fractal coding is still widely discussed and is a relatively different compression technique, we discuss the fundamental principles of the approach here (Wornell 1996; Fisher 1995).

Fractals generate an image by starting with a set of contractive maps that tile two-dimensional space and an initial or starting image and then successively apply the maps to the starting image until convergence. The final image is called the *attractor*, and for fractal coding, the attractor is supposed to be an approximation to the source image to be encoded. Of course, we need the set of contractive maps, so the real problem is: Given a source image to be encoded, find a collection of contractive mappings for which this image, the source, is the attractor. In the fractal literature, this is called the *inverse problem*. The fractal coding problem is broken down a little more by partitioning the given source image such that the succession of maps on the partitions yields the image. Each partition is the range of one of the mappings. The problem now becomes

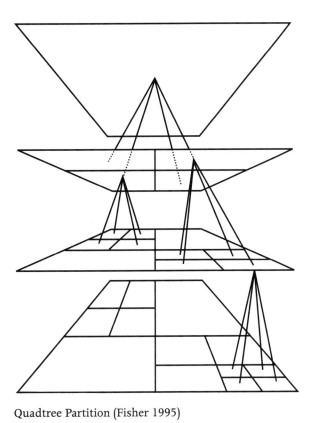

7.19   Quadtree Partition (Fisher 1995)

finding the sequence of mappings and the domains corresponding to the ranges (partitions). If the final image generated by the succession of mappings is close enough to the source image, then the encoding consists of storing the bits describing the sequence of mappings.

Picking the partitions of the source image is an important step and has been approached in several ways. One method would be to just break the image into squares, say, 8 × 8, as in transform coding, and use these as the range partitions. A popular method for doing this is *quadtree partitioning*, illustrated in Figure 7.19. Here the original image is broken into four quadrants. If these quadrants can be well approximated by an appropriate transformation, then no further partitioning is performed; otherwise, the quadrants can be further partitioned, as indicated in the figure, until an appropriate approximation is possible. Another partitioning method, called *HV partitioning*, consists of horizontally or vertically subdividing the image according to some criterion that is chosen to make the ranges include horizontal or vertical edges. Figure 7.20 illustrates the HV partitioning idea. This technique has the advantage over quadtree partitioning of allowing a greater choice of range shapes, but it has the disadvantage that the number of ranges may be larger than with quadtrees, which increases the complexity of the encoding step. Of course, many other variations and approaches to selecting the range partitions are possible.

After the range partitions are selected, the domain that maps into each range must be found. When this is complete, the actual encoding step consists of assigning bits to specify the (x, y) location of each domain, its contrast and brightness, and any rotation operations necessary to generate the range corresponding to the domain. The very large compression ratios come from the fact that common implementations may code the above information with 31 bits, and this may represent a $32 \times 32 \times 8 = 8192$-pixel region, thus producing a compression ratio of about 264:1.

A common claim concerning fractal coding is that it is resolution independent and hence allows easy "zooming" on any portion of an image. This is possible because the fractal schemes will just iterate the contractive mappings a few more times to enlarge that portion of the image. Thus, the edge of a face will appear smooth even in the zoomed portion of the image, and there will be no pixelization effects; however, the detail created is artificial, and we are not really getting a higher-resolution version of the original image. This zooming capability is also sometimes used to get inflated compression ratios for fractal coding.

Because of the possibly large number of mappings or transformations, fractal coding can be slow. In fact, most reports on fractal coding indicate that for the same complexity, fractal coding yields a lower compression ratio than JPEG. Furthermore, for compression ratios of about 20:1 or less, for which JPEG is designed, JPEG produces a better-quality reconstruction at a lower complexity than fractal coding. The artifacts in fractal coding can look "artificial," as opposed to the distortions present in, say, transform coding, where the distortions may be superimposed blocking or blurring. Fractal coding distortions may look clean or noise free, but unnatural for naturally occurring images.

The mathematical basis for fractal coding is the theory of iterated function systems (IFS); an IFS is a set of contractive mappings. An important result, called the *collage theorem*, states that the attractor will be close to the original image if a mapped or transformed version of the image is close to the original image. Thus, the series of contractive mappings will converge to an attractor that is a good approximation to the original. We will not pursue the development of fractals further here, so additional details are left to the references.

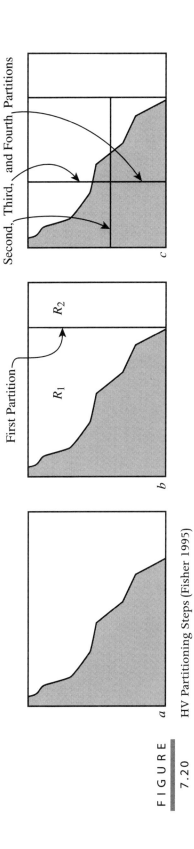

FIGURE
7.20

HV Partitioning Steps (Fisher 1995)

7.7   Summary

The frequency domain coding techniques presented in this chapter have already had substantial impact on speech, audio, and video coding standards. Chapter 8 develops several of the speech and audio standards in some detail. Chapters 9, 10, and 11 present the use of these methods in still-image and video applications. Frequency domain coding methods are also the focus of much ongoing research, primarily under the broad heading of wavelets. There is much to be learned about subband filtering, wavelet basis selection, multiresolution representations, and the exploitation of human perception. Furthermore, vector quantization and coding of the frequency domain representations is an area receiving, and deserving of, additional research effort.

The power of frequency domain methods for speech, audio, still-image, and video coding is evident throughout the remaining chapters of the book.

8 Frequency Domain Speech and Audio Coding Standards

8.1 Introduction

The frequency domain methods in Chapter 7 have proved important in many speech and audio coding standards. In particular, variants of subband coding and transform coding have been exploited to design several coders for wideband audio (50–7000 Hz) and CD-quality audio (20–20,000 Hz) that find applications in telephony and entertainment. Table 8.1 shows relevant bandwidths and sampling rates. Such coders are integral components of H.320 videoconferencing systems, of MPEG and HDTV video storage and transmission standards, and of several audio recording/storage devices.

We begin the development with a discussion of the ITU-T G.722 subband coder for wideband audio (Mermelstein 1988). This coder was standardized in 1988 and is actually a relatively straightforward subband coder. It does not use perceptual weighting or noise shaping in any form, but the subband filtering and ADPCM coding produces good performance for the coder complexity.

The general goal of the audio coders used for storage of music and for use with MPEG video and HDTV is to achieve CD quality or transparent quality; that is, there should be no discernible perceptual difference between the encoded version and the original (Noll 1997). In addition to using powerful frequency domain signal processing techniques, these coders rely very heavily on perceptual coding methods that draw upon results from psychoacoustical experiments. In Section 8.3 we develop the basic ideas behind this class of coder, which includes MUSICAM; ASPEC; MPEG Layers 1, 2, and 3; Dolby AC-2 and AC-3; AT&T PAC; Sony ATRAC; and the DCC. Table 8.2 shows the bit rates, subjective quality estimate, relative complexity, principal applications,

T A B L E
8.1

Common Bandwidths and Sampling Rates for Speech and Audio

Input	Frequency Range (Hz)	Sampling Rate (1000 samples/second)
Telephone speech	200–3400	8
Wideband speech	50–7000	16
Wideband audio	20–20,000	44.1 or 48

T A B L E
8.2

Comparison of Commercially Available Audio Coding Systems

	Bit Rate	Quality	Complexity	Main Applications	Available Since
MPEG-1 Layer 1	32–448 kbps total	transparent @ 192 kbps/ channel, as per (ISO 1991c)	low encoder/ decoder	DCC	1991
MPEG-1 Layer 2	32–384 kbps total	transparent @ 128 kbps/ channel, as per (ITU 1994)	low decoder	DAB, CD-I DVD	1991
MPEG-1 Layer 3	32–320 kbps total	transparent @ 96 kbps/ channel, as per (ITU 1994)	low decoder	ISDN, satellite radio systems, Internet audio	1993
Dolby AC-2	128–192 kbps/ channel	transparent @ 128 kbps/ channel, as per (ITU 1994)	low encoder/ decoder	point to point, cable	1989
Dolby AC-3	32–640 kbps	transparent @ 384 kbps/5.1 channel, as per (ITU 1995)	low decoder	point to multipoint, HDTV, cable, SD-DVD	1991
Sony ATRAC	140 kbps/ channel		low encoder/ decoder	MD	1992
AT&T PAC			low decoder		
MPEG-AAC (NBC)	64 kbps/ channel	transparent			1997

Adapted from Brandenburg and Bosi (1995).

and year of introduction for these high-quality audio coding methods. Details of each of these coders are presented in subsequent sections.

At the end of the chapter, we present a speech coder, called the improved multiband excitation (IMBE) coder, that has been adopted as the speech coding standard used in the International Maritime Satellite System (INMARSAT). This coder is an exotic vocoder that performs its analysis and synthesis based upon frequency domain matching calculations. It has importance beyond the INMARSAT standard because of the general approach and because it has scored well in speech intelligibility and quality tests.

8.2   ITU G.722 Wideband Audio and Lower Rate Extensions

Although most of the effort on speech coders for many years focused on telephone bandwidth speech, 200–3400 Hz, several people recognized the quality difference available by allowing the input speech to cover the bandwidth of 50–7000 Hz. Additionally, this bandwidth offered the promise of allowing music to be encoded at a much more pleasing quality level. The ITU, then the CCITT, moved quickly and established standard G.722, which is relatively simple to implement, yet achieves good performance at rates of 48, 56, and 64 kbps. It is really quite an elegant solution because of its simplicity and utilization of then-existing (1988) coding ideas and standards. The basic approach is two-band subband coding where the coding within the subbands uses a modification of the G.721 (now G.726, G.727) ITU standard ADPCM speech coder.

A block diagram of the G.722 coder is shown in Figure 8.1 (Mermelstein 1988). The audio input is assumed to be sampled at 16,000 samples/second, with a resolution of 14 bits/sample. The analysis and synthesis subband filters are identical 24-tap QMF filters that split the input into critically sampled 4-kHz bands. ADPCM coders are used in both bands, with 6 bits/sample used in the low band and 2 bits/sample used in the upper band, to yield a total rate of 64 kbps. The low-band coder is embedded ADPCM, which allows the low-band rate to be changed at the low-band coder output from 6 bits/sample down to 5 or 4 bits/sample, so that the possible rates for the overall G.722 coder are 64, 56, and 48 kbps.

The complexity of the coder is such that it can be implemented on a single chip, and it has an overall coding delay of 3 ms. The performance of the G.722 coder has been evaluated for speech using the MOS measure, and these results are presented in Table 8.3 for all three rates. The performance is quite good,

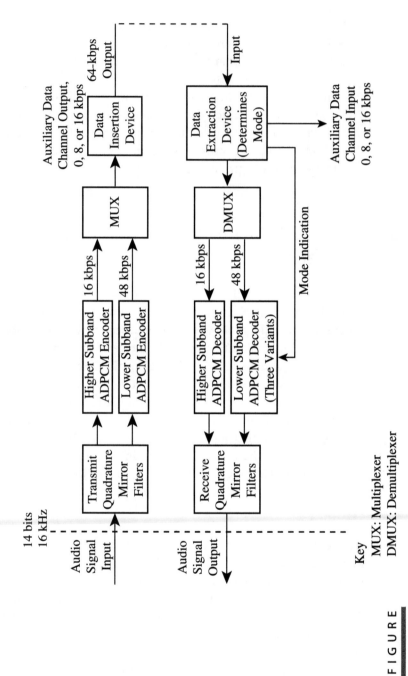

Two–Band Subband Coder for 64-kbps Coding of 7-kHz Audio

T A B L E

8.3

MOS Values of CCITT G.722 Wideband
Speech Coder at Different Bit Rates

Bit Rate	Male	Female	Mean
48 kbps	3.7	3.7	3.7
56 kbps	4.3	3.7	4.0
64 kbps	4.0	4.1	4.1

T A B L E

8.4

MOS Values of CCITT G.722 Wideband
Speech Coder from Loudspeaker Presentations

CCITT Wideband Speech Coder	$BER = 0$	$BER = 10^{-4}$	$BER = 10^{-3}$
Source signal	4.3		
64 kbps	4.3	3.8	3.0
48 kbps	3.8	3.6	3.0

especially for the coder complexity. The independent bit error rate performance
is summarized in Table 8.4, where it is seen that an error probability of 0.0001
does not cause substantial difficulties, but at 0.001, a noticeable performance
drop occurs.

There has also been an effort to extend the MPEG audio methods to cover
wideband speech coding at 32 kbps. The work has emphasized MPEG Layer 3
and required the modification of the psychoacoustic model and the quantization
accuracy as a function of frequency. The coder is not low delay but is reported
to achieve speech quality at 32 kbps better than G.722 at 64 kbps. A variable-
rate wideband speech coder has been employed in PictureTel videoconferencing
systems for several years and produces very good quality speech at an average
rate of 24–28 kbps. It is basically an adaptive transform coder, but during
silence the rate is drastically reduced by sending many fewer coefficients, and a
"noise fill-in" technique is used to replace the untransmitted coefficients during
reconstruction (Crossman 1993).

There have also been a number of efforts to code wideband speech at
16 kbps, primarily by attempting to exploit the general CELP approach. A new
technique, called *transform coded excitation* (TCX), has also been proposed and
evaluated. TCX coding is elaborated by Lefebvre et al. (1994).

8.3   Simultaneous Masking and Temporal Masking in Audio

Perceptual weighting is the key ingredient that has allowed many of the recent successes in speech and high-quality audio coding. Certainly, spectral shaping of the reconstruction error is of fundamental importance to the analysis-by-synthesis speech coders such as CELP and multipulse LPC. However, the coding of wideband audio for storage, movies, and HDTV takes even more explicit advantage of the human auditory system to decide which frequency components should be retained and with what accuracy. The basic idea is auditory masking (Noll 1997; Jayant, Johnston, and Safranek 1993).

In a quiet environment, there is a nonuniform sound pressure threshold as a function of frequency above which the sound will be audible to a human. This threshold is called the *threshold in quiet* (Figure 8.2). When a signal such as a tone is applied, the sound pressure threshold that must be exceeded by other sounds to be audible is changed. This new threshold is called the *masking threshold* and formally is defined to be the sound pressure level (SPL) below which a lower-level signal, called the *maskee,* will not be audible in the presence of a simultaneously applied stronger signal, denoted as the *masker.* In the context of audio coding, the masking threshold as a function of time is often called *just noticeable distortion* (JND).

The masking process draws upon human auditory perception, which performs what is called a *critical band analysis* in the inner ear (Zwicker 1961; Scharf 1970). This critical band analysis in the auditory system can be modeled as a bandpass filter bank but with bandwidths becoming progressively larger with increasing frequency. As shown in Table 8.5, there are roughly 25 critical bands covering the frequency range up past 20 kHz, and a strong signal in each band can mask other distortions within that band. Furthermore, masking across the critical bands can be accounted for by a spreading function. Using these ideas, a JND can be found below which a signal will not have to be coded.

Important quantities are the signal-to-mask ratio (SMR), the signal-to-noise ratio (SNR), and the noise-to-mask ratio (NMR). The SMR is the difference in sound pressure level between the level of the masker and the masking threshold. The SNR is the ratio of the masker power to the quantization noise power. The NMR (in dB) is the difference between the SMR and the SNR that describes the safety margin for audible noise. NMR should be negative.

Audio coding methods differ in the techniques used to calculate the masking threshold and, in particular, the amount of signal processing invested in these calculations. In general, a more detailed analysis in calculating masking thresholds is rewarded with improved audio quality for a given bit rate.

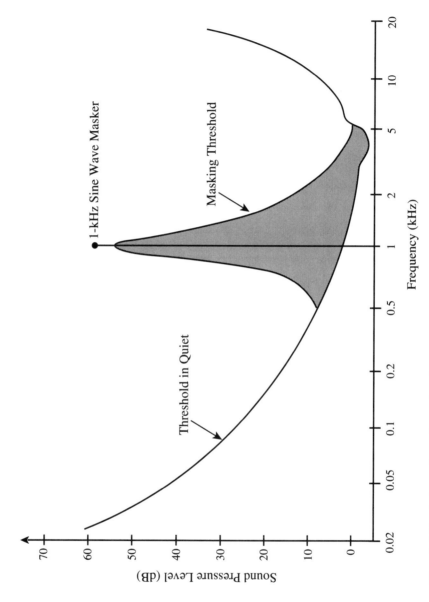

F I G U R E
8.2   Threshold in Quiet and Masking Threshold. Acoustical events in the hatched areas will not be audible.

Critical Band Center and Edge Frequencies (Scharf 1970)

Band Number	Lower Edge (Hz)	Center (Hz)	Upper Edge (Hz)
1	0	50	100
2	100	150	200
3	200	250	300
4	300	350	400
5	400	450	510
6	510	570	630
7	630	700	770
8	770	840	920
9	920	1000	1080
10	1080	1170	1270
11	1270	1370	1480
12	1480	1600	1720
13	1720	1850	2000
14	2000	2150	2320
15	2320	2500	2700
16	2700	2900	3150
17	3150	3400	3700
18	3700	4000	4400
19	4400	4800	5300
20	5300	5800	6400
21	6400	7000	7700
22	7700	8500	9500
23	9500	10,500	12,000
24	12,000	13,500	15,500
25	15,500	19,500	

Temporal masking is the idea that a particular signal can mask other signals that occur just before (premasking) and just after (postmasking) the stronger signal. It may seem contradictory that a strong signal can mask something that occurred before, but such is the memory of the human auditory mechanism. Premasking does have a much shorter possible interval than postmasking, but both are significant and must be exploited.

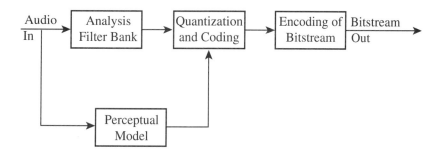

FIGURE

8.3   Basic Structure of a Perceptual Coding Scheme

The basic approach to perceptual coding is illustrated by the block diagram in Figure 8.3 (Brandenburg and Bosi 1995). Most of the operations are frequency domain based since the human auditory process is best understood in the frequency domain. The principal steps in perceptual coding are to break the input signal into spectral components, quantize and code these spectral components according to a psychoacoustical masking threshold, and generate a serial bitstream. The calculation of the masking threshold is performed using a frequency domain analysis of the input, and it may use the same frequency decomposition presented to the quantization and coding step or a separate analysis may be performed, depending upon complexity constraints and accuracy requirements.

The analysis filter bank can be a quadrature mirror filter decomposition, or it may consist of a discrete transform of some kind. Since discrete transforms can be viewed as uniform subband filter banks, any distinction is more one of historical usage than concrete differences.

Regardless of whether the masking threshold calculations are based on the original input analysis or a separate frequency domain analysis, the result is used to specify the accuracy with which the various frequency components are coded. The output of the masking threshold calculation may be a set of actual masking thresholds, the number of bits allocated to each frequency component, or a set of frequency-dependent SNRs needed to achieve transparent quality.

The quantization and coding step may be accomplished in several ways, ranging from directly using the calculated bit allocations in scalar quantizers to implementing an analysis-by-synthesis system. Analysis-by-synthesis in this context means to compare the quantized and the unquantized spectral components to find the actual quantization noise for each spectral component and then compare this to the masking threshold.

8.4   High-Quality Audio for Video Standards

The rapidly developing standards for video coding also have associated standards for coding high-quality audio. The general goal is to achieve "transparent"-quality or CD-quality audio, which is often considered to be 14- to 16-bit PCM. The initial efforts were for two-channel stereo, but more recently, work has turned toward developing high-quality coding methods for five-channel surround sound that is also compatible with the two-channel standards. In the following sections, we describe the audio coding standards that are part of MPEG-1 and MPEG-2 (Mitchell et al. 1996) and the audio coding method chosen for the U.S. HDTV standard (Petajan 1997).

The MPEG standards are combinations of systems developed by the MU-SICAM and ASPEC research groups, and all of the current high-quality audio coding methods share a common block diagram and the same philosophy: use auditory masking to shape the quantization noise, and keep the noise level below the signal-dependent masking level as a function of frequency.

8.4.1 MPEG-1 Audio

The MPEG-1 audio coding standard actually has three parts, designated as Layers 1, 2, and 3; as the layer number increases, the performance and complexity also increase. The block diagram in Figure 8.4 represents the MPEG-1 Layers 1 and 2 encoder/decoder pair. These coders use the auditory masking ideas summarized in Section 8.3 to determine which frequency components are to be coded and how accurately. Specifically, in Figure 8.4, the analysis filter bank consists of 32 equally spaced subbands that are 750 Hz wide at a sampling rate of 48 kHz, and the subband bandpass filters are implemented as 511-tap polyphase filters, which corresponds to an impulse response of length 5.33 ms. The SMR is calculated based upon a 512-point FFT. A dynamic bit allocation selects one of 15 possible quantizers for each subband such that the trade-off between SMR and rate is best accommodated. The reconstruction takes place by using the scale factors to decode 12 sample blocks for each subband and then applying these subband samples to the synthesis filter bank. At 384 kbps the MPEG-1 Layer 1 coder produces transparent-quality stereo audio equivalent to CD quality.

The MPEG-1 Layer 2 coder also fits the block diagram in Figure 8.4, but improved quality is obtained by using a 1024-sample FFT to generate the SMR, having finer quantization tables, and reducing redundancy in coding the scale factors for adjacent blocks. This coder is able to achieve transparent-quality stereo audio at 256 kbps.

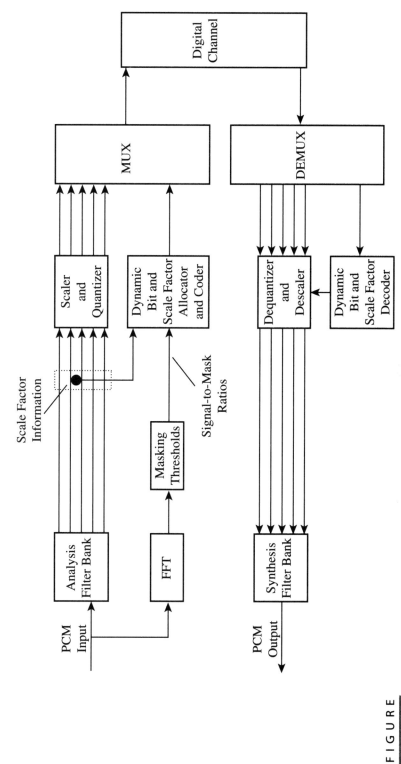

FIGURE
8.4

Block Structure of ISO/MPEG Audio Encoder and Decoder, Layers 1 and 2

There is also a joint stereo coding mode that is available to all layers, called *intensity stereo mode,* where the higher-frequency subbands are coded jointly. That is, the left and right signals in each subband have a separately determined scale factor, but the left and right signals are added together, and common quantization, bit allocation, and coding is used for the summed signals; then, after the combined signal is reconstructed, the separate scale factors are employed to produce the separate left and right stereo channels. Tests show that this technique can save 10–30 kbps. Using joint stereo coding, the MPEG-1 Layer 2 coder can achieve transparent-quality stereo at 192 kbps.

The MPEG-1 Layer 3 audio coder has the block diagram shown in Figure 8.5, which, while still trying to exploit the theory of auditory masking as for Layers 1 and 2, exhibits some substantive differences in approach. In particular, the 32 subbands are decomposed further using a modified DCT (MDCT) to produce either 6 or 18 additional frequency components per subband. Thus, if the 18-point MDCT is used, the frequency resolution provided is $750/18 = 41.67$ Hz. The shorter 6-point MDCT is employed whenever it is necessary to control time artifacts or pre-echoes (Section 8.3). A nonuniform quantizer is applied to the frequency components, and the output is coded using one of 18 Huffman coding tables. There are iteration loops in the encoder to satisfy the bit rate and masking criteria for each block.

8.4.2   MPEG-2 Audio

For MPEG-2 audio, the desire is to create a multichannel movie theater style sound system, and hence MPEG-2 allows for the inclusion of center mode and left and right surround channels in addition to the two stereo channels. Figure 8.6 shows the speaker configuration; Table 8.6 lists the various channel designations. One can imagine that compatibility with MPEG-1 audio might be an important issue; for example, we might be interested in forward-compatible audio, which means that the MPEG-2 multichannel decoder can decode MPEG-1 stereo or mono bitstreams, or in backward-compatible audio, where MPEG-1 can decode the MPEG-2 multichannel bitstream to produce MPEG-1 stereo signals. We might also not want to emphasize compatibility with MPEG-1 audio and, hence, simplify the MPEG-2 audio coding task.

The ISO has established two MPEG-2 audio coding standards: one addresses compatibility in both directions, and the other is simply nonbackward compatible. Forward compatibility places a burden on the decoder, but backward compatibility requires special matrixing of the five-channel components to

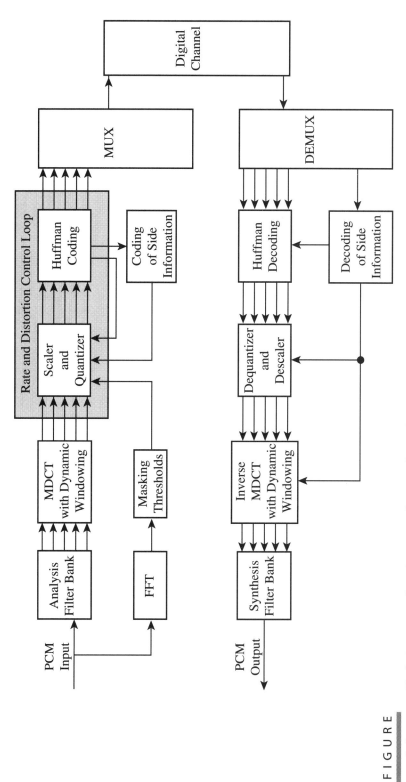

FIGURE

8.5

Block Structure of ISO/MPEG Audio Encoder and Decoder, Layer 3

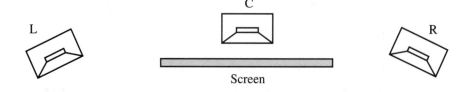

FIGURE
8.6

Speaker Configuration for Multichannel MPEG-2 Audio

TABLE
8.6

Channel Designations for Multichannel MPEG-2 Audio

Number of Channels	Channel Designations	Description
1	1/0 mode	center (mono)
2	2/0 stereo	left, right (stereo)
3	3/0 stereo	left, right, center
4	3/1 stereo	left, right, center, surround
5	3/2 stereo	left, right, center, surround left, surround right

allow the MPEG-1 decoder to obtain left and right channel stereo. Figure 8.7 shows the formats of the MPEG-1 and MPEG-2 data streams. Figure 8.8 shows one way the stereo compatibility with MPEG-1 can be achieved; that is, the MPEG-1 left and right stereo channels, L0 and R0, are transmitted in the T0 and T1 positions in the MPEG-2 stream. The quantities L0 and R0 can be chosen simply to be the left and right channels, L and R, or they can include contributions from the center and surround channels as

$$L0 = L + 0.707C + 0.707LS \qquad (8.1a)$$

$$R0 = R + 0.707C + 0.707RS \qquad (8.1b)$$

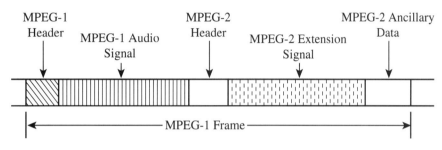

FIGURE

8.7   Data Format of MPEG Audio Bitstreams

with T2 = C, T3 = LS, and T4 = RS, in both cases. To make the MPEG-2 matrixing selection, it is necessary to take into account redundancies between channels and masking effects.

There is much to be done in determining the minimum bit rate required for MPEG-2 coding in order to take advantage of interchannel masking effects and redundancies, but certainly it should be possible to code each channel transparently at 128 kbps per channel for a multichannel rate of 640 kbps. Another consideration is the fact that matrixing for backward compatibility can cause some difficulty in MPEG-2 decoding because dematrixing may cancel some signal components that were being counted on to mask some quantization noise. This possibility requires some care when matrixing is used.

The nonbackward-compatible audio work was motivated by the results of listening tests performed in early 1994 that compared MPEG-2 backward-compatible (BC) coders with nonbackward-compatible (NBC) designs. The test results showed that NBC coders can perform statistically better than BC designs, even though at that time NBC coders were not yet broadcast quality. Since then, however, further work on NBC coders indicates that multichannel broadcast-quality audio is achievable at 320 kbps in the 3/2 channel configuration.

The MPEG-2 NBC work uses a reference model (RM) approach with six modules. The basic idea behind pursuing a modular approach is that designs for each of the modules can be contributed by different laboratories, companies,

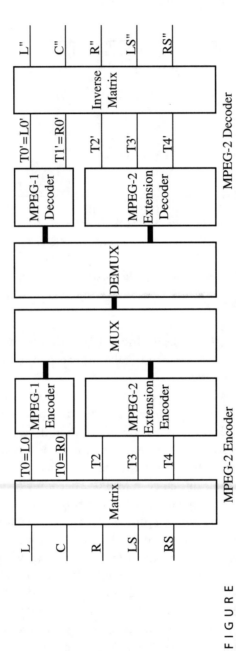

F I G U R E

8.8

Compatibility of MPEG-2 Multichannel Audio Bitstreams

or groups, thus taking advantage of the full range of expertise of the participants. The current baseline system for NBC is called "reference model 2" and designated RM2. If an improved module is proposed, a "core experiment" is performed, where the proposed improved module is inserted into the RM2 system and the quality of this modified system is compared to the baseline. If a quality improvement is produced, the new module replaces the old one. If the quality is equivalent, other issues are considered, such as scalability, editibility, and complexity, to make a selection.

The expectation for MPEG-2 NBC is that it will achieve broadcast-quality audio at about 64 kbps per channel, with provisions for multichannel and two-channel stereo.

8.4.3   Dolby AC-2 and AC-3

Dolby AC-2

Dolby AC-2 (Davidson and Bosi 1992) uses a technique, called *time domain aliasing cancellation* (TDAC), that is somewhat the dual of the aliasing cancellation achieved in the frequency domain by quadrature mirror filters in subband coding (Princen, Johnson, and Bradley 1987). Every 256 samples, the AC-2 coder performs a modified discrete cosine transform (MDCT) and a modified discrete sine transform (MDST) on successive overlapping 512-sample frames of the input audio. Block diagrams of the encoder and decoder are shown in Figure 8.9. After the forward transform operation, the transform coefficients are grouped into bands corresponding to critical bands, and an estimate of the log spectral envelope is formed to be used for dynamic bit allocation, which attempts to use more bits for perceptually important subbands while still maintaining a constant overall bit rate. For AC-2 only 17–20% of the total data rate is varied in relation to the input signal characteristics. The log spectral envelope information is transmitted to the decoder along with the quantized transform coefficients.

The frequency resolution provided by the transforms is 93.75 Hz, and the time resolution corresponding to the 512 block size is 5.33 ms. In rapidly changing segments that may be subject to pre-echoes, the block size can be reduced to 256 samples to yield a time resolution of 2.67 ms. The AC-2 system has similar encoder and decoder complexity and had the lowest complexity of coders that achieved transparent quality at 128 kbps per channel in past tests. The delay of the AC-2 system varies from 7 to 60 ms, depending upon

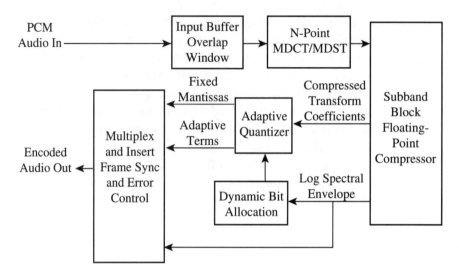

a

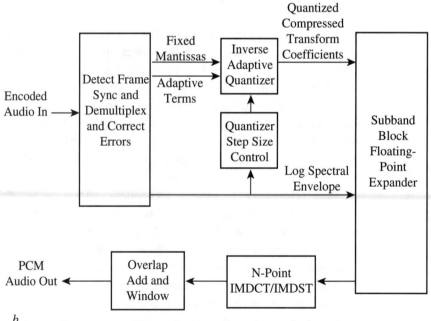

F I G U R E   *b*

8.9   *(a)* AC-2 Encoder; *(b)* AC-2 Decoder

the particular implementation. In subjective tests, the AC-2 coder has demonstrated performance close to MPEG-1 audio coders at the stereo bit rate of 256 kbps.

Dolby AC-3

The Dolby AC-3 multichannel audio coder is built around the AC-2 coder just described. It is a 5/1 multichannel system that is noncompatible with the MPEG-1 audio coder. It is the audio coding algorithm to be used in the U.S. Grand Alliance HDTV system and one of the systems adopted for the digital video disk (DVD) technology. As part of what is called the Dolby Digital film system, AC-3 is used for commercial cinema at a total bit rate of 320 kbps.

The Dolby AC-3 system improves on AC-2 by having a completely (100%) adaptive bit allocation and allows for an adjustable data rate from 32 to 640 kbps. The result is higher quality but with a more complex encoder and with a higher delay of 100 ms. The AC-3 uses an oddly stacked TDAC transform for its filter bank and provides for variable time/frequency resolution. The default transform block length is 256 samples (512-sample overlapped windows), which at a sampling rate of 48 kHz yields a frame length of 32 ms and a frequency resolution of 93.75 Hz. To minimize pre-echoes, a finer time resolution of 2.67 ms is used during rapidly varying transients.

Block diagrams of the encoder and decoder for the AC-3 system are shown in Figure 8.10. The spectral envelope information in the bit allocation has the same frequency resolution as the analysis/synthesis filter bank; that is, each and every coefficient can be coded independently and are not combined to produce wider bands (and thus simplifications) such as critical bands. The bit allocation routine is a hybrid forward/backward scheme, to be described, and the core bit allocation does use some combining, but this can be augmented by the forward adaptive allocation.

Backward adaptive bit allocation as used in this context means that the bit allocation is calculated from the coded audio data based upon an assumed psychoacoustic model, and explicit transmission of the bit allocation by the encoder is not required. An advantage of this scheme is that all bits transmitted are actually used to code the audio signal; that is, there is no side information. A disadvantage is that the bit allocation calculation must be performed at the decoder as well as the encoder, thus increasing the decoder complexity. A second disadvantage is that the bit allocation method cannot be modified to implement a better psychoacoustic model once decoders are in the field. For forward adaptive bit allocations, the encoder calculates the bit allocation and

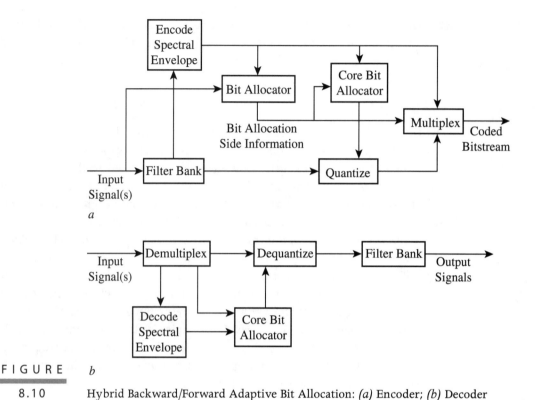

b

Hybrid Backward/Forward Adaptive Bit Allocation: *(a)* Encoder; *(b)* Decoder

sends it as part of the transmitted bitstream. This has the advantage that the input signal is available and an "optimum" bit allocation can be computed limited only by the signal processing complexity and the psychoacoustic model employed. Additionally, the bit allocation can be changed with advances in signal processing and psychoacoustic models, and the decoder can be kept relatively simple.

The spectral envelope consists of the coded exponent and mantissa of each transform coefficient, and the core bit allocation decodes the exponents and treats them as the power spectral density (psd) of the signal. Depending upon the audio sampling rate and bandwidth, there may be as many as 252 exponents. To model the ear's masking curve, the input psd should be convolved with a spreading function, but a full computation implies added complexity. To simplify the convolution, the psd values (as many as 252) are collapsed to 64 values by combining band sizes of 1 at low frequencies and of 16 at high frequencies, with the size varying in proportion to the critical bands in Table 8.5.

A much simplified model of the ear's spreading function is also used to simplify the convolution.

The result of the convolution of the psd and the spreading function is a masking curve, as indicated by the dark line in Figure 8.11. This masking curve is then subtracted from the original coded psd to obtain the SNR needed to code the unmasked coefficients, which, in turn, is used to select a quantizer for each component. The allocated bit rate is available for all coefficients, and the bits used may be adjusted up or down to achieve the desired bit rate.

The actual spectral envelope values are coded differentially with respect to the DC value for efficiency. After the DC coefficient, the immediately following coefficients can be adjusted by integer steps of −2 to +2 units, where each unit corresponds to 6 dB. In AC-3, each coded block has a 2-bit "exponent strategy" field that tells the decoder which of four coding strategies have been used, D15, D25, D45, or REUSE. The D15 strategy groups every three differentials and codes them with 7 bits, thus yielding 2.33 bits per coefficient. This is a fairly generous bit allocation and, as such, is usually only employed when the spectral content is relatively stable. Thus, it is typical to use D15 at the beginning of a stable sound and then REUSE for five subsequent blocks; thus the 2.33 bits/coefficient is actually used over 6 blocks × 5.33 ms = 32 ms, with the effective data rate working out to be about 0.39 bits/coefficient.

When the spectral content is less stable, the other two coding strategies are used. The D25 method codes a delta for every other coefficient, thus producing half the data rate of D15 and yielding half the frequency resolution. This mode is preferred for sounds that remain stable over two or three blocks. To code transients, the D45 strategy is used, where a delta is sent for only every four coefficients, but may be changed every 5.33-ms block to obtain better time resolution.

At very low bit rates, the AC-3 has the ability to couple channels so as to reduce the number of channels to be coded. The basic idea is that above certain frequencies, called the *coupling frequency* here, the human ear can detect only the spectral envelope and not the individual frequencies. The encoder has the flexibility to specify and vary the coupling frequency, the bands coupled together, and how often the coupling strategy is changed. As long as the reproduced power levels are close to the original above the coupling frequency, the audible differences will not be great. In recent AC-3 systems, the coupling frequency is 10 kHz.

The AC-3 coder sends an independent representation of every transform frequency coefficient rather than grouping them into critical bands to get the exponent information as in AC-2. Furthermore, AC-3 uses a hybrid

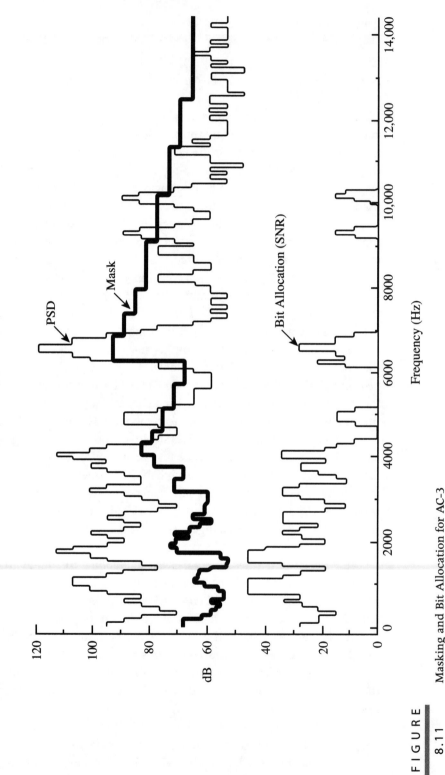

Masking and Bit Allocation for AC–3

forward/backward bit allocation routine; spectral envelope information is sent using a delta coding method, and this spectral envelope is used in a backward adaptive bit allocation routine at the encoder and decoder that incorporates psychoacoustic modeling. The core bit allocation routine can be modified somewhat by the encoder sending a correction to the decoder if necessary.

An interesting innovation is that, in the stereo mode, the AC-3 coder can code the two channels as either left and right or sum-difference pairs on a frequency band basis. This approach, sometimes called *rematrixing,* reduces the audibility of quantization errors when matrix surround techniques are used.

8.4.4 AT&T's Perceptual Audio Coder

The Perceptual Audio Coder (PAC) developed by AT&T builds on two earlier coding algorithms, the Perceptual Transform Coder (PXFM) and ASPEC (Johnston 1988a, 1988b, 1990; Johnston and Ferreira 1992). The PXFM algorithm came first and was motivated by studies showing that the entropy of a music signal above the masking threshold was much less than the statistical entropy of the source. Defining this quantity as the *perceptual entropy,* the designers used perceptual entropy as the basic coding paradigm. PXFM employed a 2048-point real FFT with a window overlap of 1/16th. This produces good frequency resolution but a loss in coding efficiency due to the window overlap. The ASPEC algorithm improved on PXFM by using the MDCT (no overlap), two window sizes of 1024 and 256 (the smaller of which helps reduce pre-echoes), and more sophisticated bit allocation and buffer control methods.

The PAC algorithm is again a substantial refinement that uses window sizes of 2048 and 256 and incorporates many of the critical details mentioned in the previous section on AC-3. PAC tested well in the ISO-MPEG-2 five-channel test in 1994 and has a low-complexity decoder implementation. There are versions of PAC that operate at 32 kbps for monophonic audio up to 1024 kbps for a 5/1 channel format.

The monophonic PAC algorithm has five components: an analysis filter bank, a perceptual model, a noise allocation routine, a noiseless compression step, and the bitstream former. We discuss each of these steps briefly. The analysis filter bank, the MDCT, switches between using 1024 or 128 uniformly spaced filter bands; these filter banks are used for both the analysis step and the coding stage. The monophonic perceptual model has several steps, but basically computes the just noticeable difference (JND) as a function of frequency. The way it does this is to calculate the energy in the signal versus frequency with $\frac{1}{3}$ critical band partitions, calculate whether the signal is noiselike or tonal to be used in the masking determination, and map the masking result onto the input spectrum. The noise allocation is accomplished iteratively to achieve an equal loudness criterion across the frequency bands while achieving the target compression ratio. However, the coder bands are not the critical band partitions; instead 49 coder bands are used for the 1024-component filter bank, and 14 coder bands for the 128-line case. Each band is coded by selecting one out of 128 possible exponentially distributed quantization step sizes. Noiseless compression consists of selecting one of eight possible Huffman codes for each frequency band. Since this can add significant overhead, a special grouping technique is employed to improve efficiency. Bitstream formation is important if the coder is to be used for a variety of applications. In PAC, the coded information for each 1024 samples (either one block of 1024 or eight blocks of 128 samples) are included in one frame. The frame has additional header information, which may include the number of channels, sampling rate, synchronization, and error recovery data.

For the stereo case, the perceptual threshold calculation must consider the fact that even though signals may be masked by the left channel or the right channel individually, they may not be masked by the combined stereo signal. This is called *binary masking level difference* (BMLD), and PAC computes four thresholds to prevent such unmasking. The coder may also switch between coding the information as monaural-stereo MS and left-right LR modes on a per band basis, depending upon which is more efficient.

There are also multichannel versions of PAC (MPAC) that employ composite coding modes to gain efficiencies.

8.5 Coding for Audio Storage Devices

For a number of years, consumers were satisfied with vinyl records and analog compact cassette recordings. More recently, however, compact disc (CD) technology has exposed consumers to high-quality audio recording and raised expectations as to what can be achieved. The convenience of making personal audio recordings on analog cassette is valued by the public, and recently products have been introduced that provide rewritable media capability but with much higher-quality audio reproduction than analog cassette tape.

In this section we discuss some of the basic principles behind two such products, the digital compact cassette (DCC) and the rewritable minidisc system.

Interestingly, both of these devices use lossy compression technology to record audio that may be considered perceptually lossless. Thus, these products rely on human auditory masking properties as discussed in Section 8.3 and as exploited by the MPEG audio coding methods.

8.5.1   DCC PASC Coder

The compression technique used in the DCC, called the precision adaptive subband coding (PASC) algorithm, has a basic coding rate of 384 kbps (Hoogendorn 1994). The PASC coder breaks the input signal into 32 subbands, each 750 Hz in width. A single prototype FIR filter with 512 coefficients is used for the subband filtering. In fact, this is the same subband structure that is used in MUSICAM. The masking levels are determined by calculating the average power in a frame of 12 samples in each subband and then referring to an empirically determined 32×32 matrix. A comparison of the peak power to the calculated masking level is used to estimate the number of bits per subband for coding. Each sample in a subband is coded as a mantissa and an exponent. The 6-bit exponent is the same for all samples in the subband and is determined from the peak power level; the mantissa of 2 to 15 bits is found from the masking calculations. Bits are allocated to the subbands starting with the subbands needing the highest number of bits and proceeding until the target bit rate is achieved.

8.5.2   Minidisc ATRAC Coder

The minidisc adaptive transform acoustic coding (ATRAC) system has the block diagram shown in Figure 8.12 (Yoshida 1994). The two cascaded quadrature mirror filters separate the 44.1-kHz sampled input into three subbands: 0–5.5125 kHz, 5.5125–11.025 kHz, and 11.025–22.05 kHz. A modified DCT is then taken on 50% overlapping blocks in each band to yield 128 coefficients in the low and medium bands and 256 coefficients in the high band. The block sizes can be adaptively adjusted to a shorter length during the "attack" portions of the audio to avoid pre-echoes. The MDCT coefficients are grouped into a block and coded. The ATRAC does not specify a bit allocation algorithm so that encoder improvements can be accommodated without changing the minidisc format. At a stereo bit rate of 292 kbps, the ATRAC coder achieves transparent quality.

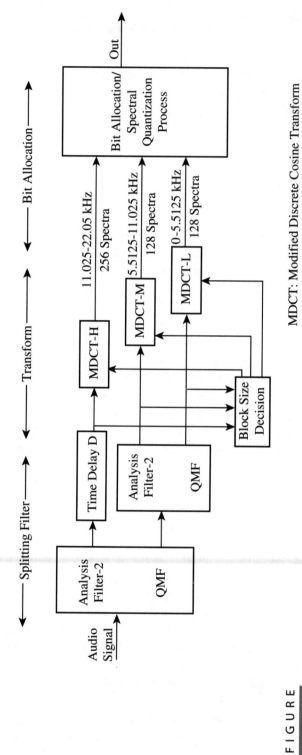

MDCT: Modified Discrete Cosine Transform

FIGURE

8.12   Block Diagram of ATRAC Encoder

8.6   INMARSAT Speech Coder

A speech coder that is quite different in its approach to high-quality speech coding at low bit rates is the improved multiband excitation (IMBE) coder that has been adopted as the international mobile satellite (INMARSAT) standard (Griffin and Lim 1988; Brandstein et al. 1990; Brandstein, Hardwick, and Lim 1991). Block diagrams of the IMBE encoder and decoder are shown in Figure 8.13. Generally, it is evident from this figure that the IMBE uses a frequency domain approach, but there is a twist in that voicing decisions are being made. Unlike LPC, however, separate voicing decisions are made on several different spectral bands, thus allowing better excitation modeling than in LPC. Although

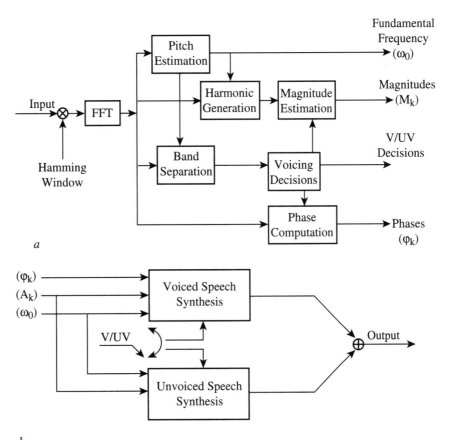

FIGURE   *b*

8.13   *(a)* Simplified Block Diagram of an MBE Encoder; *(b)* MBE Decoder there are sometimes similarities, in actual fact, the details of IMBE are quite a bit different from the other speech coders discussed in this book.

From Figure 8.13, we see that the input speech is windowed and an FFT applied to obtain the magnitude and phase of the various frequency components. Next, fundamental frequency or pitch estimation is performed, and the spectral components are grouped into bands, each containing three pitch harmonics. There are up to 12 bands, with the highest band being extended to include frequencies up to 3.8 kHz. Analyses are then conducted to classify each of these three-harmonic bands as voiced or unvoiced. There are 83 bits available for coding the speech model parameters, with 8 bits used for the pitch, and K (up to 12) bits for voicing in the bands, leaving $83 - 8 - K$ bits for coding the spectral coefficients. Coding of the spectral parameters is accomplished in several different ways, depending upon the particular application.

Several of the IMBE parameters can be sensitive to bit errors, and so for mobile communications environments, error control coding of selected parameters is essential. In fact, at a rate of 6.4 kbps and a frame size of 20 ms, 128 bits/frame are available, and in the INMARSAT application, 45 bits/frame are reserved for error control coding. The INMARSAT IMBE has achieved an MOS of 3.4 in subjective testing, a DRT score of 93.4, and has an algorithmic delay of 78.75 ms.

8.7   Summary

It should be clear from this chapter that one of the principal themes running through frequency domain speech and audio coding today is modeling perceptual effects via the theory of auditory masking. Extraordinary compression ratios have been achieved for "transparent coding" of high-quality audio, and innovations continue. In fact, at the time of this writing, there is still considerable flux in MPEG-1 and -2 audio coding, causing those involved in designing and manufacturing equipment to have to plan for several eventualities.

The fact that audio compression methods have become a part of many aspects of our entertainment systems, even while improving the delivered product, is really quite a tribute to what is being done in the field today. With competition and innovation, algorithms in the field should continue to evolve rapidly.

9

CHAPTER

JPEG Still-Image Compression Standard

9.1 Introduction

Although several standards for voice and facsimile compression have existed for a number of years, the JPEG still-image compression standard has to be one of the most widely recognized standards in existence today. The baseline JPEG compression method has truly become ubiquitous, with a wide variety of hardware and software implementations available for a host of applications. The broad goal of the Joint Photographic Experts Group (JPEG), meeting as a working group under the ISO but closely coordinated with CCITT SGVIII, was to develop a general-purpose still-image compression standard that would be applicable to virtually all continuous-tone still-image transmission and storage problems. To achieve this, JPEG draws upon years of prior research in image compression and complements this with numerous innovations and refinements that bring both performance and complexity to levels that allow it to have the wide utility that it has today.

The goals of JPEG are the following (Wallace 1991; Pennebaker and Mitchell 1993):

1. Achieve rate and reconstructed image quality "at or near the state of the art" with image fidelity classifiable as "very good" to "excellent"

2. Be useful for compressing almost any continuous-tone still image, including both gray-scale and color, any color space, and most image sizes

3. Have complexity that would allow software implementations on many common computing platforms and affordable hardware implementations

The JPEG standard has several lossy encoding modes, starting with the baseline sequential mode, and a lossless encoding mode. In the following sections, we provide an overview of the JPEG compression methods, a discussion of relative performance, and insights on what led to various parameter selections and approaches.

9.2 Baseline JPEG

The basic JPEG encoder and decoder structures are illustrated in Figure 9.1; FDCT stands for forward DCT and IDCT stands for inverse DCT. The baseline JPEG encoding method is called *sequential encoding*. First the image is partitioned into 8 × 8 blocks of pixels that are ordered according to a "rasterlike" left-to-right, top-to-bottom scan, as depicted in Figure 9.2. The FDCT is computed on each of the 8 × 8 blocks of pixels, and the resulting 64 DCT coefficients are scalar quantized using uniform quantization tables based upon psychovisual experiments (Lohscheller 1984). These scalar quantization tables are provided as part of the standard but are not a requirement. After the DCT coefficients are quantized, the coefficients within the block are ordered according to the zigzag scan in Figure 9.3, the resulting bitstream is runlength coded to generate an intermediate symbol sequence, and then these symbols are Huffman coded for transmission or storage.

Figure 9.4 illustrates the transmission sequence for all blocks in an image. Each set of DCT coefficients for an 8 × 8 block is shown as a square slice, with the rows corresponding to the bits representing the coefficients, starting in the top row with the DC coefficient, followed in subsequent rows by the AC coefficients arranged following the zigzag ordering. The zigzag scan increases the runlengths, thereby increasing the efficiency of the lossless coding step. The DC coefficients from block to block are actually differenced before scalar quantization because the DC values of adjacent blocks are often very close to being the same.

Luminance and chrominance quantization tables drawn from the CCIR-601 experiments by Lohscheller (1984) are shown in Figure 9.5; the step size for the differenced DC coefficient is shown in the upper left, followed by the step size for the first horizontal harmonic to the right, and so on. Note that the step size is presented rather than the bit allocation, so that a large step size indicates a coarse quantization, or a low bit allocation, and a small step size represents a higher bit allocation. The perceptually designed quantization tables take advantage of

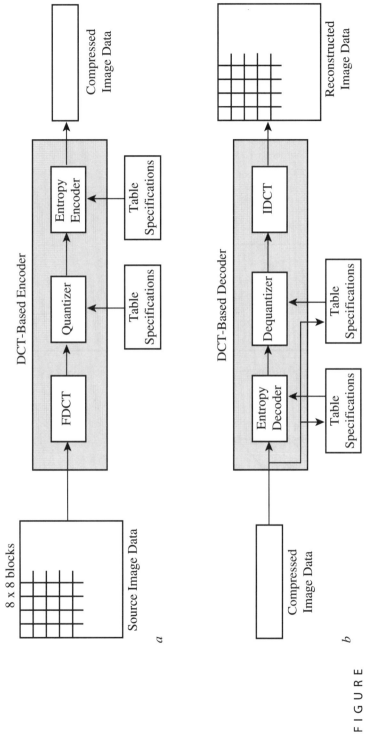

JPEG: (a) Encoder; (b) Decoder

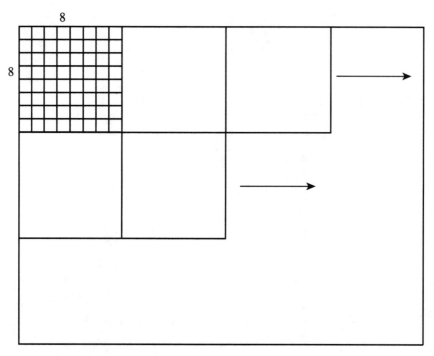

FIGURE

9.2 Partitioning of an Image into 8 × 8 Blocks of Pixels

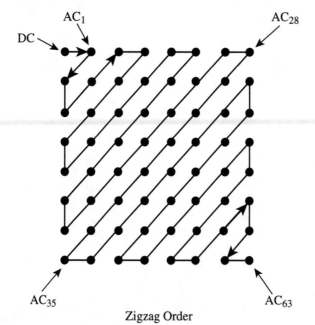

Zigzag Order

Zigzag Coefficient Ordering

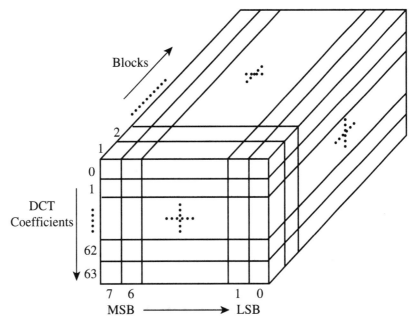

Sequential Lossy Encoding

Luminance quantization table									Chrominance quantization table							
16	11	10	16	24	40	51	61		17	18	24	47	99	99	99	99
12	12	14	19	26	58	60	55		18	21	26	66	99	99	99	99
14	13	16	24	40	57	69	56		24	26	56	99	99	99	99	99
14	17	22	29	51	87	80	62		47	66	99	99	99	99	99	99
18	22	37	56	68	109	103	77		99	99	99	99	99	99	99	99
24	35	55	64	81	104	113	92		99	99	99	99	99	99	99	99
49	64	78	87	103	121	120	101		99	99	99	99	99	99	99	99
72	92	95	98	112	100	103	99		99	99	99	99	99	99	99	99

Suggested Step Sizes for CCIR-601

masking properties of the eye and zero out many small coefficient values, which shows up in Figure 9.5 as large step size values.

The JPEG sequential baseline encoder accommodates only 8-bit sample inputs and has two Huffman tables each for the DC and AC coefficients. The entropy coding methods are detailed in Section 9.5.

9.3   Progressive Encoding

Progressive encoding modes are provided to allow a coarse version of an image to be transmitted at a low rate and then progressively improved by subsequent transmissions. This is convenient for browsing applications so that the user does not have to wait for an entire image to be received before being able to view its contents. Implementation of progressive encoding requires the availability of a sufficient buffer to store the quantized DCT coefficients for an entire image. The entropy coding then transmits selected sets of these coefficients.

The two progressive encoding modes in the JPEG standard, spectral selection and successive approximation, are illustrated in Figure 9.6. Spectral selection involves sending sets of DCT coefficients starting with lower frequencies and progressing to higher frequencies. For example, the first scan might include the DC coefficient and the two AC coefficients corresponding to the first harmonic in the horizontal and vertical directions, followed by a second scan that includes the next three AC coefficients, and so on, according to the zigzag scan in Figure 9.3. This scheme is simple to implement, but all high-frequency information is postponed to the later scans. The result is that the reconstructed images from the early scans are blurred.

Successive approximation encoding improves on spectral selection by sending the DCT coefficients corresponding to all frequencies but keeping the transmission rate down by sending only the n_1 most significant bits of each coefficient first ($n_1 = 4$ in Figure 9.6 (b)), followed by the n_2 most significant bits ($n_2 = 1$ in Figure 9.6 (b)), and so on. This method gives very good reconstructed image quality, even for the very early scans. Figure 9.6 contrasts the two progressive encoding methods.

A combination of spectral selection and successive approximation can yield very efficient compression results with good reconstruction quality. Pennebaker and Mitchell (1993) report that using all bits of the DC coefficients and reducing precision on all of the AC coefficients for a rate of 0.24 bit/pixel produces quality slightly superior to spectral selection at 0.36 bit/pixel with the DC and the first five AC coefficients sent with full precision. This is an intuitive result: the DC coefficient is often the highest energy transform coefficient in a block, and DC mismatch in adjacent blocks is a common cause of blocking artifacts, so the DC coefficient requires an accurate representation. Further, the representation of higher frequencies is impossible in the early scans of spectral selection, and even a coarse representation makes high-frequency spectral content evident to the viewer. Pennebaker and Mitchell (1993) summarize this by saying that the spectral selection mode produces no distortion below cutoff, but maximum

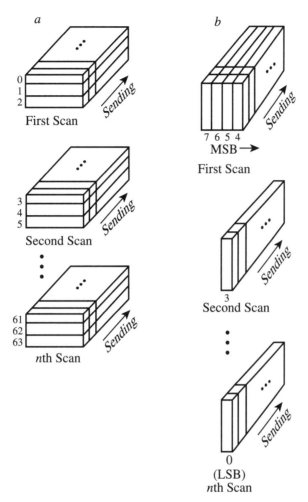

FIGURE

9.6   Progressive Encoding: *(a)* Spectral Selection; *(b)* Successive Approximation

distortion above cutoff, while successive approximation gives more of a constant distortion across spatial frequencies.

9.4   Hierarchical (Pyramidal) Encoding

It may sometimes be necessary to view a high-resolution image on a lower-resolution display device; in these situations, it would be inefficient to transmit the DCT coefficients for the entire high-resolution image to the low-resolution

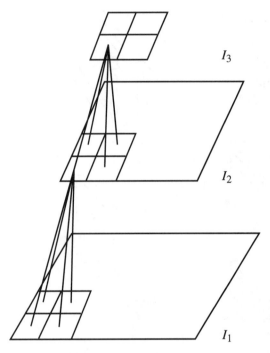

I_3

I_2

I_1

FIGURE

9.7   Pyramidal Filtering and Decimation of an Image

display. The JPEG standard accommodates these applications by specifying a hierarchical encoding mode based upon pyramidal encoding techniques, where each resolution can differ from adjacent ones by a factor of two in either the horizontal or vertical directions, or both. The hierarchical (pyramidal) encoding procedure is as follows.

The original image is filtered and downsampled by the required multiples of two, and the low-resolution image is coded using any of the lossy modes or even the lossless encoding mode. The compressed image is then decoded and upsampled, and subtracted from the next-higher-resolution image. The resulting difference image is then encoded by one of the encoding modes. This procedure is continued until all resolutions are coded. Note that all encodings may be lossy, lossless, or lossy followed by a final lossless encoding.

Figure 9.7 shows the generation of the pyramidal image structure by filtering and decimation. Figure 9.8 shows a block diagram of a hierarchical or pyramidal encoder that has the images in Figure 9.7 as input. Note that this figure represents the encoder only, yet decoders for all but the base-level image must be implemented in the encoder because the decoded and interpolated im-

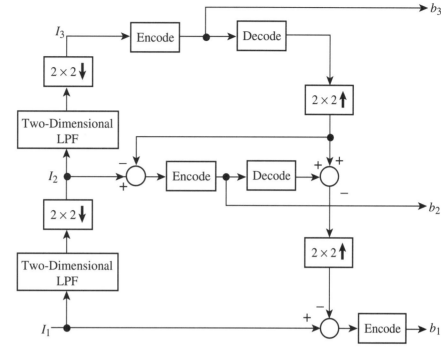

F I G U R E

9.8   Encoder for Three-Level Pyramidal Coding

ages from the upper levels are needed to encode all lower levels. The original filtered and decimated images cannot be used directly because encoding errors from upper levels will accumulate at lower levels. In Figure 9.8, b_1, b_2, and b_3 are the transmitted data streams needed at the decoder.

The encoded and transmitted images are depicted in Figure 9.9 by the labels on the left of the pyramid, or alternatively, this pyramid can represent the decoded images, as labeled to the right of the pyramid. If lossy coding of the upper three levels is employed, lossless reconstruction is still possible by sending an appropriate additional data sequence, indicated in the figure by b_0. This bitstream would be generated at the encoder to represent the difference between I_1 and $\hat{I}_1$. Completely lossless transmission of all levels in the pyramid is also possible with appropriate lossless encoders in Figure 9.8. Notice that hierarchical encoding can also be viewed as a version of progressive transmission where the progression is in spatial resolution not image reconstruction quality.

Since scaling of images on a platform can consume substantial CPU time, hierarchical coding can be a nice enhancement. Of course, it is generated at the expense of greater storage requirements at the encoder and an increase in

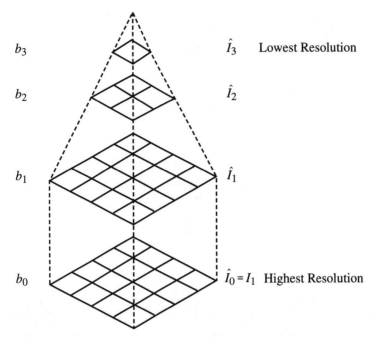

b_3 $\hat{I}_3$ Lowest Resolution

b_2 $\hat{I}_2$

b_1 $\hat{I}_1$

b_0 $\hat{I}_0 = I_1$ Highest Resolution

FIGURE

9.9   Encoded Levels and Decoded Image Pyramid

data rate of up to 33%. This increase in data rate is implied by the increased number of pixels in all of the levels combined. Specifically, if the original image is $N \times N$, then with repeated factor-of-two decimation, the next levels will be $N/2 \times N/2$, $N/4 \times N/4$, and so on, and the total number of pixels in any number of levels is upper bounded by

$$N^2 \left[1 + \frac{1}{4} + \frac{1}{4^2} + \cdots \right] \le \frac{4N^2}{3}$$

Performance of the hierarchical mode is better than other JPEG modes at very low bit rates, so this might also be an attraction for some applications. Consistent with the JPEG decoder syntax approach, the downsampling filter is not specified, but the upsampling filter is. The interpolated value between two pixels from the lower-resolution image is a truncated average of the two pixels. The left column and the top row of the upsampled and lower-resolution image are aligned, and the rightmost column and bottom row of the lower-resolution image are replicated to produce the necessary interpolations in the upsampled image. A suggested compatible downsampling filter is given in the standard.

9.5 Entropy Coding

Entropy coding in the JPEG standard is accomplished in two steps. First, the coefficients are converted into an intermediate sequence of symbols, and then these symbols are coded using Huffman coding or arithmetic coding. Since the DC value of an 8×8 block is differentially encoded, intermediate symbol sequence generation is slightly different for the AC coefficients than for the differenced DC coefficients, and since the statistics of the DC and AC coefficients are quite different, they use separate Huffman tables. We begin with a description of the intermediate sequence generation and coding for the AC coefficients.

The baseline sequential JPEG only allows 8-bit integer pixel inputs, but the AC coefficients can be 3 bits larger, so the AC amplitudes fall in the range $[-1023, 1023]$. The zigzag ordering of the AC coefficients is mapped into an intermediate sequence of what are called "symbol-1" and "symbol-2" pairs. Symbol-1 consists of (RUNLENGTH, SIZE), where RUNLENGTH is the length of zero values preceding the next nonzero AC coefficient and SIZE is the number of bits needed to code the next nonzero coefficient amplitude, which is symbol-2. So, symbol-2 is (AMPLITUDE), which is the value of the AC coefficient. RUNLENGTH takes the values 0 to 15, and a symbol-1 pair of (15, 0) represents a runlength of 16 zero-valued AC coefficients. Since there can be long runs of zero-valued coefficients, up to three consecutive (15, 0) pairs followed by a symbol-1 that completes the runlength and a single symbol-2 are allowed. There are 63 possible AC coefficients in the 8×8 block, and this coding method allows for the possibility of 63 zero values. If the last run of zeros includes the last AC coefficient in the block, no symbol-2 is sent after the final run of zeros, but instead, the (0, 0) end-of-block (EOB) symbol is sent that denotes the end of the 8×8 block.

The symbol-1 sequence is entropy coded, Huffman coded in the baseline, but symbol-2 is assigned its direct binary representation if positive, or the one's complement representation if it is negative. Thus, only the symbol-1 sequence is Huffman compressed. Note that direct Huffman coding of all of the AC coefficient amplitudes would require 2047 entries, but by Huffman coding only the (RUNLENGTH, SIZE) pairs, only 16 (RUNLENGTH values) $\times$ 10 (SIZE bits)+ EOB = 161 entries, are needed. A partial sample table for this Huffman code is given in Table 9.1, and a table for the SIZE classifications is given in Table 9.2. Only the first 12 categories are used here.

The differenced DC coefficient stream covers the range $[-2047, 2047]$ because of the differencing, and the symbol-1 sequence now just consists of SIZE. The

T A B L E
9.1

Partial Huffman Code for AC Coefficient
(RUNLENGTH, SIZE) Pairs

Run/Size	Code Length	Codeword
0/0 (EOB)	4	1010
0/1	2	00
0/2	2	01
0/3	3	100
0/4	4	1011
0/5	5	11010
0/6	7	1111000
0/7	8	11111000
0/8	10	1111110110
0/9	16	1111111110000010
0/A	16	1111111110000011
1/1	4	1100
1/2	5	11011
1/3	7	1111001
1/4	9	111110110
1/5	11	11111110110
1/6	16	1111111110000100
1/7	16	1111111110000101
1/8	16	1111111110000110
1/9	16	1111111110000111
1/A	16	1111111110001000
2/1	5	11100
2/2	8	11111001
2/3	10	1111110111
2/4	12	111111110100
2/5	16	1111111110001001
2/6	16	1111111110001010
2/7	16	1111111110001011
2/8	16	1111111110001100
2/9	16	1111111110001101
2/A	16	1111111110001110

T A B L E   SIZE Categories

9.2

SIZE	DC Difference	Code
0	0	—
1	−1, 1	0, 1
2	−3, −2, 2, 3	00, 01, 10, 11
3	−7, . . . , −4, 4, . . . , 7	000, . . . , 011, 100, . . . , 111
4	−15, . . . , −8, 8, . . . , 15	0000, . . . , 0111, 1000, . . . , 1111
⋮	⋮	⋮
16	32,768	—

T A B L E   Huffman Code for the Luminance Difference DC SIZE

9.3

SIZE Category	Code Length	Codeword
0	2	00
1	3	010
2	3	011
3	3	100
4	3	101
5	3	110
6	4	1110
7	5	11110
8	6	111110
9	7	1111110
10	8	11111110
11	9	111111110

symbol-2 sequence for the differenced DC values is again AMPLITUDE. As for the AC coefficients, only the symbol-1 sequence is entropy coded. Thus, rather than requiring a Huffman code with 4095 entries, only 12 entries are needed to Huffman code the SIZE information. Table 9.3 gives a typical Huffman code assignment for the differenced DC SIZE.

9.5.1 Example of DCT Coefficient Encoding

Let the DCT coefficients in a particular 8×8 image block be as shown below:

```
 48   12   0   0   0   0   0   0
-10    8   0   0   0   0   0   0
  2    0   0   0   0   0   0   0
  0    0   0   0   0   0   0   0
  0    0   0   0   0   0   0   0
  0    0   0   0   0   0   0   0
  0    0   0   0   0   0   0   0
  0    0   0   0   0   0   0   0
```

If we assume that the DC coefficient in the previous block was 40, the difference is thus 8. To encode this differenced DC value, we first find the SIZE in Table 9.2, refer to Table 9.3 to find the Huffman code for this SIZE, then append the code for the AMPLITUDE in this SIZE category. Thus, for the differenced DC value of 8, the assigned binary code is 1011000. To code the AC coefficients, we arrange them in order using the zigzag scan, find the correct combinations of RUNLENGTH and SIZE, look up the Huffman code for this pair in Table 9.1, and then append the appropriate code from Table 9.2. Thus, the ordered coefficients are 12, −10, 2, and 8, followed by 58 zeros to complete the block. To get the code for 12, we have no zeros before it and it falls in SIZE category 4, so from Table 9.1, we find the code for (0, 4) to be 1011 and then the 4-bit binary code for 12 is 1100, so that the complete codeword for 12 is 10111100. For −10, we have no preceding zeros and it falls into SIZE category 4, so the code for −10 is 10110101. Proceeding in this fashion, we code 2 as 0110 and 8 as 10111000. Since there are no intervening nonzero coefficients before the end of the block, the 58 zeros are encoded as EOB or 1010.

9.6 Image Data Conventions

While JPEG's goal was interoperability, there are a number of details that are not specified, including the image resolution, the color space for natural images, and methods for converting pixels with other than 8- or 12-bit accuracy. JPEG does have specifications for how to handle multicomponent images and flexibility in how a user might want to encode and play back the compressed image data. Certainly, since JPEG is intended to address a wide range of applications, it has to encompass images with several color components and varying resolutions.

JPEG provides for a maximum of 255 image components, each component represented by a rectangular array of pixels, denoted here by x_i horizontal pixels and y_i vertical pixels for the ith component. Each of these pixels has two levels of precision for lossy DCT coding, 8 and 12 bits; for lossless coding, the pixels can have 2 to 16 bits accuracy. The components are also allowed to have differing resolutions, which are expressed in JPEG as a fraction of a maximum resolution by ratios of sampling factors. That is, if we let $X = \max(x_i)$ and $Y = \max(y_i)$ denote the maximum horizontal and vertical resolutions, respectively, then x_i and y_i for the ith component can be expressed as

$$x_i = [X \times H_i/H_{max}] \tag{9.1}$$

$$y_i = [Y \times V_i/V_{max}] \tag{9.2}$$

where H_{max} and V_{max} are the maximum horizontal and vertical relative sampling factors, and H_i and V_i are the relative sampling factors of the ith components.

For example, if we have a YCbCr color space image that is 512×512, the baseline JPEG would support 8-bit precision pixels, and the luminance component would have $x_1 = y_1 = 512$. Since the chrominance components are usually subsampled by a factor of two, $x_2 = y_2 = x_3 = y_3 = 256$, so we get $X = \max(512, 256) = 512 = Y$, with relative sampling factors $H_1 = V_1 = 2$ and $H_2 = V_2 = 1$, so that $H_{max} = V_{max} = 2$. Thus, we can calculate

$$x_1 = [512 \times 2/2] = 512 = y_1$$

$$x_2 = [512 \times 1/2] = 256 = y_2 = x_3 = y_3$$

from equations (9.1) and (9.2).

With this information, it is still necessary to consider how a user might wish to encode and decode a multiple-component image. For instance, with a three-component image, it is possible that you might want to encode and store the luminance component for the entire image first, then encode and store the Cb chrominance for the entire image, then the Cr chrominance. Alternatively, you might wish to interleave coded versions of the three components for subsets of the image, which would then allow all components for a small portion of the image to be retrieved and decoded without waiting for this process for the complete image.

JPEG supports this interleaving by defining terms called *data units* and *minimum coded units* (MCUs). A data unit is the smallest possible unit of data that can be encoded and stored in JPEG; it is different for lossy and lossless coding modes. For lossy coding, the data unit is a block of 8×8 pixels processed by the DCT; for lossless coding, the data unit is a single sample or just one pixel.

The MCU specifies the number of data units per interleaved component when interleaving is used. For our previous example of a 512×512 image coded into YCbCr components with 2:1 subsampling of both chrominance components, we might have an 8×8 luminance data unit followed by one 4×4 Cb data unit and one 4×4 Cr data unit as one MCU.

9.7   Lossless Encoding Mode

Since lossless encoding with the DCT is difficult to specify, the lossless encoding mode chosen by the JPEG committee consists of a very simple predictive encoder that does not involve the DCT at all. Figure 9.10 illustrates the JPEG lossless predictive encoding operations. In this figure, the pixel to be predicted, denoted by X, can be predicted using the three pixels already available in the scanned image, labeled as A, B, and C. There are eight possible choices for the

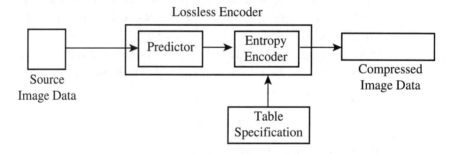

	Predictors for Lossless Coding	
Selection Value		Prediction
0		No Prediction
1		A
2		B
3		C
4		$A + B - C$
5		$A + ((B - C)/2)$
6		$B + ((A - C)/2)$
7		$(A + B)/2$

FIGURE

9.10   Predictive Lossless JPEG Encoding

predictor, as shown in the lower right of Figure 9.10, and the particular predictor used by the encoder is specified in the header sent to the decoder. The "no prediction" selection is only available for hierarchical encoding. Depending upon the image, one of the predictors may outperform the others; however, various image coding experiments in the literature indicate that their performance can be relatively close on the average.

Similar to the coding methods used for the DCT coefficients, the prediction residual is encoded by representing each value as a SIZE category and AMPLI-TUDE. The input sample can have an accuracy from 2^2 to 2^{16}, and the prediction residual may be any value up to 2^{16}. The SIZE category symbol is taken from Table 9.2 and specifies the number of bits used to represent the amplitude of the prediction residual. The AMPLITUDE symbol is the actual encoded value of the residual. The SIZE category symbols are entropy coded. Thus, if the prediction residual error is 128, the SIZE category is 8 from Table 9.2; the binary codeword for an amplitude of 128 is 10000000. The SIZE category symbols are entropy coded.

9.8   Summary

An overview of the several encoding options available with JPEG is given in Table 9.4. From the table we can see that baseline JPEG supports 8-bit input samples and has default Huffman coding tables, but does not support arithmetic coding. Extended modes include twice as many Huffman tables as the baseline and four sets of arithmetic coding tables.

JPEG performance, in terms of quality versus bit rate, is really quite impressive, especially considering the relatively low complexity and the fact that these approaches have been around for a relatively long time. The lossy mode performance is summarized in Table 9.5 for 8-bit color photographs. The rate given is in total bits per pixel. This number basically comes from the fact that the luminance component has 8-bit accuracy and the two chrominance components have 8-bit accuracy each but half the sample rate. Thus, there is an average of 16 bits/pixel in the input image, and a rate of 0.5 bit/pixel is a 32:1 compression. The 2-bit/pixel images are considered "indistinguishable" from the original; the 0.25-bit/pixel performance is only classified as "fair." A rate of 0.083 bit/pixel was tested in the JPEG evaluations, but the quality of the image at that rate need only be "recognizable," and this rate is not specified as a part of the baseline.

The entropy coding step can have an impact on coder performance. As noted by Pennebaker and Mitchell (1993) for experiments on standard test images,

T A B L E

9.4

JPEG Encoding Options

	Baseline (All DCT Decoders)	Extended Processes	Lossless Processes
DCT-based	yes	yes	
Predictive-based			yes
8-bit samples	yes	yes	
12-bit samples		yes	
2-bit to 16-bit samples			yes
Sequential	yes	yes	yes
Progressive		yes	
Maximum Huffman tables	2 DC + 2 AC	4 DC + 4 AC	4 DC
Maximum Arithmetic tables	0	4 DC + 4 AC	4 DC
Decodes 4 comps	yes	yes	yes
Interleaved scans	yes	yes	yes
Noninterleaved	yes	yes	yes

T A B L E

9.5

JPEG Lossy Mode Performance 8-Bit Color Photographs

Rate (bits/pixel)	Perceived Quality	Applications
0.25	fair to good	few
0.50	good to very good	some
0.75	very good to excellent	many
1.50	excellent to indistinguishable	most
above 2.00	indistinguishable	nearly all

custom Huffman tables provide a rate reduction of 2.4–7.9% over the fixed Huffman tables, and the arithmetic coding allows an average reduction of 2.5% over the custom Huffman tables. Lossless coder performance yields about a 2:1 compression.

Multimedia Conferencing Standards

10.1 Introduction

The International Telecommunication Union Telecommunication Standardization Sector (ITU-T, known before 1993 as the CCITT) has long been the most important international body for telecommunications standards. Now part of the United Nations, the ITU-T's roots began in 1865 with the standardization of technology for early long-distance telegraph lines.

In recent years, ITU-T has produced a number of international standards ("Recommendations," in ITU parlance) for real-time digital multimedia communication, including video and data conferencing. This chapter covers the most important of these standards, the ITU-T H-series, including H.320 through H.324, and H.310, together with their associated video and audio codecs and component standards, as well as the ITU-T T.120 series for data/graphics conferencing and conference control. Audio and video codecs used by the ITU-T H-series are covered from a systems viewpoint, focusing on what the codecs do, not how they do it. The final section discusses delay issues in these systems, an often misunderstood subject.

Table 10.1 summarizes the ITU-T H-series standards, their target networks, and the basic video, audio, multiplex, and control standards for each.

All ITU-T H-series systems standards support real-time conversational two-way video and audio (limited to one stream of each in H.320, H.321, and H.322), with provisions for optional data channels for T.120 data/graphics conferencing and other purposes. Extensions allow multipoint operation (in which three or more sites can join in a group conference), and in some systems encryption, remote control of far-end cameras, and broadcast applications. Each

T A B L E   ITU-T Multimedia Conferencing Standards (Basic Modes)

10.1

Standard	Network	Video	Audio	Multiplex	Control
H.320 (1990)	ISDN	H.261	G.711	H.221	H.242
H.321 (1995)	ATM/B-ISDN	adapts H.320 to ATM/B-ISDN network			
H.322 (1995)	IsoEthernet	adapts H.320 to IsoEthernet network			
H.323 (1996)	LANs/Internet	H.261	G.711	H.225.0	H.245
H.324 (1995)	PSTN	H.263	G.723.1	H.223	H.245
H.310 (1996)	ATM/B-ISDN	H.262	MPEG-1	H.222	H.245

standard specifies a common baseline mode to guarantee interoperability but allows the use of other optional modes, both standard and nonstandard, to be automatically negotiated using the control protocol.

These systems fall into two generations. H.320, H.321, and H.322 are first-generation standards, based on H.320 for ISDN networks approved in 1990. H.321 and H.322 specify the adaptation of H.320 terminals for use on ATM and IsoEthernet networks, respectively.

H.323, H.324, and H.310 are the second-generation H-series system standards. Approved in 1995 and 1996, they benefit from industry's experience with H.320, avoiding the problems and limitations that were discovered. They all use the new H.245 control protocol and support a common set of improved media codecs. H.324, which like H.320 is intended for low-bit-rate circuit switched networks (initially analog PSTN, often known as POTS), makes use of some H.320 extension standards, including H.233/H.234 encryption and H.224/H.281 far-end camera control.

All these H-series terminals can interoperate with each other through appropriate gateways and can participate in multipoint conferences, as illustrated in Figure 10.1.

10.2   H.320 for ISDN Videoconferencing

The ITU-T H.320 standard, known during its development as "px64" for its use of bandwidth in 64-kbps increments, covers videoconferencing and videotelephony over ISDN and switched-56 circuits at rates from 56 kbps to 2 Mbps.

Like the other H-series systems, H.320 supports real-time conversational two-way video and audio (one channel each), with provisions for optional data

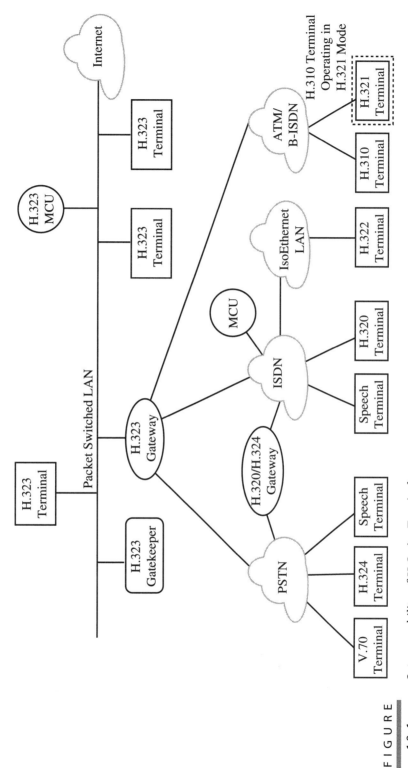

Interoperability of H-Series Terminals

FIGURE
10.1

channels. Extensions allow multipoint operation (in which three or more sites can join in a group conference), encryption, remote control of far-end cameras, and broadcast applications.

H.320 was developed during the late 1980s and approved by the CCITT (now ITU-T) in 1990. It was the first successful low-bit-rate video communications standard and remains the universally accepted standard for ISDN videoconferencing.

10.2.1 The H.320 Standards Suite

The H.320 document is a "systems standard" that calls out a number of other ITU-T standards for various parts of the system, as shown in Figure 10.2. The core components of H.320 are the following:

- H.221 multiplex: Mixes audio, video, data, and control information into a single bitstream. Uses synchronous time division multiplexing with 10-ms frames.

- H.230/H.242 control: Mode control commands and indications, capabilities exchange. Operates over a fixed 400-bps channel (BAS) in the H.221 multiplex.

- H.231/H.243 multipoint: Specifies central multipoint bridges and operation for multiway group conferences. (Optional in the H.320 standard, but universally implemented.)

- H.261 video coding: Compresses color motion video into a low-rate bitstream. QCIF (176 × 144) and CIF (352 × 288) resolutions.

- G.711 audio coding: 8-kHz sample rate, 8-bit log-PCM (64 kbps total) for toll-quality narrowband audio (3-kHz bandwidth).

Baseline H.320 components are shown in bold in Figure 10.2 and include QCIF resolution H.261 video, G.711 log-PCM audio, the H.221 multiplexer, and H.230/H.242 control. Improved standard modes such as H.263 and CIF resolution H.261 video and improved-quality or lower-bit-rate audio modes (leaving more bandwidth for video) can be negotiated using control protocol procedures, as can nonstandard or proprietary modes.

In addition to the core components of H.320, optional standard extensions support remote control and pointing of far-end cameras (H.224/H.281), encryption according to H.233/H.234, and data conferencing using T.120 for sophisticated graphics and conference control. T.120 supports applications like JPEG still-image transfer, shared document annotation, and PC application sharing.

Conferencing Applications and User Interface

H.242 Ctrl	H.243 Multi-point	H.234 Key Exchange	Preprocessing Postprocessing	AEC AGC Noise Suppression	Time-Critical Applications	Application Protocols T.126 T.127
			H.261 H.262 H.263 Video	G.711 G.722 G.728 G.723.1 G.729 Audio	H.281 Far-end Camera Control	T.124 Generic Conference Control
H.230						T.122/T.125 MCS
					H.224	T.123
BAS		ECS	H.223 Encryption			
			H.221 Multiplex and Framing			
			Transport Network (ISDN, Switched-56, . . .)			

FIGURE
10.2

H.320 Protocol Stack

The H.331 standard (not shown) specifies how H.320 terminals can be used for low-bit-rate broadcast (send or receive only) applications.

10.2.2 H.221 Multiplex

The multiplexer component of a multimedia conferencing system mixes together the audio, video, data, and control streams into a single bitstream for transmission. In H.320, the H.221 time division multiplexer (TDM) is used for this purpose.

H.221 supports a total of eight independent media channels, not all of which are present in every call. The BAS and FAS channels carry H.320 system control and frame synchronization information and are always required. There is provision for one channel each of audio and video and three user data channels, LSD, HSD, and MLP. The optional ECS channel carries encryption control messages if encryption is used.

The multiplexing scheme uses repeating 10-ms frames of 80 bytes (640 bits) each. Various bit positions within each frame are allocated to the different channels in use. This system makes efficient use of the available bandwidth, except that the allocation of bits to different channels can change among only a small number of allowed configurations.

H.221 Channel Structure

H.221 is based on the ISDN channel structure, which consists of synchronous, low-error-rate digital channels of 64 kbps each, either in individual 64-kbps connections called *B channels* or grouped into larger channels in multiples of 64 kbps, such as the 384-kbps H_0 connection, which contains six timeslots of 64 kbps each. In H.320 systems, the H.221 multiplex normally uses two or more 64-kbps channels, which are synchronized with each other using information in the FAS channel.

Each 64-kbps channel is treated as a sequence of 8-bit bytes sent at a rate of 8 kHz (125 μs per byte). In ordinary ISDN voice telephony, each 64-kbps channel carries a single voice call using G.711 log-PCM, which sends 8-bit samples at a rate of 8 kHz, for toll-quality 3-kHz audio bandwidth speech.

In H.221, the sequence of bytes is divided into 10-ms frames, 80 bytes long. Each bit position of the byte stream is considered a subchannel of 8 kbps, as shown in Figure 10.3. The low-order bit position subchannel (bit 8 in the ITU numbering) is called the *service channel* (SC) and carries frame synchronization and control information. This allows H.221 framing and control information to

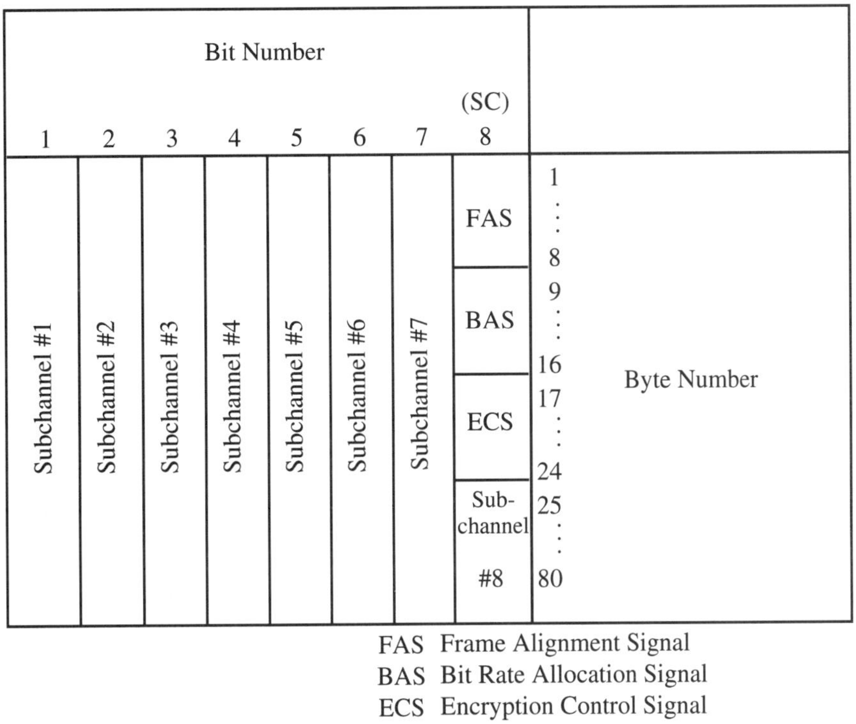

	Bit Number							(SC)	
	1	2	3	4	5	6	7	8	

FAS   Frame Alignment Signal
BAS   Bit Rate Allocation Signal
ECS   Encryption Control Signal

FIGURE 10.3   H.221 Frame

be sent in the low-order bit of G.711 audio samples during voice transmission, with minimal impact on voice quality.

Different parts of each 80-byte frame are allocated for video, audio, and data channels, with portions of the service channel reserved for the special FAS, BAS, and, when encryption is in use, ECS channels. Each bit of the H.221 frame can be considered a separately allocable channel of 100 bps.

On some (mostly North American) networks, only 7 bits are sent in each 125-μs G.711 sample period, for an aggregate bit rate of 56 kbps. On these "restricted" networks, the H.221 service channel is sent in bit 7, but the H.221 frame structure is otherwise the same. This chapter will discuss H.221 assuming the more common 64-kbps "unrestricted" channel structure.

Frame Alignment Signal (FAS)

The frame alignment signal (FAS) is used for H.221 frame synchronization and is carried in bits 1 to 8 of the service channel. Bits 2 to 8 contain a frame alignment word that repeats on even-numbered frames. Receivers discover the alignment of the H.221 frame structure in the byte stream by detecting multiple frame alignment words, properly spaced at 160-byte intervals.

H.221 frames are grouped into 16-frame "multiframes" of 160 ms each. Bit 1 of the FAS contains multichannel synchronization information transmitted at 1 bit per frame over each sequence of 16 frames in the multiframe. This includes a multiframe alignment signal and a number identifying each channel in a multichannel connection. These are used to identify and synchronize the different 64-kbps channels in an H.320 connection, equalizing any delay differences that may be caused by each channel taking a different path through the network.

Additional bits in the FAS are used to indicate when a receiver has successfully detected frame alignment, and for an optional 4-bit CRC and corresponding error indication, which are used only to monitor the quality of the connection. No retransmission or error recovery is performed based on these CRC bits.

The set of synchronized multiple 64-kbps channels deliver to the receiver a corresponding number of bytes in each 125-μs (8-kHz) period, with each byte identified as coming from a numbered channel, resulting in a single synchronous aggregate channel.

Bit Rate Allocation Signal (BAS)

The bit rate allocation signal (BAS) specifies the allocation of bit positions in H.221 frames between video, audio, and data channels, so that the required bit rates for each channel are provided. It also carries other control information, by which the terminal communicates its capabilities and commands to the other end. The BAS is carried in bits 9 to 16 of the service channel.

BAS messages are sent in units of 8-bit bytes. Each even-numbered H.221 frame carries a single byte of BAS message, while odd-numbered frames carry 8 error correction bits for the preceding byte. The result is that the BAS carries net 400 bps of control information, 1 byte per 20 ms.

As the name indicates, BAS messages were initially intended to communicate the allocation of bits in the H.221 frame among audio, video, and data channels. BAS messages are used for this purpose, but the range of possible bit allocations is limited to the small set defined in H.221, so dynamic bit rate allocation in response to the needs of bursty data traffic is difficult.

The BAS is also used to carry general control and indication messages, which compete with each other and with bit rate allocation messages for BAS bandwidth, sometimes resulting in delayed transmission when too many messages are queued for the narrow BAS bandwidth (especially at the start of a call). This has proven to be a major limitation of the H.221 multiplexer. At other times, no control messages need to be sent, so the fixed 800 bps consumed by the BAS is wasted.

One advantage of the BAS for control purposes is that messages are inherently synchronized with the audio and video data. For instance, when a BAS message is announcing a switch from one audio coding mode to another, there is no ambiguity about the point in the audio bitstream where the change occurs, since it is specified relative to the H.221 frame in which the BAS message was sent.

Encryption Control Signal (ECS)

The encryption control signal (ECS) is carried in bits 17 to 24 of the service channel only when encryption according to H.233 is in use. At other times, the service channel bits occupied by ECS, as with the remaining unoccupied service channel bits, are used to carry video or data channel information.

The ECS is used to exchange encryption control information, including algorithm in use, selection of channels to be encrypted, initialization vectors, and public key exchange according to H.234.

10.2.3 System Control Protocol

The control protocol operates between a pair of H.320 systems to govern the terminal's overall operational mode including negotiation of common capabilities, selection of video and audio modes, opening and closing of channels, and transmission of miscellaneous commands and indications to the far end. H.242 and H.230 together define the basic H.320 control protocol and procedures.

All H.320 control messages are drawn from tables in the H.221 standard, with each 8-bit code assigned a particular meaning. Each table entry is called a *codepoint*. Longer or less frequently used messages can be sent as multibyte messages, using escape values in the initial table. The meaning of and procedures for using the messages are defined variously in H.221, H.230, H.242, and, for multipoint-related messages, H.243.

The messages are sent directly in the (net) 400-bps H.221 BAS without any packetization, headers, or CRC and without the use of any acknowledgment or retransmission protocol. The low error rate of ISDN channels, combined with the forward error correction applied to all BAS messages, ensures that control messages are nearly always received without error. Although this system has worked well for H.320 terminals, the potential for undetected errors in the control channel sometimes results in added procedural complexity, such as redundant transmission. The newer H.245 control protocol, which replaces H.230/H.242 control in the second-generation ITU-T conferencing standards, is based instead on a reliable link layer that retransmits errored messages automatically until a positive acknowledgment is received, thus allowing the control protocol to assume that messages are guaranteed to arrive correctly.

Capabilities, Commands, and Indications

H.320 control messages can be generally categorized as capabilities, commands, or indications.

Capabilities (or caps) are used by terminals to state what modes they are capable of receiving or operating in, such as audio algorithms, video resolutions, or data protocols. At the start of an H.320 call, each terminal sends its entire set of capabilities, so that the far end can limit its transmission to modes that can be accepted by the receiver.

H.320 has no provision for transmit caps, which would let a terminal list its available transmission modes (as opposed to reception modes). Since all H.320 capabilities are receive caps, transmitters choose a mode arbitrarily from the set of available receiver capabilities. A recent addition to H.242 is a simple system for receivers to express mode preferences, but this is addressed more completely in the second-generation H.245 control protocol, which supports transmit caps as well as explicit receiver-driven mode requests.

H.320 capabilities are considered independent of each other, as there is no way to express that a mode could be used only if some other (perhaps highly complex) mode was not in use. H.245 corrects this limitation by adding simultaneous capabilities, which can directly express such dependencies.

Commands are used to cause the far end to take some action. This may be a simple action such as freezing the video picture or entering a loopback mode, or a command may instruct the receiver to start accepting a new media type such as an audio algorithm or video mode. Such commands generally require the receiver not only to switch its receiving decoder algorithm, but also to immediately interpret the received bits of each H.221 multiplex frame as assigned to different channels, in accordance with the new multiplex being transmitted. For example, when a transmitter switches from 56-kbps G.711 audio to 16-kbps G.728 audio, it sends a command for the new audio mode. The receiver changes audio decoders, but also redefines 400 bits in each H.221 frame (40 kbps) from audio to video. Since BAS messages are sent synchronously to the H.221 frame structure, there is no ambiguity about the point of switchover: it is defined to occur on the next even-numbered H.221 frame after the BAS command.

Indications are messages that contain useful information about events at the far end, but that don't require any response or action. For example, indications are sent when local microphones are muted and unmuted, which the far end could use to indicate the reason for the lack of audio. In multipoint conferences, indications assign terminal addresses, implement data channel token transfers, and are used to request various modes from the MCU.

H.230 Message Set

H.230 defines a set of commands and indications—for example, messages to indicate when valid audio and video are and are not being sent, requests for video picture freeze or INTRA frames, and loopback commands for diagnostic purposes. Multipoint-related messages are defined that can be used by an MCU to force all terminals into a common operating mode and to support various multipoint features. H.230 messages fall into the following categories:

- Video-related: indicate transmission of valid video signals, picture freeze commands, fast update (INTRA coded frame) requests, and so on

- Audio-related: microphone muting indications

- Loopback commands: used for diagnostic purposes

- Multipoint-related: used by an MCU to force common modes on all terminals and so on

- Characters and digits: used in text strings

H.230, together with the H.221 codepoint tables, define the basic set of messages used by H.320 control.

H.242 Control Protocol

H.242 covers the basic procedures for H.320 call setup and operation, including capability exchange, mode initialization and switching, opening various channel types, and general H.320 terminal procedures.

The H.242 call model is based on the assumption of one video and one audio channel; the BAS message syntax makes no provision for selecting among multiple channels. Aside from audio and video, H.242 supports three data channels, called LSD (low speed data), HSD (high speed data), and MLP (multi-layer protocol). LSD and HSD are mainly used by proprietary protocols and by the H.224/H.281 far-end camera control protocol. In a multipoint call, LSD and HSD are token-controlled broadcast channels; the terminal currently holding the broadcast token can send to all other terminals. The MLP channel is used primarily for the T.120 protocol and is not controlled by a token. Instead, the

MLP channel terminates at the MCU, where a T.120 entity (the T.122/T.125 MCS layer) manages data flow and routing among the terminals.

H.242 contains a great deal of complex procedure for mode switching and error recovery. This complexity stems from possible errors on the BAS channel, the need to connect and synchronize among a sometimes-varying number of 64-kbps channels, and the need to deal with "restricted" networks carrying 56 kbps per channel, of which there are several types. H.242 has been revised more than once to deal better with these issues and has gradually become a sometimes-inconsistent patchwork of fixes. The long-term solution to these problems will likely be a switch from H.320 to H.324, with its more consistent and flexible H.223 multiplexer and H.245 control system.

10.2.4 Audio Coding

G.711 Baseline Audio

The baseline audio mode for H.320 is the G.711 log-PCM codec, a simple 8-kHz sample rate logarithmic pulse code modulation scheme that has long been used as the primary voice telephony codec for digital telephone networks (long-distance voice telephone calls are today carried on digital networks even if they originate from analog telephones).

G.711 is defined to use 8-bit samples, for a total bit rate of 64 kbps, but for use with H.320 each sample is truncated to 6 or 7 bits, resulting in alternative bit rates of 48 or 56 kbps. G.711 provides excellent toll-quality narrowband (3-kHz audio bandwidth) audio with insignificant codec delay (well under 1 ms) and very low implementation complexity.

In order to provide compatibility with normal G.711 voice telephone calls, all H.320 calls start by sending and receiving G.711 audio while performing initial synchronization and mode negotiation in the H.221 FAS and BAS channels. Unfortunately, G.711 specifies two alternative encoding laws, A-law and μ-law; both schemes were already in use in different parts of the world at the adoption of G.711, and the CCITT was unable to agree on a single law. As a result, H.320 systems must attempt to automatically detect the coding law in use by the far end at the start of each call or avoid using audio until H.320 control procedures can be used to establish another audio mode.

Lip Sync

Audio codecs generally involve less delay than video codecs. H.320 provides lip synchronization, in which the decoded audio output matches lip movements displayed in the video, by adding delay in the audio path of both the transmitter

T A B L E	Current and Planned Audio Codecs Used in Multimedia Conferencing					
10.2	Standard	Bit Rates	Audio Bandwidth	Complexity (Fixed-Point)	Frame Size	Delay
	G.711 (1977)	48, 56, 64 kbps	3 kHz	near zero	125 μs	$\ll$ 1 ms
	G.728 (1992)	16 kbps	3 kHz	$\sim$ 35 to 40 MIPS	625 μs	< 2 ms
	G.723.1 (1995)	5.3, 6.4 kbps	3 kHz	$\sim$ 18 to 20 MIPS	30 ms	97.5 ms
	G.729 (1995)	8 kbps	3 kHz	$\sim$ 18 MIPS	10 ms	35 ms
	G.729A (1996)	8 kbps	3 kHz	$\sim$ 11 MIPS	10 ms	35 ms
	G.722 (1988)	48, 56, 64 kbps	7 kHz	$\sim$ 10 MIPS	125 μs	< 2 ms
	G.16K (planned 1999)	16, 24, 32 kbps	7 kHz	likely < 15 MIPS	$\leq$ 20 ms	$\leq$ 60 ms

and receiver, keeping the audio and video signals roughly synchronized as they are transmitted. This makes it impossible for receivers to present audio with minimal delay if the user does not want lip sync. Second-generation systems support lip sync without adding audio delay at the transmitter, instead using timestamp or time-skew methods that let the receiver alone add all necessary audio delay if desired.

Optional Audio Modes

G.711 was chosen as the baseline H.320 audio mode for its low complexity and compatibility with ordinary telephone traffic, but it is quite inefficient in its use of bandwidth compared to optional H.320 audio modes. The data bandwidth saved by switching to an alternative audio mode can be used to send additional video bits, making a big difference to H.320 video quality, especially on common 2-B (128-kbps) H.320 calls.

Table 10.2 summarizes the set of approved and planned ITU-T audio codecs used in H-series conferencing. Note that narrowband codecs pass 200–3400 Hz audio, and wideband codecs pass 50–7000 Hz. In Table 10.2 and throughout this chapter, these are referred to as "3-kHz" and "7-kHz" audio bandwidth codecs, respectively. Also note that audio codec delay is highly dependent on implementation. The delay values in Table 10.2, and in the rest of this chapter, use a (3 * frame size) + lookahead rule of thumb, which includes algorithmic delay, one frame time for processing, and one frame time for buffering. Section 10.6 provides a more complete discussion of codec delay and other noncodec factors contributing to total end-to-end delay.

The most important and commonly supported optional H.320 audio modes are G.728, for 16-kbps narrowband audio, and G.722, for 56-kbps wideband (7-kHz audio bandwidth) audio.

G.728, described in more detail in Chapter 6, is the preferred and most commonly used narrowband audio mode for H.320. A low-delay code excited linear prediction (LD-CELP) algorithm based on the usual 8-kHz narrowband sample rate and audio frames of five samples (0.625 ms), it uses 16 kbps to provide excellent toll-quality audio with a total codec delay of about 1.875 ms.

Audio quality is even more important to successful videoconferencing than video quality. For this reason wideband audio (7-kHz audio bandwidth) is popular for use with H.320 conferencing systems. G.722, described in Chapter 8, is used for wideband coding at 56 kbps and, like G.711, has alternative bit rates of 64 and 48 kbps. ITU-T is developing a new 16-kbps wideband audio codec standard with the working name "G.16K," which is intended to eventually replace G.722. G.16K is planned for approval in late 1999.

Recent work on improved narrowband audio codecs has produced ITU-T G.723.1, a 5.3/6.4-kbps codec with about 100 ms of codec delay, and G.729, an 8-kbps codec with about 35 ms of codec delay. Both codecs will be options in H.320 but are not yet widely implemented. These codecs are described later in this chapter, and their algorithms covered in Chapter 6.

10.2.5 Video Coding

Video is optional in the H.320 standard, but is included in essentially all products. The H.261 video codec, approved with H.320 in 1990, is the baseline video mode for H.320 systems.

The MPEG-2 video codec H.262, which supports a variety of picture formats and both interlaced and progressive scanning patterns, is an option in H.320, but since it is intended for use at high bit rates (many megabits per second), it is not widely implemented in H.320 systems.

The newer H.263 low-bit-rate video codec, approved in 1995 as part of the H.324 set, offers significantly improved video compression and additional features and is an option that is expected to be commonly implemented in H.320 systems. H.263 is described later in this chapter.

H.261 Video Codec

H.261 codes video frames using a DCT on blocks of size 8 × 8 pixels. An initial frame (called an INTRA frame) is coded and transmitted based on an input video picture. In typical video scenes, subsequent frames are often very similar to immediately preceding ones, except for small motions of objects in the scene. These can be coded efficiently (in the INTER mode) using motion compensation from the previous frame; the displacement of groups of pixels from their position in the previous frame (called *motion vectors*) are transmitted together with the DCT coded difference between the thus predicted and original images, rather than retransmitting the coded pixels themselves.

H.261 supports two video picture formats, CIF (common intermediate format) and QCIF (quarter CIF). Only QCIF is part of the H.320 baseline requirements; CIF format support is optional but widely implemented.

CIF has 352×288 luminance pixels. Color is sent at half this resolution in each dimension (176×144) because the human eye is less sensitive to color resolution than brightness resolution. This pixel array is mapped onto the 4:3 aspect ratio television screen and results in nonsquare individual pixels.

QCIF has one-quarter of the CIF resolution, 176×144 luminance pixels. It uses the same pixel aspect ratio and color sampling format as CIF.

A third H.261 image format, Annex D graphics, is used only for still-image transmission and not for motion video. Annex D mode doubles the CIF resolution in each dimension, for a 704×576 pixel still image. Annex D graphics are being replaced by more sophisticated still-image transfer methods in T.120, including the JPEG and JBIG formats used by T.126.

All H.261 video is noninterlaced, using a simple progressive scanning pattern. The video frame rate is based on the NTSC standard rate of 30,000/1001 (29.97) Hz. The low video bit rates used in H.320 often make it impossible to code each 30-Hz frame with reasonable detail, so the effective frame rate can be reduced by skipping frames at the encoder, allowing more bits to be sent for each remaining frame.

H.261 receivers may be limited in the rate at which they can decode incoming video, so included in the H.320 video capabilities are minimum picture intervals (MPI) for each supported H.261 resolution. The MPI values are the minimum number of frame periods (0, 1, 2, or 3 frames) the H.261 decoder requires between each coded frame and correspond to maximum frame rates of 30, 15, 10, or 7.5 frames per second.

H.261 specifies a standard coded video syntax and decoding procedure, but most choices about encoding methods, such as allocation of bits to different parts of the picture, are left to the discretion of the implementor. The result is that the quality of H.261 video, even at a given bit rate, greatly depends on the cleverness of the encoder implementation and on the number of computing cycles available to the encoder in real time.

10.2.6 H.231 and H.243—Multipoint

Multipoint operation, in which three or more terminals can participate in a single joint conference, is a widely implemented option in H.320. H.231 and H.243 define multipoint operation for H.320.

H.320 is oriented around ISDN switched circuit network connections, which are inherently point-to-point in nature. Multipoint calls work by connecting all participating terminals to a central bridge device, called a *multipoint control unit* (MCU). Each connection is equivalent to an ordinary point-to-point call. The MCU receives audio and video from all connected terminals and sends selected audio and video out to all the terminals. The MCU can also include participants in the conference using regular voice-only telephones or other standards supported by the MCU.

The MCU has great flexibility in choosing what to send to each terminal, but usually it mixes the few loudest audio signals and sends this to all receivers. The video signal from the current speaker (based on automatic speech detection or manually selected in various ways) is normally sent to all receiving terminals. The speaker is sent video of the previous speaker and audio without her own speech. Many other methods of choosing who is seen and heard are possible, but this common implementation allows all sites to see and hear the current speaker and the speaker to view the reactions of the preceding speaker.

MCUs themselves may be connected together to create a larger joint conference or to save on communications costs—for example, with one MCU on each continent, with a single overseas connection between the MCUs. Figure 10.4 illustrates the connections in a multipoint call.

H.231 specifies the requirements for H.320 MCUs, in which each port of the MCU behaves much like an H.320 terminal. H.243 specifies procedures for setting up H.320 multipoint calls, including terminal addressing and choosing a single common audio and video mode for the conference.

In a multipoint call, T.120 data conferencing and conference control on the MLP data channel terminates at the MCU, where the T.120 protocol stack routes messages among the terminals. The LSD and HSD data channels operate in a broadcast mode; one terminal transmits at a time, and all others receive the data, relayed through the MCU. H.243 specifies procedures for passing the LSD and HSD tokens, which grant permission to transmit, between the terminals. The bit rate assigned to these channels in the H.221 multiplex must be the same for all terminals, or receivers may be unable to accept the bit rate being transmitted.

Similarly, video switching in the MCU requires that terminals be able to receive the exact video bit rate being transmitted by the source terminal, so video bit rates must match among all terminals in a multipoint conference. The

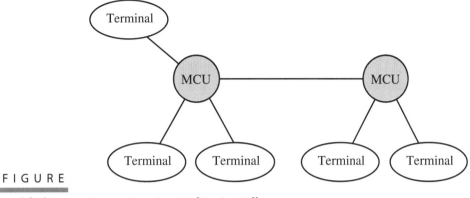

FIGURE

10.4   Connections in a Multipoint Call

H.320 video bit rate is determined by the bandwidth consumed by audio and data channels. H.243 provides procedures for an MCU to force all connected terminals into a selected communication mode (SCM), in which all terminals use the same video, audio, and data modes and bit rates to facilitate data and video switching in the MCU.

The audio and video processing that takes place in an MCU adds more end-to-end delay to the already undesirably long delays in videoconferencing, but this has not been a big problem in practice. Perhaps this is because group conferences are usually more formally structured than one-on-one conversations, with participants speaking one at a time, making the end-to-end delay less obvious.

H.243 also specifies various optional multipoint features, such as passwords for entry into a group conference and a chair control mode, in which the chairperson of a conference can control who is seen, drop terminals from the conference, and so on. These optional functions of H.243 are being replaced with more sophisticated equivalents from the T.120 standards.

A video mixing mode is described in H.243, where the MCU combines scaled-down video images from several terminals into a single output video image. This results in a *Hollywood Squares*–style output picture, with video from many different sites visible at all times in adjoining rectangular regions, without the need to switch away from any participant. This mode provides continuous presence for participants and is an indirect way to deal with the limitation of a single channel of video in H.320. Aside from the greatly reduced resolution, this method involves significantly larger end-to-end delay because the MCU must decode, frame synchronize, compose, and recode the input video streams. For these reasons, this method of supporting continuous presence operation is discouraged in the second-generation conferencing systems based on H.245. Instead, second-generation systems have the option of simultaneously decoding separate channels of video from each site.

10.2.7 H.233 and H.234—Encryption

Encryption is an option in H.320 and makes use of ITU-T H.233 and H.234, both of which are also used with H.324.

H.233 covers encryption procedures and algorithm selection; FEAL, B-CRYPT, and DES may be used as well as other ISO-registered algorithms and, in H.324, nonstandard algorithms. Key length is dependent on the algorithm in use and is practically unlimited. The interests of different national governments unfortunately made it impossible for the ITU to agree on a single baseline encryption algorithm.

H.234 covers key exchange and authentication using the ISO 8732, extended Diffie-Hellman, or RSA algorithms.

In H.320, encryption can be applied to any or all of the audio, video, and data channels in the H.221 multiplex. Initialization vectors (IV), which are used to resynchronize the encryptor and decryptor periodically, and H.233 session exchange (SE) messages, which are used to negotiate encryption mode, algorithm, and H.234 key exchange, are sent unencrypted via the ECS channel of the H.221 multiplexer.

In the encryption process, the encryptor algorithm produces a pseudorandom bitstream (cipher stream) that is exclusive-ORed with the output of the H.221 multiplexer. The exclusive-OR procedure is not applied to the H.221 FAS, BAS, or ECS channels. The receiver reverses this process.

In a multipoint encrypted call, the link between each terminal and MCU is encrypted. The MCU decrypts and reencrypts all channels, acting as a "trusted entity."

10.2.8 H.224 and H.281—Real-Time Far-End Camera Control

H.224 provides an optional H.320 data protocol for real-time remote device control. H.281 is the only standardized application, for remote control of far-end cameras. H.224 and H.281 can also be used with H.324 systems.

H.224 is simple one-way real-time data protocol for traffic that requires delivery with consistent end-to-end time latency. It operates over the LSD, HSD, or MLP channels of the H.221 multiplexer (or in its own data channel in an H.324 system) and works by sending Q.922 unnumbered information (UI)

HDLC frames (ISO 1991a). UI frames make use of HDLC framing, packet headers, and a 16-bit CRC, but don't require any response or acknowledgment from the receiver.

In H.224, large low-priority messages are segmented into short (less than 60-ms) UI frames, so that time-critical high-priority messages can be transmitted without a long wait for completion of a previous frame. This ensures that high-priority messages can be sent with only small variations in end-to-end latency. H.224 message headers contain H.243 multipoint terminal addresses, so receivers on LSD or HSD broadcast channels can identify those messages that were intended for them.

H.281 uses H.224 to send high-priority messages to remotely control pan, tilt, and zoom motions of motorized far-end cameras as well as to select among multiple cameras and preset camera positions. H.281 is the only standardized H.224 application protocol, but many nonstandard applications use H.224, often simultaneously with H.281 far-end camera control.

The H.281 control model is based on video picture feedback from the camera to the controlling user. In the usual implementation, the user starts remote camera movement by pushing a button to send a message commanding the motion to begin. As the camera moves, the user watches the video scene pan, tilt, or zoom. When the camera points in the desired direction (or a little before, since the user must lead the camera to compensate for video delay), the user releases the control button, sending an H.281 message commanding the motion to stop.

This motion model depends strongly on consistent timing between user button action and video display output and therefore on consistent control message and video delays. Although this scheme has worked well and been found to be intuitive for users, it is unsuitable for networks that have inherently unpredictable control and video delay, such as the packet switched networks addressed by H.323, and it is incompatible with other motion control models, such as those involving pointing to a subject of interest. For these reasons, a more general and sophisticated far-end camera control system is being developed as part of the T.120 protocol series.

10.2.9 H.331 Broadcast

Standard H.320 terminals can, with only small modifications, be used on networks that provide one-way data transmission, to provide essentially a low-bit-rate one-way digital television service. Applications include classroom broadcasts, with a teacher transmitting video and audio to many receiving students at different locations, large corporate or political broadcasts, and so on. Often low-bit-rate digital satellite transmission is used for such services, with one uplink site sending H.320 video and many receiving stations.

H.331 specifies how to use H.320 terminals in situations where there is no data path from receivers back to transmitters, so normal two-way control negotiation is impossible. In such situations, no MCU is needed because there is no coordination of modes or combining of video and audio, since there is only a single transmitter. All receivers simply decode audio and video modes as commanded in the H.221 BAS channel; there is no two-way H.242 negotiation.

10.3 H.320 Network Adaptation Standards: H.321 and H.322

Two standards have recently appeared that broaden the use of H.320 to networks other than ISDN. They directly adapt standard H.320 terminals to other networks and offer simple interworking with ISDN-based terminals and features identical to H.320 on ISDN. H.321 covers adaptation of H.320 terminals to ATM-based broadband ISDN (B-ISDN) networks. H.322 covers H.320 on IsoEthernet (ISLAN-16T) LANs.

10.3.1 H.321—Adaptation of H.320 to ATM and B-ISDN

H.321 specifies the use of standard H.320 terminals, intended for ISDN use, on ATM and B-ISDN networks. It uses the services of ATM Adaptation Layer 1 (AAL1), with both the segmentation and reassembly (SAR) and convergence sublayer (CS) functions of I.363, to provide data transport channels equivalent to ISDN channels.

Interworking between H.321 and H.320 terminals on ISDN can be achieved directly through a standard ISDN/B-ISDN gateway according to I.580, with the H.321 terminal using one ATM virtual channel (VC) for each ISDN channel. H.321 is also a subset of the more flexible second-generation native ATM/B-ISDN standard, H.310, described later in this chapter. H.321 terminals are compatible with the H.321/H.320 mode of H.310.

10.3.2 H.322—Adaptation of H.320 to IsoEthernet

Like H.321, H.322 adapts standard ISDN H.320 terminals to a different network type. H.322 is described as intended for "local area networks which provide a guaranteed quality of service"—LANs that provide what are essentially virtual ISDN B channels. The only existing LAN that meets this criterion is the IEEE 802.9a isochronous Ethernet, ISLAN-16T (IsoEthernet), which provides 96 virtual B channels in addition to 10-Mbps Ethernet. The H.322 standard itself, only two pages long, is almost null, stating that a standard H.320 terminal is adapted to work on the LAN via an unspecified LAN interface.

10.4 A New Generation: H.323, H.324, and H.310

The success of the original H.320 standard sparked the development of many extensions, including H.233/H.234 for encryption, H.224/H.281 for real-time far-end camera control, and H.331 for broadcast applications, as already described. The H.321 and H.322 standards for adapting H.320 terminals to new networks were also a result of the popularity of H.320.

At the same time, industry experience with H.320 since its 1990 approval revealed limitations in the standard, and improved techniques for video and audio compression appeared. A new generation of standards has been developed that avoid the problems in H.320 and take advantage of the latest compression technology: H.323 for packet switched networks, H.324 for low-bit-rate circuit switched networks, and H.310 for ATM-based broadband ISDN.

Some of the major improvements over H.320 common to all the second-generation standards include

- faster call start-up upon initial connection
- support for multiple channels of video, audio, and data
- simpler and more flexible assignment of bandwidth among the various channels
- separate transmit and receive capabilities
- means to express dependencies between capabilities
- explicit description of mode symmetry requirements
- receiver-driven mode request mechanism
- improved audio and video coding
- larger range of video modes and resolutions
- cleaner mechanisms for extension to future standard and nonstandard features

Many of these improvements come from the new, more flexible H.245 control protocol, which replaces the functions formerly provided by H.242, H.230, and part of H.221.

H.323, H.324, and H.310 all support the improved compression standards G.723.1, G.729, and H.263 (which are now also optional in H.320), share the same basic system architecture, and fully support T.120 data, graphics, and control. Smooth H.320 interworking, as well as interworking with each other, was a prime design consideration, which is why H.261 video has been retained as a baseline video mode for all the new standards.

Like H.320, these new standards can be used in both point-to-point and multipoint calls and start with a baseline for guaranteed interoperability, with many additional features as options. H.323, H.324, and H.310 are all "systems standards," calling out H.245 and other component standards that together make up the complete conferencing system.

10.4.1 H.245 Control Protocol

The new H.245 multimedia system control protocol benefits from the experience gained with H.320 system control. The control model of H.245 is based on *logical channels,* independent unidirectional bitstreams with defined content, identified by unique numbers arbitrarily chosen by the transmitter. There may be up to 65,535 logical channels.

H.245 operates in its own logical channel and carries end-to-end control messages governing system operation, including capabilities exchange, opening and closing of logical channels, mode preference requests, flow control messages, and general commands and indications. The H.245 structure allows future expansion to additional capabilities as well as manufacturer-defined nonstandard extensions to support additional features. Messages specific to particular system standards, such as multiplex table entries (for H.324) and network transport addresses (for H.323), are also present.

H.245 messages are defined using ASN.1 syntax, coded according to the packed encoding rules (PER) of ITU-T X.691, which provides both clarity of definition and flexibility of specification. The H.245 control channel runs over logical channel (LC) 0, a separate channel out of band from the various media streams. LC 0 is considered to be already open, in terms of H.245 procedures, when the call starts up. In all cases, H.245 requires an underlying reliable link layer such as TCP/IP (for H.323), V.42 (for H.324), or Q.922 (for H.310). The H.245 protocol assumes that this link layer guarantees correct, in-order delivery of messages.

Capability Exchange

The large set of optional features in all the systems standards necessitates a method for the exchange of capabilities, so terminals can become aware of the common subset of capabilities supported by both ends.

H.245 capabilities exchange provides for separate receive and transmit capabilities as well as a system by which the terminal may describe its ability (or inability) to operate in various combinations of modes simultaneously, as some implementations will be limited in processing cycles or memory availability. This sophisticated capability exchange avoids the problems experienced with the more limited capabilities exchange of H.320 systems.

Receive capabilities describe the terminal's ability to receive and process incoming information streams. Transmitters are required to limit their transmitted modes to those which the receiver has indicated it is capable of receiving. The absence of a receive capability indicates that the terminal cannot receive (is a transmitter only).

Transmit capabilities describe the terminal's ability to transmit various modes. They serve to offer receivers a choice of possible modes of operation, so the receiver can request the mode it prefers to receive using the H.245 `RequestMode` message. This is an important feature because local terminals directly control only what they transmit, but users care about controlling what they receive. The absence of a transmit capability indicates that the terminal is not offering a choice of preferred modes to the receiver (but it may still transmit anything within the capability of the receiver).

After the terminals have exchanged their capabilities, each terminal can request the modes it wants to receive. The transmitter decides what to send, based on the common capabilities as well as the receiver's wishes.

Terminals can dynamically add or remove capabilities during a call. Since many modern conferencing systems are implemented on general-purpose PCs, other application activity on the machine may result in varying resource levels. H.245 is flexible enough to handle such a scenario.

Nonstandard capabilities and control messages can be issued using the `NonStandardParameter` structure defined in H.245. This allows proprietary, or public but nonstandardized, features to be supported using the same automatic negotiation mechanisms used for standardized options.

Logical Channel Signaling

Terminals transmit media information from transmitter to receiver over unidirectional streams called "logical channels" (LC). Each LC carries exactly one channel of one media type and is identified by a logical channel number (LCN) arbitrarily chosen by the transmitter. Since transmitters completely control allocation of LCNs, there is no need for end-to-end negotiation of LCNs.

When a transmitter opens a logical channel, the H.245 `OpenLogicalChannel` message fully describes the content of the logical channel, including media type, codec in use, network adaptation layer and any options, and all other information needed for the receiver to interpret the content of the logical channel. Logical channels can be closed when no longer needed. Open logical channels may be inactive if the information source has nothing to send.

Logical channels are unidirectional, so asymmetrical operation, in which the number and type of information streams are different in each direction of transmission, is allowed. However, if a terminal is capable only of certain symmetrical modes of operation, it can send a capability set that reflects its limitations.

Bidirectional Logical Channels

Certain media types, including data protocols like T.120, inherently require a bidirectional channel for their operation. In such cases, the H.245 bidirectional channel procedure opens a pair of unidirectional logical channels, one in each direction, and associates them together to form a bidirectional channel. Such pairs of associated channels need not share the same logical channel number, since logical channel numbers are independent in each direction of transmission.

Dependent Logical Channels

A new mechanism planned for the 1998 revision of H.245 will allow logical channels to be marked as logically dependent on other channels flowing in the same direction. This simple but powerful method allows the construction of a hierarchy of channels and subchannels in a tree structure. This technique was introduced to support layered video codecs, which construct video output from a series of overlay layers (such as a weather forecaster overlaid on a weather map), but may also be used in the future to support new features such as bit-rate-scalable media codecs.

10.4.2 Audio and Video Codecs

All the second-generation standards use H.261 video as a baseline for backward compatibility with H.320. H.323 and H.310 require G.711 log-PCM audio.

However, new, more efficient codecs have recently been developed, including the G.723.1 5.3/6.4-kbps speech codec, the G.729 8-kbps speech codec offering lower delay, and the H.263 video codec. These improved codecs, while generally optional, are expected to be widely implemented in second-generation systems.

G.723.1 and G.729 both provide for silence suppression, in which the average audio bit rate is reduced by not transmitting during silence or by sending smaller frames carrying background noise information. In typical conversations, both ends rarely speak at the same time, so this can save significant bandwidth for use by video or data channels. As with most code excited linear prediction (CELP) codecs, G.723.1 and G.729 work best on speech and less well on other audio sources such as music.

G.723.1—5.3/6.4-kbps Audio

G.723.1 was developed as part of the H.324 suite, originally for use on V.34 modems at very low bit rates. It uses only 5.3 or 6.4 kbps and is estimated to require about 18–20 MIPS in a general-purpose DSP. Transmitters may use either of the two rates and can change rates for each transmitted frame, since the coder rate is sent as part of the syntax of each audio frame.

The codec provides near-toll-quality speech based on 8-kHz audio sampling. The 6.4-kbps rate provides better audio quality than the 5.3-kbps rate, especially in the presence of background noise. Coders can switch between the two rates on every 30-ms frame if desired. When coding each frame, G.723.1 looks ahead 60 samples (7.5 ms) into the following audio frame, resulting in a typical codec delay of 97.5 ms. This amount of delay is quite large for voice telephony applications (especially since codec delay is only one component of total end-to-end delay), but it is suitable for use in low-bit-rate video telephony, as even more delay is normally needed in the audio path to achieve lip synchronization with video. The G.723.1 algorithm is discussed in Chapter 6.

G.729—8-kbps Low-Delay Audio

G.729 is a high-quality, high-complexity 8-kbps narrowband (8-kHz sample rate) speech codec using conjugate-structure algebraic code excited linear prediction (CS-ACELP), as was covered in Chapter 6. The codec produces 10-ms frames and uses 5 ms of lookahead, for about 35 ms of total codec delay. While the data rate used by G.729 is higher than that of G.723.1, its considerably lower delay, higher voice quality, and improved ability to withstand sequential encoding and decoding ("tandeming") make it a better choice for applications that don't require lip synchronization or that don't use video at all.

Annex A of G.729 (sometimes called "G.729A") specifies a lower-complexity (about 11 fixed-point MIPS) encoding scheme that produces a bitstream fully compatible with the standard G.729 decoder and that shares the same frame size and delay. This provides a low-complexity codec that can interoperate with G.729, suitable for inexpensive DSPs and PC software implementation. However, both the full G.729 and the 6.4-kbps mode of G.723.1 offer better audio quality than G.729A.

H.263 Video Codec

The new H.263 video codec is optional in all the H-series standards except H.324, where both H.263 and H.261 are required in systems that support video. Approved in 1995 as part of the H.324 suite, H.263 is a general-purpose low-bit-rate video codec based on the same DCT and motion compensation techniques as H.261 and targeted at the same set of applications.

H.263 is the result of many small incremental improvements to the techniques used in H.261, which together add up to a very large improvement in video quality. At the low video bit rates typical in H.324 operation on V.34 modems (10–20 kbps of video signal), H.263 video quality is considered equivalent to that of H.261 at up to double the bit rate, although the difference is less at the higher bit rates used by H.320 and H.323. H.263 is expected to gradually replace H.261 in all applications, except that H.261 support will continue to be needed for backward compatibility.

Video coding improvements in H.263 include half-pixel precision motion compensation (H.261 uses full pixel precision and a loop filter), improved variable-length coding, reduced overhead, and optional modes including unrestricted motion vectors (where MVs are allowed to point outside the picture), arithmetic coding instead of variable-length (Huffman) coding, an advanced motion prediction mode including overlapped block motion compensation (OBMC), and a PB-frames mode, which combines a bidirectionally predicted picture with a normal forward predicted picture.

H.263 supports the same CIF and QCIF picture formats used in H.261, as well as new formats, as shown in Table 10.3.

Like H.261, H.263 works with noninterlaced pictures at frame rates up to 30 fps. New extensions are being added to H.263 that will enable it to handle square pixels and picture formats of arbitrary size.

H.263 does not contain any equivalent to the Annex D still-image mode of H.261. This still-image transfer function is provided instead by the T.120 series standards, specifically the still-image transfer protocol of T.126.

T A B L E   H.263 Video Picture Formats

10.3

Picture Format	Luminance Pixels	Video Decoder Requirements	
		H.261	H.263
SQCIF	128 × 96	not defined	required
QCIF	176 × 144	required	required
CIF	352 × 288	optional	optional
4CIF	704 × 576	not defined	optional
16CIF	1408 × 1152	not defined	optional

10.4.3   H.323 for Packet Switched Networks

Originally titled "Visual Telephone Systems and Equipment for Local Area Networks Which Provide a Non-Guaranteed Quality of Service," ITU-T H.323 at its conception was intended exclusively for real-time multimedia conferencing on corporate LANs. As H.323 matured toward its 1996 approval, it became a generic conferencing standard for all types of packet switched networks (PSNs), including Novell IPX/SPX, Ethernet and token-ring corporate LANs, and, most importantly, TCP/IP networks such as corporate intranets and the public Internet. This expanded scope is reflected in H.323's revised title planned for the 1998 revision: "Packet Based Multimedia Communication Systems."

In packet switched networks, each packet is a variable-sized unit of data containing headers and payload, which is routed hop-by-hop to its destination. Each packet may follow a different path through the network, resulting in variable and unpredictable packet arrival times, potential packet loss, out-of-order arrival, and so on. By far the most popular type of packet network is IP, which is used on the Internet as well as on many corporate LANs.

Figure 10.5 illustrates the H.323 terminal, which can provide multiple channels of real-time, two-way audio, video, and data. The H.323 standard specifies H.245 for control; defines the use of audio codecs, video codecs, and T.120 data channels; and calls out H.225.0 for audio and video packetization as well as call setup. When each logical channel is opened using H.245 procedures, the responding terminal returns a network address and port number, which together form a *transport address* to which packets carrying that channel should be addressed. Most H.323 calls consume only a small fraction of a fast network's

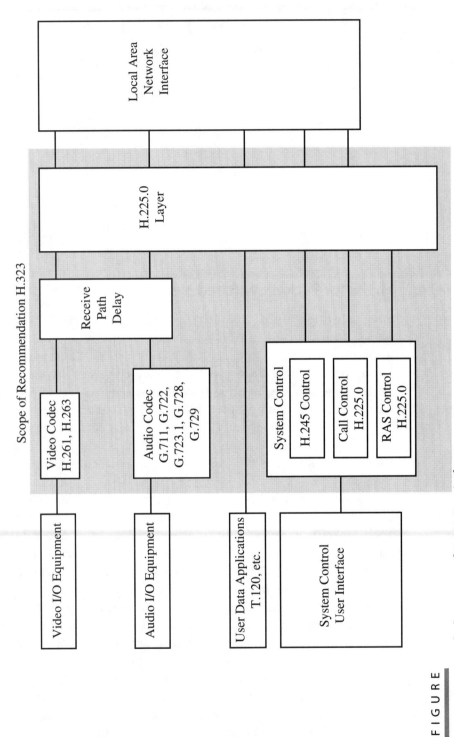

FIGURE
10.5

Block Diagram of H.323 Terminal

capacity, usually 100–500 kbps for each call, with the remainder of network bit rate available for other uses.

The multiplex for H.323 is the packet structure of the network itself, as each packet can contain a different type of content (audio, video, data, control, etc.) as specified by the packet header.

G.711 audio is mandatory in H.323 terminals, with G.723.1 and G.729 among the optional audio modes. Video is optional, but if provided, QCIF format H.261 is the baseline video mode, with H.263 the most important optional video mode.

H.225.0—Media Packetization and Call Setup

The H.225.0 standard specifies procedures for setting up H.323 calls on the network, as well as audio and video packetization for H.323.

Call setup makes use of a small subset of the Q.931 messages and procedures originally defined to implement ringing, busy, answer, and related call setup functions in ISDN telephony. Terminals can be addressed using their network address (such as an IP address) or, more commonly, alias addresses such as telephone numbers or email addresses. Alias addresses are simply text strings that are automatically mapped into network addresses.

H.225.0 specifies that the output of the audio and video codecs is packetized and transported using the Real-Time Transport Protocol (RTP/RTCP) (Schulzrinne et al. 1996) defined by the Internet Engineering Task Force (IETF) for sending real-time data on the Internet. RTP uses *unreliable* channels, such as UDP/IP or Novell IPX, to carry video and audio streams. On unreliable channels, lost or corrupted packets are not retransmitted. This ensures that all audio and video packets are delivered with minimal delay and allows multicast operation, but it means that receivers must deal with missing packets through error concealment or other means. Timestamps are included on RTP packets to allow received audio and video to be synchronized.

The H.245 control channel, call setup messages, and data channels such as T.120 are carried on *reliable* channels such as TCP/IP, which use retransmission to guarantee correct, in-order delivery of all data packets. These data types require delivery of all packets and are less time-critical than audio and video, so they can tolerate the larger and more variable delays resulting from retransmission in the network.

Two main factors influence the performance of H.323 systems: the bit rate of the underlying packet network carrying H.323, and congestion and delay in the network.

Modems and Internet Telephony

On current IP networks, H.323 packets carry headers of 40–54 bytes. In order to have a reasonably high ratio of payload to header, and therefore reasonable line efficiency, packets must be quite large. At network bit rates above 1 Mbps, such large, efficient packets can be sent quickly.

At very low bit rates, these large packets can block transmission of small urgent packets such as audio frames, thereby causing significant blocking delay. As a result, H.323 is not well suited to operation at very low bit rates, such as on V.34 modems that run at up to 33,600 bps. Alternatively, small packets can be used, but this can result in extremely poor efficiency. The IETF is addressing this problem with proposals for header compression (Bormann 1997a, 1997c; Casner and Jacobson 1997) and mechanisms for urgent packets to interrupt large packets (Bormann 1997b), but these techniques may take some years to be fully deployed in the public Internet. In the meantime, real-time Internet communication must trade off delay against efficiency when running at low bit rates.

For example, carriage of each 24-byte G.723.1 audio frame in a packet with 40 bytes of header results in the 6.4-kbps audio codec occupying over 17 kbps of network bandwidth. Reducing the header overhead to 5% would require grouping together 32 audio frames in each packet, representing 960 ms of audio, which would then take an additional 270 ms to transmit at a typical modem connect rate of 24,000 bps. Sending a video packet of the same size would block transmission of audio for 270 ms.

While this delay is not significant for one-way applications, it is a serious problem in two-way communications where data must be carried reasonably efficiently to achieve good video quality or net data throughput. If only an audio channel is to be transmitted, the high overhead associated with small, low-latency packets can be tolerated because it still results in a bit rate that can be carried by the modem.

This is how Internet telephony is possible today using H.323 over V.34 modems, even without header compression. The Voice on IP (VoIP) activity group of the International Multimedia Teleconferencing Consortium (IMTC) has selected H.323 as the standard for Internet telephony. When operating on V.34 modem links, the VoIP has recommended use of the G.723.1 audio codec, but H.323 itself suggests G.729 for low-bit-rate audio-only use and G.723.1 for low-bit-rate multimedia applications. As the only multivendor interoperable Internet telephony standard, H.323 is being supported by almost all manufacturers and service providers for Internet telephony. At this writing, it seems that G.723.1 will be the predominant low-bit-rate codec for H.323, but G.729 may eventually also be widely supported.

Network Congestion and the Internet

The other factor influencing H.323 performance is network congestion and delay.

If network routers drop packets because of congestion, audio and video quality will be reduced because the unreliable channels used for audio and video do not retransmit lost packets.

If packets are delayed in routers or take roundabout paths to avoid congestion, end-to-end delay will be increased, and audio and video quality will be reduced when receivers discard excessively late-arriving packets. Receiver implementations must buffer all incoming packets for a time sufficient to allow almost all packets to arrive and must discard any packets that arrive after the buffering period, since audio and video packets arriving after their intended playback time cannot be used.

For this reason, good-quality low-latency H.323 performance requires networks that are lightly loaded or that are quality-controlled, such as Ethernet LANs with switched hubs and reservation protocols like RSVP (Braden et al. 1996). Many corporate LANs and intranets are able to provide this, but the public Internet currently cannot.

H.323 can be used on the public Internet, and in some cases will work well, but network congestion problems can require very large delays (often well over 1 second each way) to buffer unpredictable packet arrival times, even when most packets arrive quickly.

Further work is ongoing to make H.323 more robust to packet loss, but until the public Internet is upgraded to support effective resource allocation methods, guaranteeing some limits on end-to-end latency and packet loss, low-delay H.323 operation on the Internet will be problematic. Such an upgraded Internet may require some kind of pricing mechanism to distinguish between different classes of service and encourage efficient allocation of resources.

Nevertheless, H.323 is the only accepted standard for Internet multimedia communication, and its performance is limited only by the quality of service offered by the network.

Aside from the H.323 terminal, three additional major system components are described by H.323: gateways, gatekeepers, and multipoint controllers. Each of these components is optional in H.323 systems but provide important services.

Gateways

H.323 gateways provide interworking between H.323 terminals on the packet switched network and other network and terminal types, such as H.320 on

ISDN, H.310 on ATM/B-ISDN, and H.324 and regular analog telephones on the PSTN.

Smooth, low-delay operation between H.323 and other H-series terminals should be possible through H.323 gateways, since all H-series conferencing systems support QCIF H.261 video in common, which ensures that time-consuming video transcoding is not needed.

Except for H.324, all H-series systems support G.711 log-PCM audio, but in many situations it will be desirable for gateways to use a more efficient audio codec when connecting an H.323 terminal to an H-series terminal on the ISDN or PSTN. Transcoding the G.711 audio to another codec saves limited bandwidth for use by video. This transcoding normally takes less time than is already needed to delay audio to synchronize with video, so if lip sync is being used, no additional net delay need be added by audio transcoding.

Other functions of the gateway include mapping H.245 control messages into H.242 when interworking with H.320, mapping H.225.0 RTP media packetization into the H.221 or H.223 multiplexes, initiating or accepting calls on other network types, and forwarding incoming calls to the appropriate terminal on the H.323 network.

Gatekeepers

Gatekeepers are logical entities that grant or deny permission for terminals to make calls, as a way of controlling network traffic. When permitting a call, a gatekeeper can place a limit on the amount of bandwidth to be used for the call. Decision rules for gatekeepers are not defined by the standard and are under the control of implementors and system administrators.

Another function of the gatekeeper is to locate users by translating alias addresses into network addresses. Terminals can be identified both with a network address, appropriate to the particular network type in use, and with an alias address, such as a telephone number or email address. Alias addresses can be used to provide users with an easily remembered address, perhaps the same as their office telephone number, and can provide an address to be used for incoming calls from an H.320 or H.324 terminal, which may not be aware of network addressing schemes. Similarly, the gatekeeper can locate gateways and direct calls through an appropriate gateway when needed.

Multipoint and Multicast

Unlike H.320 and H.324 multipoint, which requires all terminals to connect to a central MCU, H.323 allows the terminals in a multipoint conference to directly send audio and video streams to other participating terminals using multicast network mechanisms. H.323 multipoint calls can also use a traditional centralized MCU or a combination of both techniques (Thom 1996). These three modes are called *decentralized multipoint, centralized multipoint,* and *hybrid multipoint,* in which some media types are centrally mixed or switched, and others are multicast.

H.323 divides the functions of a traditional MCU into two separate logical entities, the multipoint controller (MC) and the multipoint processor (MP). The MC and MP can be located in different places, or integrated into terminals, allowing multipoint calls without the need for a separate MCU.

The MC coordinates control functions among the terminals in a multipoint conference, with each terminal's H.245 control channel communicating only with the MC. The MC controls selection of common video and audio modes and establishment of logical channels for the conference. The MC is used for all three types of multipoint conference.

The MP performs any centralized media processing, such as audio mixing, video switching, and so on, and sends the resulting processed media streams to all participating terminals. The MP is used only for centralized and hybrid multipoint conferences. If terminals can support reception of multiple media streams, the need for centralized media processing is reduced.

Ongoing Work

The great interest in H.323 systems has spurred efforts to further extend the capabilities of H.323 through the definition of additional standards:

- H.235 is planned to cover encryption and authentication for H.323 systems.

- H.246 will define specific requirements for gateways interconnecting the various H-series terminal types with each other and with ordinary telephones.

- The H.450.x series will define supplementary call services, such as call forwarding and call diversion.

- Annex C of H.323 will define operation over ATM using AAL5. H.245, H.225.0, and RTCP control packets will use TCP/IP over AAL5, while audio and video RTP packets are carried directly on ATM AAL5 without UDP/IP. This mode will offer consistent low delay and high quality, since packet switching of media streams will be avoided by use of a point-to-point ATM virtual circuit.

At this writing, these new standards are planned for approval in 1998, as are accompanying revisions of H.323, H.225.0, and H.245.

10.4.4 H.324 for Low-Bit-Rate Circuit Switched Networks

H.324, approved in 1995, was the first of the second-generation ITU-T multimedia conferencing standards. H.324 defines multimedia terminals for low-bit-rate circuit switched networks (CSNs), initially PSTN analog phone lines (often known as "plain old telephone service," or POTS) using V.34 modems at up to 33,600 bps. H.324 is being extended to other CSN networks, including ISDN and wireless networks (digital cellular and satellite). In the future, H.324 may eventually replace H.320 on ISDN networks, just as Group 3 fax replaced Group 2, while still retaining backward compatibility for many years.

Unlike the packet switched networks covered by H.323, CSNs are characterized by direct point-to-point synchronous data links, operating at constant bit rates over long periods of time. End-to-end latency across the CSN link is fixed, and no routing is performed, so there is no need for packet addressing or other overhead to cope with unpredictable arrival times or out-of-order delivery. Above all, H.324 was designed to provide the best performance possible (video and audio quality, delay, and so on) at low bit rates.

H.324 is a "toolkit standard," which allows implementors to choose the elements needed in a given application. Figure 10.6 illustrates the major elements of the H.324 system, which can support real-time video, audio, and data, or any combination. The mandatory components are the V.34 modem (for PSTN use), H.223 multiplexer, and H.245 control protocol. Video, audio, and data streams are all optional, and several of each kind may be used simultaneously. H.324 enables a wide variety of interoperable terminal devices, including PC-based multimedia videoconferencing systems, inexpensive voice/data modems, encrypted telephones, World Wide Web browsers with live video, remote security cameras, and stand-alone videophones.

H.324 is the most direct successor to H.320, making use of existing H.320 component standards such as H.233/H.234 encryption and H.224/H.281 far-end camera control. Multipoint H.324 calls are possible using the same centralized MCU techniques described for H.320 systems. H.324 shares H.320's basic architecture, consisting of a multiplexer that mixes the various media types into a single bitstream (H.223), audio and video compression algorithms (G.723.1 and H.263, previously described), and a control protocol that performs automatic capability negotiation and logical channel control (H.245). For low-delay compatibility with H.320 systems, H.324 video systems must support QCIF format H.261 video as well as H.263, the preferred mode that was developed as part of the H.324 suite.

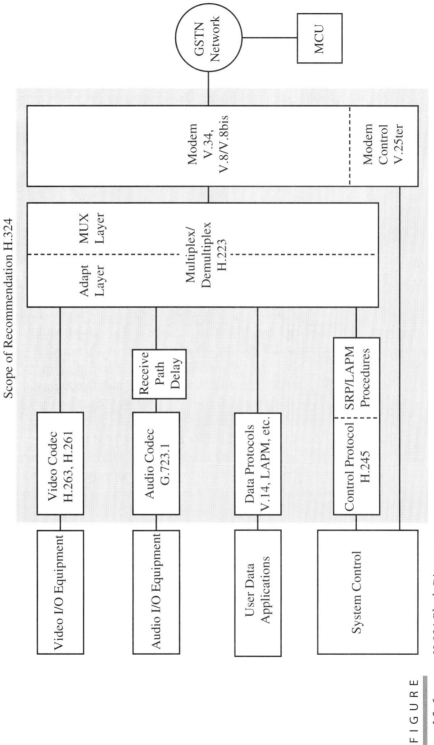

Scope of Recommendation H.324

FIGURE
10.6

H.324 Block Diagram

Modem

When operating on PSTN analog phone lines (POTS), H.324 uses the V.34 modem, which has a maximum speed of 33,600 bps. Typical telephone connections are too noisy to support this maximum rate, so the usual long-distance V.34 connect rate is in the range of 20–26 kbps. V.8 or V.8bis protocol is used at call start-up to identify the modem type and operation mode. The preferred V.8bis protocol allows a normal voice call to switch into a multimedia call at any time. ITU-T V.25ter (the AT command set) is used to control local modem functions such as dialing and answering.

H.324 uses the modem directly as a synchronous data pump. V.42bis data compression and V.42 retransmission are not used at the modem level, although these same protocols can be used within an individual H.223 logical channel to support data applications. Since most PCs have only asynchronous RS-232 interfaces, PC-based H.324 terminals need a synchronous interface to the modem or another method to pass the synchronous bitstream to the modem. ITU-T V.80 provides a standard sync-over-async tunneling protocol, commonly used between PC and modem to transport the H.324 synchronous bitstream over the PC's asynchronous RS-232 interface.

The error burst behavior of V.34 modems is important to H.324 system design. V.34 provides bit rates between 2400 and 33,600 bps, in steps of 2400 bps. On a given telephone connection, each step changes the bit error rate by more than an order of magnitude. Most modems are designed for V.42 data transfer, so modem DSP is tuned for a target error rate such that retransmissions will consume, on average, less than 2400 bps. Since in H.324 errored audio is not retransmitted, it may be desirable to run the modem at the next lower 2400-bps rate step to avoid excessive audio dropouts or errors in decoded video.

H.223 Multiplex

H.324 uses the new H.223 multiplexer standard, which, much like H.221, mixes the various streams of video, audio, data, and control information into a single bitstream for transmission. H.324 required the development of a new multiplexing method suitable for very low bit rates that combined low multiplexer delay with high efficiency and the ability to handle bursty data traffic from a variable number of logical channels.

The H.221 time division multiplexer (TDM) used in H.320 was not suitable because of its dependence on 64-kbps channels. In addition, H.221 is difficult to implement in software because of its complex frame synchronization and bit-oriented channel allocation, and because multiplex changes require control channel signaling, slowing adaptation to changing modem and payload data rates. Other TDM schemes that corrected these problems were considered but were ultimately rejected because the non-unique frame delimiters of a TDM make it impossible to add "fill" data between valid frames to adapt a low-rate stream to a higher-rate channel, as would be needed, for instance, on two tandemed V.34 modem links (perhaps through an MCU), each of which was running at a slightly different data rate.

Packet multiplexers, such as V.42 (LAPM) and Q.922 (LAPF), avoid these problems and were considered, but suffer from blocking delay, as described for H.323, where transmission of urgent data, such as audio, must wait for the completion of a large packet already started. This problem occurs when the underlying channel bit rate is low enough to make the transmission time of a single packet significant. In a classical packet multiplexer, this delay can be reduced only by limiting the maximum packet size or aborting large packets, both of which reduce efficiency.

The H.223 multiplexer met the goals for H.324. It incurs less delay than TDM and packet multiplexers, has low overhead, and is extensible to multiple channels of each data type. It is byte-oriented for ease of implementation, able to byte-fill to match differing data rates, and uses a unique synchronization bit pattern, the HDLC flag, which cannot occur in valid data. Fully dynamic allocation of bandwidth to the different channels is possible, as each variable-length multiplex protocol data unit (MUX-PDU) can carry a mix of different channels in different proportions.

H.223 consists of a lower multiplex layer, which performs the actual mixing of data streams, and a set of adaptation layers, analogous to ATM adaptation layers, which perform logical framing, sequence numbering, error detection, and error correction by retransmission, as appropriate to each media type.

MULTIPLEX LAYER.   Each H.223 MUX-PDU transmitted on the network is a variable-length sequence of bytes framed using normal HDLC bit-stuffing, which inserts a 0 bit after every sequence of five 1 bits, making the HDLC frame demarcation flag (01111110) unique. It is similar to an HDLC packet, except that the contents of the frame do not contain the usual HDLC header, payload, and CRC, but instead a 1-byte header, followed by a mix of bytes from different logical channels. If needed, extra HDLC flags may be sent between MUX-PDUs as filler, as shown in Figure 10.7.

The header byte includes a multiplex code that specifies, by reference to a multiplex table, the mapping of byte positions within the frame to various logical channels. Each MUX-PDU can contain a different multiplex code and therefore a different mix of logical channels. This allows many logical channels, low-overhead reallocation of bandwidth, and many different types of channel interleave and priority. This is all under control of the transmitter, which may choose any appropriate multiplex for the application and change the 16 multiplex table entries as needed. Many syntactically compliant multiplexing algorithms, optimized for different applications, are possible (Lindbergh and Malvar 1995).

While the H.223 multiplex is often described as a packet-like structure, it may be more useful to think of it as a repeating pattern of logical channel byte positions, similar to a TDM, with occasional escape sequences (the HDLC flag and 1-byte header) that indicate a change in the pattern. This "pattern with escape sequences" model better captures the ability of H.223 to adapt to changing patterns of media traffic flows.

Figure 10.8 illustrates four logical channels (audio, video, data, and control), but there may be any number of channels, as specified by multiplex table entries. This allows multiple audio, video, and data channels for different data protocols, multiple languages, continuous presence, or other uses.

Logical "packet-like" data structures at the adaptation layer of H.223 are segmented into individual bytes for transmission in the byte positions allocated for that logical channel. These individual bytes might end up being transported in a single MUX-PDU or spread across many MUX-PDUs.

This segmentation isolates the multiplexing function from the logical framing function. Generally, a new MUX-PDU can begin on any byte boundary, so unlike classical packet multiplexers, H.223 can terminate a frame at any arbitrary byte boundary to reallocate bandwidth, such as when urgent real-time data must be sent. The reallocation can occur within 16–24 bit times (16 bits for the flag and header, plus 0–8 bits for the byte already being transmitted), less than 1 ms at 28,800 bps. This compares favorably with TDM multiplexers and avoids the blocking delay of traditional packet multiplexers.

The header byte consists of the 4-bit multiplex code, a 3-bit CRC on the header only, and the packet marker (PM) bit, used for marking the boundaries of some packet types at the adaptation layer level.

ADAPTATION LAYER. The three H.223 adaptation layers, AL1, AL2, and AL3, provide error protection and, where needed, retransmission services according to the needs of different media types. Each logical channel is processed by a single AL before it is multiplexed with other LCs at the multiplex layer.

AL1 is intended primarily for variable-rate framed information, such as HDLC protocols and the H.245 control channel. AL2 is intended primarily for digital audio, such as G.723.1, and includes an 8-bit CRC and optional sequence numbers. AL3 is intended primarily for digital video, such as H.261 and H.263, and includes provision for retransmission using sequence numbers and a 16-bit CRC. The different adaptation layers allow each data type to use an error-handling scheme with the proper trade-off of overhead, robustness, and delay.

. . . **F F F H** information field **F F H** information field **F H** information field **F** . . .

←——— Fill Flags

←——— MUX-PDU ———→

(F = HDLC Flag, H = Header Byte)

FIGURE
10.7

Example of an H.223 Multiplex Bitstream

'

. . . VVVCVVVCV **FH** AAAAVVDCAAAAVV **FH** VDVDVDVDVDV **FH** CCCCCC **FH** AAAAVVDCAAA . . .

(Each letter represents one byte. F = Flag, H = Header, A = Audio, V = Video, D = Data, C = Control)

FIGURE
10.8

MUX-PDU in an H.223 Multiplex Stream

Audio Channels

Audio support is optional in H.324 and may not be present in some types of terminals, such as remote surveillance cameras. When audio is provided, the baseline mode is the 5.3/6.4-kbps G.723.1 codec, described earlier. The most important optional audio mode is the reduced-delay 8-kbps G.729 codec, which is useful for applications that don't require audio/video synchronization. The forthcoming G.16K 16-kbps wideband (7-kHz audio bandwidth) codec will likely be used in H.324 systems to provide audio quality much better than conventional telephone lines.

Silence suppression, by which the audio bit rate can be saved for use by video or data channels when one end of the conversation is silent, can be important to H.324 performance. The preferred (but optional) silence suppression technique sends "comfort noise" to simulate normal background noise during silent periods, as described in Annex A of G.723.1. The comfort noise frame is much shorter than a normal audio frame and often needs to be sent only once for each silent period. A simpler method supported by H.324 does not offer comfort noise, but allows transmitters to temporarily stop sending audio frames during quiet periods, after first sending a frame of silence.

Lip sync between audio and video is accomplished by adding audio delay only in the receiver, rather than in both the transmitter and receiver, as was done in H.320. H.245 is used to send a message containing the time skew between the transmitted video and audio signals. Since the receiver knows its decoding delay for each stream, the time-skew message lets the receiver insert the correct audio delay or alternatively skip lip synchronization and present the audio with minimal delay.

Video Channels

As with audio, H.324 video support is optional and may not be present in some applications. One-way video is also allowed and may be popular for PCs that don't have video cameras or video capture hardware. The baseline video mode includes both H.263 and QCIF format H.261.

Among H.324's improvements over H.320 is the videoTemporalSpatial-TradeOff message in H.245, which allows the receiver to specify a preference for the trade-off between frame rate and picture resolution.

Data Channels

H.324 can carry data channels as well as video and audio. These can be used for any data protocol or application in the same way as an ordinary modem.

Standardized protocols include T.120, user data via V.14 or V.42 (with retransmission), and H.224/H.281 for remote control of far-end cameras, among others.

An important H.324 data mode allows an IETF PPP (point-to-point protocol) (Simpson 1994) data channel to be opened in addition to normal audio and video channels. When an H.324 terminal calls an H.323 gateway on an IP network, perhaps located at an Internet service provider (ISP), real-time video and audio can be transferred efficiently to the gateway over the H.223 multiplex, while the PPP channel carries IP traffic such as World Wide Web browser data. This mode represents a big gain in delay and efficiency (and therefore video quality) over running H.323 directly on low-bit-rate channels, and the H.323 gateway can convert the video and audio streams to standard IETF RTP/RTCP protocol for transport over the Internet.

The same capability exchange and logical channel signaling procedures defined for video and audio are also used for data channels, so automatic negotiation of data capabilities is possible. This represents a big step forward from normal practice on data-only modems, where data protocols and applications must be set up manually by users before a call.

As with all other H.424 media, data application channels are carried as distinct logical channels over the H.224 multiplex, which accommodates bursty data traffic by dynamically altering the allocation of bandwidth among the different channels in use. For instance, a video channel can be reduced in rate (or stopped) when a data channel needs extra bandwidth, such as during a file transfer.

H.324 on Other Networks

H.324 is being extended to operate on other circuit switched networks besides the PSTN. When operating on these networks, the V.34 modem is replaced by another network interface as appropriate. At this writing, these extensions are not yet complete, but are planned for approval in 1998.

H.324/M FOR WIRELESS NETWORKS.   H.324 Annex C will specify operation of H.324 on the large variety of different wireless (digital cellular and satellite) mobile networks in use around the world. This mode is often called H.324/M (for "mobile"). While the usefulness of video in moving vehicles may be limited, H.324/M may enjoy great success on laptop computers or other battery-operated wireless devices.

The main technical challenge to be met by H.324/M is the very high bit error rates encountered on many wireless data links, sometimes as poor as 5×10^{-2}. The error rate can also be quite variable, and on some networks is often much better, while at other times no useful signal at all can be delivered, such as when a user is in a tunnel or under a bridge.

At this writing, H.324/M is still an active work item, but currently three error-protection modes are planned to be specified by H.324 Annex C and annexes to H.223.

In the first, called H.223 Level 1, the H.223 multiplex will be made more robust to errors by a simple substitution of a longer 16-bit sequence for the HDLC flag. The body of each MUX-PDU will not receive any additional protection. Initial studies indicate that this should allow H.324 operation on many wireless networks. It is hoped that this mode will be sufficiently simple that it will be widely implemented even in H.324 terminals intended only for use on PSTN modems, so that the error-robust bitstream can be transported directly between a mobile user and a PSTN user, without the need for any gateway to perform multiplex transcoding.

The second mode, H.223 Level 2, applies error protection also to the H.223 MUX-PDU header, to accommodate higher bit error rates.

In the third and strongest mode, H.223 Level 3, the techniques of Levels 1 and 2 are combined with a modified set of H.223 adaptation layers to protect the body of each MUX-PDU with very strong forward error correction and options for limited retransmission of errored data. This mode involves increased overhead and delay compared to normal H.223, but, combined with an optional scalable error protection scheme for G.723.1 audio (which preferentially protects the "most important" bits of each frame), it will provide a robust standardized method for running H.324 on very high error rate networks. Interoperation between H.324/M terminals in this mode and wired H.324 terminals on the PSTN will require a gateway to translate between the error-robust multiplex and the normal H.223 multiplex.

Aside from these standardized modes, it is possible for a wireless network service provider, such as a cell network operator, to define their own error protection scheme for real-time data on their network. If the network operator provides equipment at both ends of the radio link, they can use their intimate knowledge of the particular network to define an optimized error protection scheme for that network. This method would present a simulated modem or PSTN interface to the H.324 terminal and allow use of standard, off-the-shelf H.324 terminals.

H.324/I FOR ISDN. Annex D of H.324 is planned to specify operation of H.324 on ISDN and similar switched-circuit digital networks. This mode is called H.324/I (for "ISDN") and may eventually become a second-generation replacement for H.320.

Technically, H.324 can be operated directly on a single 64-kbps ISDN B channel simply by replacing the V.34 modem with the B channel. Annex D is primarily concerned with specifying the use of a draft standard, given the working name "H.DISPATCH." This will be an automatic negotiation mechanism that can select between H.320, H.324, voice, and other protocols on ISDN networks automatically, performing for digital networks much the same function that V.8bis does for the PSTN.

A related effort has the working name "H.MULTILINK," which is intended to define a low-delay, low-overhead channel aggregation method to allow multiple ISDN B channels to be treated as a single higher-rate channel. Early proposals for H.MULTILINK suggest a protocol that, unlike H.221 and the ISO/IEC CD 13871 BONDING protocol, can be used on V.34 modems as well as on fixed-rate ISDN channels.

10.4.5   H.310 for ATM and B-ISDN Networks

H.310 defines a native ATM/B-ISDN standard for videoconferencing, as well as one-way video for applications like video surveillance. Broadband ISDN (B-ISDN) is based on asynchronous transfer mode (ATM) and operates at rates of up to several hundred megabits per second. H.310 offers very high-quality video, using much higher bit rates than those available on narrowband ISDN. Many people expect B-ISDN to become the next-generation public telecommunications network; this view is especially widespread in Japan.

Like the other second-generation H-series standards, H.310 uses the H.245 control protocol, supports T.120, and was designed with interworking with other H-series terminals in mind.

H.310 includes as a subset the H.321 ATM network adaptation standard for H.320, described earlier. This is included primarily for interworking with H.320 and H.321 terminals. The native H.310 mode is based on MPEG-2 systems and video coding. Terminals are required to support MPEG-2 video coding (H.262 | ISO/IEC 13818-2) as well as H.261 video and G.711 audio for two-way conversational use. H.263 is optional. MPEG-1 audio (ISO/IEC 11172-3 Layer II) is mandatory for unidirectional terminals and optional for conversational terminals (Okubo et al. 1997).

The H.310 native mode multiplexer is described in H.222.1 and H.222.0, which is the MPEG-2 systems standard (H.222.0 | ISO/IEC 13818-1), covering multiplexing of various logical channels into a single ATM virtual channel (VC), as well as media synchronization. Data protocols can be multiplexed with audio and video using H.222.1, or they can be multiplexed at the ATM layer in a different VC. As with H.323, lip synchronization is accomplished in H.310 using timestamps on audio and video data.

A block diagram for the H.310 system, including both the H.321 and native H.310 modes, is shown in Figure 10.9.

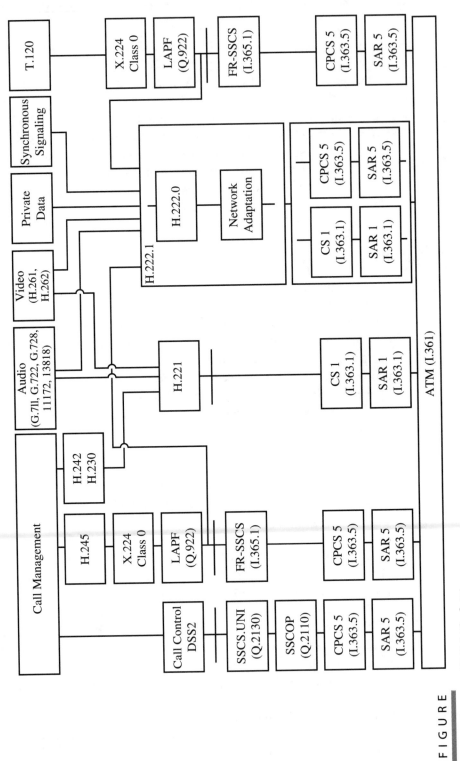

FIGURE
10.9

H.310 Block Diagram

An H.310 call is established by using Q.2931 procedures to set up an initial ATM VC, using AAL5 to carry the H.245 control channel. Once this channel is operating and H.245 has performed its capability exchange, a second ATM VC is set up to carry the H.222.1 multiplexed audio and video. This VC can use either AAL1 or AAL5. Additional VCs can be set up later if desired.

H.310 terminals can operate at a wide variety of data rates, but all terminals must support the common rates of 6.144 and 9.216 Mbps, corresponding to the MPEG-2 Main Profile at Main Level for medium- and high-quality services, respectively. Multipoint operation is possible in H.310 using a centralized MCU, as with H.320.

10.5   T.120 for Data Conferencing and Conference Control

The ITU-T T.120 series standardizes data and graphics conferencing as well as high-level conference control. T.120 supports point-to-point and multipoint video, audio, data, and graphics conferencing with a sophisticated, flexible, and powerful set of features, including support of nonstandardized application protocols. T.120 multipoint data transport is based on a hierarchy of T.120 MCUs that route data to its proper destination.

Early in its development, T.120 was called "MLP" (Multi-Layer Protocol), after the data channel MLP in H.221 intended to carry T.120.

T.120 is network independent, so terminals using H.320 on ISDN, H.323 on packet networks, H.324 on PSTN, H.310 on ATM, voice/data modems, and so on, can all join in the same T.120 conference. Figure 10.10 illustrates the T.120 protocol stack.

The T.120 series does not directly process audio or video, but relies on the H-series standards for audio and video transport. T.120 is intended to coordinate a complete conference across network types.

T.120 itself provides a general overview of the suite, describing the relationship of the standards that make up the T.120 series, and specifies requirements for T.120 compliance.

T.121, "Generic Application Template," provides procedures and requirements on T.120-based application protocols for proper use of the T.120 infrastructure, so that different applications can coexist in the same conference without conflicts.

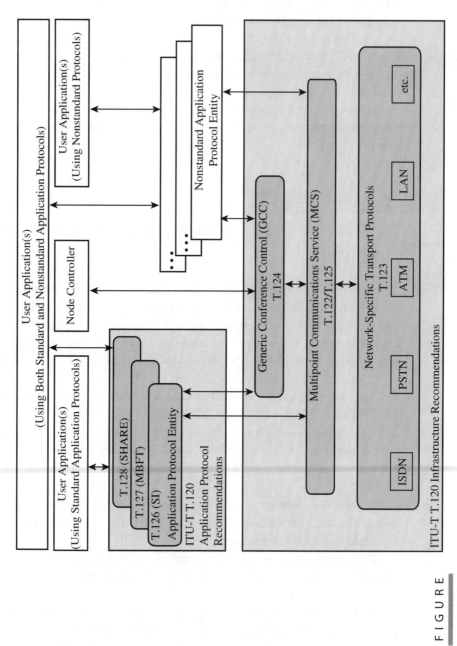

FIGURE
10.10

ITU-T T.120 System Model

10.5.1   T.120 Infrastructure

The T.122 through T.125 standards form the "infrastructure" T.120 components, which are present in both T.120 terminals and MCUs.

T.123 defines a set of transport protocol stacks for running T.120 on various networks, presenting a uniform OSI transport layer interface to the MCS layer above it. T.120 requires reliable, guaranteed delivery of messages; this is normally provided in T.123 by a reliable link layer using retransmission of errored messages.

T.122 is the service definition, and T.125 the protocol, for MCS (multipoint communication service). MCS provides many channels of one-to-one, one-to-many, and many-to-many communication among conference participants, routing messages to their appropriate destinations. MCS also provides token services, which applications may use to coordinate events in a conference.

An important MCS feature is the *uniformly sequenced* data transmission mode, which ensures that related data sent simultaneously from various sites is received in the same order at all sites. Messages such as draw and erase commands in a group whiteboard protocol must be processed in the same order at all receivers; this is accomplished by routing all such data through a central site, the *Top MCS provider*, which redistributes the data in a uniform order to all receivers.

T.124, "Generic Conference Control," provides services and procedures for setting up and managing conferences. It controls the addition and removal of sites in conferences, coordinates the use of MCS channels and tokens, and maintains a registry of active and available application protocols based on the capabilities of each participating terminal, among other functions.

10.5.2   T.120 Application Protocols

Above this infrastructure, T.120 application protocols are defined. Applications are present only in terminals; T.120 MCUs need to support only the infrastructure protocols.

The T.126 application protocol covers multipoint still-image transfer (JPEG, JBIG) and annotation, which allows high-resolution still images to be shared and discussed in real time. A lecturer can use a T.126 application to point out items in a picture or slide, draw diagrams, or write notes like on a whiteboard or overhead projector. Multiple users at different sites can work collaboratively in a common graphical work space.

T.127 provides a multipoint binary file transfer protocol that supports binary file distribution during a conference. It can be used by any application that needs to share files of any type among conference participants.

T.128, scheduled for approval in 1998, will provide a PC application sharing protocol that will let two or more conferees work together on a computer-based project such as a document or spreadsheet.

New T.120 application protocols are being developed, including a reservation protocol (which will allow MCU ports and other conference resources to be reserved in advance) and the T.130 series audio/video control protocols (which will provide management of media processing, remote device control, and routing of audio and video streams in conferences).

10.6   Delay in Multimedia Conferencing Systems

End-to-end audio delay is an extremely important characteristic of any voice telecommunications system. User perception of the spontaneity and interactivity of a conversation or group conference is very dependent on the amount of audio delay in the system. If net system delay is sufficiently long to make one-on-one conversational use difficult or impossible, such systems will simply not be used by the general public. This makes delay one of the most important parameters to be considered in the design of voice communications systems.

The perception of delay varies tremendously from person to person and in different situations. Some people appear to be far more sensitive to delay than others; this may have to do with conversational style and personality, such as the propensity to interrupt or to make "acknowledgment sounds," such as "uh-huh" and "yes," which can become missynchronized with the far-end speaker. Jokes particularly highlight delay problems; delayed laughter sounds forced.

Users of group videoconferencing systems have shown a willingness to accept increased audio delay in exchange for provision of video, which adds a new dimension to a conversation or conference. However, end-to-end delays that are acceptable (although annoying) in group conferences have a very different subjective effect in one-on-one conversations. Group conferences are typically much more structured, with one speaker and many listeners, and interruptions of the speaker are rare.

Naive users of one-on-one H.320 videotelephone systems have been known to complain about "half-duplex" audio, when in fact full-duplex audio was in use. Such users perceive the inability to interrupt the far-end user as due to half-duplex audio, when in fact the problem is delay.

There may be cultural factors at work as well. Japanese users of videoconferencing systems frequently disable the lip sync function so that the audio will not be additionally delayed to sync up with the video, perhaps because of the custom of frequent "Hai" acknowledgment sounds in one-on-one conversations.

In some cases the presence of video can compensate directly for problems with audio delay. Instead of making the acknowledgment sounds used on a telephone, some users learn to nod their head, smile, or make other nonverbal responses in video calls.

The amount of delay that is tolerable in voice communications systems therefore varies greatly depending on circumstance. Most observers conclude that one-way delays of less than 50–100 ms are generally not noticed. ITU-T G.114 considers one-way delays up to 150 ms "acceptable for most user applications," but notes:

> Some highly interactive voice and data applications may experience degradation for values below 150 ms. Therefore, increases in processing delay on connections with transmission times even well below 150 ms should be discouraged unless there are clear service and application benefits.

For comparison, one-hop geosynchronous satellite telephone circuits have about 250 ms of one-way propagation delay to and from the satellite in orbit. Many users find this extremely annoying—one reason why much intercontinental telephone traffic has moved to undersea cables.

Kitawaki and Itoh (1991) discuss human factors studies of the effects of delay on telecommunications. On a measure of conversational efficiency at tasks such as verifying numbers and names, a 250-ms one-way delay was found to impair efficiency by 20–30% from the zero delay value. They conclude that "the long round-trip transmission delay in the range of 500 ms [250 ms one-way] gives considerable subscriber difficulties in telecommunications."

10.6.1   Sources of Audio Delay

Audio delay in multimedia conferencing systems can be considered to originate from seven sources:

- Algorithmic delay (the time to accumulate audio samples before coding begins)
- Processing delay (the time to execute the coding and decoding algorithms)
- Multiplex delay (the time coded audio must wait before transmission begins)

- Transmission delay (the time needed to transmit the bits representing audio)
- Modulation delay (the time used to modulate and demodulate the signal)
- Propagation delay (the time for the signal to reach its destination)
- Buffering delay (the time data is passively stored, including time for smoothing out jitter in signal arrival times)

Of these, the algorithmic delay, processing delay, and a portion of the buffering delay can be considered as attributable to the audio codec in use, independent of other system elements.

In addition, in practical implementations, interrupt response time sometimes adds additional delay, although synchronous implementations may be able to minimize this. Unlike the other sources, this is purely a matter of implementation and will not be further discussed.

Algorithmic Delay

Algorithmic delay is the time needed to acquire audio samples before coding can begin. For frame-based audio codecs like G.723.1 and G.729, it is the duration of one frame plus the lookahead of the coding algorithm. This is the minimum possible delay for the codec, assuming zero time for coding and decoding (an infinitely fast processor).

For G.723.1, the algorithmic delay is 30 + 7.5 ms, total 37.5 ms. For G.729, it is 10 + 5 ms, total 15 ms.

Processing Delay

The processing delay is the time to execute the coding and decoding algorithms on the CPU or DSP chip. It is equal to the complexity of the codec algorithm (in MIPS), divided by the speed of the CPU or DSP executing it (in MIPS), times the duration of the audio frame:

$$\text{Processing delay} = \text{complexity} / \text{DSP speed} * \text{frame size} \tag{10.1}$$

When an ITU-T codec is described as requiring, say, 20 fixed-point MIPS, this means the algorithm requires 20 million DSP instructions to be executed for each second of audio to be coded and decoded.

A codec implementation could, in principle, finely divide DSP cycles between encoding and decoding, or it could perform encoding and decoding sequentially. This choice simply exchanges elapsed processing time for queuing time, as described below, without affecting the total delay.

Real implementations normally use the slowest DSP that can keep up with real time (this is the cheapest adequate DSP chip), so processing time is usually the same as the codec frame size. For G.723.1, this would be 30 ms; for G.729, 10 ms.

Software implementations on general-purpose CPUs may be able to devote the entire processing power of the CPU to audio processing for short periods, decreasing the audio processing delay. However, the significant interrupt latency in PC operating systems may offset any advantage from this gain.

Multiplex Delay

Multiplex delay is simply the time between when a unit of data, such as a coded audio frame, is ready for transmission and when it can actually be transmitted on the line through whatever multiplexer is in use. If some other data is already being transmitted, the new unit of data may have to wait some period, perhaps related to the frame length in TDM multiplexers, or to the maximum packet length in packet multiplexers, before the new data can begin transmission. While this delay is often variable, practical systems must buffer for the maximum possible delay, to allow smooth playout of audio at the receiver.

A naive view of an ideal multiplexer would envisage one that accurately simulated a number of slower constant-bit-rate channels carried over a single higher-rate channel. Indeed, such a multiplexer would be ideal for media sources that produced a constant-rate bitstream for transmission. However, real media sources do not fit this model because they typically produce data in bursts.

An audio codec such as G.729 with 10-ms frames is an example. Within the 10-ms intervals between frame generation, the audio codec produces no output bits at all. At the end of the frame interval, the entire bitstream representing the 10-ms frame becomes available at once. Spreading these bits over the next 10-ms frame time (to generate a constant-bit-rate stream) only serves to impose an additional 10 ms of end-to-end delay. Instead, an ideal multiplexer would switch 100% of the available bandwidth to sending each audio frame instantly upon its availability. As soon as the frame's bits are sent, the remaining time left before the next frame is ready can be used to send other data types.

The H.223 multiplexer approaches this model. Its multiplex delay for audio is 16–24 bit times, the time needed to complete transmission of the current byte, then send an HDLC flag and 1-byte header to begin transmission of the audio frame. This takes about 1 ms at typical H.324 rates.

Transmission Delay

Transmission delay is the time needed to send the bits representing the minimum decodable unit of audio signal. In audio-only telephony systems, the transmission delay is the same as the frame size, since the transmission channel carries nothing but audio information.

In multimedia communications systems, the transmission delay is less because the transmission medium is running at a higher rate than needed for audio alone. The transmission delay is the length of the audio frame divided by the bit rate in use. For G.723.1 using the 5.3-kbps audio rate (21-byte frame including CRC) at 24 kbps, the transmission delay is 7 ms. For G.729 (11-byte frame including CRC), it is 3.67 ms.

Modulation Delay

The modulation delay is the time needed to modulate and demodulate the digital signal onto and off of the physical transmission medium. For V.34 modems, it is estimated to be about 35 ms because the V.34 modulation is quite complex.

Propagation Delay

Propagation delay is the time for the signal to travel to its destination over the physical transmission medium. It varies greatly, depending on the network topology, the physics of the transmission medium, and the physical distance to be covered. For the PSTN, propagation delay will vary from near zero for local calls to over 250 ms for calls routed through geosynchronous satellite circuits.

When analyzing multimedia communications systems, propagation delay is sometimes considered to include all delay present in the network itself from any source, including amplifiers and repeaters, satellite transponders, packet routers, network congestion, and so on.

Buffering Delay

Buffering delay is caused by passive storage of real-time data and is often necessary to allow for unpredictable arrival times of audio frames ("jitter"), to smooth out asynchronous processing, and to match differing data rates.

Smooth audio playback requires enough buffering of received data to avoid audio gaps caused by late-arriving frames. The H.324 standard allows up to 10 ms of transmitter audio jitter, which can be used to increase line efficiency by waiting for a natural break point in the multiplex stream or simply to allow for interrupt latency in transmitter implementations. Synchronous multimedia

TABLE 10.4	Audio Delay Budget for H.324			
		G.723.1	G.729	Notes
	Algorithmic delay	37.5 ms	15 ms	
	Processing delay	30	10	
	Multiplex delay	1	1	
	Transmission delay	7	3.67	
	Modulation delay	35	35	
	Buffering delay	40	20	10-ms jitter + 1 frame
	Total (one-way)	150.5 ms	84.67 ms	not including propagation

systems such as H.320 have less jitter, while packet switched systems like H.323 can have much more, as discussed earlier.

Buffering may also be needed for DSP scheduling, especially when frame arrival times are unpredictable. When an audio frame is ready for processing, the DSP may already be busy with audio going in the opposite direction or may be scheduled to be busy soon. The audio may have to wait for up to an entire frame period before being processed. As with the processing delay, this queuing delay can be reduced by using a faster DSP, but normally cost considerations mean using the slowest DSP that can keep up with real time.

So for the H.324 delay budget, we will allow 10 ms for transmitter jitter, plus one frame time for DSP scheduling, resulting in $10 + 30 = 40$ ms of buffering delay for G.723.1, and $10 + 10 = 20$ ms for G.729.

Audio Delay Budget

Adding these terms together, we can produce an audio delay budget for H.324 (see Table 10.4).

When evaluating multimedia terminal alternatives, propagation delay is usually not an explicit factor, since it is outside the control of the terminal design and implementation. However, likely propagation delay on real networks, as well as video delay and delays from pre- and postprocessing, must be considered when evaluating the overall performance of communications systems.

10.7   Summary

This chapter discussed the two generations of ITU-T H-series standards for real-time multimedia conferencing and the T.120 standard for data/graphics conferencing and multimedia conference control. The subjective effects of end-to-end delay in real-time conferences were reviewed, and an analysis of the components of audio delay presented.

Multimedia and videoconferencing systems have so far achieved practical and commercial success in specific applications such as business meetings, telecommuting, and education. Consumer desire for video telephony is still mostly speculative, but at a minimum, issues of cost, end-to-end delay, video quality, and ease of use will have to be addressed before multimedia communication can hope to supplant traditional telephone service.

The standards described in this chapter, together with efforts by manufacturers and industry organizations like IMTC, seem likely to address the ease-of-use and interoperability issues. The cost of the necessary hardware is steadily declining and will reach consumer levels very soon. But major improvements in end-to-end delay and video quality may require higher bit rates than those available to consumers thus far. Happily, new high-bit-rate access technologies such as cable modems and xDSL seem to be coming quickly. These, possibly combined with effective Internet resource allocation mechanisms, may allow a real revolution in the communication tools we use every day. At the least, we can be sure multimedia standards and networks will continue to evolve rapidly for the foreseeable future.

The next chapter covers the MPEG-1 and MPEG-2 standards for audio and video compression. Unlike the ITU-T standards, the MPEG standards are primarily focused on storage, playback, and broadcast applications, rather than two-way real-time communication.

11 MPEG Compression

11.1 Introduction

The Moving Pictures Experts Group (MPEG), an international standards committee, has produced a set of standards for audio and video compression that are good examples of sophisticated compression strategies and that are also commercially important. Starting from an initial focus on video compression at approximately 1.2 Mbps on CD-ROM, the MPEG standards have expanded to become the lingua franca of high-quality audio-video compression in the 1990s.

Formally, MPEG is Working Group 11 of Subcommittee 29 of Joint Technical Committee 1 of the International Standards Organization and the International Electrotechnical Commission. As an international standards body, MPEG follows a strict set of rules aimed at maximizing consensus decision making and international endorsement and minimizing the dominance of specific proprietary interests. The resulting process can be cumbersome, but with effective leadership, surprisingly good standards with widespread acceptance can be produced in a short time. Such has been the case with MPEG.

The focus of this chapter is the completed work embodied in the MPEG-1 and -2 standards. As of this writing, MPEG continues to work to produce new standards in several important areas, including advanced audio compression (AAC), digital storage media command and control, and MPEG-4, work targeted at very low-bit-rate (less than 64-kbps) audio-video communication. These efforts are described briefly at the end of the chapter. This chapter is not an exhaustive restatement of the standards (which run to several hundred pages); rather, it describes the major methods by which MPEG achieves compression and organizes information, in order to illuminate the potential effectiveness and applications of the standard.

11.2   The MPEG Model

A key to understanding MPEG is understanding both the problems that MPEG set out to address in developing MPEG-1 and -2 (although it is likely MPEG will be applied in many unanticipated places as well) and the fundamental models that underlie the algorithms and that are used to foster interoperability.

11.2.1 Key Applications and Problems

Some of the most important applications to drive the development of MPEG include disk-storage-based multimedia, broadcast of digital video, switched digital video, high-definition television, and networked multimedia.

Disk Storage

MPEG-1 had its genesis as the solution to a very specific compression problem: how to best compress an audio-video source to fit into the data rate of a medium (CD-ROM) originally designed to handle uncompressed audio alone. At the time MPEG started, this was considered a difficult goal. Using an uncompressed video rate for 8-bit active video samples (CCIR-601 chroma sampling) of approximately 210 Mbps, this requires a rather aggressive 200:1 compression ratio to achieve the slightly greater than 1 Mbps or so available after forward error correction and compressed audio on a typical CD-ROM.

Aside from the substantial compression requirement, another requirement of many video on CD-ROM applications is a reasonable random access capability, that is, the ability to start displaying compressed material at any point in a sequence with predictable and small delay. This is a key attribute, for example, of many interactive game and training materials.

More recently, a new optical disk format with much higher capacity than CD-ROM has been developed. Called digital versatile disc (DVD) (renamed from the original "digital video disc" to include data storage applications), its higher rates, combined with the use of variable-rate encoding, can provide video quality that surpasses that currently available to consumers through other video media (e.g., VHS tape, laserdisc, cable and off-air analog television), as well as cinematic audio and a number of unique access and format features.

Broadcast of Digital Video

Electromagnetic spectrum is a scarce and valuable resource. It allows widespread and inexpensive broadcast capabilities: a single transmitting site can illuminate a city, country, or continent, without the need for digging trenches or stringing wires. But electromagnetic spectrum is also key to many existing and planned services, especially mobile radio applications of various types. For this reason, the electromagnetic spectrum available for distribution of audio-video material is limited. This has created a strong economic motivation to develop compression technology for digital broadcast applications. Already, digital broadcast of compressed video over satellite has been deployed in several countries. Application to terrestrial broadcast (typically at VHF and UHF frequencies) and point-to-multipoint microwave will emerge in the very near future.

Broadcast digital video is typically introduced within bands originally sized for analog video and capable of carrying 20–40 Mbps of digital material. Since this is sufficient for multiple channels of compressed audio and video, packet-based multiplexing is used to allow carriage of multiple programs within a single digital signal. Also, digital broadcast often occurs over channels with a high noise level and potentially with phenomena such as fading. This leads to a higher attention to the behavior of decoders in the presence of errors and interruptions in the data stream.

Broadcast video can also be carried over wired networks, such as the typical "hybrid fiber coax" networks used in cable television. These networks consist of a backbone of high-capacity fiber distributing analog modulated signals to hubs, which further distribute the signals over copper coaxial cables to multiple homes.

Switched Digital Video

Switched digital video involves establishment of a dedicated communication path between the source of the video (a real-time encoder or a storage system) and a decoder. Although such systems often contemplate carrying signals over very high-capacity fiber plant, the sheer number of such signals as well as the load on switching gear makes compression attractive. As important is the existence of a strong and complete standard allowing deployment of compatible equipment from multiple vendors at dispersed geographical and functional locations in a network, as well as additional work to detail how to transport material encapsulated within typical telecommunications protocols.

In some cases, switched digital video networks use a special modem technology, called *asymmetric digital subscriber line* (ADSL), to deliver the signal digitally over the last stretch to the home using existing copper twisted pair installed to provide basic telephone service. This technology imposes its own bit rate limit, typically between 1.5 and 6 Mbps, depending on range and the exact type of modulation used.

HDTV

High-definition television (HDTV) promises a substantial increase in the detail available in a video transmission. When combined with multichannel high-fidelity audio transmission and a wider screen aspect ratio (16:9 as opposed to the 4:3 ratio of horizontal to vertical length in current television standards), HDTV promises a near-cinematic viewing experience. However, HDTV must be delivered in the same frequency bands originally allocated for standard television (although in many cases unused to avoid interference between close-by transmitters). Substantial compression reduces the spectrum required to be comparable to that of conventional, uncompressed analog television transmission, making the introduction of HDTV achievable without a radical reallocation of the VHF and UHF frequency bands.

Networked Multimedia

The advent of a widely available and endorsed standard for representation of digital video in compressed form helps developers realize multimedia applications without a dedicated local storage device (such as CD-ROM). Should MPEG decoding become widely included in personal computers and workstations, as appears likely, delivery of multimedia including MPEG-compressed material over different computer networks is possible, although many current networks present their own problems for time-sensitive data such as audio and video. Given the sometimes high utilization on computer networks for nonvideo applications, such as file transfers, aggressive compression is often a necessity for achieving more than a trivial number of sessions over a network. Networked multimedia applications stress the ability of a technology to deliver multiple different types of data streams—some synchronized and some not—and to coexist with (encapsulating or being encapsulated in) a variety of existing and emerging computer networking protocols.

11.2.2 Strategy for Standardization

A key purpose of a standard is to facilitate interoperability. A good standard achieves this while maximizing support for current and as-yet-unknown applications and the development of a variety of implementations. For MPEG, this is achieved by focusing standardization on two related questions:

- What is a legal MPEG bitstream?
- What should be done with it to generate displayable audio-video material?

The first question is answered by a careful specification of the legal syntax of an MPEG bitstream, that is, rules that must be followed in constructing a bitstream. The second is answered by explaining how an idealized decoder would process a legal bitstream to produce decoded audio and video. The standardization process applies the principles to yield the following definitions:

- A *legal bitstream* is one that does not violate any syntactical or semantic rule of MPEG, including being decodable on an idealized decoder.
- A *legal encoder* never produces an illegal bitstream.
- A *legal decoder* successfully decodes all legal bitstreams.
- A *good encoder* generates bitstreams that use less bits for a given perceived video and audio quality level when decoded on an idealized decoder.
- A *good decoder* produces good audio and video quality on the final display device and is robust in the presence of errors in the received bitstream.

This particular strategy for standardization allows a great deal of latitude in the design of encoding systems because the range between truly efficient bitstreams (in terms of quality preserved versus bits spent) and inefficient but legal bitstreams can be quite large. There is less latitude in decoder design, since the decoder must not deviate from the idealized decoder in terms of the bitstreams it can process, but there is still room for different and clever implementations designed to reduce cost in specific applications, improve robustness to slightly damaged bitstreams, and provide different levels of quality in post-MPEG processing designed to prepare a signal for display (e.g., interpolation, digital-to-analog conversion, and composite modulation).

The actual details of what constitutes a legal bitstream are largely conveyed through the specification of the syntax and semantics of such a bitstream.

Syntax and Semantics

Syntax is specified in MPEG using a pseudocode-style notation based on the C programming language. The syntax explains how the individual defined data elements may be combined to produce a legal bitstream. The data elements themselves have specified types and lengths, with the length being either fixed or variable. The syntax is further organized by allowing a syntactical statement to include "subroutines," which are in fact syntactical statements expanded elsewhere, as well as a small number of special "functions" that describe specific local properties required of the bitstream. An example of such a function is `next_start_code()`. This function specifies that the bitstream consists of only

Syntax	Number of Bits	Mnemonic
slice() {		
slice_start_code	32	bslbf
quantizer_scale	5	uimsbf
while (nextbits() == '1') {		
extra_bit_slice	1	"1"
extra_information_slice	8	
}		
extra_bit_slice	1	"0"
do {		
macroblock()		
} while (nextbits() != '000 0000 0000 0000 0000 0000')		
next_start_code()		
}		

FIGURE

11.1   Slice Syntax

0 bits and bytes of at least 23 total bits (but possibly more) followed by a 1 bit and then 8 bits defining the particular start code found.

As an example, Figure 11.1 shows the syntactical specification for the slice layer of MPEG-1 video (ISO/IEC 11172-2 1993 (E), Section 2.4.2.6) (the *slice* is the smallest collection of compressed video data at which resynchronization can occur in case a channel error has corrupted the decoding process). It defines a slice as starting with a particular 32-bit pattern, the slice_start_code, which is a bit string left bit first (bslbf). This is followed by a 5-bit unsigned integer most significant bit first (uimsbf), the quantizer_scale. If the next bit (extra_bit_slice) is a 1, another byte (extra_information_slice) follows. Indeed several such combinations of an extra_bit_slice set to 1 and an extra_information_slice byte may follow until finally an extra_bit_slice of 0 occurs. The function nextbits() used here observes for comparison purposes the next bits in the stream. Once we have allowed for the possible occurrence of extra_information_slice bytes, we then have a sequence of macroblock() until a new start code is observed (the final nextbits() condition recognizes the 23 0 bits that can only occur at the start of a start code or the 0 bit and byte stuffing that may precede it). The syntactical definition of macroblock() is further defined elsewhere in the standard, as are the semantics (meaning) of each of the boldfaced data elements. In summary, a slice consists

slice_start_code—The slice_start_code is a string of 32-bits. The first 24-bits have the value 000001 in hexadecimal and the last 8 bits are the slice_vertical_position having a value in the range 01 through AF hexadecimal inclusive.

slice_vertical_position—This is given by the last eight bits of the slice_start_ code. It is an unsigned integer giving the vertical position in macroblock units of the first macroblock in the slice. The slice_vertical_position of the first row of macroblocks is one. Some slices may have the same slice_vertical_position, since slices may start or finish anywhere. Note that the slice_vertical_position is constrained by 2.4.1 to define non-overlapping slices with no gaps between them. The maximum value of slice_vertical_position is 175.

quantizer_scale—An unsigned integer in the range 1 to 31 used to scale the reconstruction level of the retrieved DCT coefficient levels. The decoder shall use this value until another quantizer_scale is encountered either at the slice layer or the macroblock layer. The value zero is forbidden.

extra_bit_slice—A bit indicates the presence of the following extra information. If extra_bit_slice is set to "1", extra_information_slice will follow it. If it is set to "0", there are no data following it.

extra_information_slice—Reserved.

F I G U R E

11.2   Slice Semantics

of a unique start code, the possibility of some extra information bytes, and then a sequence of macroblocks, terminating with the next start code (which typically would be another slice start code or the start code that begins a picture, the collection of compressed video material from a single video frame or video field).

Corresponding to each syntactical definition is a semantical definition describing how a particular data element is to be interpreted by a decoder. For the slice layer in Figure 11.1, Figure 11.2 gives the semantical definitions (ISO/IEC 11172-2 1993(E), Section 2.4.3.5).

We see here that the MPEG committee is reserving itself the right in the future to extend the standard through the extra_information_slice bytes. This is in contrast to providing locations where a user can insert private information (defined by the user) while generating a legal syntax (which occur at several other places in the standard).

The definition of syntax and semantics as well as the tabular definition of various variable-length codes make up the bulk of the MPEG standards. In addition, there are some critical general constraints and requirements describing

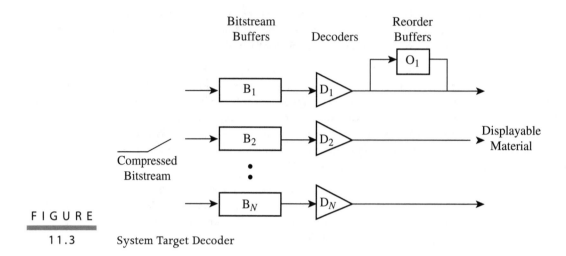

FIGURE

11.3   System Target Decoder

general timing and precision issues. A key such constraint is defined by the system target decoder.

The System Target Decoder

The *system target decoder* is a hypothetical target decoder used to provide precise definition for allowable synchronization and buffer states that can be produced by a legal bitstream (see Figure 11.3).

Conceptually, a bitstream to be decoded is demultiplexed as it arrives into elementary streams destined for various audio and video decoders, and placed in buffers $B_1, \ldots, B_N$ awaiting decoding. The decoders themselves, $D_1, \ldots, D_N$ have the idealized characteristic of instantaneously removing the bits required to decode a video or audio element at the time specified in the bitstream and decoding them ready for display. In some cases, the decoded material may wait in an additional buffer $O_1, \ldots, O_N$ until the display time, also encoded in the bitstream, occurs (such reordering buffers are often required for video decoding depending on the type of motion prediction allowed, but are not used in audio decoding).

The exact size required in the buffers $B_1, \ldots, B_N$ is specified in the bitstream (and limited by the standard). The system target decoder imposes the following key requirement on a legal bitstream: if the elements are decoded and displayed using the times given in the bitstream, the buffers $B_1, \ldots, B_N$ must never overflow or, except for the case of a special low-delay mode in MPEG-2, underflow. This requirement allows decoder designers to safely use a specific amount of memory for these buffers. On the other hand, no real decoder can instantaneously remove all bits for a video or audio element and decode them. To the extent an actual decoder design varies from the system target decoder, it is up to the decoder system designer to insure that his or her design will be able to decode any bitstream that the system target decoder could decode.

11.2.3 Parts of the MPEG-1 and MPEG-2 Standards

The MPEG-1 and MPEG-2 standards are divided into several parts. In both cases, Part 1, "System," describes how various streams (video, audio, or generic data) are multiplexed and synchronized. Part 2, "Video," defines the video compression decoder, and Part 3, "Audio," defines the audio compression decoder. Part 4, "Conformance," defines a set of tests designed to aid in establishing that particular implementations conform to the design. Beyond these, MPEG is adding several new parts, discussed at the end of this chapter.

11.3   MPEG Video

The MPEG video algorithm is a highly refined version of a popular and effective class of video compression algorithms called motion-compensated discrete cosine transform (MC-DCT) algorithms. While not universally used for video compression, these algorithms have served as a basis for many proprietary and standard video compression solutions developed in the 1980s and 1990s. The algorithms use the same basic building blocks developed throughout this book and applied to many different signals, including

- temporal prediction—to exploit redundancy between video pictures
- frequency domain decomposition—the use of the DCT to decompose spatial blocks of image data in order to exploit statistical and perceptual spatial redundancy
- quantization—selective reduction in precision with which information is transmitted to reduce bit rate while minimizing loss of perceptual quality
- variable-length coding—to exploit statistical redundancy in the symbol sequence resulting from quantization as well as in various types of side information

These basic building blocks provide the bulk of the compression efficiency achieved by the MPEG video algorithm. They are enhanced, however, by a number of detailed special techniques designed to absolutely maximize efficiency and flexibility.

11.3.1 The Basic Algorithm

Figure 11.4 shows the basic encoding and decoding algorithms. The incoming video sequence is preprocessed (interpolated, filtered), then motion estimation is used to help form an effective predictor for the current picture from previously transmitted pictures. The motion vectors from motion estimation are sent as side information if used. The predictor for each block is subtracted, and the resulting prediction residual undergoes a DCT. The DCT coefficients are quantized, and the quantized coefficients are variable-length-coded for transmission. The quantized coefficients also undergo reconstruction, inverse DCT, and combination with the predictor, just as they will in the decoder, before forming reference pictures for future motion estimation and prediction.

The decoder decodes the variable-length codes, performs reconstruction of DCT coefficients, inverse DCT, formation of the predictor from previous reconstructed pictures, and summing to form the current reconstructed picture (which may itself serve to predict future received pictures). Postprocessing interpolates and filters the resulting video pictures for display.

Representation of Video

The video that MPEG expects to process is composed of a sequence of frames or fields of luma and chroma.

FRAME-BASED REPRESENTATION.   MPEG-1 is restricted to representing video as a sequence of frames. Each frame consists of three rectangular arrays of pixels, one for the luma (Y, black and white) component, and one each for the chroma (Cr and Cb, color difference) components. The luma and chroma definitions are taken from the CCIR-601 standard for representation of uncompressed digital video.

The chroma arrays in MPEG-1 are subsampled by a factor of two both vertically and horizontally relative to the luma array. While MPEG does not specify exactly how the subsampling is to be performed, it does make clear that the decoder will assume subsampling was designed so as to spatially locate the subsampled pixels according to Figure 11.5 and will design its interpolation of chroma samples accordingly.

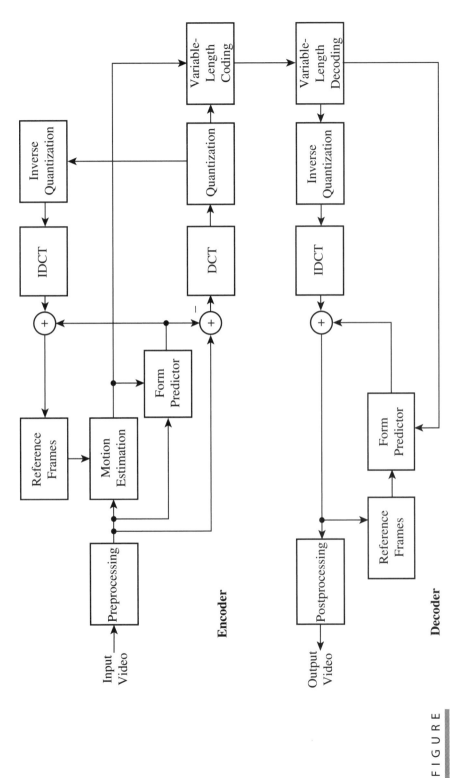

Encoder

Decoder

Block Diagram of MPEG Encoding and Decoding

FIGURE

11.5

Relationship between Luma and Chroma Subsampling for MPEG-1

FIGURE

11.6

Relationship between Luma and Chroma Subsampling for MPEG-2

Typically, MPEG-2 expects chroma subsampling to be consistent with CCIR-601 prescribed horizontal subsampling. Spatially, this implies the chroma sub-sampling pattern shown in Figure 11.6, termed 4:2:0 sampling.

FIELD-BASED REPRESENTATION.   MPEG-2 is optimized for a wider class of video representations, including, most importantly, field-based sequences. *Fields* are created by dividing each frame into a set of two interlaced fields, with odd lines from the frame belonging to one field and even lines to the other. The

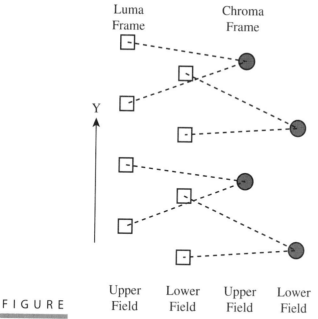

Luma   Chroma
Frame   Frame

Y

Upper   Lower   Upper   Lower
Field   Field   Field   Field

FIGURE

11.7   Relationship between Luma and Chroma Samples Vertically and in Time for
            Field-Based Video Material

fields are transmitted in interlaced video one after the other, separated by half a frame time. Interlacing of video is in fact a simple form of compression by subsampling. It exploits the fact that the human visual system is least sensitive to scene content that has both high spatial and temporal frequencies (such as a fast-moving item with much detail). An interlaced source cannot represent such scenes effectively, but can build up the full detail of a frame (within two field times) and can also update low-resolution items that are changing every field time; these latter types of material are the most visually important.

Unfortunately, field-based representations are somewhat awkward for digital compression. Most contemporary compression scientists would prefer to work with a rectangular sampled array in both space and time and apply more sophisticated techniques than simple subsampling to achieve compression. However, a great deal of material has been, and will continue to be, produced in interlaced form, so efficient compression is necessary.

For field-based sequences, MPEG-2 expects the chroma associated with each field to be vertically subsampled within the field, yet maintain an expected alignment consistent with frame-based sequences. This leads to a vertical resampling pattern as shown in Figure 11.7.

11.3.2 Temporal Prediction

Temporal prediction exploits the intrinsic redundancy between video pictures. Often in video sequences, temporally adjacent pictures have a great deal of similarity. For instance, the background of a scene may be unchanged, with only disturbances in the foreground. In such a case, application of the classic differential pulse code modulation (DPCM) compression strategy (see Section 5.3) can provide substantial compression, with the prediction being applied to entire video pictures. The typical application of this strategy uses the last picture to predict the current picture and is called *picture differencing*.

We can go beyond picture differencing, however, by noting that when there are changes in the current picture, many times they are caused by the motion of objects. Another common occurrence is motion of the entire picture caused by panning of a camera. Such observations motivate the inclusion of a motion model in the prediction to further reduce the amount of spatial information that must be encoded as a prediction residual. Motion compensation, then, is the application of a motion model to prediction.

Temporal prediction with motion compensation is not universally effective, however. For instance, a scene change involves an abrupt discontinuity from one video picture to another. No form of temporal prediction can be particularly effective across such a discontinuity, and the compression algorithm must rely on other capabilities to adequately process such changes. Also, types of changes in the video scene that are not well modeled by the particular motion model chosen may reduce the efficiency of motion compensation. For instance, a motion model based on translation will be less effective in handling rotations or zooms.

Motion Compensation

The motion model used by MPEG is blockwise translation. For simplicity, the blocks are chosen to be a single fixed size: 16×16 pixels in the luma component. Since for typical 4:2:0 chroma subsampling, the chroma components are vertically subsampled by a factor of two in both dimensions relative to the luma, each chroma component includes an 8×8 block of pixels corresponding to the same spatial region as a 16×16 block from the luma picture. The collection of the 16×16 region from the luma and the two corresponding 8×8 regions from the chroma components is called a *macroblock*.

Motion compensation consists of taking a macroblock from the current picture and determining a spatial offset in the reference picture at which a good prediction of the current macroblock can be found. The offset is called a *motion vector*. The mechanics of motion compensation are to use the vector to extract the predicting block from the reference picture, subtract it, and pass the difference on for further compression. The vector chosen for a macroblock is applied directly to determine the luma predictor, but is scaled by half in both dimensions (corresponding to their subsampled size) before being applied to find the chroma predictors.

Motion estimation consists of finding the best vector to be used in predicting the current macroblock. This is typically the most expensive activity in an MPEG encoder, but can have a substantial impact on compression efficiency. The straightforward approach to motion estimation is to evaluate each individual motion vector from the allowed range of possible vectors and select the best one. A reasonable criterion for which is best would be the number of bits consumed in coding the block using that specified offset. In practice, the criterion is often simplified to measuring the mean absolute error (MAE) between the current macroblock and the macroblock at the specified offset (often evaluated between the luma components only), and the search itself is structured in some manner to reduce the total number of comparisons to be made. The most common strategy for such motion estimation is a pyramid-based search. Pyramid searches rely on forming a collection of increasingly low-pass and subsampled versions of the image (a low-pass image pyramid) for the current and reference picture. The search begins by comparing regions between the lowest-resolution versions of the current and reference images; the result of this search initializes a local search at the next higher resolution, which again initializes a search at the next higher resolution, and so on. Such pyramidal searches may require many fewer comparisons since the local searches may be quite restricted. They are effective for most image sequence types, but can be less effective if the difference between a good and bad motion estimation match is restricted to detail that is not apparent in the lower resolution levels of the pyramid.

The effectiveness of motion compensation can be enhanced by allowing the search for an effective prediction region in the reference picture to include not only positions at integral pixel offsets but also fractional pixel offsets. For a fractional pixel offset, the predicting macroblock is constructed by linearly interpolating pixel values relative to the nearest actual pixels. An example of a $\frac{1}{2}$, $\frac{1}{2}$ pixel offset prediction block is shown in Figure 11.8. The dark circle locations have pixel values x calculated as

$$x = (a + b + c + d)/4 \tag{11.1}$$

where a, b, c, and d are the closest pixels in the original reference picture.

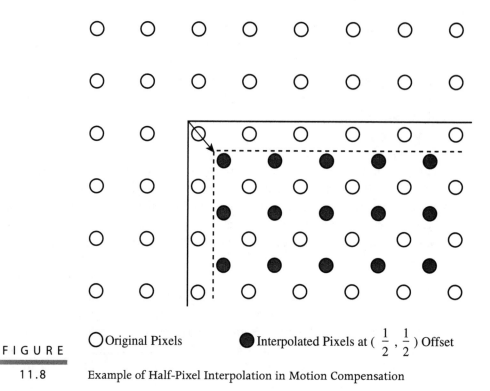

○ Original Pixels   ● Interpolated Pixels at ($\frac{1}{2}$, $\frac{1}{2}$) Offset

FIGURE
━━━━━━
11.8   Example of Half-Pixel Interpolation in Motion Compensation

MPEG allows half-pixel interpolation vertically, horizontally, and both (the previous example being both). The crudeness of linear interpolation does not provide perfect motion tracking at higher resolution, but does bring the benefit of effectively low-pass filtering the image content at interpolated locations. This sometimes removes substantial noise from a reference image and provides a better predictor than might otherwise be expected.

This 32 × 32 region size motion compensation provides a reasonably good compromise between a calculus style approximation to arbitrary motion fields (which becomes more and more accurate as block size decreases) and the bit rate absorbed as overhead in transmitting motion vectors. It will not be effective, though, on complicated motion fields involving substantial rotation, zoom, or deformation. In such cases, as with scene cuts, we must rely on the lower sensitivity of the human visual system to distortion in such complicated material as well as the compression capabilities of other elements of the standard.

Picture and Macroblock Prediction Types

One of the key requirements of MPEG is reasonable support for random access. Random access into an arbitrary motion-compensated sequence is difficult for the same reason that starting decoding in a delta modulation or DPCM sequence is difficult: the received sequence consists of a lot of information about changes from one picture to another, but not necessarily the starting point or original reference. This is a dangerous situation in any case from the point of view of dealing with transmission imperfections; the effect of such imperfections on the decoded images can persist indefinitely. These are usually managed through one of two main strategies: refresh and leaky prediction.

Refresh involves periodically sending an entire picture (picture-based refresh) or portion of a picture (region-based refresh) without any prediction, allowing the decoder to resynchronize at that point. Region-based refresh is achieved by guaranteeing a particular subset of macroblocks are encoded without prediction and rotating this subset through subsequent pictures used in prediction until all macroblocks have been forced to be encoded without prediction. This mechanism reduces the burst of bits required for a picture compressed entirely without prediction, but does not provide a guaranteed random access entry point nor a deterministic time to complete refresh (since nonrefreshed material may be shifted into a just refreshed area by motion compensation before the refresh cycle is complete).

Leaky prediction involves slightly reducing the effectiveness of the prediction in order that the decoder will progressively "forget" any perturbations in the decoded sequence caused by transmission errors. Both encoder and decoder predictors are multiplied by an agreed upon leak factor less than one. Since this reduces the accuracy of the predictor, it causes an increase in the bits required to transmit the compressed residual. However, any discrepancy between decoder and encoder predictor memories is reduced during each iteration of prediction, resulting in an exponential decay in the difference.

Only picture-based refresh aids in random access, however, as it allows a predictable location to begin decoding and a bounded time to decode to any target picture. For instance, if we want to decode picture 303 and we know every 10th picture is not predicted starting at picture 0, then we can decode picture 300, followed by picture 301, 302, and 303 (all of which may consist mainly of differences relative to the previous picture). We will never need to decode more than 10 pictures to get to any desired picture, and we know where to start decoding. To facilitate this strategy, MPEG defines an *I-picture* as being composed entirely of macroblocks compressed without the use of temporal prediction.

T A B L E   Allowed Prediction Modes by Macroblock Type

11.1

Macroblock Type	Prediction
Nonpredicted macroblock	none
Backward-predicted macroblock	references temporally nearest subsequent anchor picture
Forward-predicted macroblock	references temporally nearest previous anchor picture
Bidirectionally predicted macroblock	averages predictions from temporally nearest previous and subsequent anchor pictures

T A B L E   Allowed Macroblock Types and Anchor Picture Definition by Picture Type

11.2

Picture Type	Anchor Picture	Macroblock Types
I-picture	yes	nonpredicted
P-picture	yes	nonpredicted forward predicted
B-picture	no	nonpredicted forward predicted backward predicted bidirectionally predicted

Given the likelihood that streams would be generated with the regular use of nonpredicted pictures, the MPEG committee decided to investigate some new prediction strategies that might further improve compression efficiency and developed the concept of forward and backward prediction. We first define an *anchor picture* as one that can be used for prediction. Then we define four different prediction strategies that can be used for a particular macroblock, as shown in Table 11.1. Each picture has a declared type that limits the type of macroblock allowed in that picture, as shown in Table 11.2.

Figure 11.9 uses arrows to show which pictures can be referenced for motion estimation in a typical sequence of pictures. In fact, while not required by the standard, the set of sequences in which there is a fixed spacing between I-pictures and between anchor pictures (I- and P-pictures) is widely used, so widely that a pair of parameters are commonly used to describe these spacings: N is the number of pictures from one I-picture (inclusive) to the next (exclusive), and M is the number of pictures from one anchor picture (inclusive) to the next

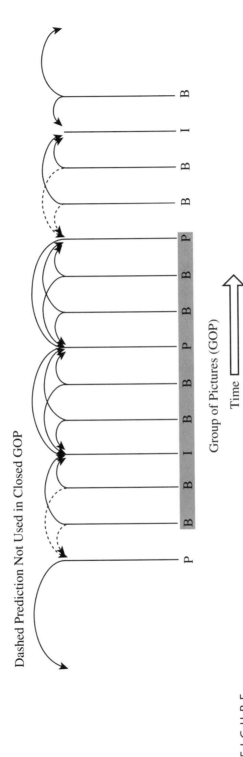

Dashed Prediction Not Used in Closed GOP

P B B I B B P B B P B B B B I B B

Group of Pictures (GOP)

Time

Typical Group of Pictures Collection of Pictures and Allowed Predictors for Pictures

FIGURE

11.9

(exclusive). So, the pattern shown in Figure 11.9 would be called an $N = 9$, $M = 3$ pattern.

There are several implications to this set of possible predictions:

- Using bidirectionally predicted blocks allows effective prediction of uncovered background, areas of the current picture that were not visible in the past but are visible in the future.

- Bidirectional prediction can provide for interpolation equivalent to an even finer degree than the half-pixel interpolation for motion compensation already allowed. Imagine an object located at offset 0 in a temporally adjacent preceding anchor picture and at offset $\frac{1}{2}$ in a temporally adjacent subsequent anchor picture. By using bidirectional prediction, we can provide the equivalent to a $\frac{1}{4}$-pixel linear interpolation of the object.

- Bidirectional prediction can reduce noise in the predictor. If a good prediction is available in both preceding and subsequent anchor pictures, then averaging the two predictors reduces noise and hence increases prediction efficiency.

- Bidirectional prediction increases motion estimation complexity in two ways: first, it obviously requires twice as much work to perform motion estimation in two different anchor pictures. More significantly, though, since anchor pictures are now possibly separated by several picture times, we need a larger overall motion estimation range in order to track objects of a given velocity. For instance, if an object is moving 10 pixels per picture, then a motion estimation range of 10 pixels is adequate to find a good predictor for the object in the absence of B-pictures. With B-pictures, however, the required range to track the object increases to $10M$, where M is the distance from one anchor picture (inclusive) to the next (exclusive).

- Since B-pictures cannot themselves be used to predict other pictures, the quality of compression is solely determined by the visual acceptability of the result. For P- and I-pictures, since the reconstruction will also be used for other predictions, quality must reflect both perceptual fidelity and prediction efficiency. This allows a substantial reduction in the bits allocated to B-pictures relative to I- and P-pictures. A ratio of 5:3:1 in bits spent on I-, P-, and B-pictures is not uncommon. These ratios can and should vary dynamically, though. For instance, an unchanging scene would tend to put almost all the bits in the I-pictures (since the others would be extremely predictable); a scene that changes so thoroughly as to render motion estimation ineffective would tend to spread bits out evenly between all three picture types (indeed, almost all blocks in all pictures would be

Picture Time	−3	−2	−1	0	1	2	3	4	5	6	7	8	9
Encoder Order	P_{-3}	B_{-2}	B_{-1}	I_0	B_1	B_2	P_3	B_4	B_5	P_6	B_7	B_8	I_9
Transmit Order			...	I_0	B_{-2}	B_{-1}	P_3	B_1	B_2	P_6	B_4	B_5	I_9
Decoder Memory 1			...	P_{-3}	P_{-3}	P_{-3}	P_{-3}	P_3	P_3	P_3	P_3	P_3	I_9
Decoder Memory 2			...	I_0	I_0	I_0	I_0	I_0	I_0	P_6	P_6	P_6	P_6
Decoder Scratch Memory			...	—	B_{-2}	B_{-1}	—	B_1	B_2	—	B_4	B_5	—
Displayed Picture			...	P_{-3}	B_{-2}	B_{-1}	I_0	B_1	B_2	P_3	B_4	B_5	P_6

FIGURE

11.10   Pictures in Encode and Transmit Order and Decoder Memory Usage

nonpredicted). Also, since B-pictures are not used as predictors, bit errors in a received bitstream that occur within a B-picture can often have their effects limited to that picture, reducing error propagation.

Display and Transmit Order

Combining the use of B-pictures with a desire to economize on the use of memory in high-volume decoders leads to a difference in the order in which pictures are transmitted versus the order in which they are displayed. The reordering is intended to ensure that, regardless of the spacing between anchor pictures, a decoder need only have enough memory to store two anchor pictures and the scratch memory for the picture currently being decoded. This is achieved by transmitting the anchor picture's compressed version before those of the B-pictures that will precede it in display. Hence the anchor picture will arrive ahead of the time it is needed and be available for reconstructing the B-pictures for immediate display. An example is shown in Figure 11.10. The boxed area shows a single Group of Pictures (GOP), defined as a contiguous sequence of pictures beginning with an I-picture (inclusive) and ending with an I-picture (exclusive) in transmit order.

Although the decoder escapes the requirement for additional buffers as the spacing between anchor pictures increases, the encoder does not: the brunt of providing memory for reordering falls on it.

The first set of B-pictures following the I-picture that starts a GOP will in general require the last anchor picture from the previous GOP in order to decode (the examples are B_{-1} and B_{-2} in Figure 11.10). So if we try to start decoding from the beginning of a GOP, although we can decode and display the I-picture, we can't decode and display the next set of B-pictures and must instead wait until the next anchor picture to be able to decode and display continuously. MPEG allows the specification of a *closed GOP*, which requires that the first B-pictures following an I-picture in transmit order cannot use motion references to the last anchor picture in the previous GOP (e.g., B_{-1} and B_{-2} cannot use P_{-3} as a reference). In this case, display can begin as soon as B_{-2} is decoded.

The actual memory required in a specific decoder implementation can vary depending on how tightly the decoder synchronizes decoding and display processes. For instance, by advocating a "display while decoding" strategy yet dealing with interlaced source, it is possible to drive the total memory required from 3 frames to 2.75 or even below.

Field and Frame Prediction

While MPEG-1 does not consider the possibility of field-based video representations, MPEG-2 specifically does allow for increased compression efficiency on interlaced material. One way in which this is accommodated is by allowing either field- or frame-based prediction for each macroblock (often termed *adaptive field/frame compression*). In the case of field-based prediction, the macroblock is divided into two field macroblocks. The top field macroblock is predicted from the top fields in one or two anchor pictures using the modes appropriate for the picture type. The lower field macroblock is predicted from the lower fields in one or two anchor pictures. Note that the subdivision of chroma here corresponds to the chroma subsampling constraints for field representation described previously.

Field-based prediction can be highly effective in instances of substantial horizontal acceleration. In these cases, an object captured in two different fields appears to have serrated vertical edges when viewed as a frame, with the depth of the serration varying with time due to acceleration. Frame-based motion estimation is quite ineffective in this case and leaves a good deal of difficult-to-compress high-frequency serrations left over. Field-based prediction can perform quite well. On the other hand, for more benign motion cases, frame-based prediction can more effectively exploit vertical redundancy. Allowing a choice between the modes to occur on a macroblock basis gives the best of both worlds at the cost of a slight increase in overhead (the net effect being in favor of allowing the choice). This type of prediction is most important on some of the most difficult-to-compress material, such as a basketball game in which a fast-moving foreground is combined with a highly detailed slow-moving background. The ability of adaptive field/frame motion compensation to improve some of this worst-case material makes it even more valuable than the average improvement alone would imply.

A special version of field-based motion estimation, *dual prime,* is also available. Dual prime can only be used in P-pictures in the absence of any B-pictures between the reference picture and the current picture. Each field in the current macroblock is predicted using the average of field macroblocks from each field in the preceding picture. Rather than sending four separate vectors in order to identify the offset between each of the current field macroblocks and their predictors in each of the previous fields, a single vector is sent and extrapolated to calculate the four vectors using a constant-velocity model. Let v_{ij} be the vector from field i in the current picture to field j in the reference picture, and let v be the transmitted vector. Then we have

$$v_{11} = v_{22} = v \tag{11.2}$$

$$v_{21} = \left(\frac{3}{2}\right) v \tag{11.3}$$

$$v_{12} = \left(\frac{1}{2}\right) v \tag{11.4}$$

These formulas can be understood from the constant-velocity model, since if a region being tracked was translating with constant velocity, the displacement between fields 1 and 1 in the current and reference picture and between fields 2 and 2 would be identical; the displacement between field 2 in the current picture and field 1 in the reference picture would be $\frac{3}{2}$ as large (since the temporal distance is $\frac{3}{2}$ as large as between fields 1 and 1 or 2 and 2) and between field 1 in the current picture and field 2 in the reference picture would be $\frac{1}{2}$ as large (since the temporal difference is $\frac{1}{2}$ as large). An additional ±1 pixel offset is available to make minor corrections in the model. Dual prime achieves some of the gains of B-pictures through the averaging effect between fields, which can reduce noise and synthesize a finer degree of motion compensation offset resolution.

11.3.3 Frequency Domain Decomposition

After motion compensation has been performed, the residual information (or original picture information in the case of a nonpredicted block) is transformed using the DCT. To prepare the macroblock for transformation, six 8×8 blocks are extracted from the macroblock, four from the luma picture and one each from each of the chroma pictures. The luma blocks for MPEG-1 and the frame DCT mode of MPEG-2 are shown in Figure 11.11; for the field DCT mode of MPEG-2, in Figure 11.12.

The field DCT mode is useful for much the same reason that field motion compensation is useful: material with a high degree of horizontal motion, especially

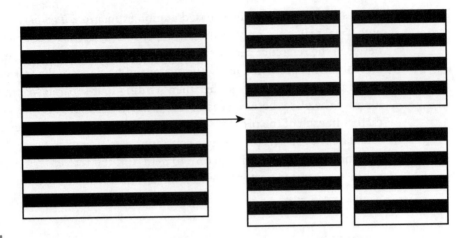

FIGURE
11.11   Mapping from 16 × 16 Block to 8 × 8 Blocks for Frame-Organized Data

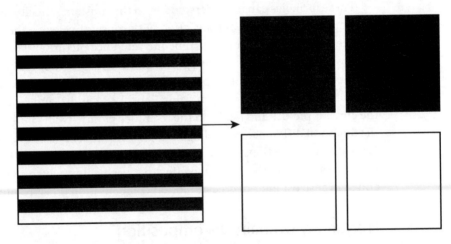

FIGURE
11.12   Mapping from 16 × 16 Block to 8 × 8 Blocks for Field-Organized Data

acceleration, captured using an interlaced video standard, tends to produce difficult-to-compress high frequencies when transformed using a frame-based DCT. The choice of frame versus field mode for motion compensation and DCT are not bound together, and there is a small benefit to be had by making the decision independently.

Discrete Cosine Transform

The MPEG standard does not specify exactly how to perform the 8×8 DCT and inverse discrete cosine transform (IDCT) required. This is too limiting given that many different software and hardware implementations of MPEG are expected. Instead, MPEG calls for the IDCT as implemented to be able to pass a test developed as part of the ITU-T standardization of H.261, a videoconferencing standard. In this test, IEEE P1180/D2, the proposed IDCT inverse transforms a particular set of blocks, and the results are compared to an idealized set of results. Providing the proposed IDCT has less than a specified number of discrepancies at each of several magnitudes, it is an acceptable IDCT.

Allowing similar but not identical IDCTs in different implementations will cause mismatch in the encoders and decoders of different manufacturers. Since the encoder includes an IDCT for the purpose of reproducing the pictures that the decoder generates, the fact that an encoder and decoder have slightly different DCTs will introduce a gradually increasing difference between these pictures, resulting in inappropriate coding decisions on the encoder's part. This phenomenon is managed by limiting to 132 the number of times a specific macroblock location may be coded as predicted in P-pictures before that macroblock location must be coded without prediction. Moreover, MPEG-2 added some specific quantization rules that were found to further mitigate the problem of mismatch.

11.3.4 Quantization

After transformation, the DCT coefficients typically have 12 bits or more of precision. On the face of it, this is not a very auspicious compression, since the data started with 8 bits per pixel. Quantization is the key step that exploits the efforts provided by motion compensation and the DCT to reduce the bits required since the information has now been organized so that many coefficients are essentially irrelevant to the final reproduction quality and only a few need be treated with care.

Quantizer Step Size

MPEG applies a uniform step size quantizer to each coefficient. However, the step size of the quantizer may vary from coefficient to coefficient and macroblock to macroblock. In fact, the quantizer step size is determined at the decoder by the following equation:

$$ss = qf[m, n] \times qs \qquad (11.5)$$

*	16	19	22	26	27	29	34
16	16	22	24	27	29	34	37
19	22	26	27	29	34	34	38
22	22	26	27	29	34	37	40
22	26	27	29	32	35	40	48
26	27	29	32	35	40	48	58
26	27	29	34	38	46	56	69
27	29	35	38	46	56	69	83

FIGURE

11.13   Intraframe Quantizer Weighting Matrix

16	16	16	16	16	16	16	16
16	16	16	16	16	16	16	16
16	16	16	16	16	16	16	16
16	16	16	16	16	16	16	16
16	16	16	16	16	16	16	16
16	16	16	16	16	16	16	16
16	16	16	16	16	16	16	16

FIGURE

11.14   Interframe Quantizer Weighting Matrix

The factor $qf[m, n]$ is dependent on the location of the coefficient within a block. The factor qs is the base quantizer step size. This allows emphasis on more perceptually important lower frequencies. MPEG provides two default weighting matrices $qf[m, n]$ for use on predicted blocks and nonpredicted blocks, shown in Figures 11.13 and 11.14. Note that for nonpredicted blocks, the DCT DC coefficient, the upper left-hand coefficient that is proportional to the average value of the space domain block, is not quantized using a weighting matrix value; hence that location in the weighting matrix has an * in Figure 11.13. This unusual treatment reflects the fact that the eye is highly sensitive to errors in the DC level of nonpredicted blocks and tends to quickly recognize these as blocking or tiling distortion in the reconstructed picture.

The default matrix for nonpredicted blocks shows a strong bias towards lower frequencies, consistent with other DCT-based algorithms applied to non-predicted material, such as JPEG (Chapter 9). However, the default matrix for predicted blocks is flat. In fact, it has been found empirically that since motion compensation itself tends to remove much of the low frequencies in any case, there is little benefit at the quantization stage to further emphasizing them.

MPEG allows encoders to override the default matrices (in the video sequence header, a header inserted at least at the beginning of the sequence and then periodically at the beginning of pictures at the discretion of the encoder); many contemporary encoders do this.

While the manner in which the decoder will map quantized values to reconstructions is precisely prescribed, the choice as to how to map the incoming values at the encoder to quantized values is not. A typical strategy for optimizing the encoder quantization is to increase the absolute threshold that bounds the range that will be mapped to the quantized value 0. This is because the coding strategy described in the next section is very efficient at compressing long runs of 0 quantized values, and the slight increase in distortion suffered by the more inaccurate values is more than offset by the savings in bits, a savings that can be applied to allow finer quantization in more critical areas. Further, for interframe material in particular, low-level random noise is also effectively reduced by a wider range for the 0 quantized value.

11.3.5   Variable-Length Coding

Both the quantized coefficients and several different types of side information (macroblock prediction type, motion vectors, etc.) exhibit statistical concentration so that the overall average bit rate can be lowered by using variable-length coding. Note that the use of variable-length coding will necessitate buffering when MPEG is to operate over a fixed-rate channel.

Modified Huffman Codes

The type of variable-length code used throughout MPEG is a modified Huffman code. Huffman coding, discussed in Chapter 2, provides optimal variable-length coding for the chosen alphabet. However, for large alphabets, storing, encoding, and decoding the Huffman code can be expensive. Hence, the table size is generally restricted to a subset consisting of the most probable symbols. An additional codeword is added to the code, termed "ESCAPE." When an input symbol is observed that does not belong to the chosen high-probability symbol set, it does not have its own Huffman codeword; instead, the ESCAPE codeword is issued followed by the explicit (i.e., standard indexed value) of the input symbol. The use of an ESCAPE strategy does increase the average bit rate of the code, but if the total probability of all symbols that will use the ESCAPE is sufficiently small, the impact is negligible. A second modification to the MPEG

TABLE 11.3 Example of a Simple Modified Huffman Code

Symbol	Code
0	01
1	10
2	110
3	111 011
4	111 100
5	111 101
6	111 110
7	111 111

Huffman codes for video is that the all-zero codeword is not used, in order to avoid emulation of a start code via a legitimate sequence of other codes. Since the start code begins with 23 zeros and is used as a resynchronization point when decoding an errored bitstream, the occurrence of 23 zeros as a sequence of other codewords could cause a spurious resynchronization with disastrous effect. Table 11.3 shows an example of a simple modified Huffman code using these rules for an alphabet consisting of {0, 1, 2, 3, 4, 5, 6, 7}. The symbols 3–7 are escaped; the codeword of all zeros is not allowed.

Two-Dimension to One-Dimension Conversion

The quantized DCT coefficients form the bulk of the material that needs to be variable-length encoded. Empirically, though, after quantization, the 8×8 blocks of DCT coefficients tend to exhibit a substantial number of zeros, particularly in the higher frequencies, as in Figure 11.15.

MPEG exploits this phenomenon by first converting the 8×8 array into a one-dimensional array and then applying coding that can exploit long runs of zeros. Both MPEG-1 and MPEG-2 use a zigzag scan for cases, such as in Figure 11.15, where there are a large number of zeros in the lower right-hand quadrant. MPEG-2 provides an alternative, vertical scan, which is often more effective, especially when a field-based DCT has been applied. The scan path of zigzag and vertical scans is shown in Figure 11.16.

Zigzag scanning applied to the example array results in the sequence:

−42 12 −19 16 14 3 −1 −8 8 3 3 −2 −9 0 0 0 2 3 0 0 0 0 0 0 0 0 0 1 0
0 1 1 0 0 0 0 0 0 0 −1 0 . . . 0

				Increasing Horizontal Frequency →			
−42	12	3	−1	0	0	0	1
−19	14	−8	0	2	0	0	0
16	8	−9	3	0	0	0	0
3	−2	0	0	1	0	0	0
3	0	0	1	−1	0	0	0
0	0	0	0	0	0	0	0
0	0	0	0	0	0	0	0
0	0	0	0	0	0	0	0

Increasing Vertical Frequency ↓

FIGURE

11.15   Example of an 8 × 8 Array of Quantized DCT Coefficients

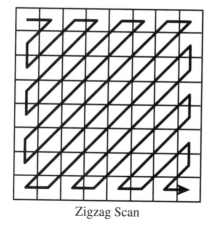
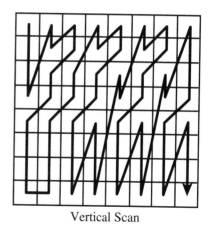

Zigzag Scan   Vertical Scan

FIGURE

11.16   Coefficient Scan Pattern for Zigzag and Vertical Scans

The decoder will perform the inverse scanning as part of its reconstruction process.

Runlength Amplitude Coding

Once a 64-symbol vector has been created by scanning the 8 × 8 array for each block, runlength amplitude coding is used. First, the DC quantized coefficient (containing the block average) is treated specially, receiving its own dedicated Huffman code, because the DC quantized coefficient tends to have a unique statistical characteristic relative to other quantized coefficients. Moreover, since there is some redundancy between adjacent DC quantized coefficients in non-predicted blocks, only the difference between these is Huffman coded. The remaining quantized coefficients are parsed into a sequence of runs, where a run is defined as zero or more 0s followed by a single nonzero value. This becomes a new symbol for Huffman coding, consisting of a runlength-amplitude pair. The parsing into runlength-amplitude pairs for the example of the last section is

$$(0, -42), (0, 12), (0, -19), (0, 16), (0, 14), (0, 3), (0, -1), (0, -8), (0, 8),$$
$$(0, 3), (0, 3), (0, -2), (0, -9), (3, 2), (0, 3), (10, 1), (2, 1), (0, 1), (6, -1),$$
$$(EOB)$$

Note that a special codeword is reserved to indicate nothing but 0 quantized coefficients from that point until the end of the block (EOB).

MPEG-1 and MPEG-2 share a modified Huffman code for runlength-amplitude pairs. MPEG-2 also provides an additional modified Huffman code that has been specifically optimized and found to provide a slight improvement on coding nonpredicted (or intraframe blocks), called the *alternative intra Huffman code*.

Side Information Coding

There are a variety of different types of side information, designed in general to reduce the number of blocks that actually have to undergo runlength-amplitude coding and to reduce the amount of information in those that do. The most important of these are summarized below.

MACROBLOCK ADDRESS.   MPEG includes a mechanism for skipping macroblocks if the decoder should reconstruct the contents of the macroblock simply using the collocated macroblock in another picture. This is enabled by starting each macroblock with the increment with which the macroblock address should be increased; if the increment is greater than one, the macroblock is skipped.

MACROBLOCK TYPE.   The macroblock type indicates whether a macroblock is not predicted, forward predicted or backward predicted, or both; whether the quantizer step size should change; whether (in MPEG-2) the macroblock is field or frame motion compensated and field or frame transformed; and whether all the blocks within the macroblock are coded.

CODED PATTERN.   Just as with skipped macroblocks, not all of the blocks within a macroblock may have significant enough information after motion compensation, DCT, and quantization to be worth coding. The coded pattern code allows the encoder to select and signal one of several patterns indicating which blocks are coded and which are not. Uncoded blocks are reconstructed using the predictor only.

MOTION VECTORS.   In the case of a motion-compensated macroblock, motion vectors are sent. Motion vectors are themselves coded using prediction: a set of rules allows construction of a predictor for the current motion vector from the last transmitted motion, and only the difference is actually transmitted. The motion vector prediction loop is restarted at the beginning of a slice and a few other conditions.

11.3.6 Syntactical Layering in MPEG

The MPEG syntax includes several distinct layers, many of which we have already discussed:

- Sequence: The sequence layer defines picture size, picture rate, expected buffer sizes, and a number of other near static parameters. It also provides an opportunity to define nondefault quantizer matrices for MPEG-1 (this can happen every picture in MPEG-2).

- Group of Pictures: A contiguous set of pictures in transmit order that aid random access. The first picture in transmit order in the GOP must be an I-picture. The GOP header can indicate whether it is open or closed, whether it has been separated from the original preceding GOP (broken_link), and SMPTE time code for the start of GOP. The GOP structure is mandatory in MPEG-1 and optional in MPEG-2.

- Picture: The picture header defines picture type (I, B, or P) as well as motion vector range in that picture.

- Slice: The unit of resynchronization. A collection of macroblocks preceded by a unique resynchronization pattern (a start code).

- Macroblock: The unit of motion compensation. A 16×16 region in the luma combined with the corresponding 8×8 regions in both chroma components. The macroblock header gives the prediction mode for the block, macroblock address, coded block pattern, and, if desired, can cause an overall change in quantizer step size through the base quantizer step size variable.

- Block: The unit of transformation. An 8×8 collection of pixels.

11.3.7 Rate Control

One of the most important encoder design issues is how to include an effective rate control system into a compressor. As mentioned earlier, once variable-length coding has been applied, some buffering is required to absorb instantaneous fluctuations in bit rate if the stream is to be delivered over a fixed-rate channel. Such buffering must be available at both encoder and decoder. A tenet of MPEG is that once the decoder buffer size has been specified, it must be possible to decode a legal bitstream in that buffer without overflowing or underflowing (except for the low-delay mode of MPEG-2, which does allow underflows).

Fixed-Rate Channels

For fixed-rate channels, with a little effort, the requirement on the decoder buffer can be made equivalent to a requirement on the encoder buffer as follows:

- If the encoder and decoder buffer are of the same size,
- and the encoder compresses units at the pace at which they arrive (i.e., each unit of information is compressed in a period that is the inverse of the number of units per second),
- and the decoder decompresses units at the pace at which they are to be displayed,
- and the decoding starts when the decoder buffer's fullness equals the buffer size minus the encoder's buffer fullness,
- and the encoder ensures that the encoder buffer never overflows (by throttling information when necessary) and never underflows (by using stuffing to send filler bits when necessary),
- then the decoder buffer will never underflow or overflow.

More specifically, the decoder buffer will persist in "mirror state" relative to the encoder buffer: its fullness will always be equal to the buffer size minus the encoder buffer fullness at a time earlier by the channel rate divided by the buffer size. Hence, a strategy for fixed-rate channels is to ensure that an encoder buffer never underflows or overflows.

Variable-Rate Channels

MPEG supports variable-rate channels. The overriding constraint is that the decoder's buffer not overflow or underflow during decoding. Variable-rate channels come in two major classes: slave and master. A slave variable-rate channel has the rate selected by the MPEG system. A master variable-rate channel tells the MPEG system what the current rate is. Variable-rate channels are often also constrained by a maximum and minimum allowable instantaneous bit rate. In the very special case of a slave variable-rate channel with no limit on maximum instantaneous bit rate and a zero minimum instantaneous bit rate, the MPEG system can effectively ignore the presence of a buffer at the decoder, and encoding can proceed with the aim of minimizing the long-term average bit rate without regard to instantaneous fluctuations (with the exception that no picture could exceed in total the entire buffer size since a picture must be decoded instantaneously in the STD model). All other variable-rate channels require the encoding to take into account the state of the decoder's buffer. In many cases, a generalized version of the theorem stated in the previous section can be applied; in some, though, it may be necessary to directly model the decoder's buffer.

Storage systems can often be used as slave variable-rate channels with specific minimum and maximum instantaneous bit rates. For instance, an MPEG-2 laser-disk-based system with a minimum transfer rate of 2 Mbps and a maximum of 8 Mbps could provide good handling of much difficult material, but could also be expected to achieve generous total stored time for most entertainment source material, which frequently varies in overall source difficulty (e.g., for basketball, the commentators versus the game).

A special case of a master variable-rate channel is statistical multiplexing. This technique considers a group of channels that are encoded together. The total bit rate available to all channels is dynamically allocated to each of the channels in order to maximize the minimum quality across the set. An external algorithm must perform the rate allocation, and although each encoder will attempt to obtain the bit rate it deems necessary, there is no guarantee it will receive it. Statistical multiplexing can be quite effective in improving average quality, even on a small number of video channels; however, it is difficult to mix and match precompressed channels from multiple statistically multiplexed streams because there is no guarantee that a new combination of channels will meet any fixed bit rate target (other than the sum of the maximum possible bit rate of all streams).

Rate Control Strategies

In most cases, for fixed- or variable-rate channels, it is necessary to (implicitly or explicitly) track the decoder buffer state and take appropriate action to avoid overflows or underflows. For fixed-rate channels, using the relationship between encoder and decoder buffer states, it is sufficient to ensure that an equivalent-size encoder buffer never underflows or overflows. Avoiding underflow is achieved by using stuffing, a way to continue to generate bits for the channel without sending actual encoded image information. MPEG provides for stuffing in several places—for instance, before video start codes and as part of the macroblock address code. Preventing overflows is more difficult. Overflows occur because the material is exhibiting a sustained difficulty relative to the bit rate that has been allocated. The only option available to the encoder is to reduce the fidelity with which the material is compressed in order to avoid overflowing the buffer. The first line of defense is generally the quantizer step size. As described previously, a key in determining quantizer step size is the base quantizer step size variable, which is selected at the encoder's discretion and may be varied on a macroblock-by-macroblock basis. Usually, the base quantizer step size depends, at least partly, on the deviation between expected and observed buffer fullness. Other options for preventing buffer overflow are increasing the number of skipped macroblocks (i.e., increasing the distortion threshold below which we will simply not bother encoding a macroblock) and modulating an external filter to reduce information (particularly high frequencies) entering an encoder. Because of the very long feedback loop involved in the MPEG compression, this latter technique requires great care to avoid instability.

An additional task of rate control is to assign bits to each of the picture types (I, B, and P). As noted earlier, this needs to be highly dynamic to reflect the change in temporal redundancy of the material. The goal is to provide enough bits to each picture type to keep the perceived reconstruction quality constant.

Finally, contemporary encoder rate control often combines some method of scene analysis to additionally modulate quantizer step size. Since the human visual system is less sensitive to distortion in the presence of coarse random texture and more sensitive in flat regions, an encoder will often vary the quantizer step size to spend more bits in areas that are more important to the human visual system.

Good rate control is the parsimonious use of every bit available to the encoding system and can achieve better visual quality at lower bit rates than mediocre rate control. Bad rate control can actually create visible artifacts of its own; the most frequent is a visible pulsing associated with an inappropriate allocation of bits across different picture types.

11.3.8 Constrained Parameters, Levels, and Profiles

The MPEG video algorithm provides an enormous flexibility in terms of the image sizes, bit rates, and other key parameters that can be supported. It is unreasonable to expect simple applications to bear the cost of decoding at the substantially higher complexity of the worst-case use of the standard,

T A B L E   Defined Levels and Profiles for MPEG-2

11.4

Level	Profile				
	Simple	Main	SNR	Spatial	High
High		X			X
High 1440		X		X	X
Main	X	X	X		X
Low		X	X		

particularly if the simpler applications will be built in highly cost-sensitive high-volume applications. Hence, MPEG has defined compliance points within the standard.

For MPEG-1, the *constrained parameters* case provides the following set of specific restrictions that are reasonable for the kind of moderate-resolution, multimedia applications in the 1–3 Mbps range for which MPEG-1 was optimized.

- Horizontal size less than or equal to 720 pixels

- Vertical size less than or equal to 576 pixels

- Total number of macroblocks/picture less than or equal to 396

- Total number of macroblocks/second less than or equal to $396 \times 25 = 330 \times 30$

- Picture rate less than or equal to 30 pictures/second

- Bit rate less than or equal to 1.86 Mbps

- Decoder buffer less than or equal to 376,832 bits

Although the first two constraints seem to allow large image sizes (up to the full resolution of broadcast digital CCIR-601), the third and fourth constraints are more limiting in this regard. For instance, the Standard Intermediate Format (SIF) sizes of 352H × 240V (NTSC countries) and 352H × 288V (PAL countries) just satisfy these constraints; a CCIR-601 resolution would not. Much of the commodity silicon targeted at MPEG-1 applications is designed to the constrained parameters level.

MPEG-2 is designed to address a much larger number of potential applications, and in order to be cost-effective in each, it has a much larger set of compliance points. These are indexed by *levels,* which set a rough limit on processing power based on image size, and *profiles,* which restrict the algorithmic features available. Table 11.4 shows the grid of compliance points for MPEG-2.

The compliance point addressed by a particular system is stated as "x profile at y level." The most popular compliance point is, not surprisingly, main profile at main level (or MP @ ML, for short). Following are brief discussions of each of the levels:

- Low—This sets constraints on image size of approximately half CCIR-601 vertically and horizontally, namely, 352H×288V.

- Main—CCIR-601 size images, 720H×576V×25Hz or 720H×480V×29.97Hz.

- High 1440—HDTV up to 1440H×1152V.

- High—HDTV up to 1920H×1152V.

Following are brief descriptions of the profiles:

- Simple—No B-pictures. This allows a reduction in the memory required at decoders of as much as 8 Mbits, at some cost in bit rate efficiency.

- Main—The material in this chapter describes most of the aspects of the main profile.

- SNR—Adds a type of scalability based on transmitting two bitstreams. The first, when decoded, will provide a reasonable reproduction. The second provides additional information to refine the reconstructed DCT coefficients, so that when both are decoded together, an excellent reconstruction results. Such scalability allows simpler and more complex decoders to share the same bitstream.

- Spatial—Adds a different type of scalability, in which the first stream provides a low-resolution reproduction and the combination of both streams provides a full-resolution reproduction.

- High—Allows SNR, spatial, and an additional type of scalability based on the first stream providing a low picture rate reconstruction and both streams providing full picture rate, as well as a number of other high-complexity options.

11.4   MPEG Audio

The MPEG audio compression standard defines a family of algorithms appropriate for a wide range of audio material (e.g., speech, music, and the range of special effects that might be expected on a movie soundtrack) based on a combination of subband compression with techniques to explicitly exploit properties of human hearing.

Encoder

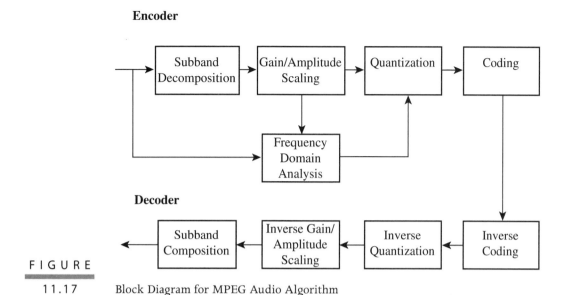

FIGURE

11.17   Block Diagram for MPEG Audio Algorithm

11.4.1 Layers

Like the MPEG video standard, the MPEG audio standard addresses different
compliance points so as to be cost-effective for a variety of applications. The
compliance points in MPEG audio are called *layers,* ordered from 1 to 3 in
increasing complexity, and if a decoder can decode layer n, it must also be able
to decode all lesser layers.

For typical music and soundtrack material, a stereo pair can be encoded well
at rates of around 64 kbps per channel for Layer 3, 128 kbps per channel for
Layer 2, and 192 kbps per channel for Layer 1. Layer 1 has the advantage of
simple encoding; both Layers 1 and 2 have already seen low-cost commodity
silicon decoder implementations.

Since rates around 128 kbps tend to be quite small when compared to the
video rate, and given the availability of commodity silicon, Layer 2 has proven
the most popular compliance point in widespread use.

11.4.2 The Basic Algorithm

Figure 11.17 shows the basic MPEG audio algorithm. Subband decomposition
separates the incoming audio signal into multiple frequency bands, which are
subsequently scaled (by a slowly varying scale factor in each subband) and
quantized. Additional analysis for selection of the quantizer step size in each
subband is provided by the frequency domain analysis function. The samples

are coded (fixed-rate coding in Layers 1 and 2, but variable-rate Huffman coding in Layer 3) and formatted with side information for transmission. The decoder unpacks and decodes coefficients and side information, performs inverse quantization to map each sample back to a reconstructed value, multiplies by the appropriate scale factor in each band, and applies subband composition to recover a time domain signal.

Digital audio source material, mono or stereo, is provided at one of three sampling rates (32, 44.1, or 48 kHz) for MPEG-1 or one of six sampling rates (16, 22.05, 24, 32, 44.1, or 48 kHz) for MPEG-2. The material undergoes a subband decomposition, scaling (separation into a slowly varying gain quantity and a residual), quantization, and then coding. Quantization is typically controlled by a perceptual model driven by a detailed frequency analysis.

Decoding first performs the inverse coding, then inverse quantization, inverse scaling, and subband composition to produce reconstructed audio. As with video and systems, MPEG carefully specifies the decoding algorithm and bitstream syntax, but allows arbitrary encoding algorithms.

11.4.3 Subband Decomposition

For Layers 1 and 2, decomposition is performed using a 32-band quadrature mirror filter (QMF) subband analysis/synthesis system like those described in Chapters 7 and 8.

For Layer 3, the QMF filter is followed by a modified discrete cosine transform (MDCT). The combination yields a much finer degree of frequency resolution, effectively a maximum of 576 bands in the filter bank. The filter bank can switch between long-time (high-frequency resolution) and short-time (low-frequency resolution) analysis based on the presence of strong temporal changes. This choice is available based on the audible distortion that occurs when a sudden change in content (attack) is compressed and coded with a long-analysis time window, resulting in distortion that either precedes or follows the attack by a substantial amount.

For all layers, the subband decomposition is *critically sampled*—the number of samples per unit time in each subband times the number of subbands equals the original number of samples per unit time in the original time domain.

11.4.4 Scaling, Quantization, and Coding

This section focuses on scaling, quantization, and coding for the predominant Layer 2 format. For each subband, a frame consists of 36 consecutive subband samples. During decoding, a scale factor for the subband (acting as a gain) will multiply the samples in a frame. A single scale factor may apply to all the samples in the frame, or separate scale factors may be applied to each successive group of 12 samples in the frame. By separating into this gain/amplitude format, quantization can focus on the much narrower dynamic range of the samples after division by the scale factor. Note that this strategy is implicitly aligned with the concept of audio masking, which states that larger distortions are acceptable in frequency bands with large signal energy. The gain/amplitude model tends to produce lower quantization noise (since the noise, like the signal, is multiplied by the scale factor) in bands with low input energy.

In addition to the gain/amplitude affect, an explicit frequency domain analysis is generally applied during encoding (although, as usual, the specific encoding technique to be used is not specified by MPEG, only the decoding). This analysis is used to drive a psychoacoustic model for the amount of masking available in each subband, yielding a *signal-to-mask-ratio* (SMR), the signal-to-noise ratio below which masking can be expected to prevent any audible distortion. Bits are then allocated between subbands so as to minimize the total of the differences between the signal-to-noise ratio in each band that will result after quantization and the SMR in that band.

The exploitation of the appropriate psychoacoustic model represents a substantial contribution to encoder performance. More sophisticated models generally require a higher degree of frequency resolution than is provided by the subband filter bank itself (which is optimized to a shorter time window in order to minimize pre-echoes, the spreading of distortion in advance of an attack). These models can be quite complex. Two example models (one primarily used with Layer 1 and 2 encoders and the other with Layer 3 encoder) are described in an informative annex to the MPEG-1 audio standard.

Using the number of bits allocated per sample in a subband, uniform step size quantization is applied to each amplitude value (i.e., subband sample after division by the scale factor).

Layer 1 encoding is similar to Layer 2 encoding, except that there is less freedom in determining whether to provide scale factors for groups of 12 samples within each audio frame's subband samples. Layer 1 also lacks Layer 2's ability to completely ignore subbands above a limit specified as side information. Layer 3 encoding adds substantial additional coding options, the most important of which is the use of Huffman coding for the amplitude (gain normalized) subband samples. This adds compression efficiency but entails the same use of buffering to smooth instantaneous rate as in MPEG video compression.

11.4.5 Multichannel Compression

MPEG-1 explicitly considers stereo compression. The four modes that address single and dual channel encoding are single_channel (mono), dual_channel (an unrelated pair of mono channels), stereo (two channels meant as a stereo pair, but without special compression), and joint_stereo. The last mode exploits a specific characteristic of human stereo perception: the spatial localization of a sound source depends on both amplitude and phase characteristics for low frequencies but only on amplitude characteristics for high frequencies. In other words, it is sufficient to have the correct loudness ratio between left and right ears for a high frequency for it to appear to be at a specific spatial location without regard to the relative phase at the two ears, but this is not sufficient at low frequencies. Joint stereo coding allows the encoder to specify a subband above which (in frequency) the subband samples from left and right signals have their scale factors independently calculated (so that the output amplitude will be maintained), but the values after division by the scale factor are averaged. These averages are what are actually transmitted and used to reconstruct samples for both left and right signals at the decoder. This destroys relative phase information between the left and right channels. Below the specified subband limit, compression occurs as normal. This technique can provide bit rate savings on the order of 5–10% in typical applications, but is incompatible with surround sound encoding techniques that rely on phase information in the analog reconstruction to synthesize surround channels.

MPEG-2 provides support for a backward-compatible extension to discrete multichannel sound typical in modern cinema (i.e., an MPEG-1 stereo bitstream is embedded and easily extractable from the multichannel compressed bitstream). Multichannel sound typically consists of left front (L) and right front (R) channels (used for most general and music material), a center channel (C) (used for dialog), a left surround (LS) and right surround (RS) channel (used for effects), and a low-frequency effects (LFE) channel, typically up to 100 Hz. The relationship between the embedded MPEG-1 left (L0) and right (R0) channels, the supplementary encoded information (T2, T3, T4), and the multichannel reconstructions is made through a decoding matrix, for which a number of choices are available. A typical one is

$$L = L0 - T2 - T3 \tag{11.6}$$

$$R = R0 - T2 - T4 \tag{11.7}$$

$$C = T2 \tag{11.8}$$

$$LS = T3 \tag{11.9}$$

$$RS = T4 \tag{11.10}$$

Note that this implies that

$$L0 = L + C + LS \tag{11.11}$$

$$R0 = R + C + RS \tag{11.12}$$

so that the embedded MPEG-1 stereo signal includes a reasonable set of components in its left and right signals. A number of mechanisms are included in the algorithm to reduce the bit rate that needs to be allocated to the T2, T3, and T4 channels based on the material already being transmitted in the L0 and R0 channels.

Although MPEG-2 multichannel encoding achieves its goal of providing a backward-compatible system that reduces total bit rate over that required for five separate channels, it is less efficient in lowering bit rate relative to algorithms without a backward-compatibility constraint. MPEG decided to develop a more efficient nonbackward-compatible multichannel algorithm, the advanced audio coding (AAC) algorithm, for applications beyond stereo. This development is ongoing at this writing and is described later in this chapter.

11.5   MPEG Systems

MPEG Systems supports the key roles of multiplexing and synchronization required to provide meaningful decoding of multimedia material. The MPEG-1 Systems layer was optimized for storage devices and personal computer implementations, resulting in long variable-length packets (long packets being supportable because of a presumed low media error rate and desirable to allow processing of packet headers in software by a general-purpose multiprocessor). The MPEG-2 Systems layer actually has two versions: the program stream, which was optimized with similar criteria to the MPEG-1 Systems layer, and the transport stream, which uses short, fixed-length packets in order to facilitate operation over more noisy channels and the multichannel multiplexing and demultiplexing operations expected in many broadcast applications. All versions share a philosophy of timing based on communicating a common reference time between encoder and decoder and timestamping desired decode and presentation events against this common reference.

11.5.1 Timing

The system or program clock is a common time base maintained by an encoder and decoder. For MPEG-1, it is a 33-bit system clock reference counter driven by a 90-kHz frequency; for MPEG-2, it consists of a 33-bit program clock reference counter incremented by a 9-bit modulo 300 counter driven at 27 MHz (this implies that the 33 most significant bits of the MPEG-2 program clock appear as if they are driven by a 90-kHz frequency and hence equivalent to the MPEG-1 system clock). The encoder periodically samples the value of the system or program clock and sends the current value to the decoder. The decoder compares this value to its own version and either speeds up or slows down its frequency source depending on whether its version is ahead or behind the received reference timestamp. In this manner, the decoder locks its time to the encoder's time.

Given the common system or program clock, the encoder explicitly encodes the value of the system time at which it wants the following key events to occur in the decoder:

- *Presentation time*—the time at which an access unit (a video or audio frame) is to be played in the system target decoder

- *Decode time*—the time at which an access unit is to be decoded in the system target decoder

Because of the assumption of the system target decoder that decode time is instantaneous, presentation and decode times only differ if a reorder buffer is present after the decoding process. In fact, this only occurs for anchor pictures when B-pictures are present in the MPEG video. For B-pictures and for audio frames, presentation and decode times are identical, and only the presentation time is actually sent.

The decode time is critical to establishing one of the key conditions described in the section on rate control above: namely, how to delay the start of decoding until mirror state is obtained (critical during random access for storage media or when first tuning to a stream for broadcast media). If the decode time is ignored, there is no guarantee that the decode buffer will avoid underflow or overflow at some point in the future.

The MPEG-2 Transport Stream makes another specific constraint on the program clock, namely, that the decoder can frequency-lock its audio and video decode sample clocks to the program clock. This allows an MPEG-2 Transport Stream decoder to forgo the necessity of an additional phase locked loop based on presentation timestamps in order to recover each sample clock. This also imposes a higher expectation of fidelity on the MPEG-2 program clock. The key case in which this can become an issue is when the arriving

MPEG-2 stream includes program clock references that arrive earlier or later than they were originally intended, as might occur during remultiplexing or protocol adaptation processes that do not explicitly adjust timestamps (such as ATM transmission). The variation between expected and actual arrival time is equivalent to a noise source being introduced into the decoder's program clock recovery loop, resulting in frequency and phase variations. In extreme cases, these can cause audio pitch variations and color subcarrier (hue) variations in the decoded material, although more typical induced jitter can be readily accommodated in the decoder's loop design.

11.5.2 System and Program Streams

The MPEG-1 System and MPEG-2 Program Streams were both defined primarily for storage applications. A simplified diagram of the MPEG-1 System layer is shown in Figure 11.18.

The MPEG-1 Systems Stream consists of a sequence of *packs*; each pack is actually a collection of packets, one from each elementary stream (video, audio, or data). The pack header includes a system clock reference for use in system timing recovery, as discussed in Section 11.5.1, and miscellaneous other parameters. Packs occasionally include system headers (in a stored stream, typically the first pack contains a system header; other packs might include them if the system header parameters change). The system header includes information required to configure the decoder, or at least verify whether it will be capable of decoding the elementary streams. This information includes number and type of streams; bounds on bit rates in the streams; the relationship between system, audio, and video clocks (which are not necessarily locked together for these streams); and elementary stream decoder buffer sizes required. The system header also indicates whether the stream satisfies the "constrained system parameter stream" limitations on packet rate and system target decoder buffer sizes.

A simplified diagram of the MPEG-2 Program Stream is shown in Figure 11.19. As with MPEG-1 System Streams, MPEG-2 Program Streams include a header to identify the start of the variable-length pack. The PES packet in the Program Stream plays the same role as the packet in an MPEG-1 System Stream and is further described in Section 11.5.4 below.

11.5.3 Transport Streams

A simplified diagram of an MPEG-2 Transport Stream is shown in Figure 11.20. The Transport Stream is composed of fixed-length 188-byte packets, always

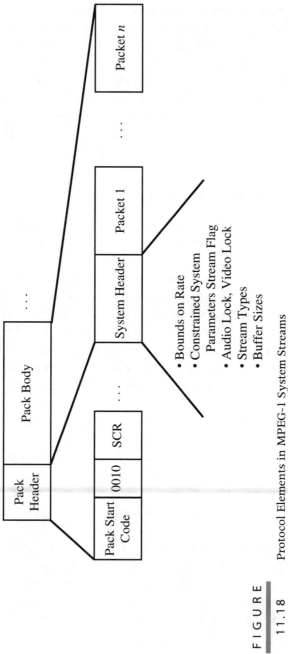

FIGURE

11.18

Protocol Elements in MPEG-1 System Streams

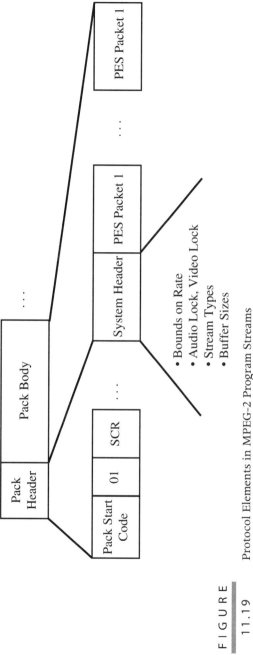

FIGURE
11.19

Protocol Elements in MPEG-2 Program Streams

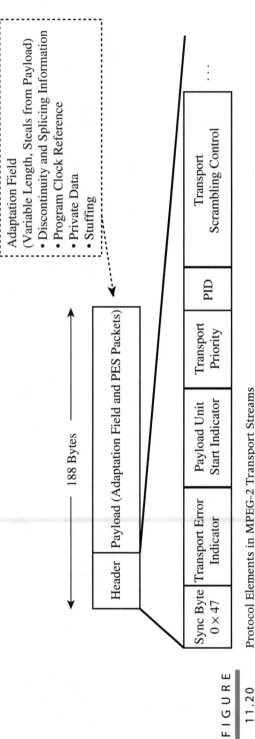

Adaptation Field
(Variable Length, Steals from Payload)
• Discontinuity and Splicing Information
• Program Clock Reference
• Private Data
• Stuffing

188 Bytes

| Header | Payload (Adaptation Field and PES Packets) |

| Sync Byte 0 × 47 | Transport Error Indicator | Payload Unit Start Indicator | Transport Priority | PID | Transport Scrambling Control | ... |

FIGURE
11.20

Protocol Elements in MPEG-2 Transport Streams

including a sync byte of a known value (hexadecimal 47). Since this value may also occur in the data, acquisition of packet boundaries normally consists of looking for the sync byte first, then verifying that it occurs 188 bytes later several times in a row. The remainder of the Transport Stream packet header includes a single-bit error indicator (to signal to a decoder to take concealment action, as the current packet has been damaged somewhere in transmission). The payload unit start indicator provides an easily extracted signal to a decoder that a PES packet or other payload is starting in the current transport packet; this facilitates start-up of decoding. The transport priority is a single bit indicating whether the current packet is high or low priority, although the exact choice of when a packet should be marked high or low priority and how this information should be used are not specified (but sending packets out of order is not allowed). The packet ID (PID) is a 13-bit address that indicates which elementary stream is carried by this packet (or, alternatively, which table type or private data stream is carried by this packet). The transport stream scrambling control is present (as are several other features of the transport stream) to facilitate secure transmission without actually defining the security protocol.

Occasionally, the later 184 bytes of a transport packet will include an adaptation field, whose most important content is the program clock reference, as discussed in Section 10.5.1. This field can also include indicators on discontinuities and on how to splice MPEG streams, private data, stuffing to adjust the Transport Stream rate, and a number of other parameters.

11.5.4   Packetized Elementary Stream (PES) and MPEG-1 Packets

Both MPEG-2 Transport and Program Streams carry a common subelement, the packetized elementary stream (PES) packets. Each PES packet contains information from a unique elementary stream. A simplified diagram of PES packet contents is shown in Figure 11.21.

The PES packet consists of a packet header, including a start code prefix and a stream ID, which identifies the elementary stream that is carried by this PES, in particular 32 for audio and 16 for video. In the case of Program Streams, this is used to determine to which audio or video decoder to send the contents of the packet. In the case of a Transport Stream, the information is redundant because only the PES packets from a single elementary stream may be carried by transport packets with a given PID. The header also contains the packet length and a number of optional fields, the most important of which is the presentation time stamp (PTS), which can be present if an audio or video frame's compressed data starts in this packet, and the decode time stamp (DTS), if a PTS is present and the DTS differs from the PTS.

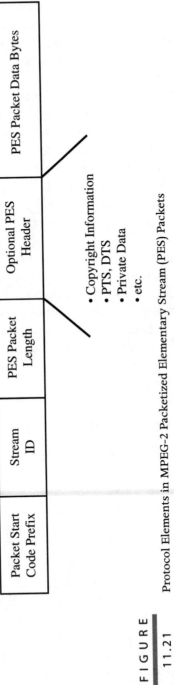

FIGURE
11.21

Protocol Elements in MPEG-2 Packetized Elementary Stream (PES) Packets

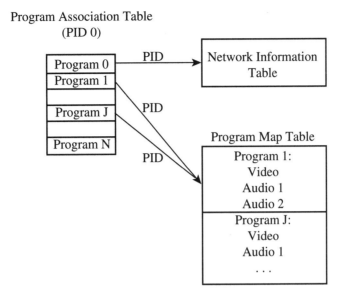

Program Association Table
(PID 0)

| Program 0 |
| Program 1 |
| |
| Program J |
| |
| Program N |

PID → Network Information Table

PID

PID

Program Map Table

Program 1:
Video
Audio 1
Audio 2

Program J:
Video
Audio 1
. . .

FIGURE

11.22   Protocol Elements in MPEG-2 Program-Specific Information

The MPEG-1 packet is essentially identical to the PES packet with the exception that the only fields in the optional PES header area are stuffing, the buffer size for the system target decoder buffer corresponding to this elementary stream, PTS, and DTS.

11.5.5   Program-Specific Information

MPEG-2 defines a key set of tables designed to facilitate the association of specific audio and video elementary streams into collections termed "programs." The typical program consists of one video stream, one or more audio streams (perhaps multiple languages), and zero or more data streams (perhaps teletext or security messages). Figure 11.22 shows how the most important tables are related.

The Program Association Table is always carried on PID 0 in a transport stream. For each program that is contained in the stream, it provides the location (by PID) of the Program Map Table that describes the streams associated with that program. It also provides the PID (associated with the dummy Program 0) of a special table, the Network Information Table, which provides global information about this Transport Stream and others that might be available on the same network.

The Program Map Table contains descriptions for one or more programs of the location (by PID) and characteristics of the individual elementary streams (video, audio, and data) that should be associated to make up that program.

11.6 More MPEG

MPEG continues to work on standardizing several extensions on its current work. This section briefly reviews these efforts to date.

11.6.1 MPEG-4

MPEG-4 started as an effort to target the other extreme of audio-video compression from the moderate to high bit rate entertainment applications of MPEG-1 and MPEG-2, in particular, audio-video compression at bit rates below 64 kbps. (In between MPEG-1 and MPEG-4 lies the ITU-T H.320, H.323, and H.324 standard suites.) This was driven by an interest in video telephony over standard telephone lines.

However, as the work progressed, the need for a standard that would also be well suited to multimedia representations on computer networks, particularly the Internet, became evident. Such networks are characterized by both a high degree of variability and flexibility in both the computational capability of terminals and in transmission characteristics, including bandwidth, and quality of service issues, such as variability in delay and loss of data. MPEG-4 has evolved into a framework designed both to allow for representations of multimedia that rely on more flexible terminals (e.g, with capabilities of rendering and compositing) in order to achieve very high compression efficiency on susceptible material, scaling from extremely low bit rates (a few kbps) to moderately high bit rates (4 Mbps) with many options to match network capabilities.

The MPEG-4 standard embraces several major areas:

- *Coding of visual objects*—extended from MPEG-1 and 2 to include both more algorithmic flexibility in basic pixel-oriented video coding (to extend applicability down to lower bit rates) and the addition of tools for compositing and rendering other graphical elements in addition to pixel-oriented compressed material.

- *Coding of audio objects*—extended to support audio compression algorithms for lower bit rates (generally speech specific) and to allow compositing of synthesized sounds and effects.

- *Scene description and user interaction*—tools for the (potentially user-modifiable) hierarchical description of elements of a scene that are to be combined to generate the displayed image.

- *Systems*—protocols for handling demultiplexing, buffer management, and timing as well as the delivery multimedia integration framework (DMIF), a sophisticated protocol to provide a transparent interface and control between distributed MPEG-4 applications connected over a variety of transport networks.

Video Objects

MPEG-4 builds around a core designed for very low bit rate video coding. This core is a motion compensated DCT algorithm but with extensions from the MPEG-1 and 2 video compression algorithms discussed earlier in the chapter. In particular, MPEG-4 allows much more content specific motion compensation, including standard 8×8 or 16×16 block-based motion estimation, global motion compensation based on eight motion parameters describing an affine transformation, or motion compensation of "sprites" (a *static sprite,* such as a large still image describing panoramic background, and motion compensated from image to image; or a set of small regions of the image, *dynamic sprites,* generated throughout the scene and then motion compensated).

MPEG-4 adds tools and algorithms for efficient encoding of visual objects beyond images and video, including tools for compression of textures and texture mapping on 2D and 3D meshes, compression of implicit 2D meshes, and compression of time-varying geometry streams that animate meshes. In addition, care is given to scaleable algorithms, that is, the ability to decode only a part of a bit stream and reconstruct images or image sequences with either reduced spatial resolution, reduced temporal resolution, or reduced quality.

Scene Description and User Interaction

MPEG-4 provides a facility for combining individual visual objects into a scene using a hierarchical description. The top level of the hierarchy defines the global coordinate system (in space and time) for the scene. Each child has a local coordinate system, which is located by reference to its offset within its parent's coordinate system. The nodes of this description tree can be dynamically added and deleted, and attributes (such as position within the parent's coordinate system) can be changed. The ability to manipulate the elements of the scene description at the decoder enables user interaction with the visual objects, for example, the ability to add, delete, or relocate elements of the scene before compositing.

Audio Objects

Audio objects are defined for several types of audio material. Natural sound can be compressed at bit rates ranging from 2–64 kbps. Three types of compression algorithms are used to span this range. For the lowest bit rate of 2–6 kbps, parametric speech coding for 8 kHz sampling is used. For intermediate bit rates of 6–24 kbps, MPEG-4 uses code excited linear prediction optimized for speech coding at 8 or 16 kHz sampling frequency. Starting at 16 kbps, MPEG-4 allows the use of the AAC compression algorithm described later in this chapter for very high-quality general purpose audio compression.

In addition to compression of natural sound, MPEG-4 supports tools for representation of synthesized sound, both text-to-speech synthesis and score driven synthesis. The latter is a generalized version of the MIDI protocol for describing musical score information to a synthesizer.

Multiplexing and Transport

The audio-video objects of MPEG-4 are transmitted in *elementary streams*. Such streams include information about parameters, such as required decoder resources (e.g, image size, buffer size) and expectations for the quality of service that will be maintained during transmission. The access unit layer collects information from each elementary stream into independently addressable elements, for example, video frames.

Two layers of multiplexing are applied to access units. The first, an internal MPEG-4 multiplexing, is termed FlexMux. This allows low-overhead grouping of access units with similar characteristics, for instance, similar expectations on quality of service. The transport multiplexing, or TransMux, layer is a transport mechanism defined outside of MPEG-4. If the TransMux provides all the necessary functionality, then no FlexMux is required. Examples of TransMux layers are RTP/UDP/IP, AAL5/ATM, or MPEG-2's Transport Stream. Similar to the MPEG Systems Layer previously discussed, display- or playout-timing information is carried with each access unit, and a decoder model of buffer state is used to define a legal MPEG-4 stream as one that does not overflow or underflow an idealized decoder with buffers of the sizes specified in the stream.

In addition to multiplexing mechanisms, MPEG-4 includes the *delivery multimedia integration framework* (DMIF). This is a transparent interface for interacting MPEG-4 peers, regardless of whether these peers are located remotely from each other across a network or are collocated. DMIF can support multiple peers, both interactive (able to react to signals from other peers) and not. DMIF can be responsible for establishing channels for elementary streams (or

FlexMux combinations of elementary streams) with the desired quality of service and bandwidth, or even for modifying these dynamically during a session, for instance when a user asks to obtain dedicated high-quality channels to improve the received quality over that achieved using only a ubiquitous but lower-quality network (e.g., the Internet).

11.6.2   Digital Storage Media Command and Control

Digital storage media command and control (DSM-CC) addresses the issues of how decoding terminals should interact with either local or remote storage devices containing MPEG material. Typical applications are CD-based playback terminals and interactive video services over a network. The DSM-CC standard provides a protocol for client-server interactions over possibly heterogeneous networks with varying capacities in both directions. It includes specific protocols for establishing connections, allocating resources, and exchanging control messages during sessions. The primary functions addressed by DSM-CC are

- configuration
- session management
- resource management
- compatibility assurance
- download
- service gateway management
- stream service control
- file service control
- database service control
- event management
- stream timelines

11.6.3   Advanced Audio Coding

The advanced audio coding (AAC) algorithm is an alternative for MPEG-2 audio, developed to overcome experimentation that showed the backward-compatible multichannel version of the original MPEG-1 audio algorithm performed relatively poorly compared to algorithms optimized with the requirement of multichannel capability in mind. The AAC algorithm does not require backward compatibility with two-channel MPEG-1 audio compression.

AAC audio provides very high-quality audio encoding at 64 kbps per channel compressed. It can support up to 48 main audio channels, 16 low-frequency effect channels, 16 overdub/multilingual channels, and 16 data streams in a single compressed audio stream, organized into up to 16 programs. AAC provides several levels of complexity through its profiles: Main Profile, Low Complexity Profile, and Scaleable Sampling Rate Profile.

AAC is able to achieve substantially better compression efficiency than other contemporary multichannel audio compression algorithms by using several compression techniques:

- a fine-frequency filter bank for frequency domain decomposition
- temporal noise shaping
- backward-adaptive linear prediction
- joint stereo coding
- Huffman coding of quantized components
- a large range of sampling rates, bit rates, and number of channels

AAC coding has been shown to provide slightly better audio quality at 320 kbps than MPEG-2 backward-compatible multichannel encoding provides at 640 kbps.

11.6.4   The Professional or 4:2:2 Profile

An additional profile is under consideration for applications that allow substantially higher bit rate than the main profile, but which demand both higher quality and often simplified editing properties (for instance, in professional studio applications). The professional profile supports the 4:2:2 chroma subsampling format of professional uncompressed digital video as well as slightly larger image sizes than the main profile (to ensure coverage into the blanking in traditional analog video formats), larger rates (up to 50 Mbps), and larger buffer sizes (up to 9.5 Mbits).

11.6.5   MPEG-7

MPEG-7 is a new effort to define a standard for description of various types of multimedia information. While text can be relatively easily searched by computer, it is more difficult to find particular pieces of audio and video based on their content. MPEG-7 descriptions may be located either with data, such as still pictures, graphics, 3-D models, audio, speech, and video, or located remotely with a bidirectional link to the data described. The syntax for description will be optimized to permit fast searching.

11.7   Summary

The MPEG standard suite is a comprehensive set of video and audio de-compression algorithm specifications, as well as specifications of how the compressed bitstreams can be multiplexed together and how the resulting decoded media can be synchronized. MPEG is used in a number of substantial commercial applications, including playback of media from disk storage, digital broadcast of audio-video programming over a variety of channels, point-to-point switched connections for delivery of digital audio-video material, high-definition televi-sion, and networked multimedia, as well as in a larger number of specialized commercial and noncommercial applications.

MPEG compression relies on a number of fundamental techniques described in the abstract and in other specific applications throughout this book. For video, these include temporal prediction from video frame to video frame based on a simple model of motion, the application of the DCT to prediction residuals, quantization to select the extent to which information about individual DCT co-efficients will be retained, and the application of both runlength and Huffman lossless variable-rate codes to extract remaining statistical redundancy in the quantized DCT coefficients. The audio standard relies on subband decomposi-tion of the audio signal, followed by different levels of quantization for samples in each subband, with quantizer resolution generally based on a sophisticated frequency domain analysis of energy to exploit human auditory masking (the tendency to not hear spectral energy near a strong tone). The MPEG Systems standards provide a number of protocols to aid in multiplexing, synchroniza-tion (based on the concept of timestamps to construct a common reference time at both encoder and decoder), and general organization and manipulation of compressed audio-video material.

A Speech Quality and Intelligibility

APPENDIX

A.1 Introduction

In order to determine the performance of a speech coder, it is necessary to measure the intelligibility and the quality of the speech produced by the coder. The term *intelligibility* usually refers to whether the output speech is easily understandable; the term *quality* ideally is an indicator of how "natural" the speech sounds. It is possible for a coder to produce highly intelligible speech that is low quality: the speech may sound very machinelike, and the speaker is not identifiable. On the other hand, it is unlikely that unintelligible speech would be called high quality, but there are situations where perceptually pleasing speech does not have high intelligibility. A particular example of this latter phenomenon is the output of a delta modulator operating on speech that has been excessively low-pass filtered. The filtering causes a loss of intelligibility, but the elimination of high frequencies produces sounds that are subjectively more pleasing to the ear.

Although there are many techniques for objectively evaluating the performance of speech coders, such as signal-to-quantization noise ratio and spectral distortion measures, which are useful for initial evaluations, the final judgment of the quality or intelligibility of speech coders requires subjective testing to account for the human perceptual mechanism. However, the design and conduct of subjective listening tests is not trivial if maximum confidence in the test results is desired.

For each speech coder tested, the spoken utterances must be carefully selected to guarantee that the various speech sounds are well represented. For example, it is known that some speech coders perform well for all-voiced speech but do not accurately reproduce unvoiced sounds. Similarly, some coders perform better for low-pitched voices than for higher-pitched voices, and hence, the speakers chosen for the experiment should be representative of the real-world environment, with female as well as male speakers, if appropriate. The experience or training required of the listeners must also be considered with respect to what will be encountered in the user environment. Finally, the utterances must be presented to the listeners in an order that does not bias the results.

In this appendix, we will briefly describe objective performance indicators, intelligibility measures, and measures of speech quality.

A.2 Phases of Speech Coder Evaluation

When a speech coder is being developed, a combination of informal objective and subjective tests, and then formal subjective tests, are used to evaluate performance. Informal objective measures such as signal-to-noise ratios or spectral distance measures are used for initial screening; when these objective values seem acceptable, informal listening tests, perhaps side-by-side comparisons with original speech and other candidate coders, are performed. If these results are promising, the coder developer may conduct, or pay someone else to conduct, formal subjective testing that gives the current best-known indicators of performance. Of course, these stages are successively more time consuming and expensive, so the last stage, formal testing, is employed sparingly compared to the first two informal stages of tests.

A.3 Informal Tests

Under the heading of informal tests we include easily calculated objective measures such as signal-to-noise ratio and spectral distance, in addition to informal subjective listening tests. None of these tests are well calibrated, and they can be misinterpreted easily, but they can be useful to experienced speech researchers.

A.3.1 Objective Measures

An easily computed measure of waveform coder performance is the signal-to-noise ratio (SNR), which is given in decibels by

$$\text{SNR(dB)} = 10 \log_{10} \frac{<s^2(n)>}{<[s(n) - \hat{s}(n)]^2>} \qquad \text{(A.1)}$$

where $s(n)$ is the input speech, $\hat{s}(n)$ is the coder output speech, and $< \cdot >$ denotes time averaging over the entire utterance. The segmental SNR (SNRSEG) is often claimed to be more indicative of subjective performance for speech inputs. It is obtained by first computing the SNR in equation (A.1) over many nonoverlapping blocks of data (often excluding silence) and then taking the arithmetic mean over the blocks. Thus, following Jayant and Noll (1984), and letting SNRB_j denote the SNR for the jth block, for K blocks of data,

$$\text{SNRSEG} = \frac{1}{K} \sum_{j=1}^{K} \text{SNRB}_j \qquad \text{(A.2)}$$

Both SNR and SNRSEG usually rank-order the performance of coders within a particular class, such as DPCM, correctly, but how much of a difference is perceptually significant is not clear. Furthermore, using SNR or SNRSEG to compare PCM with DPCM can be completely misleading.

A spectral distance measure introduced by Itakura (1975b) that is computable from LPC coefficients is

$$d = \ln \left[\frac{\mathbf{AVA}^T}{\mathbf{BVB}^T} \right] \qquad \text{(A.3)}$$

where the row vectors $\mathbf{A}$ and $\mathbf{B}$ are augmented predictor coefficient vectors, $\mathbf{A} = [1 - a_1 - a_2 \cdots - a_N]$ and $\mathbf{B} = [1 - b_1 - b_2 \cdots - b_N]$. The a_k coefficients are calculated from the original input speech, the b_k coefficients are calculated from the speech coder output speech, and $\mathbf{V}$ is the autocorrelation matrix of the speech coder output. The quantity $d \geq 0$ and, according to Sambur and Jayant (1976), $d \leq 0.3$ implies that the spectra of the input speech and the speech coder output speech are not significantly different.

Another spectral distance measure that is often used is given by

$$\text{CD} \cong \frac{10}{\ln 10 \sqrt{2 \sum_{j=1}^{N} [c_s(j) - c_{\hat{s}}(j)]^2}} \qquad \text{(A.4)}$$

where $c_s(j)$ and $c_{\hat{s}}(j)$, $j = 1, 2, \ldots, N$, are the cepstral coefficients of the input speech and the coder output speech, respectively. Cepstral coefficients are the inverse Fourier transform of the logarithm of the power spectrum, but they can also be calculated from the LPC coefficients $\{a_i, i = 1, \ldots, N\}$ as

$$c_s(j) = a_j + \sum_{k=1}^{j-1} \left(\frac{k}{j}\right) c_s(k) a_{j-k} \tag{A.5}$$

$j \geq 1$ (Rabiner and Schafer 1978). A CD value of about 0.5 dB corresponds to 8-bit μ-law PCM, with larger CD values indicating poorer performance.

A.3.2 Subjective Tests

One of the most effective ways to compare two speech coders is simply to perform side-by-side listening tests. Such tests are relatively easy to conduct, but they only give binary preference results. They do not indicate in any way how close the two coders are, and if the two coders have different types of distortion, it may be difficult for the listeners to choose one over the other. When a coder is compared to 8-bit μ-law PCM, if the coder is not equivalent in performance, it is difficult to say exactly how close in performance it really is. Additionally, if, say, a delta modulator is compared to a subband coder, the delta modulator may have a "hissing" distortion, while the subband coder may produce reverberation. The listener then makes a somewhat arbitrary choice based upon which type of distortion is less offensive to the individual, which is not a reliable performance indicator. However, side-by-side listening tests continue to enjoy widespread use.

For a particular application, such as cellular communications or voice messaging, it is advantageous to let potential users actually experiment with a version of the coder in as natural an environment as possible. This approach has the advantage of not using relatively short, recorded, unrepresentative speech segments for evaluation, and it puts the user in the mind-set of using the system rather than evaluating synthesized speech. In other words, the user becomes more concerned with whether the system achieves the desired goal, rather than trying to listen for "problems" in the output speech. Of course, the difficulty with this approach is that achieving a natural environment implies the implementation of a complete prototype system.

A.4   Formal Tests

There are a number of formal testing procedures that are commonly employed to establish the intelligibility and quality of speech coders. The discussion is separated into tests for intelligibility and tests for quality; however, some tests clearly measure both, and these are discussed in Section A.4.2.

A.4.1   Intelligibility

The Diagnostic Rhyme Test (DRT) was devised by Voiers (1977b) to test the intelligibility of coders known to produce speech of lower quality. Rhyme tests are so named because the listener must determine which consonant was spoken when presented with a pair of rhyming words; that is, the listener is asked to distinguish between word pairs such as meat-beat, pool-tool, saw-thaw, and caught-taught. Each pair of words differs in only one of the six phonemic attributes: voicing, nasality, sustention, sibilation, graveness, and compactness. Specifically, the listener is presented with one spoken word from a pair and asked to decide which word was spoken. The final DRT score is the percent correct responses computed according to

$$P = \frac{R - W}{T} \times 100 \tag{A.6}$$

where R is the number correctly chosen, W is the number of incorrect choices, and T is the total of word pairs tested. Usually, $75 \leq \text{DRT} \leq 95$, with a "good" being about 90 (Papamichalis 1987). A more detailed listing of the results is available from Dynastat (Papamichalis 1987).

There is another test, available from Dynastat, called the Modified Rhyme Test (MRT). In the MRT the listener is asked to decide which one of six words has been spoken. The six words may have different beginning or ending consonants. The MRT is not widely used at this time.

A.4.2   Quality

The Articulation Index (AI) is an objective measure of speech quality that was originally introduced in 1947 and is still frequently quoted (Beranek 1947; French and Steinberg 1947). The AI is really a frequency-weighted signal-to-noise ratio calculation. The frequency range from 200 to 6100 Hz is divided into 20 unequal-width subbands (this is the frequency weighting), as shown in Table A.1, and the signal-to-quantization-noise ratio in $\text{dB}(\text{SNR}_i)$ is computed for each of the subbands, $i = 1, 2, \ldots, 20$. The SNR_i values are limited to 30 dB, normalized to 1, and averaged, so

$$\text{AI} = 0.05 \sum_{i=1}^{20} [\min\{\text{SNR}_i, 30\}/30] \tag{A.7}$$

Note that limiting speech to the telephone band of 200 to 3200 Hz automatically reduces the AI to 90%, or 0.90. A primary impediment to the use of the AI is the complexity of implementation associated with 20 bandpass filters.

| T A B L E | Frequency Bands (in Hz) of Equal Contribution to the Articulation Index |||||
| A.1 |
Number	Limits	Mean	Number	Limits	Mean
1	200 to 330	270	11	1660 to 1830	1740
2	330 to 430	380	12	1830 to 2020	1920
3	430 to 560	490	13	2020 to 2240	2130
4	560 to 700	630	14	2240 to 2500	2370
5	700 to 840	770	15	2500 to 2820	2660
6	840 to 1000	920	16	2820 to 3200	3000
7	1000 to 1150	1070	17	3200 to 3650	3400
8	1150 to 1310	1230	18	3650 to 4250	3950
9	1310 to 1480	1400	19	4250 to 5050	4650
10	1480 to 1660	1570	20	5050 to 6100	5600

To establish a Mean Opinion Score (MOS) for a coder, the listeners are asked to classify the speech coder output as excellent (5), good (4), fair (3), poor (2), or bad (1). Alternatively, the listeners may be asked to classify the coded speech according to the perceptible distortion present by associating the output with one of the impairment categories: imperceptible (5), barely perceptible but not annoying (4), perceptible and annoying (3), annoying but not objectionable (2), or very annoying and objectionable (1).

The numbers in parentheses are used to assign a numerical value to the subjective evaluations, and the numerical ratings of all listeners are averaged to produce a MOS for the coder. Many times, the standard deviation of the numerical ratings is also computed to aid in assessing the utility of the MOS thus obtained. A MOS between 4.0 and 4.5 usually indicates high quality. For example, 8-bit $\mu = 255$ log-PCM was recently judged to have a MOS of about 4.5, with a standard deviation of near 0.6.

It is important to compute the variance of MOS values since the large variances indicate unreliability of the test. Since a large variance can occur if listeners do not know what the categories such as "good" and "bad" mean, it is sometimes useful to present examples of good and bad speech to the listeners before the test to calibrate the five-point scale (Papamichalis 1987). One study revealed that MOS scores taken under similar circuit conditions in different countries with native languages and listeners did not easily translate between locations; that is, the MOS needed to be adjusted to get a reliable indicator of

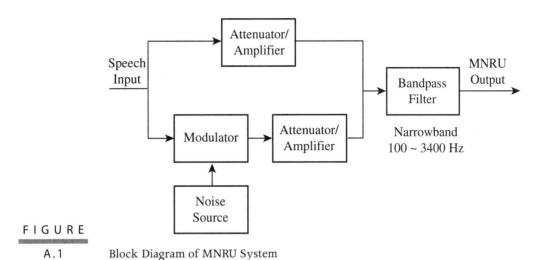

A.1   Block Diagram of MNRU System

quality (Goodman and Nash 1982). The MOSs for a variety of speech coders and noise conditions are given by Daumer (1982).

The Diagnostic Acceptability Measure (DAM), developed by Dynastat (Voiers 1977), is an attempt to make the measurement of speech quality more systematic. For the DAM, it is critical that the listener crews be highly trained and repeatedly calibrated in order to get meaningful results. The listeners are each presented with sentences taken from the Harvard 1965 list of phonetically balanced sentences, such as "Cats and dogs each hate the other" and "The pipe began to rust while new," that have been processed by the speech coder of interest. The listener is asked to assign a number between 1 and 100 to characteristics in three classifications, signal qualities, background qualities, and total effect. The ratings of each characteristic are weighted and used in a multiple nonlinear regression. Finally, adjustments are made to compensate for listener performance. A typical DAM score is 45–55%, with 50% corresponding to a "good" system.

The modulated noise reference unit (MNRU) opinion-equivalent Q is being employed more often recently because of its appearance in an ITU-T recommendation for waveform coder evaluation (CCITT 1984; Kitawaki and Nagabuchi 1988). In a paired comparison or opinion test, the coded speech is compared to a reference signal with a fixed, but adjustable, level of speech-correlated noise generated using the MNRU system shown in Figure A.1 (CCITT 1984, 1988). Reference signals with different signal-to-speech-correlated noise ratios, which is the Q in decibels, are obtained by adjusting the relative gains of the attenuator/amplifiers. That value of Q for which the subjective match of the MNRU output with the coded speech is best is the quantitative performance indicator. There are narrowband and wideband MNRU systems; the narrowband Q is denoted by Q_N. This is a fairly accurate method for speech quality assessment for waveform coders, since the MNRU distortion tends to mimic waveform coder noise. For coders with other types of distortion, it may not be as helpful.

A.5   Important Considerations

There are several important considerations that are common to all performance tests for speech coders. First, there must be enough speakers, and their characteristics sufficiently varied, to span the entire class of possible users. Second, sufficient speech data must be processed to include all eventualities. In the well-structured tests like DRT and DAM, the speech material is fixed and a tentative guideline has been obtained for the number and type of speakers. Thus, for these tests, these two issues are less controversial. However, for the AI, MOS, and side-by-side comparisons, there is no rule as to how many speakers and how much data is enough. It is certainly true that "more is better," and one possible approach is to consider new speakers and material until no new distortions are found in the speech coder output. Although this approach is somewhat open-ended, it is viable in the hands of workers familiar with speech coding.

A third important point is that for most applications, both quality and intelligibility are important, and both should be tested for. Often, perceptually pleasing speech is accepted without evaluating intelligibility.

B

Proof that Huffman Codes Minimize $\bar{l}$

We shall show that applying Huffman's algorithm to any given $\{p_j, 1 \le j \le M\}$ generates a prefix code tree that minimizes $\bar{l} := \sum_{j=1}^{M} p_j l_j$, where l_j is the depth of the jth terminal node. First we show that binary Huffman codes are optimum in this sense; then we extend to coding alphabets of arbitrary size D.

Assume $\mathcal{C} = \{\mathbf{x}_1, \ldots, \mathbf{x}_M\}$ is a minimum-$\bar{l}$ binary prefix code. By Morse's principle we know that $\mathcal{C}$ must assign to the least likely source symbol, a_M, a codeword $\mathbf{x}_M$ whose length l_M is at least as long as that of any other codeword. In other words, $\mathbf{x}_M$ must be assigned to one of the nodes on the deepest level of the tree. Moreover, it cannot be the lone node on that level. For, if it were, we could replace it by its ancestor on the previous level, thereby shortening it by one binary digit while leaving all other codewords unchanged; that would result in a prefix code with an $\bar{l}$ smaller than that of $\mathcal{C}$, which would contradict our assumption. Applying Morse's principle a second time, we see that $\mathbf{x}_{M-1}$ also must be assigned to a node on the deepest level. Since shuffling the assignment of codewords to nodes on any fixed level does not affect $\bar{l}$, we can assume without loss of generality that $\mathbf{x}_{M-1}$ and $\mathbf{x}_M$ stem from a common ancestor, with $\mathbf{x}_{M-1}$, say, ending in a 0 and $\mathbf{x}_M$ ending in a 1. Let us now redefine l_{M-1} to be the depth of the node that is the common ancestor of $\mathbf{x}_{M-1}$ and $\mathbf{x}_M$, while letting each l_j for $1 \le j \le M - 2$ retain its original meaning. This converts our problem into that of constructing a binary branching tree with $M - 1$ terminal nodes so as to minimize

$$\sum_{j=1}^{M-2} p_j l_j + (l_{M-1} + 1)(p_{M-1} + p_M) \tag{B.1}$$

If we now introduce a modified probability distribution $\{p_j^*, 1 \leq j \leq M - 1\}$ defined by $p_{M-1}^* = p_{M-1} + p_M$ and $p_j^* = p_j$ for $1 \leq j \leq M - 2$, then we may reexpress our goal as that of constructing a prefix tree with $M - 1$ terminal nodes that minimizes

$$\sum_{j=1}^{M-2} p_j^* l_j + (l_{M-1} + 1) p_{M-1}^* = p_{M-1}^* + \sum_{j=1}^{M-1} p_j^* l_j \qquad \text{(B.2)}$$

But $p_{M-1}^* = p_{M-1} + p_M$ is a constant of the problem that is not affected by how we construct the tree. Hence, we have converted our original problem of finding a tree with M terminal nodes that is optimum for $\{p_j, 1 \leq j \leq M\}$ to that of finding a tree with $M - 1$ terminal nodes that is optimum for the modified probabilities $\{p_j^*, 1 \leq j \leq M - 1\}$. This, in turn, can be reduced to an $(M - 2)$-node problem by assigning the codewords corresponding to the smallest two of the modified probabilities p_j^* to a pair of terminal nodes that possess a common immediate ancestor. But that is precisely what the next merge in Huffman's algorithm does! Iterating this argument a total of $M - 1$ times establishes that Huffman's algorithm produces minimum-$\bar{l}$ prefix codes in the binary case.

We may argue similarly for general D. Note first that in an optimum code any fan not on the deepest level must be a complete D-ary fan; otherwise, $\bar{l}$ could be lowered by moving a terminal node from the deepest level into a vacant spot in an incomplete fan on a shallower level. By shifting nodes among fans on the deepest level, which leaves $\bar{l}$ invariant, we can arrange things so that there is at most one incomplete fan. The reasoning in the next paragraph establishes that this lone possibly incomplete fan must contain exactly $J = 2 + (M - 2) \bmod (D - 1)$ terminal nodes to which we may without loss of generality assign the J least likely source symbols. From that point on exactly the same reasoning used in the binary case establishes the $\bar{l}$-minimizing property of Huffman codes for general D.

To see why the lone incomplete fan must contain $2 + (M - 2) \bmod (D - 1)$ terminal nodes, first consider *complete* D-ary trees, which are those in which every internal node has a full complement of D branches stemming from it. A trivial induction argument shows that a D-ary complete tree with I internal nodes has $D + I(D - 1)$ terminal nodes. (The root is not considered to be an internal node in this context.) Next recall from the previous paragraph that there is an optimum prefix code tree composed only of full fans with the possible exception of one fan on the deepest level that has J branches, where $2 \leq J \leq D$. If this tree has I internal nodes, then it has $D + (I - 1)(D - 1) + J - 1$ terminal nodes because J terminal nodes are created and one is destroyed when the fan with J branches is made to stem from what had been a terminal node in the otherwise complete tree. Since the tree in question must have M terminal nodes because it is a prefix code tree for an M-ary source, we have $M = D + (I - 1)(D - 1) + J - 1 = J + I(D - 1)$, which we rewrite in the form

$$J - 2 = M - 2 - I(D - 1) \tag{B.3}$$

Since $0 \le J - 2 \le D - 2$, we know that $J - 2 \bmod (D - 1) = J - 2$. Evaluating both sides of the above equation modulo $D - 1$ therefore yields

$$J - 2 = (M - 2) \bmod (D - 1) \tag{B.4}$$

or $J = 2 + (M - 2) \bmod (D - 1)$, as advertised.

C

Proof That Every UD Code Satisfies the Kraft Inequality

We shall show that the codeword lengths $\{l_j\}$ of *any* UD D-ary code must satisfy the Kraft inequality,

$$\sum_j D^{-l_j} \le 1 \tag{C.1}$$

For fixed n and L, let A_L denote the number of source words of length n that are assigned a code string of length L. There are only D^L distinct sequences of length L from the code alphabet, so unique decipherability requires that $A_L \le D^L$, or

$$1 \ge D^{-L} A_L \tag{C.2}$$

The length $l(\underline{u})$ of the codeword assigned to a source word $\underline{u}$ of length n must satisfy

$$nl_{\min} \le l(\underline{u}) \le nl_{\max} \tag{C.3}$$

where $l_{\min}$ and $l_{\max}$ are, respectively, the smallest and largest values of $l(u)$ for any $u \in \mathcal{U}$. Accordingly, we have

$$nl_{\max} > \sum_{L=nl_{\min}}^{L=nl_{\max}} 1 \ge \sum_{L=nl_{\min}}^{L=nl_{\max}} D^{-L} A_L \overset{(a)}{=} \sum_{L=nl_{\min}}^{L=nl_{\max}} D^{-L} \sum_{\{\underline{u}\in\mathcal{U}^n:l(\underline{u})=L\}} 1 \tag{C.4}$$

where (a) holds because

$$A_L = |\{\underline{u} : l(\underline{u}) = L\}| \tag{C.5}$$

It follows that

$$nl_{max} > \sum_{L=nl_{min}}^{L=nl_{max}} \sum_{\{\underline{u}:\in\mathcal{U}^n:l(\underline{u})=L\}} D^{-L} = \sum_{L=nl_{min}}^{L=nl_{max}} \sum_{\{\underline{u}:\in\mathcal{U}^n:l(\underline{u})=L\}} D^{-l(\underline{u})}$$

$$= \sum_{\underline{u}\in\mathcal{U}^n} D^{-l(\underline{u})} \quad \text{(C.6)}$$

Recalling that the codeword for $\underline{u} = (u_1, \ldots, u_n)$ is the concatenation of the codewords for $u_1, u_2, \ldots$ through u_n, we have $l(\underline{u}) = l(u_1) + l(u_2) + \cdots + l(u_n)$. Hence,

$$\sum_{\underline{u}\in\mathcal{U}^n} D^{-l(\underline{u})} = \sum_{u_1\in\mathcal{U}} \sum_{u_2\in\mathcal{U}} \cdots \sum_{u_n\in\mathcal{U}} D^{-[l(u_1)+l(u_2)+\cdots+l(u_n)]}$$

$$= \sum_{u_1\in\mathcal{U}} D^{-l(u_1)} \sum_{u_2\in\mathcal{U}} D^{-l(u_2)} \cdots \sum_{u_n\in\mathcal{U}} D^{-l(u_n)} \quad \text{(C.7)}$$

$$= \left(\sum_{u\in\mathcal{U}} D^{-l(u)}\right)^n$$

We conclude that UD implies that

$$nl_{max} > \left(\sum_{u\in\mathcal{U}} D^{-l(u)}\right)^n \quad \text{(C.8)}$$

and hence that

$$\frac{\log(n) + \log(l_{max})}{n} > \log\left(\sum_{u\in\mathcal{U}} D^{-l(u)}\right) \quad \text{(C.9)}$$

for every n. Sending $n \to \infty$ converts this to

$$0 \geq \log\left(\sum_{u\in\mathcal{U}} D^{-l(u)}\right) \quad \text{(C.10)}$$

or

$$1 \geq \sum_{u\in\mathcal{U}} D^{-l(u)} \quad \text{(C.11)}$$

That is, UD implies satisfaction of the Kraft inequality.

D Behavior of Approximations to Entropy Rate

Recall the definitions $H_n = n^{-1}H(U_1, \ldots, U_n)$ and $h_n = H(U_n|U_{n-1}, \ldots, U_1)$. We seek to justify the following statements in Section 2.11.2:

(a) h_n approaches a limit, call it h, in a monotonic nonincreasing manner.

(b) $h_n \leq H_n$ for all n.

(c) H_n also approaches a limit, call it H, in a monotonic nonincreasing manner.

(d) h and H are equal.

Toward establishing (a) we note that

$$h_{n+1} = H(U_{n+1}|U_n, \ldots, U_1) \leq H(U_{n+1}|U_n, \ldots, U_2) \tag{D.1}$$

where we have used the fact established in Section 2.10 that reducing the amount of conditioning can only increase entropy. Because $\{U_k\}$ is stationary, the right-hand member of the above equation will not change if we decrement all the time indices in it by 1. Thus,

$$h_{n+1} \leq H(U_n|U_{n-1}, \ldots, U_1) = h_n \tag{D.2}$$

which establishes the nonincreasing nature of $\{h_n\}$. Since $h_n \geq 0$ for every n, it follows that $\{h_n\}$ must converge to some number $h \geq 0$.

For (b) we use the chain rule to write

$$\begin{aligned} nH_n &= H(U_1, \ldots, U_n) \\ &= H(U_1) + H(U_2|U_1) + \cdots + H(U_n|U_{n-1}, \ldots, U_1) \\ &= h_1 + h_2 + \cdots + h_n \end{aligned} \tag{D.3}$$

From (a) we know that h_n is the smallest of the n terms on the right-hand side, so $nH_n \geq nh_n$, which establishes (b).

To show (c) we write

$$H_{n-1} - H_n = \frac{h_1 + h_2 + \cdots + h_{n-1}}{n-1} - \frac{h_1 + h_2 + \cdots + h_n}{n}$$

$$= (h_1 + h_2 + \cdots + h_{n-1})(\frac{1}{n-1} - \frac{1}{n}) - \frac{h_n}{n} \qquad \text{(D.4)}$$

$$= \frac{1}{n} \cdot (\frac{h_1 + h_2 + \cdots + h_{n-1}}{n-1} - h_n) \geq \frac{1}{n} \cdot (h_{n-1} - h_n) \geq 0$$

where both inequalities follow from (a). Thus, $\{H_n\}$ also is monotonic non-increasing and bounded from below by 0 and hence must converge to some number $H \geq 0$.

Taking the limit as $n \to \infty$ in (b) yields $h \leq H$. Therefore, to establish (d) it suffices to show that $H \leq h$. Toward this end we write

$$H_{n+m} = \frac{1}{n+m} \cdot [H(U_1, \ldots, U_{n-1}) + h_n + h_{n+1} + \ldots + h_{n+m}] \qquad \text{(D.5)}$$

Since $h_n + \cdots + h_{n+m} \leq (m+1)h_n$ by (a), we have

$$H_{n+m} \leq \frac{1}{n+m} \cdot H(U_1, \ldots, U_{n-1}) + \frac{m+1}{n+m} h_n \qquad \text{(D.6)}$$

Keeping n fixed and letting $m \to \infty$, we see that the left-hand side approaches H by definition, while the first term on the right-hand side approaches 0 and the second term on the right-hand side approaches h_n. Accordingly, sending $m \to \infty$ yields $H \leq h_n$. Finally, letting $n \to \infty$ in this result yields $H \leq h$. We have shown that h and H are equal.

Proof of Forward March Property for LZY

We need to show that for all $n \geq 1$, the $n + 1$st LZY word W_{n+1} always penetrates at least as deeply into the data sequence as does W_n. Observe that every W_n for $n \geq 1$ has length at least 2, since we can at least copy one of the singletons present even in D_0 before appending the one-symbol extension. Cases in which the length of W_n is exactly 2 are trivial because W_n then penetrates only to position $n + 1$, but W_{n+1} starts at position $n + 1$, has length at least 2, and therefore penetrates at least to position $n + 2 > n + 1$. In particular, W_1 always consists of the first two source symbols, so the desired result is true for $n = 1$. We use proof by induction, the inductive hypothesis being that for all $1 \leq k \leq n$, W_k ends at or to the right of where W_{k-1} ends. To prove the theorem we must show that this holds for $k = n + 1$, too. Let $\tilde{W}_n$ denote all but the terminal symbol of W_n. Since we have already handled the case in which W_n has length 2, we may assume that W_n has length at least 3, or equivalently, that $\tilde{W}_n$ has length at least 2. This implies that $\tilde{W}_n$ is a copy not of one of the singletons that was in D_0 but of one of the words $W_1, \ldots, W_{n-1}$ associated with positions 1 through $n - 1$. Let L, where $1 \leq L < n$, denote the position whose dictionary entry W_L is copied to form $\tilde{W}_n$, and let R denote the position at which W_L ends. The symbols in positions L through R match the ones in positions n through $n + R - L$, so the symbols in positions $L + 1$ through R match those in postions $n + 1$ through $n + R - L$. Since $L + 1 \leq n$, W_{L+1} is in D_n and therefore is a candidate to serve as $\tilde{W}_{n+1}$. If W_{L+1} extends at least to R, $\tilde{W}_{n+1}$ will have to penetrate at least to the depth $n + R - L$ that $\tilde{W}_n$ does. But, since $L + 1 \leq n$, the inductive hypothesis assures us that $\tilde{W}_{L+1}$ does indeed end at or to the right of where $\tilde{W}_L$ does, that is, at or to the right of position R. Hence, $\tilde{W}_{n+1}$ penetrates at least as deeply as does $\tilde{W}_n$; equivalently, W_{n+1} penetrates at least as deeply as does W_n.

F Efficient Coding of L_k for LZ77

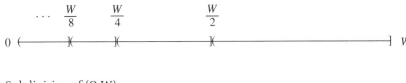

F.1   Subdivision of (O,W)

Here is a scheme for encoding the maximum match length L found within a window of width W that capitalizes on the fact that usually $L \approx \log W$. Divide the interval $(0,W]$ into $(0,W/2]$ and $(W/2, W]$. Then divide $(0,W/2]$ similarly in half into $(0,W/4]$ and $(W/4, W/2]$. Next divide $(0,W/4]$ into $(0,W/8]$ and $(W/8, W/4]$, and so on. Repeat this n times in all, where $1 \leq W/2^{n-1} < 2$; note that this implies that $n = \lceil \log_2 W \rceil$. It therefore requires only

$$\lceil \log_2 n \rceil = \lceil \log_2 (\log_2 W) \rceil \tag{F.1}$$

binary digits to specify which of the intervals contains L. Once we know that interval, we know how many integers I it contains, whereupon it would suffice to provide $\lceil \log_2 I \rceil$ more binary digits to specify L exactly. We know that the interval specified to contain L has an upper endpoint that is at least as large as L and has width equal to half that upper endpoint, so its width does not exceed $L/2$. Therefore, it can contain at most $L/2$ integers. (It is open on the left and therefore does not contain its left endpoint.) Accordingly $I \leq L/2$, so $\lceil \log_2 (L/2) \rceil$ upper-bounds the number of additional digits needed to specify L. The total number of binary digits used therefore satisfies

$$N_L \leq \lceil \log_2(\log_2 W) \rceil + \lceil \log_2(L/2) \rceil \tag{F.2}$$

In practice, we expect L to be comparable to the length of one of the extremely small intervals near the left end of Figure F.1, namely, $L \approx \log W$. Thus, we usually get

$$N_L \approx \lceil \log_2(\log_2 W) \rceil + \lceil \log_2(\log_2 W/2) \rceil < 2 \log_2(\log_2 W) \tag{F.3}$$

For the rare, large values of L, our scheme succeeds, as advertised, in using approximately $\log_2 L$ binary digits to encode L, not $\log_2 \max L = \log_2 W$.

References

All ISO and ISO/IEC standards discussed are published by the International Organization for Standardization, 1 rue de Varembé, Geneva. They are also available through http://www.iso.ch.

All ITU-T recommendations discussed are published by the International Telecommunication Union, Place des Nations, Geneva. They are also available online at http://www.itu.ch.

Abut, H., ed. 1990. *Vector quantization*. New York: IEEE Press.

Adoul, J.-P., P. Mabilleau, M. Delprat, and S. Morisette. 1987. Fast CELP coding based on algebraic codes. *Proc. Int. Conf. Acoust., Speech, Signal Process.*, 1957–1960.

Akansu, A. N., and R. Haddad. 1992. *Multiresolution signal decomposition*. San Diego, CA: Academic Press.

Antonini, M., M. Barlaud, P. Mathieu, and I. Daubechies. 1992. Image coding using wavelet transform. *IEEE Trans. Image Proc.* 1(2):205–220.

Atal, B. S. 1982. Predictive coding of speech at low bit rates. *IEEE Trans. on Communications* COM-30(April):600–614.

Atal, B. S., and S. L. Hanauer. 1971. Speech analysis and synthesis by linear prediction of the speech wave. *J. Acoust. Soc. Am.* 50(2):637–655.

Atal, B. S., and J. R. Remde. 1982. A new model of LPC excitation for producing natural sounding speech at low bit rates. *Proc. Int. Conf. Acoust., Speech, Signal Process.*, 617–917.

Atal, B. S., and M. R. Schroeder. 1979. Predictive coding of speech signals and subjective error criteria. *IEEE Trans. on Acoustics, Speech, and Signal Processing* ASSP7(3):247–254.

Atal, B. S., and M. R. Schroeder. 1984. Stochastic coding of speech at very low bit rates. *Proc. Int. Conf. Comm.*, 1610–1613.

Barnes, C. F., and S. A. Rizvi. 1996. Advances in residual vector quantization: A review. *IEEE Trans. on Image Processing* 5(2):226–262.

Bell, T. C., J. G. Cleary, J. H. Whitten. 1990. *Text*. Englewood Cliffs, NJ: Prentice Hall.

Bender, P. E., and J. K. Wolf. 1991. New asymptotic bounds and improvements on the Lempel-Ziv data compression algorithm. *IEEE Trans. on Information Theory* IT-37:721–729.

Beranek, L. L. 1947. The design of communications systems. *Proc. IRE* (September):880–890.

Berger, T. 1971. *Rate distortion theory*. Englewood Cliffs, NJ: Prentice Hall.

Berger, T., and D. J. Miller, co-inventors. 1992. U.S. Pat. No. 5,091,975. A method and apparatus for on-line compression of human signatures. Assignee: TCSI, Berkeley, CA.

Blahut, R. E. 1987. *Principles and practice of information theory*. Reading, MA: Addison-Wesley.

Bodson, D., R. A. Schaphorst, and S. J. Urban. 1989. Gray scale pictures via Group 3 facsimile. *IEEE Comm. Magazine* (September):42–49.

Bormann, C. 1997a (date accessed). The Multi-Class Extension to Multi-Link PPP. Internet draft, May. `ftp://ietf.org/internet-drafts/draft-ietf-issll-isslow-mcml-02.txt`

Bormann, C. 1997b (date accessed). PPP in a real-time oriented HDLC-like framing. Internet draft, July. `ftp://ietf.org/internet-drafts/draft-ietf-issll-isslow-rtf-01.txt`

Bormann, C. 1997c (date accessed). Providing integrated services over low-bitrate links. Internet draft, May. `ftp://ietf.org/internet-drafts/draft-ietf-issll-isslow-02.txt`

Boyd, I., and C. B. Southcott. 1988. A speech codec for skyphone service. *Br. Telecom. Tech. J.* 6(2):50–59.

Braden, R., L. Zhang, S. Berson, S. Herzog, and S. Jamin. 1997 (date accessed). Resource reservation protocol (RSVP)-Version 1 functional specification. Internet draft, June. `ftp://ds.internic.net/internet-drafts/draft-ietf-rsvp-spec-16.txt`

Brandenburg, K., and M. Bosi. 1995. Overview of MPEG-audio: Current and future standards for low bit-rate audio coding. 99th Audio Engineering Society Convention, New York, preprint 4130.

Brandstein, M., J. Hardwick, and J. Lim. 1991. The multi-band excitation speech coder. In *Advances in speech coding*, eds. B. S. Atal, V. Cuperman, and A. Gersho, ch.20. Norwell, MA: Kluwer Academic Publishers.

Brandstein, M. S., P. A. Monta, J. C. Hardwick, and J. S. Lim. 1990. A real-time implementation of the improved MBE speech coder. *Proc. IEEE Int. Conf. Acoust., Speech, Signal Process.* (April).

Burrows, M., and D. J. Wheeler. 1994. A block-sorting lossless data compression algorithm. SRC Research Report 124, Digital Systems Research Center, Palo Alto, CA. `http://gatekeeper.dec.com/pub/DEC/SRC/research-reports/abstracts/src-rr-124.html`

Campbell, J. P., V. C. Welch, and T. E. Tremain. 1989. The new 4800 bps voice coding standard. *Proc. Military Speech Tech.*, 64–70.

Casner, S., and V. Jacobson. 1997 (date accessed). Compressing IP/UDP/RTP headers for low-speed serial links. Internet draft, July. `ftp://ietf.org/internet-drafts/draft-ietf-avt-crtp-03.txt`

CCITT. 1980. Standardization of Group 3 facsimile apparatus for document transmission. Geneva. Amended at Malaga-Torremolinos, 1984, and Melbourne, 1988.

CCITT. 1984. Facsimile coding schemes and coding control functions for Group 4 facsimile apparatus. Malaga-Torremolinos, 1984. Amended at Melbourne, 1988.

CCITT. 1984, 1988. Recommendations of the P series. *Red Book V.* Amended 1988, Melbourne. Malaga-Torremolinos, 198–203.

Chan, W.-Y., I. Gerson, and T. Miki. 1996. Half-rate standards. In *The mobile communications handbook,* ed. J. D. Gibson, ch.32, 511–525. Boca Raton, FL: CRC Press.

Chellappa, R., and A. A. Sawchuk. 1985. *Digital image processing and analysis, Volume 1: Digital image processing.* Los Angeles: Computer Society Press.

Chen, J.-H., and A. Gersho. 1995. Adaptive postfiltering for quality enhancement of coded speech. *IEEE Trans. on Acoustics, Speech, and Signal Processing* 3(1):59–71.

Chen, J.-H., R. V. Cox, Y.-C. Lin, N. Jayant, and M. J. Melchner. 1992. A low-delay CELP coder for the CCITT 16 kb/s speech coding standard. *IEEE J. Selected Areas Comm.* 10(5):830–849.

Clarke, R. J. 1985. *Transform coding of images.* San Diego, CA: Academic Press.

Conway, J. H., and N. J. A. Sloane. 1982. Fast quantizing and decoding algorithms for lattice quantizers and codes. *IEEE Trans. on Information Theory* IT-28(March):227–232.

Conway, J. H., and N. J. A. Sloane. 1983. A fast encoding method for lattice codes and quantizers. *IEEE Trans. on Information Theory* IT-29:820–824.

Conway, J. H., and N. J. A. Sloane. 1988. *Sphere packings, lattices and groups.* New York: Springer-Verlag.

Cover, T. M., and J. A. Thomas. 1991. *Elements of information theory.* New York: Wiley.

Cox, R., and P. Kroon. 1996. Low bit-rate speech coders for multimedia communication. *IEEE Comm. Magazine* (December):34–41.

Crochiere, R. E., S. A. Webber, and J. L. Flanagan. 1976. Digital coding of speech in sub-bands. *Bell Syst. Tech. J.* 55(8):1069–1085.

Crossman, A. 1993. A variable bit rate audio coder for videoconferencing. *IEEE Workshop on Speech Coding for Telecomm.,* 7–8.

Daubechies, I. 1992. *Ten lectures on wavelets.* SIAM, Philadelphia, PA.

Daumer, W. R. 1982. Subjective evaluation of several efficient speech coders. *IEEE Trans. on Communications* COM-30(April):655–662.

Davidson, G. A., and M. Bosi. 1992. AC-2: High quality audio coding for broadcasting and storage. *46th Annual Broadcast Engineering Conference* (April):98–105.

Davisson, L. D., and R. M. Gray, eds. 1976. *Data compression.* Stroudsburg, PA: Halsted Press.

DeAgostino, S., and J. A. Storer. 1996. On-line versus off-line computation in dynamic text compression. *Information Processing* 59:169–1740.

DeJaco, P. J. A., W. Gardner, and C. Lee. 1993. QCELP: The North American CDMA digital cellular variable rate speech coding standard. *Proc. IEEE Workshop on Speech Coding for Telecomm.*, 5–6.

Dimolitsas, S., M. Sherif, C. South, and J. R. Rosenberger, eds. 1993. CCITT 16 kbits/s voice encoding standard. *Speech Commun.* 12(2):97–206.

Durbin, J. 1960. The fitting of time series models. *Rev. Inst. Inter. Statist.* 28:233–243.

Esteban, D., and C. Galand. 1977. Application of quadrature mirror filters to split band voice coding schemes. *Proc. ICASSP*, 191–195.

Fano, R. M. 1961. *Transmission of information.* New York: Wiley.

Fisher, Y., ed. 1995. *Fractal image compression: Theory and application.* New York: Springer-Verlag.

Flanagan, J. L. 1972. *Speech analysis, synthesis and perception.* New York: Springer-Verlag.

Flanagan, J. L., M. R. Schroeder, B. S. Atal, R. E. Crochiere, N. S. Jayant, and J. M. Tribolet. 1979. Speech coding. *IEEE Trans. on Communications* (April):710–737.

Freeman, H. 1961. On the encoding of arbitrary geometric configurations. *IRE Trans. on Electronic Computers* EC-10(June):260–268.

French, N. R., and J. C. Steinberg. 1947. Factors governing the intelligibililty of speech sounds. *J. Acoust. Soc. Am.* (January):90–119.

Gersho, A. 1979. Asymptotically optimal block quantization. *IEEE Trans. on Information Theory* IT-25:373–380.

Gersho, A. 1994. Advances in speech and audio compression. *Proc. of the IEEE* 82(6):900–918.

Gersho, A., and R. M. Gray. 1992. *Vector quantization and signal compression.* Dordrecht, The Netherlands: Kluwer.

Gerson, I. A., and M. A. Jasiuk. 1991. Vector sum excited linear prediction (VSELP). In *Advances in speech coding,* eds. B. S. Atal, V. Cuperman, and A. Gersho, 69–79. Norwell, MA: Kluwer Academic Publishers.

Gibson, J. D. 1993. Speech signal processing. In *The electrical engineering handbook,* ed. R. C. Dorf, ch.14, 279–314. Boca Raton, FL: CRC Press.

Gibson, J. D., and K. Sayood. 1988. Lattice quantization. *Advances in electronics and electron physics,* New York: Academic Press, 259–330.

Gilbert, E. N. 1971. Codes based on inaccurate source probabilities. *IEEE Trans. on Information Theory* IT-17(May):304–314.

Gonzalez, R. C., and P. Wintz. 1977. *Digital image processing.* Reading, MA: Addison-Wesley.

Goodman, D. J. 1980. Embedded DPCM for variable bit rate transmission. *IEEE Trans. on Communications* (July):1040–1066.

Goodman, D. J., and R. D. Nash. 1982. Subjective quality of the same speech transmission conditions in seven different countries. *IEEE Trans. on Communications* COM-30 (April):642–654.

Gray, A. H., and J. D. Markel. 1976. Distance measures for speech processing. *IEEE Trans. on Acoustics, Speech, and Signal Processing* ASSP-24:380–391.

Gray, R. M. 1984. Vector quantization. *IEEE ASSP Magazine.* 25:373–380.

Gray, R. M. 1990. *Source coding theory.* Dordrecht, The Netherlands: Kluwer Academic Publishers.

Gray, R. M., and L. D. Davisson. 1974. A mathematical theory of data compression? *Proceedings of the '74 Int. Conf. Commun.*, 40A-1–40A-5.

Griffin, D. W., and J. S. Lim. 1988. Multi-band excitation vocoder. *IEEE Trans. on Acoustics, Speech, and Signal Processing* ASSP-36(August):1223–1235.

Hoogendorn, A. 1994. Digital compact cassette. *Proc of the IEEE.* 82(10):1479–1489.

Huffman, D. A. 1952. A method for the construction of minimum redundancy codes. *Proceedings of the IRE* 40:1098–1101.

ISO/IEC. 1991a. Information technology-telecommunications and information exchange between systems-high-level data link control (HDLC) procedures-frame structure. ISO/IEC 3309. `http://www.iso.ch`

ISO/IEC. 1991b. Progressive bi-level image compression, Revision 4.1, ISO/IEC JTCI/SC2/WG9, CD 11544, September. (See also ITU-T T.85, Application profile for recommendation T.82-Progressive bi-level image compression (JBIG coding scheme) for facsimile apparatus, November 8, 1995.)

ISO/IEC. 1991c. The SR-report on the MPEG/AUDIO subject listening test. ISO/IEC JTCI/SC2/WG11 MPEG 91/010. Stockholm, April/May.

Itakura, F. 1975a. Line spectrum representation of linear predictive coefficients. *J. Acoust. Soc. Am.* 57(suppl. 1):S35.

Itakura, F. 1975b. Minimum prediction residual principle applied to speech recognition. *IEEE Trans. on Acoustics, Speech, and Signal Processing* ASSP-23:67–72.

ITU-R. 1994. Low bit rate audio coding. Recommendation ITU-R BS.1115. Geneva.

ITU-R. 1995. Low bit rate multichannel audio coder test results. ITU-R Document 10/51-E. Geneva, May.

Jacquet, P., and W. Szpankowski. 1995. Asymptotic behavior of the Lempel-Ziv parsing scheme and digital search trees. *Theoretical Computer Science* 144:161–197.

Jayant, N. S. 1973. Adaptive quantization with a one-word memory. *Bell Syst. Tech. J.* (September):1119–1144.

Jayant, N. S. 1976. *Waveform quantization and coding.* New York: IEEE Press.

Jayant, N. S. 1992. Signal compression: Technology targets and research directions. *IEEE J. Selected Areas Commun.* (Special Issue on Speech and Image Coding/June).

Jayant, N. S., and P. Noll. 1984. *Digital coding of waveforms: Principles and applications to speech and video.* Englewood Cliffs, NJ: Prentice Hall.

Jayant, N. S., J. Johnston, and R. J. Safranek. 1993. Signal compression based on models of human perception. *Proc. IEEE* 81(10):1385–1422.

Jelinek, F. 1968. *Probabilistic information theory.* New York: McGraw-Hill. (Cites unpublished finding by P. Elias.)

Jeong, D. G., and J. D. Gibson. 1993. Uniform and piecewise uniform lattice vector quantization for memoryless Gaussian and Laplacian sources. *IEEE Trans. on Information Theory* IT-39(3):786–804.

Johnston, J. D. 1988a. Estimation of perceptual entropy using noise masking criteria. *ICASSP-88 Conf. Record,* 2524–2527.

Johnston, J. D. 1988b. Transform coding of audio signals using perceptual noise criteria. *IEEE Journal on Selected Areas in Communications* 6(February):314–323.

Johnston, J. D. 1990. Perceptual coding of wideband stereo signals. *ICASSP-89 Conf. Record,* 1993–1996.

Johnston, J. D., and A. J. Ferreira. 1992. Sum difference stereo transform coding. *ICASSP-92 Conf. Record,* II-569-II-572.

Josenhans, J. G., J. F. Lynch, Jr., M. R. Rogers, R. R. Rosinski, and W. P. VanDame. 1986. Speech processing application standards. *AT&T Tech. Journal* 65(5):23–33.

Kitawaki, N., and K. Itoh. 1991. Pure delay effects on speech quality in telecommunications. *IEEE Journal on Selected Areas in Communications* 9(4):586–593.

Kitawaki, N., and H. Nagabuchi. 1988. Quality assessment of speech coding and speech synthesis systems. *IEEE Commun. Mag.* (October):36–44.

Kiyohara, J., and T. Kawabata. 1996. A note on the Lempel-Ziv-Yokoo algorithm. *IEICE Trans. on Fundamentals of Electronics, Communications and Computer Science.* E79-A (September):1460–1463.

Kleijn, W. B., P. Kroon, and D. Nahumi. 1994. The RCELP speech-coding algorithms. *European Trans. on Telecom.* 5(5):573–582.

Kondoz, A. M. 1994. *Digital speech coding for low bit rate communications systems.* West Sussex, England: John Wiley & Sons Ltd.

Kraft, L. G. 1949. *A device for quantizing, grouping and coding amplitude modulated pulses.* M.S. Thesis, Electrical Engineering Department, MIT, Cambridge, MA, March.

Kroon, P., E. F. Deprettere, and R. J. Sluyter. 1986. Regular-pulse excitation-A novel approach to effective and efficient multipulse coding of speech. *IEEE Trans. on Acoustics, Speech, and Signal Processing* ASSP-34(5):1054–1063.

Lefebvre, R., R. Salami, C. Laflamme, and J.-P. Adoul. 1994. High quality coding of wideband audio signals using transform coded excitation (tcx). *Proc. IEEE Int. Conf. Acoust., Speech, Signal Process.,* 193–196.

LeGall, D. 1991. MPEG. *Communications of the ACM* 34(April):47–58.

Lindbergh, D., and H. Malvar. 1995. Multimedia teleconferencing with H.324. In *Standards and common interfaces for video information systems,* ed. K. R. Rao, 206–232. Philadelphia, PA: SPIE.

Linde, Y., A. Buzo, and R. M. Gray. 1980. An algorithm for vector quantizer design. *IEEE Trans. on Communications* COM-28:84–95.

Lloyd, S. P. 1957. *Least squares quantization in PCM.* Unpublished Bell Laboratories Technical Note. Portions presented at the Institute of Mathematical Statistics Meeting, Atlantic City, NJ, September. Published in the March 1982 special issue on quantization of *IEEE Trans. on Information Theory.*

Lohscheller, H. 1984. A subjectively adapted image communication system. *IEEE Trans. on Communications* COM-32(12):1316–1322.

MacQueen, J. 1967. Some methods for classification and analysis of multivariate observations. *Proc. 5th Berkeley Symp. on Math, Statist., and Prob.* Berkeley, CA: Univ. of California Press, 281–297.

Makhoul, J. 1975. Linear prediction: A tutorial review. *Proc. IEEE* 63(April): 561–580.

Makhoul, J., S. Roucos, and H. Gish. 1985. Vector quantization in speech coding. *Proc. IEEE* 73:1551–1558.

Markel, J. D. 1972. The SIFT algorithm for fundamental frequency estimation. *IEEE Trans. on Audio Electroacoustics.* AU-20(5):367–377.

Markel, J. D., and A. H. Gray, Jr. 1976. *Linear prediction of speech.* New York: Springer-Verlag.

Max, J. 1960. Quantizing for minimum distortion. *IRE Trans. on Information Theory* IT-6(March):7–12.

McCree, A. V., and T. P. Barnwell III. 1995. A mixed excitation LPC vocoder model for low bit rate speech coding. *IEEE Trans. on Acoustics, Speech, and Signal Processing* ASSP-3(4):242–250.

McCree, A. V., K. Truong, E. B. George, T. P. Barnwell, and V. Viswanathan. 1996. A 2. 4 kbit/s MELP coder candidate for the new U.S. federal standard. *ICASSP '96*, 200–203.

Mermelstein, P. 1988. G.722, a new CCITT coding standard for digital transmission of wideband audio signals. *IEEE Comm. Magazine* 26(1):8–15.

Mitchell, J. L., W. B. Pennebaker, C. E. Fogg, and D. J. LeGall. 1996. *MPEG video compression standard.* New York: Chapman & Hall.

Nelson, M., and J.-L. Gailly. 1995. *The data compression book.* New York: M&T Books.

Noll, P. 1997. Audio coding. In *The communications handbook,* ed. J. D. Gibson, ch.104. Boca Raton, FL: CRC Press.

Okubo, S., S. Dunstan, G. Morrison, M. Nilsson, H. Radha, D. Skran, and G. Thom. 1997. ITU-T standardization of audiovisual communication systems in ATM and LAN environments. *IEEE Journal on Selected Areas in Communications,* August.

Papamichalis, P. E. 1987. *Practical approaches to speech coding.* Englewood Cliffs, NJ: Prentice Hall.

Pasco, R. 1976. Source coding algorithms for fast data compression. Ph.D. dissertation. Stanford University.

Pennebaker, W. B., and J. L. Mitchell. 1993. *JPEG still image data compression standard.* New York: Van Nostrand Reinhold.

Pennebaker, W. B., J. L. Mitchell, G. G. Langdon, and R. B. Arps. 1988. *IBM Journal of Research and Development* 32(6):771–726. (See also other articles about the Q-coder in this issue.)

Petajan, E. 1997. The high definition television grand alliance system. In *The communications handbook,* ed. J. D. Gibson, ch.103, 1462–1474. Boca Raton, FL: CRC Press.

Petr, D. W. 1982. 32 kb/s ADPCM-DLQ coding for network applications. *Proc. IEEE Global Telecomm. Conf,* A8.3–1–A8.3–5.

Pratt, W. K. 1978. *Digital image processing.* New York: John Wiley & Sons.

Princen, J. P., and A. Bradley. 1986. Analysis/synthesis filterbank design based on time domain aliasing cancellation. *IEEE Trans. on Acoustics, Speech, and Signal Processing* ASSP-34:1153–1161.

Princen, J. P., A. W. Johnson, and A. B. Bradley. 1987. Subband/transform coding using filter bank designs based on time domain aliasing cancellation. *Proc. IEEE Int. Conf. Acoust., Speech, Signal Process.,* Dallas, 2161–2164.

Rabbani, M., and P. W. Jones. 1991. *Digital image compression techniques.* Bellingham, WA: SPIE Optical Engineering Press.

Rabiner, L. R., and R. W. Schafer. 1978. *Digital processing of speech signals.* Englewood Cliffs, NJ: Prentice Hall.

Ramachandran, R. P., and P. Kabal. 1989. Pitch prediction filters in speech coding. *IEEE Trans. on Acoustics, Speech, and Signal Processing* (April):467–478.

Rao, K. R., and P. Yip. 1990. *Discrete cosine transform algorithms, advantages, applications.* San Diego, CA: Academic Press.

Rissanen, J. 1976. Generalized Kraft inequality and arithmetic coding. *IBM Journal of Research and Development* 20:198–203.

Rissanen, J. 1983. A universal data compression system. *IEEE Trans. on Information Theory* IT-29(September):656–664.

Rissanen, J. 1984. Universal coding, information, prediction and estimation. *IEEE Trans. on Information Theory* IT-30(July):629–636.

Ross, M. J., H. L. Shaffer, A. Cohen, R. Freudberg, and H. J. Manley. 1974. Average magnitude difference function pitch extractor. *IEEE Trans. on Acoustics, Speech, and Signal Processing* ASSP-22(October):353–362.

Salami, R., C. Laflamme, J.-P. Adoul, and D. Massaloux. 1994. A toll quality 8 kb/s speech codec for the personal communication system (PCS). *IEEE Trans. Veh. Technol.* 43(3):808–816.

Salami, R., C. Laflamme, B. Bessette, and J.-P. Adoul. 1997. ITU-T recommendation G. 729 annex-A: Reduced complexity 8 kbit/s CS-ACELP codec for digital simultaneous voice and data (DSVD). *IEEE Communications* 35(9):56–63.

Salami, R., ed. 1995. Descriptions of the proposed ITU-T 8kb/s speech coding standards. *Proc. IEEE Speech Coding Workshop* (September):5–8.

Sambur, M. R., and N. S. Jayant. 1976. LPC analysis/synthesis from speech inputs containing quantizing noise or additive white noise. *IEEE Trans. on Acoustics, Speech, and Signal Processing* ASSP-24:488–494.

Savari, S. A. 1997. Redundancy of the Lempel-Ziv incremental parsing rule. *IEEE Trans. on Information Theory* IT-43(January):9–21.

Sayood, K. 1996. *Introduction to data compression.* San Francisco: Morgan Kaufmann.

Scharf, B. 1970. Critical bands. In *Foundations of modern auditory theory, Vol. 1,* ed. J. V. Tobias, 159–202. London: Academic.

Schulzrinne, H., S. Casner, R. Frederick, and V. Jacobson. 1996 (date accessed). RTP: A transport protocol for real-time applications. IETF RFC 1889, January. `ftp://ds.internic.net/rfc/rfc1889.txt`

Shannon, C. E. 1948. A mathematical theory of communication. *Bell Syst. Tech. J.* 27:379–423, 623–656.

Shannon, C. E. 1959. Coding theorems for a discrete source with a fidelity criterion. *IRE Nat. Conv. Rec.* Part 4:142–163.

Shields, P. C. 1993. Waiting times: Positive and negative results on the Wyner-Ziv problem. *Journal of Theoretical Probability* 6:499–519.

Simpson, W. 1994 (date accessed). The point to point protocol. IETF RFC 1661, July. `ftp://ds.internic.net/rfc/rfc1661.txt`

Singhal, S., and B. S. Atal. 1984. Improving performance of multi-pulse LPC coders at low bit rates. *Proc. Int. Conf. Acoust., Speech, Signal Process.,* 1.3.1–1.3.4.

Smith, M. J. T., and T. P. Barnwell III. 1986. Exact reconstruction techniques for tree-structured subband coders. *IEEE Trans. on Acoustics, Speech, and Signal Processing* ASSP-38(August):1446–1456.

Soong, F. K., and B. H. Juang. 1984. Line spectrum pair (LSP) and speech data compression. *Proc. Int. Conf. Acoust., Speech, Signal Process.,* 1.10.1–1.10.4.

Spanias, A. S. 1994. Speech coding: A tutorial review. *Proc. of the IEEE* 82(10):1541–1582.

Stewart, L. C. 1981. *Trellis data compression.* Stanford University Information Systems Lab Technical Report 1905–1, Stanford University, July. Stanford University Ph. D. thesis.

Thom, G. 1996. H.323: The multimedia communications standard for local area networks. *IEEE Comm. Magazine* 34(12):52–56.

Todd, C., G. A. Davidson, M. F. Davis, L. D. Fielder, B. D. Link, and S. Vernon. 1994. AC-3: Flexible perceptual coding for audio transmission and storage. *96th Audio Engineering Society Convention,* Amsterdam, Preprint 3796.

Vaidyanathan, P. P. 1987. Quadrature mirror filter banks, m-band extensions and perfect-reconstruction techniques. *IEEE ASSP Magazine* 4(July):4–20.

Vary, P., R. Hoffman, K. Hellwig, and R. Sluyter. 1988. A regular-pulse excited linear predictive code. *Speech Comm.* 7(2):209–215.

Vetterli, M., and J. Kovacevic. 1995. *Wavelets and subband coding.* Englewood Cliffs, NJ: Prentice Hall.

Viswanathan, V., and J. Makhoul. 1975. Quantization properties of transmission parameters in linear predictive systems. *IEEE Trans. on Acoustics, Speech, and Signal Processing* ASSP-23(June):309–321.

Voiers, W. D. 1977a. Diagnostic acceptability measure for speech communication systems. *Proceedings 1977 IEEE ICASSP,* 204–207.

Voiers, W. D. 1977b. Diagnostic evaluation of speech intelligibility. In *Speech intelligibility and recognition,* ed. M. E. Hawley. Stroudsburg, PA: Dowden, Hutchinson, and Ross.

Wallace, G. K. 1991. JPEG. *Communications of the ACM* 34(April):31–44.

Welch, T. 1984. A technique for high-performance data compression. *Computer* 17(June): 8–19.

Westerink, P. H., J. Biemond, and D. E. Boekee. 1988. An optimal bit allocation algorithm for sub-band coding. *Proc. Int. Conf. Acoust., Speech, Signal Process.*, 757–760.

Westerink, P. H., J. Biemond, and D. E. Boekee. 1991. Subband coding of color images. In *Subband image coding,* ed. J. W. Woods, ch.5, 193–227. Amsterdam and Norwell, MA: Kluwer Academic Publishers.

Willems, F. M. J., Y. M. Shtarkov, and T. T. Tjalkens. 1995. The context-tree weighting method: Basic properties. *IEEE Trans. on Information Theory* IT-41(May):653–664.

Wong, P. W., and J. Koplowitz. 1992. Chain codes and their linear reconstruction. *IEEE Trans. on Information Theory* IT-38:268.

Woods, J. W., and S. D. O'Neil. 1986. Sub-band coding of images. *IEEE Trans. on Acoustics, Speech, and Signal Processing* ASSP-34(October):1278–1288.

Woods, J. W., ed. 1991. *Subband image coding.* Amsterdam and Norwell, MA: Kluwer Academic Publishers.

Wornell, G. 1996. *Signal processing with fractals: A wavelet based approach.* Upper Saddle River, NJ: Prentice Hall.

Wyner, A. D., and A. J. Wyner. 1997. *Improved redundancy of a version of the Lempel-Ziv algorithm.* Submitted for publication.

Wyner, A. D., and J. Ziv. 1994. The sliding-window Lempel-Ziv algorithm is asymptotically optimal. *Proceedings of the IEEE* 82(June):872–877.

Wyner, A. J. 1997. The redundancy and distribution of the phrase lengths of the fixed-database Lempel-Ziv algorithm. Submitted to *IEEE Trans. on Information Theory.*

Yokoo, H. 1992. Improved variations relating the Ziv-Lempel and Welch-type algorithms for sequential data compression. *IEEE Trans. on Information Theory* IT-38(January):73–81.

Yoshida., T. 1994. The rewritable minidisc system. *Proc. IEEE* 82(10):1492–1500.

Zeger, K., and A. Gersho. 1990. Pseudo-gray coding. *IEEE Trans. on Communications* 38:2147–2158.

Zelinski, R., and P. Noll. 1977. Adaptive transform coding of the speech signals. *IEEE Trans. on Acoustics, Speech, and Signal Processing* ASSP-25(August):299–309.

Ziv, J., and A. Lempel. 1977. A universal algorithm for sequential data compression. *IEEE Trans. on Information Theory* IT-23(May):337–343.

Ziv, J., and A. Lempel. 1978. Compression of individual sequences via variable-rate coding. *IEEE Trans. on Information Theory* IT-24(September):530–536.

Zwicker, E. 1961. Subdivision of the audible frequency range into critical bands (Frequenzgruppen). *J. Acoustical Society of America* 33(February):248.

Glossary

2D-DCT	two-dimensional discrete cosine transform
4:2:2 profile	profile for higher quality digital "video supporting" 4:2:2 chroma and larger image sizes, rates, and buffer sizes than main profile
4CIF	4 times the common intermediate format (in H.263)
16CIF	16 times the common intermediate format (in H.263)
AAL	ATM adaptation layer
ACELP	algebraic code excited linear prediction
adaptive pixel	nonfixed site in JBIG arithmetic coder context
ADM	adaptive delta modulation
ADPCM	adaptive differential pulse code modulation
ADSL	asymmetric digital subscriber line
AL	adaptation layer (in H.223)
AMDF	average magnitude difference function
analysis by synthesis	a technique for finding the best match by synthesizing all possibilities
APC	adaptive predictive coding
APCM	adaptive pulse code modulation
AQB	backward adaptive quantization
AQF	forward adaptive quantization
ASN.1	abstract syntax notation one
ATC	adaptive transform coding
ATM	asynchronous transfer mode

ATRAC	adaptive transform acoustic coding
average mutual information	Shannon's measure of shared content of two signals
B	bearer (B channel in ISDN)
BA	backward adaptive
bandwidth	the information carrying capacity of a network or channel, in bits per second (in the context of digital communications)
BAS	bit rate allocation signal (in H.221)
base layer	the coarsest level of resolution reduction in JBIG
baseline	a mandatory mode required by a standard for interoperability. There may be additional modes that are optional.
BC	backward compatible
Bernoulli-p source	sequence of independent binary random variables; usually p is the probability of a one and $1-p$ is the probability of a zero
B-ISDN	broadband integrated services digital network
bit	information content inherent in a binary digit that is equally likely to be a zero or a one
block code	a collection of equal-length vectors comprising a source or channel codebook
BMLD	binary masking level difference
B-picture (B-frame)	bidirectionally predicted video frame
BPS	bits per second
b/w	black/white
CAP	capability
Carleton corpus	a quasi-standard collection of textual material used to compare the performance of lossless compression algorithms
CCIR	International Consultative Committee for Radio
CCIR-601	standard for uncompressed digital video
CCITT	Comité Consultatif International de Telegraphique et Telephonique
CD	compact disc
CDMA	code-division multiple access
CD-ROM	compact disc read only memory
CELP	code excited linear prediction
chain rule	a formula for term-by-term evaluation of joint entropies
chroma	chrominance signal

CIF	common intermediate format (in H.261 and H.263)
codebook	the totality of the vectors in a vector quantizer
codec	coder/decoder
codepoint	a table entry, numeric value, or bit sequence representing some capability, command, operating mode, or control message
conditional average mutual information	mutual information between two random objects when a third random object is known by all parties
conditional entropy	uncertainty about a random object that remains after another random object has been observed
constrained system parameter stream	information in the header of an MPEG-1 pack about packet rate and decoder buffer size
context	a collection of previously encoded pixels with specified geometric relationships to the target pixel in arithmetic coding (in JBIG fax)
CPU	central processing unit
CRC	cyclic redundancy check
CS	convergence sublayer (in ATM)
CS-ACELP	conjugate structure algebraic code excited linear prediction
CSN	circuit switched network (for instance, PSTN)
DAM	Diagnostic Acceptability Measure; a speech coder quality measure
D-ary	capable of assuming any one of D distinct values
DAT	digital audiotape
DCC	digital compact cassette
DCME	digital circuit multiplication equipment
DCT	discrete cosine transform
decode time	the time at which an audio unit should be played or a video unit should be decoded
decode time stamp	information in MPEG-2 packetized elementary stream about decode time for packet payload
DFT	discrete Fourier transform
differential layers	levels with intermediate resolution reduction in JBIG
digital storage media command and control	instructions for interaction of MPEG decoders with storage devices

dithering	random or pseudo-random jittering intended to enhance perceptual quality in quantization schemes
DPCM	differential pulse code modulation
DRT	Diagnostic Rhyme Test; speech coder intelligibility measure
DSM-CC	digital storage media command and control
DSP	digital signal processor; special-purpose computer processor that facilitates common digital signal processing operations
DTMF	dual tone multifrequency
DTS	decode time stamp (in MPEG-2)
dual prime	scheme for motion vector reduction in interlaced video
DVD	digital video disc or digital versatile disc
ECS	encryption control signal (in H.221)
Elias coding	data compression scheme underlying arithmetic coding
entropy	quantitative measure of uncertainty
entropy rate	entropy per symbol or per second
EOB	end-of-block
EOL	end-of-line
ETSI	European Telecommunications Standards Institute
FA	forward adaptive
FAS	frame alignment signal (in H.221)
FDCT	forward discrete cosine transform
FEC	forward error correction
FFT	fast Fourier transform
Fibonacci	recursion in which the next number is the sum of the previous two
field	all the odd or all the even scan lines of a frame (in interlaced video)
fill	a zero-information symbol used to complete a data set
FIR	finite impulse response
FMH	Fibonacci-Markov-Huffman
fractional PEL	a form of interpolated motion compensation
GCC	generic conference control (in T.120)
GOP	group of pictures (an I-frame and the B- and P-frames thereafter until the next I-frame)
Group 3	a digital facsimile standard
Group 4	a digital facsimile standard using line-to-line differences

GSM	Global Systeme Mobile; formerly, Group Speciale Mobile
GSTN	general switched telephone network (also known as PSTN or POTS)
gzip	a commericial realization of LZ77 lossless data compression
half-tone	a dithering scheme used to make bi-level images appear to be gray-scale images; also, the extension thereof to color images
HDLC	high-level data link control
HDTV	high-definition television
horizontal mode	Group 3 submode within Group 4 facsimile
HSD	high-speed data (in H.221)
Huffman codes	prefix codes with mimimum average codeword length
Huffman's algorithm	a recursive algorithm for generation of Huffman codes
hybrid coders	coders that do not attempt to reconstruct the exact time domain waveform of an input signal but try to obtain a best-weighted match of the time domain signal
hybrid fiber coax	a cable TV wired network for broadcast video
Hz	hertz (cycles per second)
IDCT	inverse discrete cosine transform
idle channel noise	the quantization error when no input is presented to a quantizer
IEC	International Electrotechnical Commission
IEEE	Institute of Electrical and Electronics Engineers
IETF	Internet Engineering Task Force
IIR	infinite impulse response
IMBE	improved multiband execution
IMTC	International Multimedia Teleconferencing Consortium
INMARSAT	International Maritime Satellite Organization
instantaneous	type of code with no encoder or decoder delay
I-picture	(I-frame) non-predicted video frame
ISDN	integrated services digital network (N-ISDN unless otherwise specified)
ISO	International Standards Organization
ITU	International Telecommunication Union
ITU-T	ITU Telecommunication Standardization Sector (formerly CCITT)

IV	initialization vector (in H.233)
JBIG	Joint Bilevel Image Group
JDC	Japanese Digital Cellular (see also PDC)
JND	just noticeable distortion
joint entropy	entropy of two or more random variables
joint stereo coding	a stereo coding technique that uses subband thresholding, scaling, and averaging
JPEG	Joint Photographic Experts Group
kbps	kilobits per second
kHz	kilohertz (1000 cycles/second)
KLT	Karhunen-Loeve transform
Kraft inequality	inequality relating code alphabet size and codeword lengths in lossless source coding
ℓ	length of the binary codeword assigned to source symbol
LAN	local area network
LAP	link access procedure
LAR	log-area ratio
latency	end-to-end delay
LBG	Linde, Buzo, Gray: the inventors of a training mode vector quantization technique
LC	logical channel (in H.245)
LCN	logical channel number (in H.245)
LD-CELP	low-delay code excited linear prediction
leaky prediction	scheme for combatting error propagation in video
Lempel-Ziv	family of lossless compressors based on string matching
lip sync	lip synchronization; the synchronization of video with audio. Normally this is accomplished by adding delay in the audio path since video coding and decoding takes longer than audio coding and decoding.
log PCM	logarithmic pulse code modulation; a nonlinear scalar quantization method used in the public switched telephone network for voice communications
LPC	linear predictive coding
LPC-10	a tenth-order LPC system that served as the U.S. Federal Standard 1015
LPS	less probable symbol (in binary arithmetic coding)
LSD	low-speed data (in H.221)

LSP or LSF	line spectrum pair or line spectrum frequency
LSZ	numerical quantity in arithmetic Q-coder
luma	luminance signal
LZ	Lempel-Ziv
LZ77	LZ algorithm based on 1977 paper by Lempel and Ziv
LZ78	LZ algorithm based on 1978 paper by Lempel and Ziv
LZ78E	excised (or expurgated) LZ78
LZ78EP	prefix-coded LZ78E
LZ78S	LZ78 with suppression
LZ78SE	excised LZ78S
LZ78SEP	prefix-coded LZ78SE
LZW	Lempel-Ziv-Welch
LZWE	excised LZW
LZWEP	prefix-coded LZWE
LZY	Lempel-Ziv-Yokoo
LZYE	excised LZY
LZYEP	prefix-coded LZYE
macroblock	block of 16×16 luma pixels used as basic motion compensation unit together with two corresponding 8×8 chroma blocks
MAE	mean absolute error
Markov	process whose future is conditionally independent of its past given its present value
Markov chain	time-discrete Markov process
Markov string	finite segment of a Markov chain
MBE	multiband excitation
mbps	megabits per second (1,000,000 bits/second)
MC	multipoint controller (in H.323)
MC-DCT	motion-compensated DCT
MCS	multipoint communication service (in T.120)
MCU	multipoint control unit (also known as a multipoint bridge)
MCU	minimum coded unit
MDCT	modified discrete cosine transform
MDST	modified discrete sine transform
MELP	mixed excitation linear prediction

MIPS	million instructions per second (fixed point)
MLP	Multi-Layer Protocol (in H.221)
modem	modulator/demodulator
modified Huffman code	Huffman code with codeword length and/or resynchronization restriction
modified READ	modified relative element address designate (in Group 4 fax)
Morse code	classic international telegraphy standard
Morse's principle	codeword lengths should vary inversely with symbol probabilities
MOS	Mean Opinion Score; a speech coder performance rating
motion vectors	estimated displacements of image blocks from one frame to the next
MP	multipoint processor (in H.323)
MPEG	Motion Picture Experts Group
MPEG-1	a video standard for CD-ROMs and certain TV signals
MPEG-2	a broadcast quality video standard
MPEG-4	an emerging standard for low and medium bitrate video
MPEG system layer	specifications supporting multiplexing and synchronization for multimedia decoding
MPI	minimum picture interval (in H.261 and H.263)
MPLPC	multipulse linear predictive coding
MPS	more probable symbol (in JBIG arithmetic coding)
ms	milliseconds
MSE	mean squared error
MUC	make up code (in Group 3 fax)
multilink	the use of more than one physical channel to obtain a higher aggregate bit rate for a single call
multipoint	the interconnection of three or more sites in a single conference
MUSICAM	masking pattern universal subband integrated coding and multiplexing
MUX-PDU	multiplex protocol data unit (in H.223)
NBC	natural binary code (when used with quantization); nonbackward compatible (when used in high-quality audio)
N-ISDN	narrowband integrated services digital network
NMR	noise-to-mask ratio

noise spectral shaping	shaping the spectral content of the encoding error
nonbinary Huffman codes	Huffman codes using alphabets with three or more letters
nontypical	in JBIG fax, a solid pixel whose color is different from that of a neighboring resolution-reduced pixel; a line containing a nontypical pixel
NTSC	National Television Systems Committee; U.S. TV standard
Nyquist rate	the lowest rate that an analog signal can be sampled and still be reconstructed without distortion
OBMC	overlapped block motion compensation (in H.263)
PAC	perceptual audio coder
pack	part of an MPEG-1 systems stream having a header and a body and comprised of several packets
packet ID	13-bit address in MPEG-2 transport stream payload
packetized elementary stream	packet with header and data information in MPEG-2
PAL	phase alternation line; European TV standard
PARCOR coefficients	partial correlation coefficients
parsing	segmenting a data string into successive phrases
PASC	precision adaptive subband coding
pass mode	one of three basic modes in Group 4 fax coding
PC	personal computer
PCM	pulse code modulation
PCS	personal communications systems
PDC	Personal Digital Cellular
pdf	probability density function
PEL	pixel
PER	packed encoding rules (in X.691)
perceptual distortion measures	measures of distortion that model human preferences
PES	packetized elementary stream (in MPEG-2)
phase	one of four pixel offsets (JBIG fax)

phrase	segment of a parsed data sequence between two "commas"
PID	packet ID (in MPEG-2)
pixel	picture element
pkzip	commercial realization of LZ77
PM	packet marker (in H.223)
POTS	plain old telephone service (also known as GSTN)
PPDPCM	pitch-predictive differential pulse code modulation
P-picture	(P-frame) forward-predicted video frame
PPP	point-to-point protocol
preemphasis	amplifying just the higher-frequency part of a signal
prefix codes	codes that comply with the prefix condition
prefix condition	no short codeword may be a prefix of a longer codeword
presentation time	the time at which an audio unit should be played or a video unit should be displayed
presentation time stamp	information in MPEG-2 PES about play/display time for packet payload
professional profile	4:2:2 profile
profiles	compliance points within low, main, and high levels in video standards
program association table	table giving PID of program map table and network information table in an MPEG-2 program stream
program map table	table giving PID and characteristic of elementary streams (in MPEG-2)
program specific information	tables for association of audio, video, and data (in MPEG-2)
PSD	power spectral density
PSI-CELP	pitch synchronous innovation code excited linear prediction
PSN	packet switched network (as in IP)
PSTN	public switched telephone network
PTS	presentation time stamp (in MPEG-2)
p × 64	P times 64 kbps (H.320)
PXFM	Perceptual Transform Coder
pyramid	collection of increasingly low-pass subsampled versions of an image
QCELP	Qualcomm code excited linear prediction

QCIF	quarter common intermediate format; one-fourth resolution of CIF
Q-coder	a binary arithmetic coder used in JBIG fax
QMF	quadrature mirror filter
quantization	discretizing the amplitude of a parameter or signal
RAM	random access memory
rate control	local trading off of bit rate versus quality to achieve a more nearly uniform number of bits per frame in video
RCELP	relaxed code excited linear prediction
READ	relative element address designate (in Group 4 fax)
redundancy	amount by which description length exceeds source entropy
refresh	periodically sending part or all of a frame without using prediction
RELP	residual excited linear prediction
RM	reference model
RMS	root mean square
RPE	regular pulse excitation
RSA	Rivest, Shamir, Adleman encryption scheme
RTC	return to control (in G3 and G4 fax)
RTP/RTCP	Real-Time Transport Protocol/Real-Time Transport Control Protocol
runlength	amplitude coding modified Huffman compression of the combination of a scanned run of DCT coefficients quantized to zero and terminal non-zero quantized coefficient (in JPEG and MPEG)
μs	microseconds
SAR	segmentation and reassembly
SB-ADPCM	subband adaptive differential pulse code modulation
SBC	subband coding
scalar	one-dimensional
SE	session exchange (in H.233)
self information	negative logarithm of probability of a symbol or event
SELP	self-excited linear prediction
Shannon-Fano codes	prefix codes whose word lengths are self-information ceiling
SIFT	simplified inverse filter tracking; refers to a pitch extraction algorithm
signal-to-mask ratio	signal-to-noise ratio below which masking can't prevent audible distortion

slice	smallest block of MPEG compressed video at which resynchronization can occur after a channel error
SMR	signal-to-mask ratio
SNR	signal-to-noise ratio, sometimes given in dB (decibels)
solid	in JBIG fax, a pixel that's the same color as all eight of its neighbors in its differential layer
source alphabet	set of possible instantaneous source outputs
SQCIF	subquarter common intermediate format
Stacker	a commercial realization of LZ77
stationary	describing a source whose statistics are invariant with respect to choice of the time origin
STC	sinusoidal transform coder
subband decomposition	separation of a signal into multiple frequency bands that subsequently receive different treatments
super-letters	n-tuples of source letters, $n > 1$
SVGA	Super VGA; a display monitor adapter with higher resolutions and more color bits than VGA
switched digital video	video using a dedicated circuit-switched path
syntax	rules for combining defined elements to produce a legal (i.e., standard-compliant) bitstream
system clock reference	timing recovery information in the header of an MPEG-1 pack
system target decoder	hypothetical decoder providing synchronization and buffer states for CD-ROM and certain TV signals
tail-biting	treating the front of the current phrase as part of the past when encoding the back of the current phrase
tandeming	sequentially decoding and reencoding a signal using the same coding algorithm. Tandeming is often necessary when mixing encoded audio signals from different sources.
TC	terminating code (in Group 3 fax)
TCP/IP	transmission control protocol/Internet protocol
TCX	transform coded excitation
TDAC	time domain aliasing cancellation
TDM	time division multiplexer
TDMA	time division multiple access

template	configuration of pixels or voxels used as a context in arithmetic coding
TIA	Telecommunications Industry Association
TIC	Japanese Telecommunications Technology Committee
transcoding	sequentially decoding and reencoding a signal using two different coding algorithms. Transcoding is used to translate a signal from one coding algorithm to another.
transport stream	version of MPEG-2 systems layer with short packets suitable for broadcast over noisy media
TSVQ	tree-structured vector quantization
UD	unique decipherability
UDP/IP	user datagram protocol/Internet protocol
UI	unnumbered information
uncertainty	incomplete knowledge about what value a random variable assumes
unique decipherability	the requirement that two distinct source strings may not generate the same code string
universal	capable of efficiently encoding any source with a given alphabet
Unix compact	lossless compression scheme that uses adaptive Huffman coding
Unix compress	lossless compression scheme based on LZW
VC	virtual channel (in ATM)
vertical mode	one of three basic modes in Group 4 fax coding
VGA	video graphics array; a display monitor adapter
VL	variable length
VLSI	very large scale integration
VoIP	voice on IP; activity group of IMTC
Voronoi regions	nearest-neighbor regions in n-dimensional space
VQ	vector quantization; the quantization of a multidimensional entity
VSELP	vector sum excited linear prediction
V/UV	voiced/unvoiced classifications of speech
WAN	wide area network
WHT	Walsh-Hadamard transform
WWW	World Wide Web

Index

About the Authors

Jerry D. Gibson currently serves as chairman of the Department of Electrical Engineering at Southern Methodist University in Dallas, Texas. He has held positions at General Dynamics-Fort Worth, the University of Notre Dame, the University of Nebraska-Lincoln, and Texas A&M University. He served as president of the IEEE Information Theory Society in 1996.

Dr. Gibson is editor in chief of *The Mobile Communications Handbook* (1995) and of *The Communications Handbook* (1997). In 1990, Dr. Gibson received the Fredrick Emmons Terman Award from the American Society for Engineering Education and in 1992, was elected Fellow of the IEEE "for contributions to the theory and practice of adaptive prediction and speech waveform coding." He was co-recipient of the 1993 IEEE Signal Processing Society Senior Paper Award for the Speech Processing area.

His research interests include data, speech, image, and video compression, multimedia over networks, wireless communications, information theory, and digital signal processing.

Toby Berger was born in New York, NY on September 4, 1940. He received the B.E. degree in electrical engineering from Yale University, New Haven, CT in 1962, and the M.S. and Ph.D. degrees in applied mathematics from Harvard University, Cambridge, MA in 1964 and 1966, respectively.

From 1962 to 1968 he was a senior scientist at Raytheon Company, Wayland, MA, specializing in communication theory, information theory, and coherent signal processing. In 1968 he joined the faculty of Cornell University, Ithaca, NY where he is presently the J. Preston Levis Professor of Engineering. His research interests include multiterminal coding theory, the information theory of random fields, communication networks, video compression, human signature compression and verification, and coherent signal processing. He is the author of the textbook, *Rate Distortion Theory: A Mathematical Basis for Data Compression.*

Dr. Berger has served as editor in chief of the IEEE Transactions on Information Theory and as president of the IEEE Information Theory Group. He has been a Fellow of the Guggenheim Foundation, the Japan Society for Promotion of Science, the Ministry of Education of the People's Republic of China, and the Fulbright Foundation. He received the 1982 Frederick E. Terman Award of the American Society for Engineering Education for outstanding contributions by a young electrical engineering educator. Dr. Berger is a Fellow of the IEEE and a member of Tau Beta Pi and Sigma Xi.

Tom Lookabaugh is president of DiviCom. A cofounder of the company, Dr. Lookabaugh brings experience in the research and engineering of video and audio compression and high-performance multiplexing systems, as well as in developing and managing partner relationships, to his position at DiviCom.

Prior to joining DiviCom, Dr. Lookabaugh spent five years at CLI, reaching the position of executive director of research and new business technology. During his tenure at CLI, he was intimately involved in algorithm development and engineering of numerous compression-based systems, including three generations of products in videoconferencing and broadcast video. He also helped build and maintain key relationships with customers and partners involved in product development and testing. One of his responsibilities was development of an MPEG-1 decoder for video-on-demand trials.

Dr. Lookabaugh holds a bachelor's degree in engineering physics from the Colorado School of Mines; master's degrees in electrical engineering, statistics, and engineering management from Stanford University; and a Ph.D. in electrical engineering from Stanford.

Dave Lindbergh has worked in the computer and data communications industry since 1979. In 1981 he founded Lindbergh Systems, a developer of microcomputer data communications software, including the award-winning OMNITERM programs. As a consulting engineer, he designed modem protocols and software and developed the APT (Asynchronous Performance Tester) data communications measurement tool widely used in the modem industry. He was president of CD Atlas Company, a multimedia mapping firm, from 1990 to 1992.

In 1993 he joined PictureTel Corporation (NASDAQ: PCTL), the world's leading manufacturer of videoconferencing equipment, where he is currently manager of PictureTel's technical standards group. He has represented PictureTel within U.S. and international standards organizations, including ANSI T1 and TIA, and the ITU. He was a principle contributor to ITU-T H.223, H.224, and H.281, served as editor for ITU-T H.324, and is currently chairman of the ITU-T H.324 Systems Experts group. He is credited with a U.S. patent for data compression technology and is an IEEE member.

Richard L. Baker, Ph.D., vice president and chief technical officer at PictureTel Corporation, Danvers, MA, is involved in the development of key technologies for the emerging group and desktop visual communications market. Prior to joining PictureTel in January 1990, he was an assistant professor of electrical engineering at UCLA, where he taught courses in information theory, rate distortion theory, and circuit analysis and researched image and video compression techniques and their application in VLSI. Dr. Baker has over 30 technical publications.

Dr. Baker also serves as vice president, Americas, and member of the board of directors of the International Multimedia Teleconferencing Consortium (IMTC), a non-profit corporation of over 100 member companies dedicated to the development of products based on the H.32x/T.120 series of ITU-T standards. Within the IMTC, he co-chairs the activity group on Packet Network Conferencing, which facilitates the ITU-T H.323 Internet Protocol videoconferencing standards and interoperability processes.